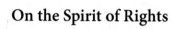

On the Spirit of Rights

the
LIFE
OF
IDEAS

SERIES EDITORS

Suzanne Marchand, *Louisiana State University*
Darrin M. McMahon, *Dartmouth College*

After a period of some eclipse, the study of intellectual history has enjoyed a broad resurgence in recent years. The Life of Ideas contributes to this revitalization through the study of ideas as they are produced, disseminated, received, and practiced in different historical contexts. The series aims to embed ideas—those that endured, and those once persuasive but now forgotten—in rich and readable cultural histories. Books in this series draw on the latest methods and theories of intellectual history while being written with elegance and élan for a broad audience of readers.

# On the Spirit of Rights

DAN EDELSTEIN

The University of Chicago Press
Chicago and London

The University of Chicago Press, Chicago 60637
The University of Chicago Press, Ltd., London
© 2019 by The University of Chicago
All rights reserved. No part of this book may be used or reproduced in any manner
whatsoever without written permission, except in the case of brief quotations in
critical articles and reviews. For more information, contact the University of Chicago
Press, 1427 E. 60th St., Chicago, IL 60637.
Published 2019
Printed in the United States of America

28  27  26  25  24  23  22  21  20  19      2  3  4  5

ISBN-13: 978-0-226-58898-8 (cloth)
ISBN-13: 978-0-226-58903-9 (e-book)
DOI: https://doi.org/10.7208/chicago/9780226589039.001.0001

Library of Congress Cataloging-in-Publication Data

Names: Edelstein, Dan, author.
Title: On the spirit of rights / Dan Edelstein.
Other titles: Life of ideas.
Description: Chicago: The University of Chicago Press, 2018. | Series: Life of ideas
Identifiers: LCCN 2018019709 | ISBN 9780226588988 (cloth: alk. paper) | ISBN
    9780226589039 (e-book)
Subjects: LCSH: Human rights—History. | Natural law—History. | Human rights—
    France—History. | Human rights—United States—History.
Classification: LCC JC571 . E357 2018 | DDC 323.09—dc23
LC record available at https://lccn.loc.gov/2018019709

♾ This paper meets the requirements of ANSI/NISO Z39.48–1992
(Permanence of Paper).

*To Keith M. Baker*

# Contents

# How to Think about Rights in Early Modern Europe

## 1. Introduction

There are some seams of political thought that, when mined, threaten to collapse the entire mountain of Western culture on your head. The history of rights is one such seam. Tug at the threads woven into the French Declaration of the Rights of Man and of the Citizen, and you are sent in dizzying directions: toward the American Revolution, the French Enlightenment, British political history, Dutch and German natural law theory, Spanish neo-Scholasticism, Huguenot resistance theory, late medieval conciliarism, and Roman law. Drop down these different rabbit holes, and a distinct sense of déjà vu sinks in. Every "original" claim about rights turns out to have precedents; when a claim does break new ground, it is usually as a variation on a theme. Little is lost, little is gained, everything is transformed.

On the surface, this book presents itself as a history of how natural rights became human rights, from the Wars of Religion to the Age of Revolutions, and ultimately up to 1948. But it would be presumptuous to describe its argument in that way: too much of that history is missing from the present account. This book is, more modestly, a genealogy of the rights regimes enshrined during the American and French Revolutions. Reconstructing this genealogy, however, requires reaching back to the sixteenth century and casting glances further back still. The purpose of these historical soundings is not to hit rock bottom and locate ground zero of revolutionary rights. It is rather to gain sufficient perspective on the sprawling series of debates between jurists, theologians, philosophers, political reformers, writers, and others pushing rival rights regimes to defend conflicting ideologies. These disputes were not merely academic quarrels, but flared up most during moments of political turmoil, when the very structure of governments was called into question.

The bone of contention in these quarrels was not whether humans possessed natural rights per se; by the mid-sixteenth century, few disputed that everyone can lay claim to some rights by virtue of natural law.[1] The real debate was over what happened to these rights in political society. Some of the early theorists of natural rights insisted that we maintained them in all circumstances. One group, the revolutionary French Huguenots, made this claim a key tenet of their arguments against the French crown; it was also central to the political demands of the Levellers during the English Civil War. And it was this same "self-evident truth" that eighteenth-century revolutionaries in America and France later proclaimed in their declarations. This conception of natural rights, which I term the "preservation" regime, remains a defining feature of human rights to this day.

But the preservation regime was not the only game in town and had two competitors. Political theorists with a more authoritarian bent privileged an "abridgment" regime, according to which upon joining a body politic, the abandonment of (most of) our rights was a prerequisite for security and peace. The most famous author to defend this thesis was Hobbes, though the outlines of this argument stretch back much earlier. It would also resonate well into the eighteenth century and even into the American Revolutionary War.[2] Against this claim, more republican-leaning authors defended a "transfer" regime of rights. In this model, we cease to enjoy our rights as individuals in a political society, because we hand them over to the body politic as a whole, or more narrowly to government. This regime typically included a proviso that we can regain these rights under certain conditions, as with Locke's famous right of resistance. These three rights regimes were not mutually exclusive, and some accounts of natural rights in political society drew upon more than one (see fig. 1.1). But together they map out the basic frameworks available for thinking about rights during this period. I examine how these frameworks came about in chapter 2.

I describe these frameworks as "regimes" for two main reasons.[3] First, this term allows me to distinguish between the *concept* of a particular kind of right and the treatment of rights in general by a given theorist. For instance, many theologians and philosophers, going back to the late medieval period, insisted that all humans have a natural right to self-preservation, which they can never give up. On that basis, one could say that these authors defended the concept of an inalienable right. But just because they believed that this one right was inalienable does not mean that they believed humans should necessarily retain all their rights. On the contrary, the concept of an inalienable right is wholly

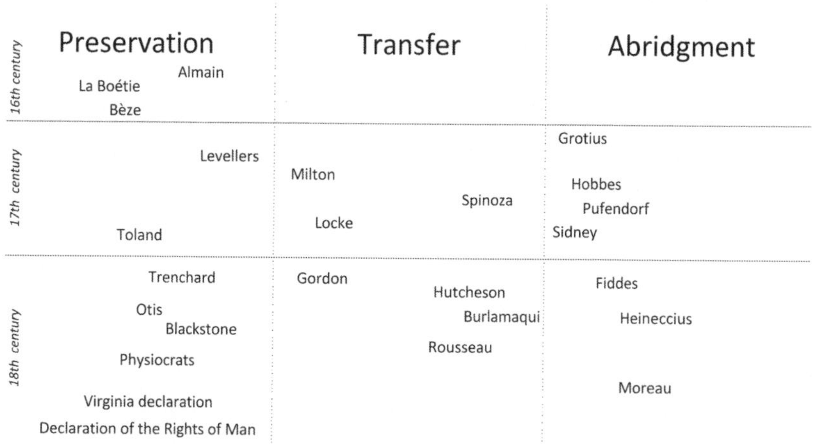

| | Preservation | Transfer | Abridgment |
|---|---|---|---|
| 16th century | La Boétie   Almain   Bèze | | |
| 17th century | Levellers     Toland | Milton   Locke   Spinoza | Grotius   Hobbes   Pufendorf   Sidney |
| 18th century | Trenchard   Otis   Blackstone   Physiocrats   Virginia declaration   Declaration of the Rights of Man | Gordon   Hutcheson   Burlamaqui   Rousseau | Fiddes   Heineccius   Moreau |

FIGURE 1.1. Major authors and documents sorted by natural rights regime, from the sixteenth to the eighteenth century. Spatial position reflects proximity to neighboring regimes.

compatible with a rights *regime* that emphasizes their general abandonment in a political state. We find precisely such a case in Hobbes, who held that even when we "laid down" our "right to all things," we still retained a right to self-preservation.[4] The retention of this right was an exception to the rule: the very precondition for political order (and by extension, for our security) in Hobbes was the "laying down" of our natural "right to all things." Hobbes thus championed the abridgment regime of rights, but this did not prevent him from granting the odd inalienable right on the side.

Second, there is a loose relation between a rights regime and political regimes. I call this relation loose because it is not inevitable nor is it one-to-one. The same rights regime can underpin multiple political regimes, but some lend themselves more to one than to others. The abridgment regime, for instance, was mostly popular with proponents of monarchic absolutism. The preservation regime, by contrast, typically supports constitutional, liberal governments (as well as libertarian utopias), whereas the transfer regime may be best suited for more classical republics. To be sure, there are many exceptions to these trends. But the trends are real and remind us that a rights regime is more than just an ideological construct. It emphasizes certain political practices: one could only contest a rights violation under the preservation and (to a lesser extent) transfer regimes. Different regimes confer different political identities: the disenfranchised subject of the abridgment regime stands apart from the rights-bearing citizen of the preservation regime. And each regime privileges particular institutions: for instance, the legislative body for the transfer regime; or the executive function for the abridgment one.

The story of how rights became "rights," in the sense that we use the word today—in Ronald Dworkin's terminology, as individual "trumps" that we can use against the state[5]—is therefore not a simple story of who got there first. It is rather a story of how one rights regime won out over two others—others that, for most of this period, were far better defended and more broadly accepted. But the success of the preservation regime in the mid-eighteenth century was only indirectly related to its emergence a century (or century and a half) earlier. If, in the American case, one can trace a faint line from the New England Puritans back to the English Levellers, in France memories of the Huguenot revolutionaries had mostly faded among the *philosophes* and their allies. The latter did not so much rediscover the preservation regime as reinvent it. Central to its French revival was a small group of economists known as the Physiocrats, whose initial focus on property rights was soon extended to include political rights, as well. These are the authors I examine in chapter 3.

By the end of the eighteenth century, revolutionaries on both sides of the Atlantic insisted that "all men [ ... ] have certain inherent rights, of which, when they enter into a state of society, they cannot, by any compact, deprive or divest their posterity," and that "the aim of all political association is the preservation of the natural and imprescriptible rights of man."[6] But this apparent meeting of fraternal minds was more illusory than it sounds, as the Americans and the French had worked their way back to the preservation regime of rights along very different paths. In France, legal and political theorists took inspiration from Roman law and its supposed Stoic underpinnings, as well as from Jansenist theology, to imagine a state that was entirely deduced from natural law principles. This doctrine of "social naturalism," which I analyze in chapters 4 and 5, largely dispensed with constitutional precedents and did not explicitly define rights as defenses against the state. Instead, it sought to buttress economic rights above all others and, in so doing, lay the intellectual and metaphysical foundations for free-market liberalism.

Anglo-American theorists, by contrast, merged natural rights with traditional constitutional liberties, creating a political doctrine that I describe as "natural constitutionalism." This doctrine allowed the American revolutionaries to claim the political right to representation and ultimately to form new governments, but also to hold on to the criminal procedural rights that were a hallmark of English common law. I recount this history, from its origins in colonial New England to its revolutionary conclusion in the United States, in chapter 6.

But the French did not entirely lack constitutional rights. A group of lawyers, centered around the Paris Parlement, brought them back into the picture in the 1770s, at the moment when Louis XV was cracking down on the judiciary system. The rights that they championed, however, belonged to the nation as a whole (*les droits nationaux*), not to individual citizens. These rights served to defend institutional bodies, such as the Parlement, against royal despotism. By the time of the French Revolution, leading rights theorists had combined these enlightened and *parlementaire* conceptions of rights, producing a tension between individual and national rights claims. Now it was the Assembly that claimed to defend the rights of the nation, or *les droits du peuple*, as they came to be called. This tension remained mostly hidden in the 1789 Declaration of the Rights of Man and of the Citizen, which hewed closely to Enlightenment ideals of social naturalism. But it came to the fore during the Terror, when individual rights would be suppressed in the name of national ones. This is the final part of my story, which I tell in chapter 7.

The 1789 Declaration of Rights, in this account, might not appear particularly original. Most of its claims, like those of its American predecessors, can be traced back to earlier statements from the eighteenth (or seventeenth—and in some cases, even sixteenth) century. But to downplay its historical novelty is not to diminish its historical importance. The rights talk of the preceding decades had mostly been just that: talk. The Declaration gave these rights the force of law, leading to new political practices and claim making. In addition to asserting their newly established rights, the French also came to understand themselves differently as citizens. What's more, the historical importance of the Declaration was not limited to France. As I show in the conclusion, it was this Declaration—as well as its 1793 cousin—that later constitutional and international lawyers looked to as a model for a genuinely universal affirmation of rights. In this capacity, the French revolutionary declarations played a central role in the interwar debates and proposals that ultimately led to the 1948 Universal Declaration.

While partial, this genealogy of natural rights nonetheless offers a major reshuffling of more standard histories. When bookended by the Wars of Religion and the Age of Revolutions, the classic seventeenth- and eighteenth-century texts of natural law theory no longer appear as central to the political history of rights. Indeed, if the thesis that rights should be preserved in society ultimately imposed itself in the late eighteenth century, it was not because the seeds planted by the major seventeenth-century theorists had finally bore fruit, but rather, on the contrary, because their influence had started to wane. More specifically, what faded was the premise of a stark divide between the state of nature and political society. By positing an ontological gulf between these two conditions, canonical theorists from Hobbes to Rousseau could more easily envisage rights that only existed in a pre-political state, but then vanished or were transformed after individuals joined together in a body politic.

It was only when, in the eighteenth century, literary authors and philosophers ceased to recognize a rift between natural and political states, that it became less evident and less appealing to conceive of rights that we do not retain at all times. The main driver behind this shift was cultural: as the "moral authority of nature" expanded, it became harder to envisage political regimes that were at odds with natural principles.[7] The profound ramifications of this shift are no doubt most visible in the realm of literature and art, but can be seen just as strongly in natural law theory. Indeed, starting with Pufendorf, philosophers and jurists ceased to define the law of nations (*ius gentium*) as a body of law that might contradict natural law. This had been the Roman understanding, found in the *Corpus juris civilis*, and was a feature of neo-Scholastic natural law theory.[8] By 1700, however, any aspect of "international law" that violated natural law was deemed suspect and condemnable. Hence Montesquieu could cite the Roman description of slavery as *contra naturam* as an argument for its abolition.[9]

To be sure, this cultural shift did not affect all authors in the same way. One of the most sentimental admirers of nature, Rousseau, simply reversed the Hobbesian polarity between state of nature and civil society, but maintained the split. Accordingly, Rousseau was one of the few French Enlightenment authors who did not endorse the preservation regime, arguing instead for "the total alienation of each associate with all of his rights to the whole community."[10] The rights we enjoy in political society, according to Rousseau, do not come from nature, but are granted to us by the sovereign (for him, the collective people). It fell on his contemporaries, most of whom were less well versed in the natural law tradition stretching back to Grotius, to describe human rights in the way that we now consider determining—as pre-political entitlements that we retain under government.[11]

Of course, this decentering of the more celebrated natural lawyers is a matter of perspective; they still feature prominently in genealogies of other concepts, such as freedom. But in excavating the roots of our contemporary human rights regime, they play a mostly negative role. As such, they figure in this story in a more dialectical manner, as unintentional bridges between the sixteenth and eighteenth centuries. In arguing against Hobbes, for instance, the French Physiocrat François Quesnay ended up echoing arguments that had been made by Huguenot revolutionaries. He was most likely unfamiliar with their texts, though Hobbes himself had probably read them.[12] In a curious fashion, then, Hobbes ended up serving as a negative conduit for the preservation regime of rights.

## 2. Tectonic Shifts and Tectonic Plates:
## Two Models for the Transformation of Culture

In *The Last Utopia*, Samuel Moyn criticizes the "classic case" for the history of human rights, which "begins with the Stoic thinkers of Greek and Roman philosophy and proceeds through medieval law and early modern natural rights, culminating in the Atlantic revolutions of America and France. [ . . . ] By that point at the very latest, it was assumed, the die was cast." Moyn's central contention against this "myth of deep roots" is that it assumes all universalisms are identical. The Greeks, Romans, and Christians may all have espoused concepts of "humanity," but this does not mean that their understandings of humanity matched our own. "[H]uman universalism alone—including the versions of universalism in Greek philosophy and monotheistic religion—is of no real relevance to a history of human rights," he concludes.[13]

There are good reasons to heed Moyn's warning. At one level, Moyn is simply expressing the methodological principle on which modern intellectual history was founded, in opposition to the earlier, Lovejoyian history of ideas. The meaning of an idea or expression can vary significantly depending on its context.[14] Any history that strips context away and merely connects the dots between ideas over time is likely to misconstrue how people understood ideas, which may turn out to have been very differently. "Virtue," to take a famous example, did not mean the same thing for Dante as it did for Machiavelli.[15]

At another level, Moyn advocates for a historical perspective that privileges moments of disruption over periods of continuity.[16] It is certain that innovations and abrupt changes are more exciting for the historian to track down. And it can be challenging to find something to say about persistent institutions or patterns of thought beyond "and there it is again!" But we must also be wary of assuming that conceptual tremors can topple all structures. In culture, as in plate tectonics, the tremors are only half the story; the other half are the plates themselves. And some cultural landmasses move only minimally over centuries, surviving even the most violent quakes. One of these plates was the Catholic Church, which curated and transmitted a remarkably stable set of texts. Paul's Epistle to the Romans, for instance, contains a famous passage on the law that was "written on the hearts of all men" (Romans 2:14–15), including the Gentiles. This passage would be incessantly cited by theologians and philosophers up through the eighteenth century and served as a lasting reference point for thinking about natural law and rights (see chapter 4).

Another institution that weathered centuries of historical turmoil was Roman law (the focus of chapter 5).[17] This legal legacy of the Roman Empire survived, in fragmented form, its fall in the West;[18] whereas in the East, the

*Corpus juris civilis*, a codification of Roman law under Justinian in the sixth century, synthesized earlier Roman legal sources, including philosophical works such as Cicero's *De legibus*.[19] Rediscovered in northern Italy at the end of the eleventh century, the *Corpus* would be incorporated in the curricula of Western European law schools; and it was in the *Institutes* (a section of the *Corpus*) where law students often first learned about natural law.[20] Even those who did not make it past the opening section would discover that natural law is what "natural reason appoints for all mankind" and "obtains equally among all nations."[21]

But continuity is not only produced by permanence. Continuity in cultural and intellectual matters can also come from regular, repeated returns to the same source. If Aristotle or Cicero had a lasting influence on medieval, early modern, and Enlightenment thinkers, it is not because they formulated the philosophical program of Western thought once and for all, but because so many philosophers in subsequent ages returned to their texts.[22] The reception of classical ideas could of course lead to very different interpretations: Aquinas's Aristotle is not Voltaire's. But the canonical place of ancient philosophy and literature in European education did entail the persistence of certain key themes and arguments, particularly with regard to natural law. Those who point to Antigone as the founder of human rights could do worse: Aristotle himself had singled out Sophocles's *Antigone* as exemplifying the belief that "there is something of which we all have an inkling, being a naturally universal right and wrong, if there should be no community between the two parties nor contract," in a text that was still read and praised in the Enlightenment.[23]

Whatever one thinks of *Antigone*, it is still a leap from Sophocles to the Déclaration des droits de l'homme et du citoyen. So what does it mean to draw a link between the two? To acknowledge a family resemblance, and even a tangible historical connection, between classical and Enlightenment ideals of universal justice is simply to recognize that the history of human rights may be more archaeological than seismic, with successive generations adding new layers of interpretation to older theses. Sometimes they drastically altered the original meaning, but they rarely started over on entirely new ground. In this additive process, both continuity and rupture are possible, though even rupture bears the imprint of what one breaks from.

The real problem with the "classic case" is not, therefore, that the different expressions of human universalism in antiquity, the Christian Middle Ages, or the European Enlightenment are wholly dissimilar, but rather Moyn's other point that, somewhere along the way, "the die was cast." If the history of human rights is indeed additive, then no such moment can exist. In this archaeological model, instances of rights talk will always owe a debt to the past, but also extend beyond it. The ghostly structure of Roman law, for instance, haunts Blackstone's legal theory but does not exhaust it. The foundational concepts of human rights are not generative ideas that only bloom in later centuries.

### 3. A Revolution in Natural Law?
### From Objective to Subjective Right (and Back Again)

It is unfortunately the case that many of the historians who do posit some degree of continuity between ancient and modern notions of universal justice seek to identify a decisive event in this longer history after which the die was cast once and for all. The most common candidate for dividing up this history is the emergence of the concept of a subjective, or individual, right. Classical philosophers and jurists tended to use the Latin word *ius* in the sense related to the idea of justice or of a system of laws.[24] Hence, in the famous definition of justice in the *Institutes* as "constans et perpetua voluntas ius suum cuique tribuens," *ius suum* did not designate "his right," but rather "his fair share" or "his due."[25] It was a relative concept that could fluctuate based on the needs of others.

Sometime around the thirteenth century, however, theologians and jurists began employing *ius* more to mean an individual right or power. The phrase *ius naturale*, which had previously designated the natural sphere of justice (what it was objectively just to do), could now be taken to mean what an individual had the right or "legal power" to do. For the French legal historian Michel Villey, who drew particular attention to this development and credited it to William of Ockham (c. 1287–1347), the introduction of a subjective concept of right was a pivotal (and in his view, catastrophic) moment in the history of the West.[26] From Ockham, it would eventually pass on to Grotius and then Hobbes, after whom the virus of subjective rights became pandemic. There was accordingly, for Villey, a direct line running from the thirteenth to the twentieth century and to human rights, which he condemned in a 1983 work dedicated to Pope John Paul II.[27]

But there was another way to tell this story. In his still-influential monograph *Natural Rights Theories*, Richard Tuck drew on Villey's insight to tell a heroic, rather than a tragic, story.[28] In Tuck's account, it wasn't Ockham but rather twelfth-century jurists who formulated "the first modern rights theory."[29] Still, Tuck largely adopted Villey's historical narrative, crediting seventeenth-century Protestant natural lawyers—Grotius and Hobbes, in particular—with embracing and ushering this subjective doctrine into the modern age. Finally, like Villey, Tuck assumed that the adoption of this subjective perspective implied a rejection of an objective understanding of natural law.

Though Tuck did not mention it at the time, his thesis bears an even closer resemblance to Leo Strauss's definition of "modern natural right." In Strauss's reading of Hobbes, "natural law must be deduced from the desire for self-preservation [. . . ;] in other words, the desire for self-preservation is the sole root of all justice and morality." And it is Hobbes's emphasis on "the primacy of natural rights" that Strauss considered to be "the fundamental change in the character of the natural law doctrine."[30] There is no reference to *Natural Right and History* in *Natural Rights Theories*, though Tuck does reference an earlier study by Strauss on Hobbes, in which we can already find an embryonic statement of his later thesis.[31] In *The Rights of War and Peace*, Tuck would acknowledge his appreciation of Strauss, noting, "I am bound to say that [Strauss's] views on early modern political thought seem to me to have been extremely penetrating."[32]

Tuck's thesis of a "modern school" of natural rights theory, founded on the precedence of natural rights over natural law, proved catching, particularly among historians associated with the Cambridge school. One promoter was Anthony Pagden, who stated that "the concept of an 'international law' has its origins in the 'modern' natural-law theorists, notably Hugo Grotius, Samuel Pufendorf, and John Selden, whose project was very different from Vitoria's, and wholly indifferent to the Thomist definition of *ius*."[33] Jerome Schneewind, in *The Invention of Autonomy*, also followed Tuck in defining a modern natural law school, starting with Grotius.[34] And Tuck's influence is evident on the *Cambridge History of Political Thought, 1450–1700*, a reference book used by many students in the field (and scholars from without).[35]

But the rigid conceptual distinction between subjective and objective right—which underpins the work of Villey, Strauss, and Tuck—has come under attack, most importantly by Brian Tierney and Annabel Brett. Villey may have been correct in identifying the late medieval period as the moment when theologians began employing *ius* more commonly to designate a subjective power, Tierney recognizes, but as he points out, one can already find instances of Roman jurisconsults employing *ius* in this individualistic sense.[36] Other scholars have further challenged Villey's claim that the concept of a subjective right was unknown in antiquity.[37] Conversely, there are plenty of cases where medieval and early modern philosophers used *ius* in the classical, objective sense. The distinction on which Villey, and Tuck after him, so adamantly insisted was thus not all that clear-cut in the minds of most of their subjects. While it could be of useful scholarly value, this opposition ran the risk of imposing an artificially neat and anachronistic polarization on historical arguments.

But the problems with Villey's thesis ran even deeper. Tierney disputed the very notion that "classical objective right [ . . . ] and modern subjective rights" are "inherently inconsistent with one another." On the contrary, they represent two sides of the same coin: "In propounding a system of jurisprudence one can emphasize either the objective pattern of relationships or the implied rights and duties of persons to one another—and then again one can focus on either the rights or the duties."[38] An example of what Tierney means by this correlation can be found in Grotius's first definition of the law of nature as "the Abstaining from that which is another's, and the Restitution of what we have of another's."[39] This statement can be parsed as the affirmation of a duty, derived from natural law (it is morally wrong to take other people's stuff), which in turn affords others a right (my stuff is my rightful property).[40] Tierney takes such correlations as an indication that we should in fact *expect* natural law theorists to mix and match objective and subjective concepts of right, since one entails the other.[41] By extension, uncovering a subjective understanding of *ius* in a treatise cannot be taken as a sign that the author has repudiated the classical, objective conception of natural right. These two concepts of right(s) are fully compatible; what's more, authors who employed *right* in a subjective sense would invariably use it in an objective sense, as well. Villey's thesis thus rested on a spurious premise. The rise of subjective rights alone cannot be taken as the point of rupture between classical and modern theories of natural right.[42]

It might seem uncontroversial to assume that a century capped off by declarations of rights on either side of the Atlantic was committed to a political theory that asserted the primacy of rights. This was a commonplace in the older history of political thought: Strauss, for instance, affirmed that "in the course of the seventeenth and eighteenth centuries a much greater emphasis was put on rights than ever had been done before."[43] But the story is not nearly so simple. As I argue in chapters 4 and 5, the moral, theological, legal, economic, and political spheres of seventeenth- and eighteenth-century continental Western Europe often rested on the belief in a natural order, which was governed by natural law. The focus of these chapters is on France, but examples abound from elsewhere, as well. In the German states, philosophers such as Leibniz and Wolff returned to Scholastic definitions of rational natural law.[44] Even in the land of Hobbes and Locke, it was only in the later part of the eighteenth century that authors began to use the language of rights with any regularity (see fig. 1.2), though still less frequently than the "law of nature."[45]

This trend is also visible in the American colonies: even as American political discourse saw an uptick in references to natural rights, natural law

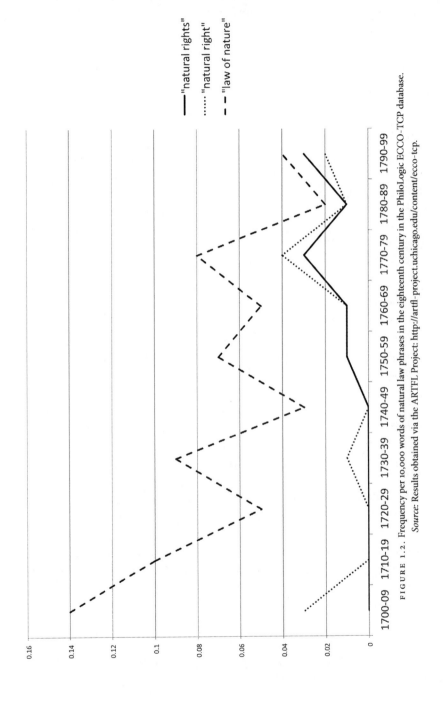

FIGURE 1.2. Frequency per 10,000 words of natural law phrases in the eighteenth century in the PhiloLogic ECCO-TCP database.

*Source:* Results obtained via the ARTFL Project: http://artfl-project.uchicago.edu/content/ecco-tcp.

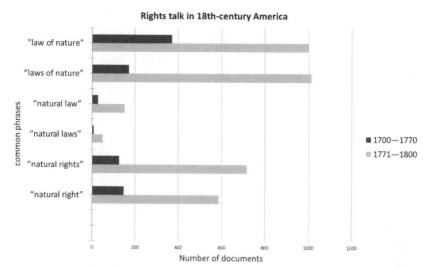

FIGURE 1.3. Number of documents containing key natural law phrases in eighteenth-century American works; results normalized based on varying sample size sets. Data from the Early American Imprints, Series I: Evans, 1639–1800 database: http://www.readex.com/content/early-american-imprints-series-i -evans-1639-1800.

continued to dominate the discussion. (see fig. 1.3). James Otis's description of the "natural rights of the Colonists" is exemplary: "The Colonists are by the law of nature free born, as indeed all men are, white or black."[46]

In France, the pattern is even starker. Between the 1740s and the 1760s, French authors increased their references to *droit naturel* by a factor of three.[47] All the major *philosophes*, as we will see, grounded their attacks on unfair laws, the slave trade, or religious intolerance in appeals to natural law, but their mentions of *droits naturels* were comparatively far fewer (see fig. 1.4).

The story of how Scholastic natural law theory gave way to revolutionary natural rights cannot be told in terms of a simple rights/law opposition. Not only does this argument fail on a quantitative level, but it also fails conceptually, since subjective and objective theories of natural right continued to intermingle all the way up through the Age of Revolutions. Indeed, even the Universal Declaration of Human Rights (UDHR) was constructed around the hidden scaffolding of natural law.[48] This foundation was subsequently removed, intentionally, as the drafters could not agree on the foundations they should cite, for fear of rendering the Declaration less "universal."[49] But its traces remain, notably in article 1, where our enjoyment of rights is premised on the fact that we are all "endowed with reason and conscience." These were precisely the faculties that in both the Stoic and Thomist objective doctrines grant us access to the natural law.[50]

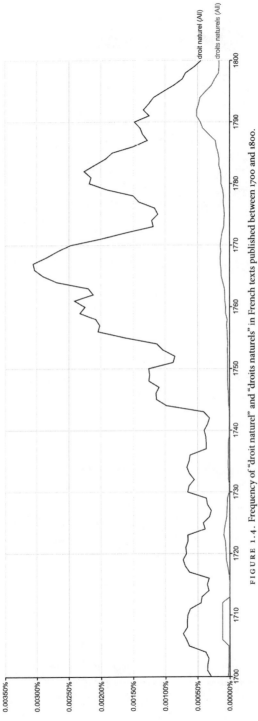

FIGURE 1.4. Frequency of "droit naturel" and "droits naturels" in French texts published between 1700 and 1800.

*Source:* From Google Books Ngram Viewer.

## 4. Rights and Sovereignty: Beyond the State

Another distinction that scholars have sought to harden between modern and early modern theories of rights is their relation to state sovereignty. While focusing primarily on the late twentieth century, Moyn, in *The Last Utopia*, also addressed the Enlightenment and revolutionary history of human rights, in order to underscore "the essential connection between rights and the state" during this period. What he means by this characterization is that "[t]he first natural rights doctrines were the children of the absolutist and expansionist state of early modern European history, not attempts to step outside and beyond the state."[51] In this account, early modern affirmations of natural rights required a sovereign state to recognize and enforce their claims; they were not appeals to universal norms that might contradict national laws.

Moyn's own source for this description of early modern natural rights theory is another influential work by Richard Tuck, *The Rights of War and Peace* (2001). The central analogy around which Tuck structured this book was the one between the sovereign state and the sovereign individual. As he wrote in his introduction, "The natural rights theorists [ ... ] simply took the jurisprudence of war which had developed among humanist lawyers, and derived a theory of individual rights from it." This "jurisprudence of war" was reason-of-state theory, according to which a sovereign state could act in whichever manner it pleased to ensure its self-preservation. For Tuck, natural rights theorists conceptualized the rights of the individual on the model of the sovereign state, proof of which can be found in their similar emphasis on self-preservation above all. The theorist who consumed this analogy, Tuck argued, was Hobbes, "who made clear the relationship between humanism and natural rights, and who demonstrated the link between the older jurisprudence of war and the new political theory."[52]

The analogy between the state and the individual is a fruitful one and does seem to have conditioned how certain theorists conceptualized the rights of both. But it fails as a historical account of how individuals came to be viewed as rights-bearing subjects, and it does not hold for all rights theorists. Chronologically, Moyn's claim that the "first natural rights doctrines" derived from absolutist political theory overlooks the much longer history of natural rights, in particular their place in conciliarism.[53] In pressing their case that the council of the Church had greater authority than the pope (or, during the Western Schism, popes), conciliarists politicized the language and concept of individual natural rights. Jean Gerson (1363–1429) argued that all humans possessed these rights "as a gift from God."[54] His later followers insisted on this same point: Jacques Almain (d. 1515), for instance, claimed a century later that

God, the author of nature, created man with a natural right or power [homi-
nem condidit cum naturali Jure, seu potestate] to obtain those things which are
necessary for his sustenance and to repel those which are harmful, on which
right is founded the power to kill anyone who attacks [one] unjustly, if the
standard of blameless response is observed. [ . . . ] In the same way, any community of people living together in civil association [ . . . ] has a natural right
to preserve itself not only in being but in peaceful being. . . .[55]

While Almain, too, makes an analogy between individual and state rights,
it is not at all with absolutist intentions. On the contrary, his argument is
designed to prove that the rights of the sovereign are both derived from, and
*limited* by, the inalienable rights of individuals. What's more, it did not take
any reason-of-state theory for Almain to insist, above all, on self-preservation
as the fundamental right: "No perfect community can abdicate this power [to
kill dangerous members], just as no individual man can abdicate the power
which he has of preserving himself."[56] This was a traditional Stoic claim, which
Aquinas himself had restated.[57]

It is also misleading to suggest that early modern theorists could not conceive of rights "outside and beyond the state." An obvious counterexample
here is Francisco de Vitoria's *De Indis* (c. 1532), in which the Spanish Do-
minican argued that native Americans had certain inalienable natural rights,
including that of property (*dominium*).[58] While he recognized in the Amerindian societies the basic outlines of a *civitas*, their rights did not proceed from
this embryonic political structure, which merely offered as evidence that they
were reasonable creatures.[59] Rather, they possessed these rights as a direct
consequence of their innate reasonableness. What's more, Vitoria portrays
their natural rights as "trumps" against the sovereign power of the Spanish
crown. While it would be grossly anachronistic to portray Vitoria as a human
rights prosecutor, he does depict his investigation as a response to the stories
of murder and pillage coming out of the New World.[60] In order to assess the
lawfulness of the Spanish actions there, he had to ground his judgment on a
higher authority than the state. This foundation was natural law, itself under-
written by God. The Amerindians may have been sinners, but even "a sinner
has a right to defend his own life."[61]

It was in similar terms of rights violations by European sovereigns that
Raynal's *Histoire philosophique* would criticize colonial practices some 250
years later.[62] But the supra-national authority of natural law was in fact long
recognized even by theoreticians of absolutism. Jean Bodin restricted sovereign power to what was allowed by "les loix de Dieu et de nature";[63] and the
actions of Hobbes's Leviathan were similarly curtailed by the laws of nature.[64]
These limits on sovereignty were not just rhetorical. Some scholars have even

claimed to find an embryonic theory of the "responsibility to protect" (R2P) in Grotius's *De jure belli ac pacis* (*The Law of War and Peace*, 1625).[65] If this responsibility still falls on sovereign states, their intervention on behalf of foreigners whose own rulers violated natural law implies that these foreigners' rights were not merely recognized and affirmed by their own state (which, in this example, it did not), but also "universally," including by those states called upon to protect them. This use of a violations threshold to determine when foreign intervention in defense of a people is warranted continues to serve as a standard for delimiting core human rights today.[66] Far from being "*subordinate* features of the creation of both state and nation,"[67] then, natural rights were foundational elements of nascent international law.

## 5. Inalienability vs. the Alienation of Rights

To some extent, the question of when rights became synonymous with individual "trumps" is another way of asking when rights became inalienable. But these are overlapping, not identical, questions, with distinct histories. The concept of inalienable rights emerged out of Roman law and was developed in the thirteenth century as a quality of sovereignty, with respect to property rights.[68] As the king could not alienate any part of his domain, he was said to possess inalienable rights over it. Ernst Kantorowicz argued that the concept of the sovereign's inalienable property rights was first developed in England, but it was also strongly associated with France. Many commentators, including Voltaire, pointed to François I as an early advocate of sovereign inalienability.[69] In a 1542 edict, this monarch had reaffirmed "nos droictz qui sont, comme dict est, dommaniaulx, & patrimoniaulx, & inalienables de nostre dicte couronne."[70] Theorists of royal absolutism later latched on to inalienability as a general feature of sovereignty. "All agree that the rights of the crown cannot be relinquished or alienated [sont incessibles, inaliénables]," wrote Bodin in his *Six livres de la République* (1576).[71] This identification of inalienable rights with sovereign power would be reasserted throughout the seventeenth century, both in France and in England, where, toward the beginning of the century, they still remained associated with the French crown.[72]

Following the Glorious Revolution, Williamites adopted the concept of inalienability for individual rights. The government spy Richard Kingston, for instance, argued that "Resistance for Self-Defence, is a Right of Nature, and Inalienable"; tellingly, he still paid heed to the earlier sense of inalienability, criticizing the "prevailing opinions of the age [ . . . ] among which this was one, viz. that Monarchy and Hereditary Succession was by Divine Right, and Inalienable."[73] During the eighteenth century, it was not uncommon for philosophers,

such as Francis Hutcheson, and theologians, such as Richard Fiddes, to refer
to our "unalienable rights" or "the natural and inalienable rights of mankind."[74]
But one had to wait until later in the century for French and American authors
to pry the concept of inalienable rights fully loose from royal power.[75] In the
American colonies, critics of British policies began referring to the "unalienable
rights" of the colonists, rather than those of the king or of churches, in the aftermath of the Stamp Act (1765).[76] In France, Diderot described natural rights as
"inaliénables" as early as 1755, in an *Encyclopédie* article, but this qualifier did
not stick.[77] It was only in the 1770s that authors began to repeat it with some
regularity. Diderot's friend the baron d'Holbach insisted in 1773 that "the rights
of nations are grounded in nature: they are inalienable. The rights of man are
as old as the human species; the rights of justice have no statute of limitation."[78]

As chapters 3, 6, and 7 will show, the 1770s were an important decade in
the history of natural rights, particularly for the preservation regime. But the
history of this regime extends much further back; the addition of the term
"inalienable" to individual rights was not a necessary step in developing the
idea that natural rights should be retained in a political state. What's more,
this idea was in fact far more radical than the limited claim that *some* natural
rights were "inalienable."

### 6. Roman Law, the *Lex Regia*, and the Genealogy of Rights Regimes

As Gerson's adoption of natural rights theory during the Western Schism indicates, the basic tenets of the preservation regime were already in place by
the fifteenth century, if not earlier. But what exactly does this mean? Before
the late sixteenth century, the preservation regime was often a default position, not a particularly well-thought-out theory of government. The question
of what happened to our natural rights in political society was not one that
authors who defended this claim necessarily asked themselves. In part, they
ignored the question because they did not share the underlying assumption
that there was a great divide between political society and the state of nature.
As we saw (and I discuss further in chapter 2), it was largely thanks to Hobbes
that these two states became seen as ontologically distinct conditions. Until
then, political thinkers were more likely to adopt a more Aristotelian perspective, according to which human beings are always to be found in some sort of
political arrangement.

Although we can detect the outlines of the preservation regime in the fifteenth century, then, we should be wary not to project back on to this period
the more robust claims of, say, the revolutionary age. Gerson was not Jefferson,
and there is no inevitable, causal chain that led from one to the other. In fact,

the preservation regime, for a long time, was not distinguished from the transfer regime. Consider the famous revolutionary Huguenot pamphlet *Vindiciae contra tyrannos* (1579). Its prefatory poem asserts that this work "defines true kings and leading men and teaches peoples their rights [iura]." And in his prefatory notes, "Cono Superantius" adds his hope that, thanks to this book, "the ancient rights of the peoples should be restored in their entirety. . . ."[79] But the treatise itself sets forth the demand that "the sovereign rights and privileges originally held by the people as a whole should be exercised [ . . . ] *on their behalf* and in their own interest."[80] The author(s) abruptly switched here from demanding that our rights be "restored" to us, to implying that we must transfer them to the government, only to retrieve them in cases of sovereign mismanagement. Similar ambiguities abound throughout this period.

It would take the repeated theoretical assaults of those authors defending the other two rights regimes to make preservation theorists articulate a more thorough and robust defense of their own position. While the primary objective of this book is to study that development, it also seeks to understand how and why these other two regimes came about. In part, they arose in response to the perceived dangers of the preservation regime, as championed by revolutionaries in 1570s France and 1640s England. But these responses also drew on earlier debates about the origins of monarchic power. Indeed, the question of what happens to our political rights when we place ourselves under the rule of government was a legacy of Roman law, and more particularly of the *lex regia*.[81]

According to the Justinian *Digest*, the *imperium*, or "right to rule," of a Roman emperor was originally conferred on him by the people: "What the Emperor wills has the force of law; seeing that, by a *lex regia* which was passed on the subject of his sovereignty, the people confer [conferat] upon him the whole of their own sovereignty and power."[82] The historical grounds of this "royal law" have long been called into question, but the medieval Glossators who retrieved and retransmitted Roman law to Western Europe firmly believed it to be true.[83] They disagreed, however, on what exactly this transfer of power entailed. One line of interpretation, notably pushed by Irnerius (c. 1050–c. 1130), took the *lex regia* to mean that the Roman people had abandoned the entirety of their legislative and executive power to the emperor once and for all. In this reading, they did not retain any original power—or what would later be called natural right—of self-government. But another group of jurists, championed by Azo of Bologna (c. 1150–1230), understood the *lex regia* to be revocable, should the body of the people so desire. Despite having transferred their power to the emperor, the people thus retained some "residual dormant right" to choose or replace their sovereign. Scholars have found in this doctrine the stirrings of modern constitutional thought.[84]

This notion of a popular consent to monarchic rule would live on in various theories of absolutism, as well as in the coronation oaths of early modern Europe.[85] In the sixteenth and seventeenth centuries, however, this debate was recast in terms of natural rights, with the two dueling interpretations of what the *lex regia* meant for popular rights forming the basis of two alternative rights regimes. The traditional "absolutist" interpretation, which held that the people irreversibly alienated their rights when choosing a sovereign, became the abridgment regime of natural rights. The common origin of these two political frameworks is evident in this passage from Grotius's *De jure belli ac pacis*:

> It is lawful for any Man to engage himself as a Slave to whom he pleases. [ . . . ] Why should it not therefore be as lawful for a People that are at their own Disposal, to deliver up themselves to any one or more Persons, and transfer [transcribat] the Right of governing them [regendi sui jus] upon him or them, without reserving any Share of that Right to themselves?[86]

Later authors defending total alienation, such as Hobbes, did not always share the view that sovereignty was an aggregate of the powers of individuals in a state of nature. And Hobbes also shifted the focus from alienation to abridgment, emphasizing not just the dispossession of rights but their disappearance. But even the renunciation of political power by individuals required some sort of decree or oath (in Hobbes's case, a "covenant of every man with every man").[87]

As we saw, however, the *lex regia* could also be read in a more conditional mode. And it was precisely on the principle that contracts should have a termination clause that the transfer regime of rights rested. In this regime, the people do "reserve a share of that right to themselves" and can overrule, or even depose, a sovereign if he fails to live up to his side of the bargain. Almain's conciliarist argument rests precisely on this alternative interpretation of the *lex regia*. If the ruler can legitimately exercise justice, it is because "[t]he community confers on the prince the authority to kill those whose life leads to harm to the commonwealth. [ . . . ] [T]he prince does not have that authority from himself." The *imperium* of the ruler, in other words, is "conferred"—the same term as in the *Digest*—by the people. But Almain then channels Azo by insisting that "if the king rules not to the edification but to the destruction of the polity, it [the people] can depose him. . . ."[88] The power transfer was reversible. In the late seventeenth century, this transfer regime would enjoy particular attention, most notably with Spinoza and Locke.

The fate of individual rights in the transfer regime is somewhat ambiguous, and this ambiguity has contributed to much confusion in the scholarship on some authors, Locke in particular. (I discuss this further in chapter 2.) Can individuals still be said to possess rights if they transferred them, even conditionally, to the body politic? What is the nature of our claim to these rights? Most authors were fairly clear on the issue: as with the abridgment regime, when we transferred our rights, we gave them up, with the added caveat that we could regain them under special circumstances. The contrast here with the preservation regime was stark. Theorists who defended the idea that we maintained our natural rights in political society insisted on the fact that we could still *enjoy* them as individuals. As Daniel Defoe put it:

> No Man Possesses what he can't enjoy;
> And all Enjoyment's Lame, but that which knows,
> A Power to Keep, as well as to dispose.[89]

While we can recognize in this theory our own conception of rights as entitlements to be enjoyed at all times, it bears noting that this definition can also lend itself to rather utopian ideas about government. Depending on the range and number of natural rights one was willing to admit, the very possibility of government could fade away. The ideal of liberty that some preservationists touted was often less republican than libertarian.[90] This rights regime could also be put to the service of representative democracies; it was, as I suggested above, a building block of modern constitutionalism. But we should be wary not to spin a Whiggish yarn around its rise. As the example of the Physiocrats shows, preservationism would become a hallmark of laissez-faire economic policy (see chapters 3 and 4). If it was instrumental in the revolutionary struggles of the late eighteenth century, it is also the intellectual forefather of free-market fundamentalism.

For better or for worse, we primarily think about rights today within the preservation regime. The following chapters explore how this regime took hold in the period between John Major's tenure in Paris and the holding of the Estates General in Versailles. Obviously, this was not just a French story, and many of its most important twists and turns occurred elsewhere (notably in England and the United States). But the gradual domination of the preservation regime over its rivals is an essential chapter in the history of human rights, and a chapter that has hitherto escaped attention.

## 7. Writing Intellectual History in a Digital Age

In terms of methodological practices, I make no grand statements in this book but will call attention to two features. First, I continue to be interested in the narrative and temporal dimensions of political theory.[91] The central insight of this book—that different rights regimes coexisted and competed during much of the early modern period—was only made possible by an awareness of this x-axis in political thought. This focus is largely absent in the two main approaches to political history found in most scholarship today. The Cambridge school, to which I am otherwise indebted, typically seeks to identify the "speech acts" or "grammar" of political languages, sometimes explicitly comparing their object of inquiry to Saussure's *langue*.[92] This more synchronic approach would seem to rule out, by definition, a diachronic analysis. In the case of rights, the differences between the three regimes outlined here would not be apparent from a more "grammatical" perspective; indeed, in one of the early methodological statements of the Cambridge school, they were treated as a single language.[93]

My focus on rival regimes might appear more closely related to the *Begriffsgeschichte* method, from which I have also learned a great deal, but the resemblance, in this specific instance, is misleading. Where Reinhart Koselleck and his followers examine debates over the meanings of individual concepts, these are not the kinds of debate at stake here. Almost all of the authors I consider in this book shared a basic understanding of "natural rights" as individual entitlements all could enjoy in a state of nature. Their disagreements only arose over what *happened* to these rights when humans transitioned from a state of nature into a political order. In other words, it was the narratives that were contested; the concepts, not so much.

The other methodological feature that may stand out in this book is my use of digital methods and databases. At the simplest level, I have availed myself, like most scholars today, of the remarkable power and efficiency of such databases as EEBO, ECCO, Gallica, FRANTEXT, Early American Imprints, and Google Books, for retrieving texts and search words. I am well aware of the limitations and challenges of using such resources, both in terms of selection bias and poor quality scanning (aka "dirty OCR"). That said, because my interest lies primarily in identifying large-scale trends, my tolerable margins of error are much larger. I mostly use these databases to extend my corpus beyond canonical works and to identify lesser-known authors, thereby revealing which debates and trends resonated most widely.

I do, however, make some use of statistical analysis, mostly in terms of word frequencies. The tables scattered throughout the book, whether from Google Book's Ngram Viewer or my own home-brew graphs, are not intended in any way to be demonstrative, but merely to provide some degree of corroboration for some of my more sweeping statements (of the sort, "rights talk was largely absent in France during the first half of the eighteenth century"). I do not consider such data visualizations to be terribly accurate in their details,

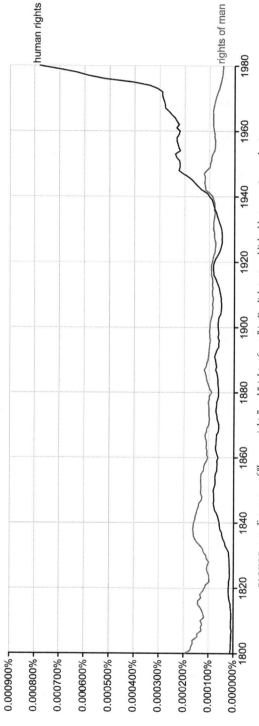

FIGURE 1.5. Frequency of "human rights" and "rights of man" in English texts published between 1800 and 1980. *Source:* From Google Books Ngram Viewer.

but they can be useful for noticing broad patterns.[94] They are a kind of theatrical backdrop, setting the scene and providing context for the more detailed interventions on the stage.

Of course, one should always treat word searches with caution. Concepts can feature under different names, which can make tracking their rise and fall tricky. For instance, the expression *droits de l'homme* may only have appeared in French in the second half of the eighteenth century.[95] But as the following chapter shows, there had been cognate expressions in circulation for the previous two centuries, including *droits humains, droits de [la] nature, droits naturels, droits des hommes*, and *droits de l'humanité*. Before 1650, the more common spelling was *droicts*, a minor difference, but one that can completely throw off word searches. *Rights of man, rights of mankind*, and many other variations thereon were similarly employed in seventeenth- and eighteenth-century England. There are no doubt differences in signification between these terms, and important reasons why, say, "human" or "mankind" became the preferred attribute over "natural."[96] At the same time, these expressions and concepts are clearly closely related (they were often used interchangeably) and belong to the same current of thought. By the late eighteenth century, the French expression *droits de l'homme* mostly eclipsed its alternatives and has remained in place ever since (though *droits humains* is sometimes preferred). In English, by contrast, *rights of man* and *human rights* were used in almost equal measure throughout the nineteenth century, with the latter only surpassing the former in frequency after 1940 (see fig. 1.5). Depending on the language one chooses, then, one could reach very different conclusions about the history of *human rights* versus the history of *droits de l'homme*.

The limitations of digital searches thus highlight a key methodological point about the history of rights: one can't be too much of a nominalist. If *droits de l'homme* replaced *droits naturels* as the choice expression in French, it was largely for a historically contingent reason, viz., the publication and immediate fame of the Déclaration des droits de l'homme et du citoyen. The decline of *rights of man* after 1940 was similarly connected to the appearance of the 1948 Universal Declaration of Human Rights. While words and documents are what provide us our access to the conceptual history of rights, they are only the surface phenomena we use to track the complex, and at times subterranean, evolution of ideas.

## PART I

# Early Modern Rights Regimes

# When Did Rights Become "Rights"? From the Wars of Religion to the Dawn of Enlightenment

In 1576 a three-volume work appeared in Geneva, with a false imprint, entitled *Mémoires de l'état de France sous Charles IX*. It contained a text that would go down in the annals of political thought: Etienne de La Boétie's *Discours sur la servitude volontaire*, published there for the first time in full.[1] The author, who died in 1563, had penned this treatise as a college student, around mid-century; since then, it had circulated only in manuscript. Its sentences still burned with youthful incandescence, castigating tyrants with the torch of liberty. But within pages redolent of Plutarch, whom La Boétie had also translated, there arose a more modern note as well, a justification of political liberty in terms of individual rights. "[M]an must [ . . . ] regain his natural right [se remettre en son droit naturel]," the author insisted, "and, so to speak, go from beast to man." Regaining our rights was both a political liberation and a return to our natural social condition: "If we lived with the rights that nature has given us [les droits que la nature nous a donnés] and the lessons she imparted, we would be naturally obedient to our parents, subject to reason, and the serfs of no-one."[2] Natural rights, as this passage clearly indicates, should remain in force in political society; to abandon them was to subject ourselves to the whims of tyrants and to alienate ourselves from our very humanity.

Already in the middle of the sixteenth century, then, there were authors who passionately defended the preservation regime of rights. In fact, La Boétie's dear friend Michel de Montaigne would later suggest that such arguments were banal, "a common theme hashed over in a thousand places in books."[3] While it is unclear which other books (ancient? contemporary?) Montaigne had in mind, there was some truth to his claim: as we saw in chapter 1, neo-Thomist theologians at the University of Paris such as John Major and Jacques Almain had put the language of individual, inalienable rights back into circulation. La Boétie was not the founder of any rights discourse. But Montaigne had other reasons to dismiss his friend's text as a piece of immature juvenilia: the volumes in which it first appeared were the work of Huguenot revolutionaries.[4] Their interest lay not in Greek tyrants, but in the sitting French king, Henri III, whose brother, Charles IX, had reigned over the massacre of Protestants on Saint Bartholomew's Day, 1572. Their appropriation of La Boétie signaled the extent to which debates about rights would henceforth be caught up in the turmoil of the religious wars and in their political consequences.

## 1. Monarchomachs and Tyrannicides: Natural Rights in the French Wars of Religion

It pays to recall that natural rights, in early modern Europe, were not only used to advance political claims. Ecclesiastical literature regularly intoned about the natural rights of the clergy and churches, the Gallican Church in particular.[5] Kings had natural rights, though in their case this expression referred to their rights by birth, following the Latin roots of "nature" (from *nascio*, to be born).[6] In the same vein, legal texts discussing the succession rights of children often referred to their "natural rights."[7]

Once hopes of a political reconciliation between Catholics and Protestants were dashed, however, Huguenot pamphleteers latched onto the idea of natural rights in order to challenge the legitimacy of the French monarch. Fragments of La Boétie's treatise had first appeared in a work that signaled the new Huguenot line after the 1572 massacre, *Le Reveille-matin des François*.[8] The author (possibly Nicolas Barnaud) struck many of the same themes as La Boétie, denouncing the bestial condition of humans who lived without rights: "[O]h wretched people! Must their condition be worse than beasts, who nature has at least taught to preserve themselves? Are they to be treated worse than the slave, whom natural right [le droict de nature], the law of nations, and also civil law grant protection from a master who he seeks to kill him?"[9] Here the author still employed *droit de nature* in the classical (objective) sense of *ius naturale*, that is, the body of natural laws. This was the more common usage throughout this work, though it came with some innovations in terminology: the author raged that "our enemies [ . . . ] attack us and violate their conscience and every right of humanity [tout droit d'humanité] to satisfy the tyrant's will."[10] This right of humanity was not a human right; it was closer to natural law. But subjective rights were not foreign to the Huguenot revolutionaries: if every individual could legitimately "defend himself from tyranny" by "withdrawing from [the tyrant's] subjection," it was because "my

right [mon droit], my fortune, my honor, and my life, even my salvation" cannot be "abandonned and lost."[11] Tellingly, one of the fragments of La Boétie's
*Discours* that the author cited was precisely the passage on the need to "regain
his natural right [son droit naturel]."[12]

These rights-based arguments also informed another important pamphlet published in the aftermath of the Saint-Bartholomew's Day Massacre,
Théodore de Bèze's *Du droit des magistrats sur leurs subjets* (1574). The Huguenot theologian, and Calvin's successor in Geneva, once again reached for
the language of subjective rights to rail against tyranny: "[W]ho is guiltier of
this crime [of *lèse-majesté*] than the Tyrant who manifestly violates all divine
and human rights [tous droits divins & humains]?"[13] This expression, "divine
and human rights," appears repeatedly throughout his text (occasionally in the
singular, as well). For Bèze, these rights functioned chiefly as a barrier against
political subjugation: "[I]t is for magistrates, and especially for sovereigns,
to rule; this I grant, but add that their power is limited by divine and human
rights [les droits divins & humains]."[14] While his early use of the expression
"human rights" is arresting, what is perhaps more significant is that these
rights were conceived in opposition to sovereign power, not as its result.[15]

If the Huguenot revolutionaries rallied around the notion of natural rights,
it was also because they provided support for their constitutional claims. Bèze
discussed the dissolution of political bonds in terms that foreshadowed the
social contract theorists of the following century: "when a sovereign becomes
a tyrant, and the people use their right against him, he is the one who unbinds
[deslié] the people by his perjury, not the contrary."[16] This appeal to constitutional, rather than confessional, arguments, was part of a concerted effort
to turn even French Catholic readers away from their ruler.[17] But it must also
be viewed within the context of the multiple constitutional documents that
Huguenot communities drafted around this time.[18] While these texts did not
contain anything resembling a declaration of rights, they did propose such
revolutionary ideas as convoking the Estates General without the first estate
(i.e., the clergy), and even proposed doubling the representation of the third
estate.[19]

There was a certain ambiguity with the natural rights that these texts affirmed. On the one hand, they were firmly affixed to individuals.[20] For the
Huguenots, religious freedom was the most fundamental of natural rights, and
it was the Catholic sovereign's violation of this deeply personal right that, in
their eyes, justified political resistance. As Bèze argued, "every individual [un
chacun particulier] must defend his oppressed fatherland with all his power,
especially when his religion and liberty are at stake." On the other hand, this
individual action only gained recognition when exercised collectively; "the

people [les peuples] use their right against [the Tyrant]," Bèze asserted else-where.[21] *Le Reveille-matin* made the same assumption: "[T]here is no statute of limitations against the rights of the people [les droits du peuple] and the estates" (2:88). In this reading, our individual natural rights are bundled into collective rights, exercised not only by the people as a whole, but by their representative bodies, namely, the Estates General. In the sixteenth century, this ambiguity does not appear to have been particularly significant, as these two conceptions of natural right (individual vs. collective) did not come into conflict. It was a different story, however, during the French Revolution, as we will see in chapter 6.

Huguenot revolutionaries were not alone in using pre-political rights to advance their political agenda. After Henri III had the duc de Guise (leader of the Catholic League) assassinated in 1588, his Catholic subjects now became even more shrill in their calls for armed resistance, adding demands for ty-rannicide. A notorious case was the *ligueur* and University of Paris professor Jean Boucher, who approved of the assassination of Henri III (in 1589) and also applauded the Jesuit-educated Jean Châtel's attempt on the life of Henri IV (in 1594). In his *Apologie pour Iehan Chastel Parisien*, Boucher invoked Cicero on tyrants: "[W]e know how they have always been described and judged, whether it be by nature, or the agreement of wise men. [ . . . ] Cicero wrote [ . . . ] that all the rights of nature are suspended with tyrants [tous droicts de nature cessent envers les tyrans]. . . ."[22] In addition to encouraging the more extreme measure of assassination, Boucher's claim here is somewhat different than, say, Bèze's, as it implies that our natural rights would normally not extend to authorizing such an act, rather than stating that sovereigns who *invade* our rights are tyrants. In both cases, however, these natural rights are presumed to remain active and exercisable in society.

What one might call the political "weaponization" of natural rights in the sixteenth century does not therefore appear to have been triggered by any theological specificities of the Protestant or Catholic faiths.[23] Huguenot revo-lutionaries published the Catholic La Boétie (himself an opponent of religious toleration); Catholic *ligueurs* advanced similar arguments to their confessional foes. There was obviously a more general Christian dimension to this story: it was, after all, the revival of neo-Thomism at the University of Paris that reintroduced the language and logic of inalienable natural rights. From there, however, rights talk flowed into both the Spanish Catholic school of natural law theory and into Calvinism. Indeed, the founders of both schools spent their formative years in Paris, with Jean Calvin studying directly under John Major, and Francisco de Vitoria under one of his pupils (Pierre Crockaert).[24]

Even before the Reformation ripped states apart, theologians who insisted on the existence of natural rights in society were of course making political claims. As we saw in the chapter 1, many of the rights-based arguments fashioned by advocates of conciliarism would later resurface in constitutionalist theory. John Major argued that it was "within the rights of the people to transfer from one race to another the kingly power," so long as it was done "with deliberation."[25] Vitoria would go so far as to place the question of natural rights, and more specifically of *dominium*, at the heart of imperial debates.[26] But if these earlier emphases on rights paved the way for their later revolutionary roles, they still lacked a crucial element—the very element that arguably made them revolutionary. What "weaponized" the preservation regime of rights was its merger with the even older political theory of tyrannicide.[27] Because classical justifications of tyrannicide already rested on natural law theory, it was a fairly seamless, almost self-evident merger, one that could have occurred to any number of students who, like La Boétie, were reading Plutarch and Cicero alongside Major and Almain. Before 1572, such accusations of tyranny in the name of natural rights still retained a bookish quality that made them seem more appropriate for the ancient world. The same words, after the Saint-Bartholomew's Day Massacre, cut much closer to home. The scholarly brio that La Boétie's friends had once admired now dazzled with subversive audacity. The revolutionary potential of rights had been fully activated.

Its threatening power revealed, rights talk itself would soon come under withering scrutiny. It would be the Catholic, and more specifically Jesuit, connection that led to its severe censorship in the first decades of the seventeenth century. Following the discovery of Châtel's connection to their Society, the Jesuits were briefly expelled from France.[28] When François Ravaillac successfully murdered Henri IV in 1610, they again fell into disrepute, notably since the Spanish Jesuit theologian Juan de Mariana had recently justified tyrannicide, and more particularly the assassination of Henri III, in his *De rege et regis institutione* (1598).[29] The Paris Parlement condemned this work to be publicly burned in the immediate aftermath of Henry IV's death; other Jesuit authors, including Francisco Suárez, would soon be banned as well. Any claim that individuals retained natural rights in political societies was viewed with suspicion: the University of Paris purged scholars who had expressed sympathy for what was now viewed as a regicidal doctrine.[30] Fifteen years later, when Grotius published *De jure belli ac pacis* in Paris, where he was living at the time, he studiously avoided citing any of these Jesuitical works, which he knew well and praised elsewhere.[31] More critically, the preservation regime of rights was no longer acceptable: where La Boétie had exhorted his reader to "live with the rights that nature gave us," Grotius claimed that we give them up, like slaves who sell themselves to a master, when we enter into a political regime.[32]

The emergence of an absolutist political culture in France thus corresponded with a general silencing of natural rights talk. Mentions could still crop up in historical accounts: in 1623 Auger de Moléon de Granier, a future member of the Académie française, published a *Recueil de divers mémoires* that contained an "Harangue de Monsieur le Chancelier [François] Olivier faicte au Parlement de Paris, l'an 1559." In this speech, delivered in front of Henri II shortly before his accidental death, the chancellor had expressed regret that "all natural rights [tous les droicts naturels] and duties [offices] of humanity have always ceased" in the face of religious zealotry.[33] Another historical document, cited by the Huguenot soldier and poet Agrippa d'Aubigné, recorded the use of natural rights by the *parlementaires* that same year (1559).[34] But texts addressing the contemporary political situation mostly shunned this language: one exception, the statesman Philippe de Béthune's treatise *Le conseiller d'estat* (1633), merely recycled without attribution the above-cited speech by Chancellor Olivier.[35]

This sudden silencing of natural rights suggests a significant degree of state- and self-censorship. This hypothesis finds support in the fact that the situation changed again dramatically after Louis XIV revoked the Edict of Nantes in 1685. As a century earlier, it was the Huguenots in particular who brandished the language of natural rights to defend themselves against a Catholic monarch who was acting in a "tyrannical" manner. The pastor and theologian Jean Claude, who sought refuge in The Hague, decried the unjust persecutions of the Protestants, which were "contrary to reason, the rights of nature [aux droits de la Nature] and the rights of society."[36] In a later work, he also denounced "the blind obedience that [the Catholic Church] expects from the faithful toward their pastors," which he claimed was "a tyrannical principle that violated the natural rights of Christianity."[37] The Genevan writer Jean Tronchin du Breuil, who had fled Paris for Amsterdam, deplored in similar terms the plight of the Protestant Vaudois, who, evicted from the Piedmont for their religious beliefs, fought for their return: there was simply no justification, he alleged, "to allow a distinguished people, resolute in their faith [ . . . ] to be deprived of their natural and civil rights."[38] And in an addendum to the article "Calvinisme" in Louis Moréri's *Grand dictionnaire historique*, the Protestant scholar Jean Le Clerc (or Leclerc), who had also sought asylum in Amsterdam, rhetorically asked, "[I]f he [the king] obliged them to adopt his religion, against divine right, would the people be in the wrong if they defended their natural rights with the same force that was opposed to them?"[39] The Huguenot refugees had forcefully reclaimed the preservation regime of rights, in whose name individuals could fight to defend themselves against a tyrannical ruler.

Where were they finding these arguments? Some seem to have been familiar with texts by Bèze and other Monarchomachs.[40] But their residence in the Netherlands may also have contributed to their political education. Indeed, the Dutch, too, grounded their arguments for political freedom in natural rights. In his *Supplication to the King's Majesty of Spain*, published during the Dutch Revolt, William I of Orange accused the Duke of Alba of enforcing laws that were "repugnant contrarie to all godly and naturall rightes."[41] A century later, the *Memoires de Jean de Wit, grand pensionnaire de Hollande* (attributed to his follower Pieter de la Court) again proclaimed the importance of preserving natural rights in society: "[I]n every country in the world the greatest happiness of a political society" comes from granting "to all inhabitants the full liberty to preserve their bodies and souls," including the liberty "to use [employer] their natural rights."[42] This was also a major theme in the French Protestant historian Jean Jennet's four-volume history of the Dutch Republic:

> But there are other rights and other privileges, that are naturally acquired by men, that naturally belong to them by virtue of their being human [par cela même qu'ils sont hommes], and which they possess even before they enter into society, and that they bring with them as they unite with their neighbors, and that they aimed to preserve by means of this confederation [ils ont eu dessein de se conserver par le moien de cette confédération].[43]

The revolutionary regime of rights is here described in all its fullness: simply by virtue of being human ("par cela même qu'ils sont hommes"), we possess pre-political and inalienable rights, and the purpose of government is to preserve them. Revolutionaries in America and France, a century later, would flesh out these claims but not significantly alter them.

For the historian interested only in the origins of the preservation regime, it might be tempting to end the story here. Conceptually hammered out by the early sixteenth century, then enriched by classical theories of tyrannicide, the rights regime that eighteenth-century declarations would enshrine had already acquired its distinctly modern revolutionary character after 1572. Told in this manner, however, this story falsely suggests that the revolutionary regime of rights was consistently available, just lying on the shelf waiting for would-be revolutionaries to come along and dust it off. Worse still, it could imply that revolutionary rights, after their "discovery" in the sixteenth century, were simply "destined" to triumph in the eighteenth. In fact, the adoption of this regime by Atlantic revolutionaries was anything but teleological. To understand how it did come to pass, we must place the story of the preservation regime within a broader history of natural rights, and of those authors who sought not to silence the revolutionaries, but to prove them wrong.

## 2. English Liberties and Natural Rights: Leveller Arguments in the English Civil War

At the time when Huguenot exiles were defending their natural rights, another French refugee, Pierre Bayle, published an attack on the preservation regime, in the anonymous *Avis important aux réfugiés sur leur prochain retour en France . . .* (1690).[44] Here he chided the oppressed Protestant minority for believing it could "regain its natural rights to independence [ses droits naturels d'independance], as soon as the promises it had received were broken." But this belief could only lead to a "strange and terrible state," since it would prove impossible to establish genuine political sovereignty. Bayle even invoked Scripture (turning the other cheek) to justify passive obedience in the face of despotic ruler.[45] His work set off a firestorm and inspired powerful refutations: from London, the French pastor Jacques Abbadie answered with a *Défense de la nation britannique* (subtitled *Les droits de Dieu, de la Nature, & de la Société*), which simultaneously defended the English Revolution and the natural rights of all Christians, concluding forcefully that "the rights of nature can never be lost [les droits de la nature ne se perdent jamais]."[46] Although Abbadie's work would enjoy an unexpected afterlife in the late eighteenth century,[47] Bayle's arguments were more in keeping with the trends of the time. These trends were coming out of England, and they were not favorable to the preservation regime of rights.

Despite France and England's geographical and intellectual proximity, French and English political thought largely developed along separate tracks in the seventeenth century. There were, to be sure, various points of intersection: as we will see, some of the arguments advanced by the radical French Huguenots resurfaced during the English Civil War;[48] and in the eighteenth century, English political thought gained increasing prominence on the Continent. But the remarkably divergent trajectories of France and England during the seventeenth century made it difficult to translate, in a conceptual sense, political claims formulated in and about one country to the other. Between 1610 and 1715, France was ruled by a mere two monarchs, from the same family; during the same period, England witnessed six kings, two queens, one lord protector, three royal dynasties, and at least three different political regimes, including a commonwealth. Accordingly, certain political questions—such as who has the right to rule, or when can a people legitimately resist their ruler—were less likely (or allowed) to be raised in France. England's turbulent conditions, conversely, provided a unique laboratory for experimenting with a whole range of political theories. The results of these experiments would shape the ways that philosophers and political actors in England, the American colonies, and post-Louisquatorzian France would think about rights up to the French Revolution.

As in other Western European countries, English legal theorists had long employed the language of natural law, and on occasion natural rights, which was part of their shared Roman law inheritance.[49] What made England more distinctive was its constitutional legacy. Where natural lawyers spoke of natural rights, English jurists and politicians routinely invoked the "rights and liberties" of English subjects, hard-won from the monarchy in the thirteenth century and inscribed in their "Great Charter of Liberties," or Magna Carta. The combination of these two kinds of rights talk—natural and constitutional—would produce a particularly resilient and lasting Anglo-American regime of rights.

Perhaps because the English had constitutional rights to preserve, they did not pay much attention to natural rights before the seventeenth century.[50] Richard Hooker, an Anglican divine who served as a respected authority on natural law in the following century, did not develop a theory of natural rights in *Of the Lawes of Ecclesiastical Politie* (1594–97).[51] Even during their early skirmishes with Charles I, the Parliamentarians stuck mainly with constitutionalist claims: Sir Edward Coke's 1628 "Petition of Right," for instance, makes no mention of natural rights or even natural laws in its remonstrances to the king. But the situation shifted dramatically once it became clear that the traditional means of parliamentary resistance permitted by constitutional doctrine were insufficient.[52] While the majority of Parliament remained committed, at least in theory, to constitutional forms—going so far, in 1642, as to declare war against the king in order to "save" him,[53] and still seeking to negotiate with Charles after the Second Civil War (1648)[54]—a group of pamphleteers known as the Levellers legitimated their appeals for more radical political reform by invoking natural rights.[55]

Historians of political thought have highlighted the conceptual debt owed by the Levellers to the radical Huguenots of the 1570s, but the Levellers also transformed these earlier arguments in an important way. The two leading Leveller pamphleteers in particular, John Lilburne and Richard Overton, combined the natural rights talk of the Huguenots with English constitutional claims. English liberties became natural rights, with Lilburne referring to them in one breath as "naturall, rationall, nationall, and legall liberties, and freedoms."[56] Overton made this identification even more explicit in *An Arrow against all Tyrants* (1646), where he argued that the charges on which he was held in the Tower of London were "illegal, and contrary to the natural rights, freedoms and properties of the free Commoners of England (confirmed to them by Magna Charta, the Petition of Right, and the Act for the abolishment of the Star-chamber)."[57] The effect of this identification was double: on the one hand, it gave greater legitimacy to civil rights and even left open the possibility of extending them beyond those spelled out in constitutional documents; on the other hand, it inscribed natural rights in a constitutional framework, which in turn "confirmed" them. Following this logic, the Levellers grounded their own constitutional proposal for near-universal male suffrage in a natural right:

> That the Supreme Authority of *England* and the Territories therewith incorporate, shall be and reside henceforward in a Representative of the People consisting of four hundred persons, but no more; in the choice of whom (according to naturall right) all men of the age of one and twenty yeers and upwards (not being servants, or receiving alms, or having served in the late King in Arms or voluntary Contributions) shall have their voices. . . .[58]

In most cases, the Levellers simply asserted their claims about the natural origins of English liberties. Accordingly, they tended to be fairly undertheorized, as can be expected from political pamphleteers, rather than philosophical scholars. One exception to this trend was Overton, most notably in his *Arrow against all Tyrants*. Addressed to Sir Henry Marten, an MP who was unusually close to the Levellers, Overton's pamphlet developed his opening thesis that "[t]o every Individual in nature, is given an individual property by nature, not to be invaded or usurped by any." As he also affirmed that "[n]o man hath power over my rights and liberties," he thus had to explain the authority of government. He did so by sketching out an argument that others would subsequently build on to reach very different conclusions. Governments owe their legitimacy, he argued, to the fact that we transfer some of our rights to them: "For their better being, discipline, government, propriety and safety have each of them communicated so much unto you (their chosen ones [i.e., members of Parliament]) of their natural rights and powers, that you might thereby become their absolute commissioners and lawful deputies."[59] Overton did not address the implicit tension in his argument—if we communicate rights and powers, in what sense do we still retain them?—but others would not sidestep this question, as we will see.[60]

The Levellers' ideas were hardly representative of the political thinking on the parliamentary side, even after Pride's Purge. Cromwell's entourage remained very skeptical of natural rights: during the Putney debates, Cromwell's son-in-law and fellow army grandee, Henry Ireton, challenged the army agitators who presented Leveller arguments: "I think you must fly for refuge to an absolute natural right and you must deny all civil right; and I am sure it will come to that in the consequence."[61] Natural rights never became part of the official discourse: they are missing from the "Act Declaring and Constituting the People of England to be a Commonwealth and Free-State" (1649), as well as from the constitution that Parliament eventually did pass in 1653, the "Instrument of Government." Politically, the Levellers were swiftly disbanded and mostly eliminated after 1649.

But the argument that we must "communicate" at least some of our natural rights to government for a political order to exist would not disappear. It features centrally, for instance, in John Milton's *The Tenure of Kings and Magistrates* (1649), written to justify the execution of Charles I and first published a month after this event. At the heart of Milton's justification of tyrannicide lay a contractual theory of government, grounded in natural law and rights:[62] "[A]ll men naturally were borne free," he asserted, echoing Justinian's *Institutes*.[63] If we joined together into commonwealths, it was for the purpose of self-defense. To this end, we inevitably agree to "ordaine som authoritie, that might restraine by force and punishment what was violated against peace and common right." But it took a transfer of our natural rights to establish this authority:

> This autoritie and power of self-defence and preservation being originally and naturally in every one of them, and unitedly in them all, for eases for order, and least each man should be his owne partial judge, they communicated and deriv'd either to one [ . . . ] or to more than one [ . . . ]: the first was call'd a King; the other Magistrates. (10)

This is a dense passage. It foreshadows Locke, both in the argument for establishing government and in the transfer of specific rights or "powers."[64] It also extends the Leveller argument about a "communication" of natural rights that must be restricted: the king and magistrates were to be "Deputies and Commissioners," not "Lords and Masters" (10). At the same time, it is only one passage. And while Milton expressly frames the transfer of power outlined here in terms of natural law, the more specific language of natural rights is missing.[65] It would take Hobbes's full-blown attack on both the preservation and the limited transfer regimes for others to defend and develop the latter two in more theoretically sophisticated manners.

*

As soon as the preservation regime entered into English political discourse, then, it gave way to, and was almost supplanted by, the transfer regime. But it did not vanish altogether. The Levellers' natural-constitutional arguments remained a fairly minor theme in English rights talk for the following century and would go on to know much greater success in the American colonies (see chapter 6). We hear them echoed in Sir Henry Vane's 1656 proposal for a republican government, founded on popular sovereignty, in the name of the people's "just natural rights in civil things, and true freedom in matters of conscience."[66] One group that embraced Leveller ideas were the Quakers (to whom Vane was also close):[67] William Penn, writing apropos the persecution of the Quakers, argued that "[N]o *English-man* can be so sottish, as to conceive that his right to *Liberty* and *Property*, came in with his Profession of the *Protestant Religion*; or that his *natural and humane Rights, are dependant on certain religious apprehensions.*" For Penn, these "humane Rights" derived rather from nature and were protected by English law: "We shall proceed to make it appear that *Magna Charta* (as recited by us) imports nothing less then [*sic*] their preservation."[68] Penn would go on to publish the first American edition of the Magna Carta, when he relocated to Philadelphia.[69]

Still, this argument in favor of the natural source of constitutional rights did not catch on. It hardly featured in the manifold celebrations and defenses of the Glorious Revolution: the few authors who did praise the Revolution for restoring natural rights tended not to make the connection with civil liberties.[70] The rare exceptions were mostly radical Whigs.[71] The mere mention of natural rights could invite accusations of firebrand republicanism: the scholar and clergyman William Hopkins, a High Church Anglican and royalist, attacked Samuel Johnson, the radical Whig author of the fiercely anti-Jamesian (and best-selling) pamphlet *Julian the Apostate* (1682), for not "bear[ing] God's own Government, as wise, just, and gracious as it is, but quarrel[ing] at his holy Laws, which restrain [men's] intemperance, their Lusts and Revenge, as intolerable Usurpations upon the natural Rights and Liberties of Mankind."[72]

With the uptick in French natural rights talk that followed the revocation of the Edict of Nantes, a handful of English authors similarly reasserted the principle that men preserved their natural rights in society. Predictably, we find in this company more radical Whigs, including John Toland, who pitched the debate over press censorship in such terms: "Whosoever therefore endeavours to hinder Men from communicating their Thoughts, (as they notoriously do that are for restraining the Press) invade the natural Rights of Mankind, and destroy the common Ties of Humanity."[73] Tory authors were not above restating this principle either, as the nonjuring clergyman John Scott showed in *The Christian Life* (1696).[74]

Soon, however, both this general claim and its more specific constitutional version would lose steam. When either did resurface, it was generally only in passing, without any attempt at justification. Hence, Daniel Defoe, in 1710, casually referred to "the Constitution [ ... ] which is founded on the natural

Rights of Mankind, and is calculated for the Preservation of their Liberties"; six years later, Joseph Addison likewise praised George I for having "regarded those which are our Civil Liberties, as the natural rights of Mankind; and therefore indulged them to a People [George's Hanoverian subjects], who pleaded no other Claim to them than from His known Goodness and Humanity."[75] But both authors also expressed contrary opinions at other times, suggesting that these comments had not been deeply thought through.[76] Despite the occasional impassioned affirmation of the natural grounds of English liberties, there was little to suggest, by the 1730s, that this argument would carry the day.[77] By this time, two alternative theories about natural rights had grown in popularity. And both challenged the assumption that we could retain such rights in society.

### 3. Abridging Natural Rights: Hobbes and the High Church Divines

Huguenot and Leveller authors had mounted fairly minimalist defenses of the preservation regime. They insisted that we all possessed natural rights, but as we saw, this argument easily morphed into an account of how in fact we transferred some of these rights to our governments. Over the course of the following decades, English and Scottish authors would increasingly differentiate between these preservation and transfer regimes, bringing both of them into greater contrast. But they also had to contend with a third regime, according to which we must simply abandon most of our natural rights when living under government. While this regime was primarily championed by High Church theologians, its most resounding theoretical defense was mounted by Thomas Hobbes.[78]

Like the preservation and transfer regimes, the abridgment regime shares the common premise that all humans are endowed with natural rights. But Hobbes ingeniously claimed that these rights are in conflict with the most desirable of human goods—namely, prosperity and security. The preservation of our natural rights is accordingly an obstacle to the establishment of a commonwealth. As he wrote in *De Cive* (1642), "[I]f each man held on to his *right to all things*, it necessarily follows that some men would be attacking and others defending themselves, and both by right. [ . . . ] *War* would ensue." For this reason, he concluded, "the right of all men to all things must not be held on to; certain rights must be transferred or abandoned."[79] He made a similar argument in *Leviathan* (1651): it was a very condition of government that "a man be willing, when others are so too, as farre-forth, as for Peace, and defence of himselfe he shall think it necessary, *to lay down this right to all things*; and be contented with so much liberty against other men, as he would allow other men against himselfe."[80]

It was not that unusual to suggest that, in transferring their political rights, the people alienated them once and for all. Grotius had said as much in *De jure belli ac pacis*, and a version of this argument could already be found in the "absolutist" interpretation of the *lex regia* (see chapter 1). But it was far more uncommon to insist that some rights simply had to be "abandoned" once and for all. This claim went beyond the assertion that we irreversibly *alienated* some rights when contracting into society, since that logic entailed someone else (an *alius*, i.e., other) taking over our rights. Hobbes seemd to be suggesting that (at least some of) our rights must simply vanish in thin air.

If these rights were natural, how could one justify their complete disappearance? The answer lay in Hobbes's introduction of a sharp caesura between the state of nature and civil society. This caesura was vividly depicted in the bottom half of the frontispiece to *De Cive* (see fig. 2.1). The stark visual contrast here between "Imperium" (Government, or Sovereignty) and "Libertas" is underscored by the very different scenes that play out in the background.[81] Under the protection of government, farmers peacefully reap their crops; in the state of nature, savage Indians attack each other.

Before Hobbes, the state of nature and civil society were not viewed as such ontologically different conditions. As Harro Höpfl points out, the Jesuit theologians who developed the concept of a state of nature (*status naturae*) did not use it to designate a "pre-civil" condition.[82] The idea that there might be a state without any government rarely appears in their work. From an Aristotelian perspective, even a single-family household constitutes a political entity. What's more, humans were naturally social, and political life was our *telos*.[83] But Hobbes's turn against "the Vain Philosophy of Aristotle," combined with accounts he read of Amerindian tribes that "have no government at all," opened up a new framework for thinking about the origins of the state.[84] Instead of an organic body politic, reflecting a natural order of society, he conceived of the state as an "artificial" entity that operates according to its own rules.[85] To be sure, the laws of nature still applied in political societies. In fact, for the most part, they *only* applied there.[86] Indeed, Hobbes further distanced the state of nature from the commonwealth by arguing that natural laws could be superseded, in that former state, by the "right of nature."[87] Accordingly, for society to exist and peace to be established, the right of nature must be "abridged":

[T]he Right of Nature, that is, the naturall Liberty of man, may by the Civill Law be abridged, and restrained: nay, the end of making Lawes is no other, but such Restraint without the which there cannot possibly be any Peace. And Law was brought into the world for nothing else, but to limit the naturall liberty of particular men. . . .[88]

FIGURE 2.1. Frontispiece of Hobbes's *De Cive* by Jean Matheus. Image courtesy of Houghton Library, Harvard University (EC65 H6525 642e).

What exactly did it mean, though, for this natural right to be "abridged" or, as he put it elsewhere, "laid down"? Hobbes outlines two options for this process, without fully explaining which one is at work in his own theory. An individual who wishes to join in civil society can either "renounce" or "transfer" this right. In the first case, "he cares not to whom the benefit thereof redoundeth," whereas in the latter case, "he intendeth the benefit therof to some certain person, or persons." To renounce, he continues, is to "abandon" a right, whereas to transfer is to "grant away." In the private domain, to transfer a right (say, to one's estate) will have a significantly different outcome than merely renouncing it.[89] But most of the time Hobbes uses these terms interchangeably:

> The way by which a man either simply Renounceth, or Transferreth his Right, is a Declaration, or Signification, by some voluntary and sufficient signe, or signes, that he doth so Renounce, or Transferre; or hath so Renounced, or Transferred the same, to him that accepteth it.[90]

If Hobbes seems here to conflate renouncing and transferring, it is in part because both actions follow the same format. It is through a contractual agreement ("a Declaration") that we give this right up. Whether we give it up unilaterally, or give it up to someone, the net result is the same: we lose our ability to enjoy it ("He that transferreth any Right, transferreth the Means of enjoying it"; 210). Even if we transfer a Right, we alienate it.

So when we "lay down this right to all things" and enter into a political contract, are we renouncing or transferring our right of nature? Hobbes is somewhat ambiguous on this point. His first statement suggests renunciation. If the future subject must "be contented with so much liberty against other men, as he would allow other men against himselfe," then presumably he must abandon (i.e., renounce) the liberties that he would not allow other men against himself.[91] When it comes to describing the foundation of the commonwealth, however, Hobbes adopts the language of transfer. The "Covenant of every man with every man," out of which the commonwealth is born, specifically details a rights transfer: "I Authorise and give up my Right of Governing my selfe, to this Man, or to this Assembly of men, on this condition, that thou give up thy Right to him, and Authorise all his Actions in like manner."[92]

One of Hobbes's earliest critics, John Bramhall, pointed out his inconsistencies around this question. "Sometimes he maketh the institution of sovereignty to be only the laying down the right of subjects. [ . . . ] At other times he maketh it to be a surrender. [ . . . ] Before, we had a transferring without transferring; now we have a giving up without giving up. [ . . . ] What is this?"[93] More recently, Noel Malcolm described this process as "a special kind of openended transfer of rights [which] creates a common authority endowed with sovereignty over a group of people."[94] One might say that it is "special" precisely because it is "open-ended." Unlike my right to a specific object, property, or action, the "right of Governing my selfe" is an extraordinarily broad and indeterminate power. What does it include? What does it not include? The illustrations that Hobbes provide suggest few limits: "They that give to a man the Right of government in Soveraignty, are understood to give him the right of levying mony to maintain Souldiers; and of appointing Magistrates for the administration of Justice."[95] It is not clear why all these rights should follow from the transfer of our political right. In the end, one could imagine that for Hobbes it took both the transfer (and alienation) of specific rights, as well as the abridgment of our general "right of nature" to create political society.[96]

In any case, the key point for Hobbes was to counter those authors who insisted that we should retain our natural rights under government. In this regard, his theory was successful: even authors who disputed his extremely broad definition of the "right of nature" would accept that some natural rights must be abandoned for society to function. As we will see below, it was these authors who pushed Hobbes's argument in the direction of a more clear-cut abridgment regime. Others would seek to pry the transfer regime away from Hobbes's description, in order to develop a theory of limited government and even political resistance.

*

Considered scandalous for its materialist premises and possibly atheistic conclusions, few English political theorists would admit to "Hobbism," particularly among the clergy.[97] Still, Hobbes's argument about the necessity of laying down natural rights in order to establish state and society would be widely repeated—even by those who purported to reject Hobbes's philosophy. One of the earliest, and most influential, clergymen to adopt Hobbes's views about rights was Edward Stillingfleet, who in 1689 became bishop of Worcester and is today mostly remembered for his debates with Locke.[98] In his *Irenicum* (1659), he chided Hobbes ("Leviathan") for implying that "no *precepts* of the *Gospel* are *Law*, till *enacted by civil authority*," but nonetheless reached a similar conclusion about the place of natural rights in society. In society, he reasoned, "there must be Laws and Bonds [ . . . ] and submission acknowledged to those Lawes, else Men might plead their Naturall Right and Freedom still, which would be destructive to the very Nature of these Societies." Accordingly, in order to enter into society, it was necessary that "men then did first part with their natural Liberties." Only under such circumstances could society hold together: "a free and voluntary consent to part with so much of their Natural Rights as was not consistent with the well being of the Society."[99] Some thirty years later, as bishop, Stillingfleet was still pushing this claim, notably in a sermon preached before Queen Mary: "[T]he mutual benefit Men have from Society with one another [ . . . ] cannot be enjoy'd without particular Persons abridging themselves of some natural Rights for a common Benefit."[100]

*Irenicum* attracted a fair deal of attention, with multiple authors weighing in for and against.[101] Though himself politically affiliated with the ruling (after 1689) Whig Party, Stillingfleet's Hobbesian take on natural rights was more common among clergymen with Stuart loyalties. The year after *Irenicum* was published, Jeremy Taylor, then a bishop in the Church of Ireland who had been close to Charles I, published *Ductor dubitantium*. Here he defined "the right of nature" in very similar terms to Hobbes: it is "a perfect and universal liberty to doe whatsoever can secure me or please me. [ . . . ] Whatsoever we naturally desire, naturally we are permitted to." But such a right did not carry any moral weight: "A Natural right is no indication of a Moral law." The needs of society thus outweighed our natural rights, which "can be impeded in their use and challenge by the Supreme Civil power."[102]

Like Hobbes himself, some of his emulators recognized that we could retain certain core rights in society: hence Samuel Parker (appointed bishop of Oxford by James II in 1686) recognized in his 1671 *A Discourse of Ecclesiastical Politie* "the natural Right that every individual man has to happiness," which he granted "cannot be obtain'd without Society." But his was hardly a Jeffersonian argument, as he distinguished between a right and its practice. "Mankind therefore have the same Natural Right to Liberty of Conscience in matters of Religious Worship, as in Affairs of Justice and Honesty, *i.e.* a Liberty of *Judgment*, but not of *practice*," he argued. "They have an inviolable freedom to examine the Goodness of all Laws Moral and Ecclesiastical [ . . . ]: but as for the Practice and all outward Actions either of Virtue or Devotion, they are equally governable by the Laws and Constitutions of Common-wealths."[103] In the end, our power to enjoy our natural rights could be limited by the state.

The abridgment regime became popular during the Exclusion crisis among the clergymen who preached passive obedience (as opposed to the right of resistance). Among them was James II's former chaplain William Sherlock, who (in 1684) hewed a similarly Hobbesian line. He, too, insisted on the absolute authority of the sovereign: "[H]e's God's Minister and Vicegerent, and Subjects are expressly forbid to resist; and it is a vain thing to pretend a natural right against the express Law of God." Those who claimed that "Christ has taught us by his example to bear servitude and sufferings with an equal mind, when we cannot help it; so he has not forbid us to vindicate and recover our *natural rights* and *liberties*, when we can," were in the wrong. And he rejected the argument that primitive Christians "were weak, and unable to resist, and therefore were taught to suffer patiently without resistance; but thanks be to God, the case is not thus now; and therefore we may vindicate our natural and religious rights and liberties against all unjust violence." To believe this is to "weaken the authority of the Gospel, and make it a very imperfect, and a very uncertain rule of Life, which every man may fit and accommodate to his own humour and inclinations."[104] As Taylor, Sherlock warned that the preservation of natural rights in society opened the doors to licentiousness and anarchy.

Such concerns remained in force among clergymen who refused to accept the revolutionary settlement. The nonjuror John Kettlewell, for instance, continued to defend passive obedience in his 1691 *Christianity, a Doctrine of the Cross*. He was more willing than his predecessors to recognize that natural rights might extend into society. But this did men little good, as Kettlewell refused to allow them the right to uphold their rights, civil or natural: "[T]here is no liberty for Subjects, to defend their Rights thus by joyning in Arms, against their lawful Sovereigns."[105]

The persuasiveness of Hobbes's abridgment regime of rights can be measured by the fact that even his philosophical or political opponents accepted it. Richard Cumberland, who became bishop of Petersborough in 1691 and who devoted many chapters of his *De legibus naturae* (1672; English trans., *A Treatise of the Laws of Nature*, 1727) to assailing Hobbes, nonetheless granted him this point: "I own, indeed, That the various Vicissitudes of Human Life and Actions, do necessarily introduce various Alienations of antient Rights, and many new Regulations concerning them."[106] Hobbes's great challenger on the Continent, Samuel von Pufendorf, also strongly criticized his definition of a "natural right," but similarly allowed for civil laws to curb our natural rights in society.[107]

Even some theorists who defended republican government, such as Algernon Sidney, firmly insisted that the institution of society was conditional on the abridgment of rights.[108] When reflecting back on his life while awaiting execution in 1683, Sidney reminisced how "I had from my youth endeavored to uphold the common rights of mankind, the laws of this land, and the true Protestant religion, against corrupt principles, arbitrary power, and Popery, and I do now willingly lay down my life for the same."[109] To some degree, this is how he was remembered in the eighteenth century.[110] But the *Discourses Concerning Government*, published posthumously in 1698, told a different story. As Hobbes before him, Sidney recognized that in the state of nature "every man is a king," but this unrestrained condition ends when "he divest[s] himself of his right [to natural liberty], in consideration of something that he thinks better for him."[111] Indeed, the loss of our natural freedom constitutes for Sidney, as it had for Hobbes, the decisive feature of civil society: "[H]ow numerous soever families may be upon the increase of mankind, they are all free, till they agree to recede from their own right, and join together in, or under one government, according to such laws as best please themselves."[112] Only individuals who are not members of a civil society, and accordingly "take their authority from the law of nature," can enjoy unfettered liberty: "[T]heir rights cannot be limited or diminished by any one man, or number of men."[113] But once we enter into society, we can, and must, accept that our rights will be curtailed.

To be sure, Sidney does not follow Hobbes in his understanding of legitimate government: the rights of citizens should "no otherwise to be restrained than by laws made with their consent."[114] But the more interesting point here is that the abridgment regime could equally well serve republican, as absolutist, political theories. Political autonomy ("laws made with [our] consent") could guarantee freedom, but it did not necessarily guarantee human rights.

By the eighteenth century, then, this regime had acquired a life of its own, detached from Hobbes's politics. In England, it often remained associated with the Tory Party. In the 1720s, for instance, it was repeatedly and strongly restated by the High Church clergyman Richard Fiddes, starting with his *Theologia speculativa*.[115] To the question "whether there are not certain natural rights of men which the authority of God is allowed to supersede," he answered in the affirmative: "[T]he power of the civil magistrate may extend in limiting and restraining, or in certain cases of totally destroying the natural rights of men."[116] He rehearsed this theme in his best-selling *Life of Cardinal Wolsey*, and again in his *General Treatise of Morality*.[117] Philosophers also persisted in upholding this rights regime: in his widely read and widely translated *Religion of Nature Delineated* (1724), William Wollaston affirmed that "[a] man may part with some of his natural Rights, and put himself under the Government of Laws, and those, who in their several stations are intrusted with the execution of them, in order to gain the protection of them, and the privileges of a regular Society."[118] This argument was echoed by the German philosopher and law professor Johann Gottlieb Heineccius, in his *Elementa juris naturae et gentium* (1737), who similarly argued that "civil laws may confine and alter natural rights, consistently with the law of nature."[119] At the onset of the Enlightenment, it was clearly not a given that natural, pre-political rights would come to be seen as entitlements that could not be curbed by government.

### 4. Entrust, but Verify? The Transfer Regime from Spinoza to Locke

For defenders of the abridgment regime in the late seventeenth century, the greatest challenge came not from those who argued for the preservation of rights in society, but rather from those who outlined a different theory of rights transfer. Where Hobbes had largely equated the transfer and renunciation of rights, these other theorists teased these two operations apart, ultimately arriving at a very distinct model. The first philosopher to explore the mechanisms of the rights transfer in detail was Spinoza, in his *Theological-Political Treatise* (1670).[120] But it was Locke who would give this regime its canonical formulation.

## 4.1. BARUCH SPINOZA

Spinoza famously distinguished his argument in *Theological-Political Treatise* from Hobbes's own political theory, claiming that "I always preserve natural right in its entirety [ego naturale jus semper sartum tectum conservo]."[121] This statement has led some commentators to conclude that Spinoza argued that individuals must preserve their natural rights in society, or that he "leaves the citizen with his natural right intact."[122] But this conclusion rests on a misreading of what Spinoza meant by "natural right." Spinoza used the expression *ius naturale* here in the singular: he is not claiming that individuals preserve their *subjective* natural rights in their entirety, only that his own argument does not contradict *objective* natural right.[123] And as we will see, he believes it possible to remain faithful to the principles of objective natural right all the while obliging citizens to renounce the individual enjoyment of subjective natural rights.

How does Spinoza achieve this intellectual balancing act? He begins by defining "the natural right of the individual" (jure naturali uniuscuiusque) in a somewhat different manner than Hobbes. This right, he argues, is simply "co-extensive with [his] determinate power."[124] Put simply, we have a natural right to do whatever we *can* do, that is, whatever it is in our power to do. Spinoza's natural rights are thus a kind of liberty rights (in Hohfeldian terms).[125] They do not entail any correlative duties. In this respect, the natural rights of humans are no different than those of animals: fish have a natural right to swim, wolves have a natural right to hunt, and we have a natural right to do whatever we desire.

While Spinoza arrives at this definition through a different reasoning than Hobbes (who limits the "right of nature" to rational creatures), the end result is fairly similar. Just as, for Hobbes, in the state of nature, "every man has a Right to every thing," for Spinoza "whatever every man [ . . . ] believes to be to his advantage [ . . . ] he may by sovereign natural right seek and get for himself by any means, by force, deceit, entreaty, or in any other way he best can" (174). Both authors similarly view this situation as untenable and violent, with Spinoza concurring that "the life of men without mutual assistance must necessarily be most wretched" (175). And both find a solution to this "wretched" situation in the establishment of government and the creation of an all-powerful sovereign who will enforce contracts between us.[126]

But Spinoza conceives of the sovereign in a very different way. Whereas for Hobbes, sovereign power is ultimately concentrated in a single "man, or Assembly of men,"[127] for Spinoza (as for Rousseau after him), it could only legitimately reside in a democratic community.[128] This community was the result of a contract, through which "everyone transfers [transferat] all the power that he possesses to [it]" (177; Latin, 179). Once created, the community "will therefore alone retain the sovereign natural right over everything" (177), meaning that our individual natural right to act as we pleased will be curtailed. Spinoza maintains that this loss is not an "infringement of natural right [sine ulla naturalis juris repugnantia]," for the simple reason that we no longer have the power to do whatever we wish, and thus are not at liberty to do it. As a member of a community, I can no longer use force or deceit, since doing so would risk punishment. In this sense, I do not technically have to "lay down" my natural rights; those rights are simply no longer available once I lose the power to act freely.[129]

These rights do not just go up in smoke, however. When we contract into a body politic, our natural rights are transferred to the community, which then enjoys "common ownership" of them (175). In this respect as well, Spinoza "preserves natural right in its entirety," by shifting its possession from the individual to the community.[130] If we enjoy these rights as members of the sovereign, as individuals we no longer possess any rights from nature and are "consequently resolved to obey the [sovereign] absolutely in all matters" (179). Spinoza grants that some rights could technically be retained by individuals, if they made a "secure provision to uphold" them at the time of contracting, but he insists that in most cases we submit ourselves to the community "without reservation" (177). In this respect, Spinoza's transfer regime of rights is similar to the abridgment regime, as we experience life under government as an alienation of our original natural rights.[131] Spinoza goes even further than Hobbes by including our "power of self-defence" (179) in the rights we transfer to the sovereign.

As should be apparent, the transfer regime does not lead to a particularly liberal conception of society. It provides very few checks against an oppressive government. Spinoza approvingly quotes Seneca's adage that "tyrannical governments never last long" (178), but he does not outline a mechanism for ensuring they will be short-lived. The duty of the subject (subditus) in Spinoza's democracy is to "acknowledge no other right but that which the sovereign power declares to be a right" (180). So restricted is this subject that Spinoza is at pains to distinguish him from a slave (servus). He does so by insisting that whoever lives in "a commonwealth whose laws are based on sound reason is the most free," as "he can live whole-heartedly under the guidance of reason" (178). Given that his subject plays little part in the legislative process, his freedom resembles that of Hobbes's subject more than, say, Rousseau's republican citizen.[132] Spinoza does not even endorse a right to resistance as a last resort against tyranny. He instead adopts a more naturalistic and passive perspective:

sovereigns who do not live up to the expectations of their subjects are simply likely to lose power.[133]

As subsequent authors emphasized the democratic, and specifically legislative, dimensions of the transfer regime, its differences with the abridgment regime would become more pronounced, and it would emerge as a genuine *via media* between the abridgment and preservation regimes. A key shift in this evolution was the insistence on a verification mechanism: how can we ensure that the government is genuinely acting in our interest? The ability to retrieve our natural rights in cases of sovereign misconduct would come to distinguish the transfer regime more clearly from the Hobbesian model, which rested on the abridgment and alienation of our natural rights (at least until the commonwealth was dissolved). We find all these elements folded into the transfer regime with John Locke. But lest it be assumed that such a conclusion was inevitable, it pays first to consider the case of another, much lesser-known British author who used the transfer regime to defend absolute monarchy.

### 4.2. JAMES CRAUFURD

Published in 1682, when Locke was most likely at work on his own *Two Treatises*, James Craufurd's *A Serious Expostulation* was one of the earliest, if now forgotten, political treatises from the British Isles to flesh out the transfer regime of rights.[134] Craufurd, a Scottish Episcopalian clergyman, was royal historiographer of Scotland under Charles II.[135] Predictably, he came down strongly against any popular right of resistance. "[I]f it were declared lawfull for Subjects only to resist in some cases, who must judge when these fall out?" he asked in terms that might seem to foreshadow Locke's.[136] But Craufurd's answer differed greatly, as he advocated patience and "lawful opposition," and accepted a bad government to be better than no government at all.[137] He also expressed fears about the judgment of the people and the risks of empowering them with such a potentially destructive weapon: "[I]f it were left to the judgment of Subjects, it is to be feared that the Determination would be highly partial on their side; the case of lawfull Resistance would then turn frequent, Obedience would be rare [ . . . ] and Subjects would at this rate only be such to whom and when they pleased" (7).

As Spinoza before him, Craufurd's treatise echoes Hobbesian themes: he warns, for instance, that "Men are apt to confound Natural Rights, and the Law of Nature, which vastly differ" (12). But his account of how governments form bears a closer resemblance to Locke than Hobbes, as it rests on a transfer of natural rights: "The Law of Nature first taught Men to give up their Natural

Rights to the Publick [ ... ] committing their Lives, Liberties and Fortunes to its Trust, to be dispos'd of at all times as the Publick should think fit" (12). Here we find all the major elements of the transfer regime: the "giving up" of natural rights *to* the body politic, which in turn operates as a sort of "trust," and must henceforth defend the three primary objects to which our natural rights had been attached.[138] This transfer, again, entails an alienation of rights ("[men] freely resign some natural Rights [ ... ] their Natural Liberties are brought under the Confinement of Laws, and are in some measure abridg'd"; 10–11), but this is made up for by greater security in the civil society ("their Condition is much more comfortable"; 11); hence, in the overall balance, it is "the wisest Bargain they could make" (12).

### 4.3. JOHN LOCKE

By the time Locke was working out his own theory, then, a sophisticated theoretical alternative was emerging for thinking about the fate of natural rights in civil society. While there is no direct evidence that Locke knew of Craufurd, he did read and annotate Spinoza's *Tractatus theologico-politicus* carefully.[139] But because Locke is fairly discreet about his political influences in the *Second Treatise*, and because his own usage of the term is less than systematic, his understanding of "rights" has remained somewhat elusive and a matter of scholarly debate. Much of this debate has taken place between philosophers, who focus on Locke's own internal arguments.[140] When considered from a broader historical perspective that spans the work of generations of theorists, however, it becomes clearer that Locke's arguments about rights are closely aligned with the transfer (rather than the preservation) regime. While this more contextual approach does not resolve all the disputed issues with Locke's theory of rights, its conclusions do find support in the fact that Locke's closest followers and emulators also appear to have read him as a transfer theorist, as I show in a subsequent section.

   This interpretation of Locke goes against what is perhaps the dominant, libertarian reading of Locke, according to which we preserve our natural rights in society.[141] Authors who defend this interpretation often speak of Locke's "inalienable natural rights."[142] This account of Locke's argument, which other scholars have also challenged,[143] appears to be validated by various passages of the *Two Treatises*, most notably the preface: here Locke praises "the people of England, whose love of their just and natural rights, *with their resolution to preserve them*, saved the nation when it was on the very brink of slavery and ruin." As this reference to the Glorious Revolution makes clear, however, the preface (which also celebrates "our present King William") was written six to ten years after the *Second Treatise*.[144] Elsewhere in the *Treatise*, Locke does sound as though he believes rights ought to be preserved: he writes, for instance, that "all men [should] be restrained from invading others [*sic*] rights, and from doing hurt to one another" (§ 7). But the context here is the state of nature, where "the execution of the law of nature is [ . . . ] put into every man's hands."[145] The real question is not what happens in the state of nature, where we have "a title to perfect freedom, and an uncontrouled enjoyment of all the rights and privileges of the law of nature" (§ 87), but in what Locke calls "political society."

And there is little doubt that the price of entry into society is steep: indeed, as a condition of forming a community, we must "give up" most of our rights and freedom.[146] When Locke's natural man "puts on the bonds of civil society," he "divests himself of his natural liberty" (§ 95); he must "give up all the power, necessary to the ends for which [he] unite[s] into society, to the majority of the community" (§ 99). This divestment is detailed in the ninth chapter. "To omit the liberty he has of innocent delights," Locke observes here, "a man has *two* powers" in the state of nature (§ 128; emphasis added).[147] These two powers are (1) "doing whatsoever he thought for the preservation of himself, and the rest of mankind," and (2) the executive "power of punishing" (§§ 129–30; see also § 87); both of these "powers" are described elsewhere as "rights."[148] Locke then details what happens to these powers or rights once we unite in society: "Both these he gives up, when he joins in a private, if I may so call it, or particular politic society, and incorporates into any common-wealth" (§ 128). Locke himself acknowledges that this "giving up" amounts to a significant loss: "if man in the state of nature be so free [ . . . ] why will he part with his freedom? why will he give up this empire, and subject himself to the dominion and controul of any other power?" (§ 130). Only the insecure conditions of the state of nature can explain such a sacrifice.

Contrary to the abridgment regime, however, this loss is not absolute, since the rights are transferred to the body politic: we give up, but we give up *to* ("men give up all their natural power *to* the society which they enter into," § 136, my emphasis; see also § 95).[149] Where for Spinoza this transfer was complete ("everyone transfers all the power that he possesses"), Locke by contrast enumerates the specific rights we must part with. Accordingly, the power of the government, for Locke, is not as absolute as it was for Spinoza: "[I]t can be no more than those persons had in a state of nature before they entered into society, and gave up to the community: no body can transfer to another more power than he has in himself" (§ 135).[150] While this rule imposes certain limitations on the legitimate activity of the state, it operates in a very different manner than rights provisions. Instead of claiming that government cannot do anything that infringes on your rights (which is how governmental power is constrained in the preservation regime), Locke insists that government cannot do anything that you could not do in the state of nature.[151] Put simply, Locke does not provide any explicit reassurances like those found in the U.S. Constitution's Ninth Amendment, a problem that his American readers would struggle with.[152]

But surely we retain our *property* rights in civil society? After all, it was to better secure their property that people formed commonwealths in the first place. We should not, however, confuse "securing our property" with "securing our *natural right to* property."[153] Property is both an object (my stuff) and a title to an object (the lawful possession of my stuff). And the very reason why we pay the price of admission into society is because our natural right to objects turns out to be a flimsy title of ownership: "[I]n the state of nature he hath such a right, yet the enjoyment of it is very uncertain, and constantly exposed to the invasion of others [. . . ;] the enjoyment of the property he has in this state is very unsafe, very unsecure" (§ 123). It is in order to place our property (i.e., "our stuff") under a better legal safeguard than that afforded by our natural right—and conversely, by the law of nature—that we form commonwealths.[154]

Here we touch upon a key point: Locke never explicitly states that we retain a *natural*, pre-political right to property once we live under government.[155] Instead, he argues that society provides us with a new, *positive* legal title for our property: "To avoid these inconveniencies, which disorder men's properties in the state of nature, men unite into societies, that they may have the united strength of the whole society to secure and defend their properties, and may have *standing rules* to bound it" (§ 136). To be sure, governments are bound by "the fundamental law of property" (§ 140), according to which they must do their utmost to preserve the property that we originally acquired in the state of nature. But though we enter into society to preserve "our stuff," our original natural right to property no longer serves to secure them: "*Men therefore in society having property*, they have such a right to the goods, which by the law of the community are their's" (§ 138; my underline). Our right to own property becomes, in society, a positive legal title, granted by "a law of the community." As Kirstie M. McClure, Alex Tuckness, and others have argued, Locke looked to the legislature, and not to any express rights provisions, to protect our "lives, liberties, and estates" in society.[156] It is "by *stated rules* of right and property [that men] secure their peace and quiet" (§ 137; my underline) under government, and not by natural rights.[157] While the government cannot arbitrarily take away anyone's property, it does have the "power to make laws, for the regulating of *property* between the subjects one amongst another" (§ 139; my underline). The institution of government is thus the result of a quasi-alchemical process, through which natural rights are transformed into positive laws.

I recognize that this reading of Locke's views on property may be controversial, so will advance a few more arguments in its defense. One might ask, first, so what happens to our natural right to property? Why doesn't Locke mention it in the course of explaining this transfer? Let us recall how the natural right to property comes about. As the fifth chapter on property makes clear in its introductory paragraph, our right to own goods in fact flows from our right to self-preservation: "[M]en, being once born, have a right to their preservation, and consequently to meat and drink, and such other things as nature affords for their subsistence" (§ 25). Nearly all of the examples of property that Locke provides in this chapter pertain to subsistence, that is, to self-preservation; even the famous proviso relates to the ability of others to nourish themselves. Giving up the right to self-preservation—a sacrifice that Locke clearly insists on (§ 128)—thus implies giving up our original natural right to property, as well (again, the "legal title," not the goods themselves).

The clearest and most decisive argument (my second) in favor of the reading I am proposing here concerns the legal power of governments to take property without unanimous personal consent. As Locke writes, in a paragraph on taxation, "it is fit every one who enjoys his share of the protection, should pay out of his estate his proportion for the maintenance of it" (§ 140). He adds, most importantly, "still it must be with his own consent," but then clarifies this comment: "*i.e.* the consent of the majority."[158] This means that if I oppose a vote to raise taxes, but am in the minority, I will still be lawfully obliged to pay more taxes. My rightful claim to property can therefore not be considered a pre-political, natural "trump," since positive law can override it.[159] This argument might appear inconsistent with Locke's assertion that "the preservation of property [is] the end of government" (§ 138), but there are in fact *two* ends of government in Locke: "the public good and preservation of property" (§ 239). Most of the time, these ends align; but they need not always. For instance, it is simple to imagine situations where "the regulating and preserving of property" could clash with "the defence of the commonwealth from foreign injury," to take two duties that Locke assigns to political power (§ 3).

A complicating factor for understanding Locke's rights regime is that there are certain circumstances under which we can regain the full enjoyment of our original natural rights. For instance, "I may kill a thief that sets on me in the high-way" (§ 182), because in that situation, "the law, which was made for my preservation[,] [ . . . ] cannot interpose to secure my life from present force"

(§ 19). Accordingly, I may take the executive right of nature back into my own hands, since between the thief and me, there is no social bond. Indeed, by attacking me, the thief removes himself from the commonwealth and becomes a foreign enemy: "Whosoever uses force without right, as every one does in society, who does it without law, puts himself into a state of war with those against whom he so uses it; and in that state all former ties are cancelled, all other rights cease, and every one has a right to defend himself" (§ 232; see also § 19). In the state of war, as in the state of nature, I possess an individual right to enforce the law of nature.

It is the same logic that underpins Locke's famous right of resistance. The right to resist a tyrant with force is not one that we always hold in reserve in society, like an ace up our sleeve, but a once-surrendered natural right that we exceptionally regain through the actions of a tyrannical sovereign. Like the thief on the highway, the tyrant "put[s] himself into a state of war with his people," thereby "dissolv[ing] the government, and leav[ing] them to that defence which belongs to every one in the state of nature," namely, the natural right of self-preservation (§ 205).[160] But if the prince does not use force without right against us, we have no natural right to resist him, since we are still bound together in a society of laws. This is the very point on which Locke concludes the *Second Treatise*: "The *power that every individual gave the society*, when he entered into it, can never revert to the individuals again, as long as the society lasts, but will always remain in the community" (§ 243). As long as the prince does not destroy our social bonds, we cannot enjoy, and thus cannot be said to possess, our natural rights. Our natural rights are as good as alienated until we change states (from political society to a state of war).

When we recall that the preservation regime still enjoyed plenty of support around the time Locke was writing (remember the French Huguenots), a simple question comes to mind: If Locke had wished to emphasize the preservation of rights in his theory, why didn't he? We know from other texts that Locke believed the natural right to free religious conscience should always remain in force, but you would not know this from reading the *Second Treatise*. There simply is no clear, unambiguous statement in this text to the effect that we retain any natural rights whatsoever in political society. To rephrase the question, then: if Locke really thought that we could enjoy our natural rights in society, why did he only insist on the rights we must give up?[161]

Of course, Locke's silence on this matter is not an indication that he really believed that we must part with them *all*; as just noted, he would make some exceptions. The point is rather that the rights *regime* adopted in the *Second Treatise* based the creation of political society in a transfer of individual natural rights. It is this argument that fundamentally distinguishes the transfer regime from the preservation regime, for which society is the best way to *maintain* our natural rights. Both regimes can incorporate elements of the other: in the transfer regime, we might still hold on to some rights; in the preservation regime, we might have to give some rights up. Nonetheless, the two regimes represent two profoundly different ways of conceptualizing the relation between natural rights and government. Locke's decision to embrace the transfer narrative must therefore be seen as deliberate choice, one that, moreover, was emerging at that precise moment as a kind of sophisticated alternative to the more conservative abridgment regime, and to the less theorized preservation regime.

A final objection to this reading might grant that it holds true when we examine the text closely, but that most people read Locke to say that we retain our natural rights in society. In fact, as the following section shows, one of his closest followers shows us that the opposite is true.

### 4.4. MATTHEW TINDAL

To gain greater clarity on how Locke thought about rights, it pays to consider how his contemporaries understood him, particularly those sympathetic to his views. An interesting case is Matthew Tindal, the controversialist best known for his defense of deism and who was a friend of Locke's in the latter's old age.[162] Tellingly, the closer Tindal drew to Locke, the further he drifted away from his early embrace of the preservation regime, and the more he insisted on the transfer of rights.[163]

In his first published work, *An Essay Concerning Obedience to the Supreme Powers* (1694), Tindal combined elements of the preservation and transfer regimes in his description of the transition from natural to civil state. "[W]hatever Rights or Liberties men did not part with to their Governors," he wrote, "those they have still retained in themselves." While this argument bears some resemblance to Locke's ("part with *to*"), it places greater emphasis on the preservation of rights, including that of self-preservation (which, let us recall, Locke held we must "give up"). "Is it not absurd to suppose," Tindal asserted, perhaps taking aim at Hobbes, "that Human Laws should be able to destroy the Law of Nature, or take away that Natural Right which people have to act for their own good and preservation, which is a Right that is superior to all Human Laws"? Accordingly, for Tindal, we did not need to *regain* this right in order to defend ourselves against a tyrannical sovereign, since we maintained it all along. Echoing a famous question from the *Second Treatise*, Tindal supposes: "*But it may be asked*, Who shall judge between them [the people and their government], if either should usurp the Right that belongs to the other?"

He offered a rather different answer than Locke's: "[W]here people have not parted with their Rights, it must be presumed they have retained a Power to judge whether those Rights are invaded, or else the design of preserving those Rights would be to no purpose."[164] As his language suggests, Tindal's argument here fell squarely within the framework of the preservation regime.

Three years later, Tindal published his *Essay Concerning the Power of the Magistrate* (1697), which he sent to Locke in their first recorded correspondence.[165] By this time, his theory of rights had evolved in a more Lockean direction, as he now left very little room for the preservation of rights:

> The only Difference between being in a State of Nature, and under Government, consists in this, that *under Government Men have debarred themselves from exercising their natural Rights*, and intrusted the Magistrate to do those things that in the State of Nature every one of them had a Right to do; so that the Magistrate's Power is not larger, but theirs more contracted than it was in that State.[166]

Where the power of the magistrate was limited, in the 1694 *Essay Concerning Obedience to the Supreme Powers*, by the natural rights that individuals preserved in society, Tindal now followed Locke to the letter in his claims that (1) we must "debar ourselves" from enjoying our natural rights in society, and (2) governmental action was only legitimate when it mirrored the powers of individuals in a state of nature. As with Locke, this theory is striking for its lack of rights provisions. Following this logic, the right of resistance is not *retained* by the people, but can only *return* to them when a government acts illegitimately.

Tindal made this claim again in *The Rights of the Christian Church Asserted* (1706), where his theory of rights was also expressed in accordance to the transfer regime: "[T]he Power every one had by the Law of Nature, is *by their receding from it solely in the Magistrate*; whose Right of punishing cannot extend further than theirs did in the State of Nature." The people can only regain this power when the magistrates cease to "act agreeably to the End for which they were constituted," at which point "the Power naturally *returns* to the Body of the People."[167] This last text attracted a great deal of criticism—it was condemned to be burned by the House of Commons—and one of the points on which Tindal's attackers pounced was precisely this claim. George Hickes, a bishop in the nonjuring church, denounced Tindal's claim that "Men first came by their own Consent, in a free Election of a Multitude, or a Select Number, or a single person, unto whom they transferred their Natural Rights, and gave them Authority to Rule" as taken from the "execrable Principles" and "Satanical Arts" of Spinoza.[168]

## 5. Into the Enlightenment: "Cato" and Hutcheson

The dispute over the proper place of natural rights in civil society would continue to simmer in early eighteenth-century England. For a long while, clergymen and pamphleteers continued to debate the right of resistance. For instance, Benjamin Hoadly, a Low Church bishop, attacked the Tory position that "the *Nature* and End of *Government* necessarily take away from the *governed Part* of *Mankind* the *Right* of *Self-Defense*," countering instead that when we enter into society, we "transfer this right of *Self-Preservation*, by empowering one, or more Persons, to ordain, and do, what should be necessary on all such Occasions."[169] Hoadly, then bishop of Bangor, would subsequently lead the charge against Hickes's defense of an independent Church, in a quarrel known as the "Bangorian controversy.[170] During this dispute, at least one clergyman entered the fray on the side of Hoadly, while advancing a preservationist argument.[171]

It is hardly surprising, then, that the status of natural rights in society was a contested issue in one of the most important political treatises of this period, *Cato's Letters*, by John Trenchard and Thomas Gordon (published 1720–23). Building on research that has revealed the importance of this work for the American colonists, Michael Zuckert has called attention to the place of natural rights in this work. But he offers a questionable interpretation of their treatment: "Cato understands the purpose behind the institution of government in the familiar Lockean manner: the securing of rights."[172] Leaving aside the fact that Locke himself did not define the purpose of government in this way, it is also a misleading account of how rights are discussed in *Cato's Letters*. To begin with, it is critical to recognize that, on this point at least, "Cato" did not speak with one voice. For his part, Trenchard did believe that "no government ought to take away men's natural rights, the business and design of government itself being to defend them."[173] His views on rights are similar to those of his friend Robert Molesworth, who similarly defended "the Rights of the People" and insisted that "the People can no more part with their legal Liberties, than Kings can alienate their Crowns," in his influential 1694 *An Account of Denmark*.[174]

But Trenchard's coauthor, who wrote frequently on this topic and delved deeper into social contract theory, was of another mind. In an early essay, Gordon seemed to concur with Trenchard, as can be seen in his praise of Algernon Sidney: "He had asserted the rights of mankind, and shewed the odiousness of tyranny."[175] But as Gordon elaborated his thoughts about government, he began to push his argument in a different direction. "[T]he necessity of government," he now maintained, involved individuals "agreeing upon certain terms of union and society, and putting themselves under penalties, if they violated these terms, which were called laws, and put into the hands of one or more men to execute." This new arrangement came at a price: "[M]en quitted part of their natural liberty to acquire civil security."[176]

At this stage, Gordon was still closer to Sidney than, say, to Locke. But in a subsequent essay on the topic, he came very close to paraphrasing the thesis of the *Second Treatise*: "That Right which, in the State of Nature, every man had, of repelling and revenging injuries, in such a manner as every man thought best, is *transferred* to the magistrate, when political societies are formed, and magistracy established; but must *return* to private men again, when the society is dissolved." This is indeed the crux of Locke's argument, though not in the way Zuckert suggests: far from *preserving* this right in society, we instead give it to another, only to regain it in extreme circumstances. In accordance with the transfer regime, Gordon continues to stress how we must "part with [our] natural rights" when we "become the members and subjects of society."[177] For Gordon, as for Locke, to transfer is also to renounce. Those who wish to credit *Cato's Letters* with providing the American founding fathers with their ideas on rights must be wary of ignoring the equal, if not greater, number of letters that insist on the transfer regime.[178]

This same warning applies to the Scottish philosopher Francis Hutcheson, who is also often heralded as a precursor of the American revolutionaries.[179] It is true that Hutcheson places an emphasis on "unalienable" rights: "Unalienable Rights are essential Limitations in all Governments."[180] But he only recognizes a very small number of "unalienable rights," fewer still than Locke. He considers that "our Right of serving God, in the manner which we think acceptable, is not alienable"; and he grants that "a direct Right over our Lives or Limbs, is not alienable to any Person," while acknowledging that in the case of military service, "We have indeed a Right to hazard our Lives in any good Action which is of importance to the Publick [ . . . ] and so far this Right is alienable" (186–87). He does not regard property as an inalienable right. What's more, as we will see, Hutcheson does not invoke these rights when he comes around to discussing the limits of government.

As their name indicates, *alienable* rights are those that, by contrast, we give up when entering into society. And Hutcheson devotes most of his energy to describing what happens to these rights (186–87, 192ff.). Most crucially, they are what gives a government its legitimacy through the transfer process: "[A]ll human Power, or Authority, must consist in a Right transferr'd to any Person or Council, to dispose of the alienable Rights of others" (192). As with Locke, it is the transfer of rights, more than any defenses supplied by inalienable rights, that determines the limits of legitimate governmental power: "[A]s far as the

People have subjected their Rights, so far their Governours have an external Right at least, to dispose of them, as their Prudence shall direct, for attaining the Ends of their Institution; and no further" (189).

A second reason why it seems unlikely that Hutcheson lay at the source of revolutionary ideas about rights is that he was more than willing to accept the legitimacy of (what he called) "absolute government." In such a government, the people transfer the entirety of their alienable rights: "[B]y absolute Government, either in Prince, or Council, or in both jointly, we understand a Right to dispose of the natural Force, and Goods of a whole People, as far as they are naturally alienable" (193). As this assertion makes clear, Hutcheson even included property ("Goods") in this list. So long as the absolute ruler acts "for the publick Good of the State," then it is not a deviant form of government. Indeed, Hutcheson distinguishes it from "despotick Power," which "is solely intended for the good of the Governours, without any tacit Trust of consulting the good of the Governed" (194).

Even in "limited government," it is not unalienable rights that constrain the actions of the ruler(s), but rather the constitution, that is, *positive* law. "A Prince, or Council, or both jointly, may be variously Limited," wrote Hutcheson, laying out two options. First, "when the consent of the one may be necessary to the validity of the Acts of the other," which implies a constitutional settlement on the separation of powers; or second, "when, in the very Constitution of this supreme Power, certain Affairs are expressly exempted from the Jurisdiction of the Prince, or Council, or both jointly" (193). But Hutcheson also grants a fair degree of leeway to such governments "in Cases of extreme Necessity": at such times, "it must certainly be Just and Good in limited Governours [ ... ] to use the Force of the State for its own preservation, beyond the Limits fix'd by the Constitution, in some transitory acts, which are not to be made Precedents" (194–95). Our "unalienable" rights, in these and other cases, may well be essential, but they do not appear to be particularly effective "limitations in all governments."

✷

This overview of rights theories at the dawn of the Enlightenment underscores how the preservation regime, which would overtake its rivals later in the eighteenth century, was by far the least developed and least defended a mere fifty years prior. While it may be possible to identify isolated passages in earlier texts that strike a similar note as the later declarations, reconstructing the genealogy of revolutionary rights in such a piecemeal fashion ignores the fact that there were significantly different frameworks for thinking about rights in society. The history of rights in the eighteenth century need not for that reason be told in terms of epistemic ruptures. The preservation regime, which the revolutionaries (and some of their immediate precursors) were to latch onto, was certainly not "unthinkable" and was indeed even present, albeit in fewer instances, in this earlier period.[181] The next chapter in this history, as well as in this book, tells the story of how and why the transfer and abridgment regimes lost their luster for subsequent rights theorists, who accordingly revived— often transforming it in the process—the preservation regime.

# From Liberalism to Liberty: Natural Rights in the French Enlightenment

The country that issued the Declaration of the Rights of Man and of the Citizen showed little indication, during the first fifty years of the eighteenth century, that it cared much about natural rights or believed that the purpose of society was to conserve "the natural and imprescriptible rights of man" (art. 2). For the most part, natural rights hardly registered in French political thought at all or in other genres of writing (see fig. 3.1). The brief surge of enthusiasm for rights among Protestant exiles after 1685 did not leave much of a mark on the early Enlightenment. Montesquieu does not mention natural rights in any of his major works; the concept is missing from La Mettrie's books of the late 1740s; and it is almost entirely absent from Voltaire's pre-1750 writings.[1] The subsequent interest in rights by French authors after 1750 is thus all the more intriguing, as is the story of how the preservation regime came to prevail. This chapter explores how and why rights ultimately became a salient feature of Enlightenment political discourse, and uncovers the critical role played in this story by a rather unexpected group—the Physiocrats.

On the rare occasions that natural rights did surface in French texts before 1750, their treatment was fairly similar to that in England. The literary critic and journalist Thémiseul de Saint-Hyacinthe, a onetime rival of Voltaire who spent his career in Holland, published a series of dialogues in 1718, the second of which outlined the transfer regime: "Man is obliged, by the very Love he feels for his natural rights, to place them in hands that can conserve them for him, and prevent him from abusing them."[2] This same process was described by Andrew Michael Ramsay, a Scottish Jacobite who had converted to Catholicism under the influence of François Fénelon and lived out most of his life in France. In his 1719 *Essay de politique*, he argued that the logical conclusion of the preservation regime was the legalization of theft. In an imaginary dialogue

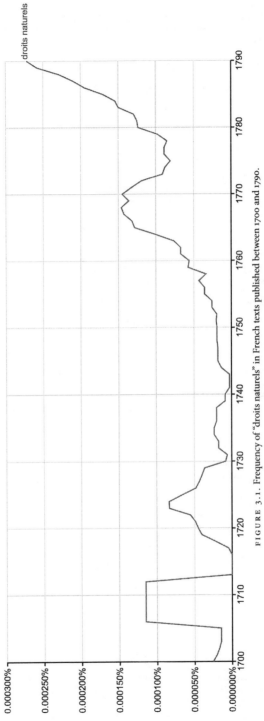

FIGURE 3.1. Frequency of "droits naturels" in French texts published between 1700 and 1790.
*Source:* From Google Books Ngram Viewer.

with an "anti-royalist," a robber affirms that "these Princes and Magistrates whom you call usurpers of the rights of humanity [les droits de l'humanité] prevent me from enjoying my natural possessions. I want to uphold my rights, and sweep up the abundance of those I encounter."[3] Ramsay's only concession to the "violent republicans" (les Republicains outrez) who accepted this logic was that even if "the source of all authority [came] from the people, and the renunciation [cession] of its natural right," then still "it does not follow that they can always retrieve [this right] once it has been given" (66). In this version, the transfer and the abridgment regimes again came close to merging.

### 1. Sources for Natural Law Theory in France, 1700–1750

French readers could have also encountered the abridgment regime in a number of older texts and translations. Pufendorf's *De jure naturae et gentium* (*Of the Law of Nature and Nations*, 1672), as well as its much shortened, simplified, and more commonly read version, *De officio hominis et civis* (*On the Duty of Man and Citizen*, 1673), were both translated and annotated by the Swiss natural law professor Jean Barbeyrac in 1706 and 1707, respectively.[4] Pufendorf insisted here that civil laws "*limit* us (as they do) in the Exercise of several Rights, to the Use whereof the Law of Nature left us much at *Liberty* [l'usage des droits que chacun avoit naturellement]."[5] This point was reinforced in the marginal note to this paragraph in the French edition: civil laws "limit the use of each person's natural rights [l'usage des Droits naturels de chacun]."[6] An abridged translation of William Wollaston's *Religion of Nature Delineated* (discussed in the previous chapter) came out in 1726, which included a similar claim: "A man may part with some of his natural rights [renoncer à quelques-uns de ses droits naturels]. . . ."[7] And the Italian philosopher Alberto Radicati di Passerano—who circulated in freethinking and reformist circles in Paris, London, and Holland—nonetheless affirmed in the first of his *Moral, Historical and Political Discourses* that "if we go back to the origin of societies, we see that the men who created them unanimously sacrificed their natural rights [leurs Droits naturels] and particular interests to produce a single interest and body of law [un Droit]."[8]

Defenders of the preservation regime were not entirely absent from this debate, but their voices were scarce. In another of Barbeyrac's translations, this time of the Dutch law professor Gerhard Noodt, we read that primitive individuals "joined together into a body politic, in order to enjoy collectively their natural rights [jouïr en commun de leurs Droits Naturels]." Indeed, the passage from a state of nature into political society is motivated, according to Noodt, by the desire to preserve individual rights: "[T]hey abandoned the savage and rough life they had previously led to taste the sweetness of Society, and to ensure the enjoyment of their Natural Rights [pour s'assurer la jouissance de leurs Droits Naturels]."[9] But this commonplace argument in Dutch republican thought did not catch on in France, where it was conspicuously absent before mid-century. One interesting exception can be found in Voltaire's English dedication to Queen Caroline in *La Henriade* (1728): "YOUR MAJESTY will find in this book [ . . . ] the Rights of Kings always asserted, and those of Mankind never set aside."[10] Curiously, he would not celebrate such rights in French for another twenty years. Authors who did tended to be expatriates, as was Voltaire himself when he penned this dedication. His friend the Jean-Baptiste de Boyer, marquis d'Argens, lamented the fact that "there have been Men who were crazy and stupid enough to submit to monacal Despotism, and to abandon their natural and civil Rights," in his widely read and reedited *Lettres juives* (1736–37); he was then living in Holland.[11] One finds a similar claim under the pen of César de Missy, who in a 1742 letter to Voltaire wrote, "I call good those who wish with all their hearts that everyone can freely enjoy their natural rights."[12] But Missy was a Berlin-born Huguenot refugee who spent most of his life in London.

Only after 1750 did it become common to encounter references to natural rights in French texts, notably those authored by the *philosophes*. In his *Siècle de Louis XIV* (1751), Voltaire claimed that the 1685 *Code Noir* was "established in favor of the negroes [nègres] in our colonies; a type of human who did not yet enjoy the rights of humanity [droits de l'humanité]," highlighting the emancipating and liberalizing clauses of a legal code that was in most other ways oppressive.[13] In his *Discours sur l'inégalité* (written in 1754, published the following year), Rousseau invoked "the rights of nature [les droits de la nature]" and gestured toward a future work in which he "would weigh the advantages and inconveniences of every government, with respect to the rights of the state of nature [droits de l'état de nature]"[14]—a work that would materialize eight years later as the *Social Contract*. In his *Encyclopédie* article "Economie," Rousseau further celebrated "the writings of those philosophers who dared to clamor for the rights of humanity [droits de l'humanité]."[15] And in the same volume, his then-friend and coeditor of the *Encyclopédie*, Diderot, signed an article on "Droit naturel," in which he affirmed, "I am human, and the only truly inalienable natural rights I have are those of humanity."[16] In *De l'esprit* (1758), Helvétius decried how tyrants sought to "violate the rights of humanity [les droits de l'humanité] with impunity," whereas the happiness of a nation was proportional to "the knowledge that a people has of the rights of humanity."[17] When an anonymous editor republished Montesquieu's *Spirit of Laws* in 1764, it seemed natural for him to add, "[H]umans, for the same reason that they constitute civil society, are also driven to conserve the natural rights of liberty [les droits naturels de la liberté]."[18] Never mind that Montesquieu had not mentioned such an idea.

What occasioned the adoption of natural rights talk by mid-eighteenth-century French authors? Before considering some of the possible reasons, two general observations are pertinent. First, the 1750s marked the moment when French authors became more interested overall in natural law theory (see fig. 3.2). The uptick in references to natural rights thus occurred in tandem with an increase in discussions of natural law.[19] A second aspect of this change may have been generational: Rousseau and Diderot only began publishing around mid-century; the writing careers of many other important figures in this story similarly took off after 1750.

But why was it at this *particular* moment that the *philosophes*, old and new, began writing about rights? Were there historical reasons? Mid-eighteenth-century France was in a period of political turmoil, with the Parlements and the crown facing off over issues of taxation and religion; but natural law arguments do not appear to have featured prominently in those debates.[20] The 1750s also witnessed a number of shocking events, including the Lisbon earthquake (1755) and the execution of the would-be regicide Robert-François Damiens (1757), but again, one would be hard-pressed to relate these to the newfound interest in natural rights. So what was going on?

## 1.1. THE *PHILOSOPHES* AGAINST THE PHILOSOPHERS: DUELING DIALECTS OF RIGHTS TALK

In much of the scholarship on rights, it is assumed that the *philosophes* simply derived their ideas about natural law theory and natural rights from seventeenth-century philosophers.[21] But this explanation overlooks an awkward problem, namely, the *philosophes'* remarkable hostility toward their predecessors. Indeed, they repeatedly attacked what they viewed as the pedantic, hyper-rational style of jusnaturalist writers.[22] The lawyer and journalist Simon-Nicholas-Henri Linguet put the case most succinctly, attacking Grotius's *De jure belli ac pacis* as "a mass of undigested and boring erudition. [ . . . ] He does not prove anything: he cites." As for Pufendorf, Linguet added, "He is equally knowledgeable, and even more diffuse."[23] In France, this antipathy toward the jusnaturalist tradition reflected the fact that natural law never quite took hold in the universities, the law faculties in particular. Hence Gabriel Bonnot de Mably could lament that "our judges [nos gens de robe], who no doubt know a great deal [ . . . ,] could not be more ignorant of the most common principles of natural right"—all the while dismissing Grotius, Hobbes,

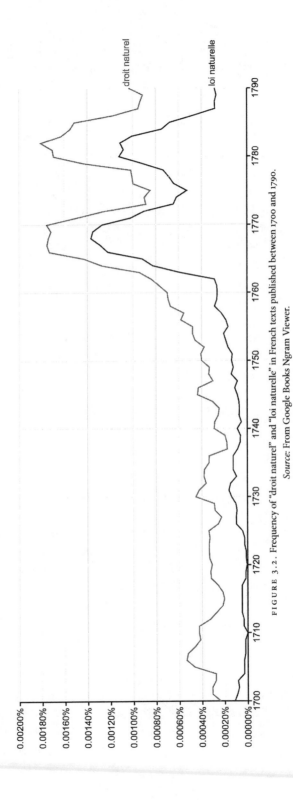

FIGURE 3.2. Frequency of "droit naturel" and "loi naturelle" in French texts published between 1700 and 1790.

*Source:* From Google Books Ngram Viewer.

Pufendorf, and Christian Wolff as peddlers of falsehoods.[24] The split between these two camps is particularly evident in the *Encyclopédie*, which uncharacteristically contains not one, but two articles on *droit naturel*, the first by the jurist Antoine-Gaspard Boucher d'Argis, who surveys the history of natural law theorists (including Grotius, John Selden, Hobbes, and Pufendorf), the other by Diderot, who cites no authorities and suggests that philosophers are inept at defining this concept.[25]

Even *philosophes* who were deeply cognizant of the natural law tradition expressed a similar distaste. In the preface to his *Discourse on Inequality* (1755), for instance, Rousseau dismissed this entire school of thought (which he knew very well) out of hand, on the grounds that its practitioners were too often in disagreement with one another. "It is not without surprise or scandal that we note the lack of agreement on this important topic among the different authors who have discussed it," he wrote, criticizing how "among the most solemn writers it is hard to find two who share an opinion on this point."[26] Up until then, it would not have seemed "scandalous" that different authors should have reached different conclusions, since natural law was viewed primarily as an academic topic, subject to philosophical dispute. But something had changed: as Rousseau's indictment, in this same text, of the philosopher who reasons himself out of sympathetic feelings for a murder victim made patently clear, natural law was no longer viewed as the prerogative of academics.[27]

While coming down less hard on philosophers, Diderot drove a similar point home in his *Encyclopédie* article "Droit naturel," which also appeared in 1755. "This interior sentiment is common to both the philosopher and the unthinking man [l'homme qui n'a point réfléchi]," he proclaimed.[28] Clearly, if both the philosopher and the unthinking man could gain access to the lessons of natural right, their common denominator was not philosophy. What, then, was the value of the learned works by those philosophers who had transformed natural right into a rigorous academic discipline? Apparently, not very high. In his 1769 *De la philosophie de la nature*, Jean-Baptiste-Claude Delisle de Sales wrote, "Europe has long begged us for an elementary treatise on natural right, which would collect the scattered truths found in the lengthy dissertations of the Pufendorfs, Cumberlands, and Burlamaquis, and which would correct these famous men, and consign them to oblivion."[29] At best, these earlier authors may have stumbled upon a few "scattered truths"; at worst, they had misled their readers. In either case, they were destined for the dustbin of philosophy. Lest these sentiments appear extravagant, let us recall that Voltaire had similarly called upon his audience to abandon such academic guides: "Let us leave aside those novels called systems / And to be elevated into ourselves descend," he wrote in his *Poème sur la Loi naturelle*.[30]

There was no use philosophizing about natural law, the *philosophe* concluded: even the wild girl of Châlons recognized their dictates.

## 1.2. WHERE IS LOCKE'S "SECOND TREATISE OF GOVERNMENT" IN THE FRENCH ENLIGHTENMENT?

Historians of the Enlightenment may at this point be impatiently raising an imaginary hand to shout out a counterexample to all that has been claimed above. Sure, the *philosophes* rejected the jusnaturalist authors and, as we will see in chapter 4, adopted a sentimental epistemology of rights. But wasn't there at least one author from this tradition who they did favor and emulate? What about John Locke? Not only was Locke more in line politically with the *philosophes* than the canonical natural law philosophers, many of whose political views tended toward absolutism, but the very epistemology on which sensibility depended derived largely from Locke's *Essay Concerning Human Understanding*. Accordingly, there has been a widespread tendency to view the *philosophes* as basically Lockean in their natural law views.[31]

As I argue in this section, however, this assumption must be revised, and to a considerable degree discarded, both for quantitative and qualitative reasons. Quantitatively, this thesis rests on shaky evidence. It is commonly stated that the French translation of Locke's *Second Treatise*, first published in 1691 in Amsterdam, went through twelve editions in the eighteenth century—clearly a bestseller![32] Unfortunately, this figure is wrong: I was only able to identify six editions that appeared before the French Revolution, in 1724, 1749, 1754, 1755, 1780, and 1783. Three subsequent editions appeared in 1794, 1795, and 1802. Excluding this last nineteenth-century edition (and the original in 1691), the total number of eighteenth-century editions is therefore eight.[33] But the stories of these individual editions are also noteworthy. The three editions that appeared in the middle of the century seem to have been propagated by "outside" interest groups. Keith Baker pointed to the role of Jansenist exiles in the publication of the 1749 and 1754 editions (both from Brussels), and Margaret Jacob noted how the 1755 edition was largely geared toward a Dutch audience (then in the throes of revolution).[34] The fact that three editions appeared in close succession between 1749 and 1755 may thus have had less to do with a sudden demand for Locke's political philosophy in Paris, and more with the political goals of parties non-affiliated with the *philosophes*.

But the quantitative problems with Locke's influence do not end there. A broader survey of Locke's presence in eighteenth-century French thought reveals that he was far less appreciated for his political theory than for his epistemological and pedagogical ideas. Put simply, people were mostly reading the *Essay Concerning Human Understanding* and *Some Thoughts Concerning Education*, and not the *Second Treatise*.[35] We can observe this tendency by examining the references to "Locke" in the works published between 1700 and 1789 in ARTFL's FRANTEXT database. Out of a total of 354 mentions, only 32 (9%) concern the "political" Locke of the *Two Treatises on Government*. These 32 references, moreover, are packed into a small number of books—7, to be precise, out of a total of 69 works that mention Locke. What's more, 3 of these 7 books account for 26 out of the 32 references to the "political" Locke, or for 81% of the total.[36] So out of the 575 documents for this date range in the ARTFL database, only 3—half a percent—engage significantly with Locke's political theory (defined here as more than 2 references).

Such numbers can of course only brush a very rough portrait of the intellectual reception of Locke's political ideas in eighteenth-century France, as the FRANTEXT database is far from exhaustive, particularly in matters of political theory.[37] But these numbers do make it difficult to argue that Locke's *Second Treatise* was the fountainhead of Enlightenment rights talk. Perhaps the number that best undermines this case is zero: that is the number of times that Voltaire, the *philosophe* who arguably played the greatest role in introducing Locke into French thought, mentions him as the author of *Du gouvernement civil* (or references Locke's political ideas) anywhere in his entire corpus.[38] It is not clear, in fact, that Voltaire ever read Locke's *Second Treatise*.[39] The same holds true for Montesquieu, whose political philosophy is so often associated with Locke's, but who never gives any indication that he read this particular work.[40]

A direct reference to Locke is of course not the only indication that his political ideas had been disseminated. The case of Mably's *Des droits et devoirs du citoyen* (written in 1758, but only published in 1789) is indicative. Locke is only cited there once, but we know from Mably's correspondence that he considered Locke to be "the supreme authority in matters of natural law."[41] Cultural transmission could also take place along more subterranean channels. It has long been known, for instance, that many of Locke's ideas were transmitted through Barbeyrac's notes to his translations of Grotius and Pufendorf.[42] Many of these notes, in turn, were cited and paraphrased in Jean-Jacques Burlamaqui's textbooks, which introduced basic natural right concepts to French and American audiences in the second half of the eighteenth century.[43] The arguments of Locke's treatise were also disseminated through reviews in the French Huguenot press.[44]

The influence of Locke's political philosophy must accordingly be assessed through more qualitative means. What such analysis uncovers is that while Locke's presence as a political thinker was certainly more widespread than the figures cited above suggest, his ideas appeared in such a disaggregated form that one can hardly speak of a "Lockean" theory—not in the least since his authorship was often not acknowledged. In other words, to the extent that his ideas were transmitted, they were also transformed. The *Encyclopédie* provides a striking example of this process: many of its articles on political subjects reproduced large chunks of *Du gouvernement civil* without ever indicating their source.[45] For the most part, this silence was strategic; it was a way to include a subversive author in an officially protected text, while avoiding censorship.[46] But it had other effects, as well. With no authorial identity in place to connect the different parts of a political theory, individual ideas could easily be separated from the original discursive whole and made to combine in new formations.[47]

One can see this atomizing process at work in the article that was the *Encyclopédie*'s most famous and controversial contribution to political theory, Diderot's entry "Autorité politique." Scholars have long detected "vague echoes of the last five chapters of the second *Treatise*" (i.e., the chapters that deal with usurpation, tyranny, and the dissolution of government), though as John Lough pointed out, "the fact remains that a careful comparison of the text of [this] article with the writings of Locke, Grotius, and Pufendorf and with Barbeyrac's notes does not reveal a single passage which [Diderot] could be said to owe directly to any one of these writers."[48] With respect to Locke in particular, it is striking to consider what Diderot did *not* borrow from the *Second Treatise*. This is the article, after all, in which Diderot (under the cover of anonymity) leads a full-on assault against absolutist theories of monarchy in the name of natural law and social contract theory. He goes so far as to argue, for instance, that "the nation has the right to maintain its contract above and against anyone; no power can change it; and when the contract no longer holds, the nation regains its full freedom and right to contract anew with whomever, and however, it pleases."[49] The one argument that Diderot doesn't make, however, is that an unjust or illegitimate monarch can be legitimately resisted: hence, his conclusion that "if ever the people were ruled by an unjust, ambitious, and violent king," they should "address this misfortune with a single remedy, which is to appease him through their submission, and to sway God by their prayers. This is the only legitimate remedy, given the contract of submission previously sworn to the reigning prince."[50] Just when we might have expected Diderot to leap to the expected Lockean conclusion, he shies away.[51] Some might invoke a fear of censorship to explain this apparent lack of nerve, but this explanation is doubtful, given that Diderot expressed the exact same sentiments in the *Supplément au voyage de Bougainville*, a text that was not published during his lifetime, and in which he could have expressed a freer opinion, had he been so inclined.[52] Indeed, none of the passages from the *Second Treatise* quoted in the *Encyclopédie* are taken from the final chapter on the dissolution of government, in which the right of resisting is discussed.

Even authors familiar with, and sympathetic to, the *Second Treatise* seem largely to have cherry-picked its arguments, without even choosing those we associate most closely with Locke. Mably may have viewed Locke as a "supreme authority," but his views on property were hardly Lockean, and, as Keith Baker has noted, his political philosophy was "much closer in tone to Sidney's classical republicanism than to Locke's *Second Treatise*."[53] Rousseau is perhaps the *philosophe* who knew Locke the best, but he also follows him the least.[54]

What this cursory assessment of the influence of Locke's political philosophy in eighteenth-century France suggests, therefore, is not that nobody was reading Locke's *Second Treatise*, but rather that Enlightenment rights talk cannot be described as "Lockean." Because many *philosophes* expressed views that look at a distance similar to those of Locke, it is tempting to apply this label to their basic narrative of rights. But as the data and observations above remind us, what looks and sounds like Locke may not, in fact, have come from Locke at all. Not only did Locke's political theory have a surprisingly limited reception in France, compared with his epistemology, but many of the specific arguments contained in the *Second Treatise* could be found in various other texts, as well.[55] The Jesuit tradition of natural law, for instance, which was in many ways similar to Locke's, lived on in schools attended by Voltaire, Diderot, Turgot, and Helvétius, as R. R. Palmer noted over seventy years ago.[56] The idea that the laws of nature should continue to govern civil societies was common to Hobbes, Spinoza, and Fénelon, among others. Nor was Locke the only Englishman (or Frenchman, for that matter) to justify a right to resistance. To the extent that the *philosophes'* views on natural right did share a certain family resemblance, they do not seem to have received this imprint from Locke.

### 1.3. EIGHTEENTH-CENTURY SOURCES: TRANSLATIONS AND TEXTBOOKS

A more promising explanation for the revival of natural law in the French Enlightenment may lie in the appearance of a series of publications, many in translation, that breathed new life into this topic. Francis Hutcheson's *An Inquiry into the Original of Our Ideas of Beauty and Virtue* (1725) came out in French in 1749, right before the resurgence of natural rights talk in France.[57] As we saw in the previous chapter, this work contained an early sketch of Hutcheson's theory of natural rights but framed in terms of the transfer regime. The French translation (*Recherches*) was somewhat abridged: it did not contain, for instance, the final paragraphs on despotism.[58] But French readers would still have found Hutcheson's typology of perfect/imperfect and alienable/inalienable rights,[59] and could have read that property rights are among "the more important Rights of Mankind [les Droits les plus importants de l'humanité]."[60] The emphasis on human rights in this text was embellished by the translator Marc-Antoine Eidous, who has the reputation of being "un traducteur peu exact."[61] To Hutcheson's account of tyranny, he added that the tyrant "is not afraid to violate the most sacred rights of justice and humanity [les droits les plus sacrés de la justice & de l'humanité]," a phrase missing in the original. With the (unintentional?) addition of a single word, Eidous also turned Hutcheson's description of the transfer regime into an account that was much closer to the preservation regime. Where Hutcheson had flagged "the Right [that] Men have to constitute Civil Government, and to subject their alienable Rights to the Disposal of their Governours," Eidous introduced a negation, so that the sentence became about the rights that men could *not* alienate ("soumettre des Droits qu'ils *ne* pouvoient aliéner, à la disposition des Magistrats qu'ils ont choisis").[62] Eidous was a friend of Diderot's and an *Encyclopédiste*; it may well have been through his influence that Diderot himself came to know Hutcheson's text, which he drew on heavily when writing the *Encyclopédie* article "Beau." Some French readers may also have been familiar with Hutcheson's Latin textbook, the *Philosophiae moralis institutio compendiaria* (1742), though the French translation of this work only appeared in 1770.[63]

A more spirited defense of natural rights, also linked to an attack on tyranny, could be found in the 1751 translation of Thomas Gordon's *Political Discourses upon Tacitus*.[64] Voltaire had already called attention to Gordon's work in the English original, and it would continue to attract interest in the second half of the century.[65] While highly critical of those authors who invented arguments that sought to "to sanctify oppression, to blast and overthrow all the natural and civil rights of men [tous les droits naturels & civils qui appartiennent aux hommes]," Gordon nonetheless stuck to the transfer regime in this work, as this quote (repurposed from his earlier, untranslated *Cato's Letters*) indicates: "In a State of Nature, every man has a right to vindicate himself; when Society is dissolved, the same right returns [il rentre dans le même droit]." By implication, individuals did *not* retain this right while in society. Still, there was a fiery republicanism to Gordon's text, particularly when it addressed the topic of tyrannicide: "By the Laws of Rome the Dominion of one, and consequently the dominion of Cæsar, was detestable and accursed, and any man was warranted to slay the Tyrant [tout homme étoit en droit de tuer le Tyran]."[66] Lines such as these would make Gordon a favorite author of some French revolutionaries, notably Camille Desmoulins.[67]

Equally fiery was Algernon Sidney, whose *Discourses Concerning Government* (posthumously published in 1698) were first translated into French in 1702, then reedited in 1755.[68] Sidney was also popular among the *philosophes*, who often name-dropped this other scourge of absolute government. But Sidney, too, did not defend the preservation regime, nor did he develop a particularly elaborate theory of natural rights.

Alongside these translations, another major publication brought about renewed interest in natural law theory. This was the Genevan law professor Jean-Jacques Burlamaqui's *Principes du droit naturel*, published in 1747.[69] Written primarily for his students at the Académie de Genève, Burlamaqui's textbook (like Hutcheson's *Institutio*) was in large part a summary of earlier works, Pufendorf's *De officio hominis et civis* in particular.[70] But it also reflected the Genevan's own political views, which supported the local patrician party in its conflict with the bourgeoisie.[71]

There is no doubting the popularity of Burlamaqui's study (along with that of its companion volume, the *Principes du droit politique*, 1751): it went through four subsequent editions before the Revolution and was translated into English the year after its initial publication.[72] Its accessibility and availability in English made the author well-known across the Atlantic.[73] Given that so much of his work merely summarized the ideas of earlier theorists, however, it is difficult to assess how, exactly, his influence exerted itself. What's more, Burlamaqui's textbook did not promote the preservation regime. He considered the abridgment of rights in society to be fully legitimate, claiming that we are "at liberty to use them [rights] or not, to retain or renounce them in the whole or in part"; and if we did renounce our rights, then "actions in themselves permitted, happen sometimes to be commanded or forbidden by the authority of the sovereign."[74] In the *Principles of Politic Law*, he came out strongly and repeatedly in favor of the transfer regime: "[T]he right of a sovereign, to punish crimes, is no other than that natural right which human society and every individual had originally to execute the law of nature, and to take care of their own safety; this natural right has been *yielded and transferred* to the sovereign. . . ."[75]

While Burlamaqui may have played a role in rekindling a general interest in natural law theory, he clearly could not have been at the source of the resurgence of the preservation regime. So what explains why, beginning sporadically in the 1750s, then accelerating in the 1760s, French authors such as Diderot, Helvétius, d'Holbach, Raynal, Condorcet, and even the future revolutionary leader Mirabeau insisted on preserving our natural rights in civil society? Gone were any arguments about the need to transfer rights from individuals to government; gone, too, suggestions that any natural rights must be sacrificed to enjoy the benefits of society.[76] Instead, author after author maintained that "society is just, good, worthy of our love, when it fulfills the physical needs of its members, and guarantees their safety, freedom, and the possession of their natural rights."[77] As I argue in the following section, the reason why the preservation regime was revived in France had nothing to do with translations of English or Latin natural law texts (or, for that matter, by the recovery of older French works). It was instead brought about by a group of French thinkers known as the Physiocrats.

## 2. Physiocracy and the Dangerous Ignorance of Natural Rights

Remembered today for their contributions to economic thought, the Physiocrats also developed an elaborate political theory, which met with considerable success in the last quarter of the eighteenth century.[78] As I've argued elsewhere, their political ideas grew out of the longer French tradition of "natural republicanism," a tradition that stretches back to Fénelon, and that can in some regards be viewed as a literary adaption of natural law theory.[79] More than any other authors in this tradition, however, the Physiocrats placed a particular emphasis on natural rights.[80]

### 2.1. POLITICAL THOUGHT BEFORE ECONOMIC THEORY: FRANÇOIS QUESNAY

The birth of Physiocratic economic theory is usually situated in the early 1750s; it enjoyed a heyday in the mid-1760s, before fading from view after 1775. The outlines of Physiocratic *political* thought, however, can be traced further back, to a work published in the 1740s by the group's founder, François Quesnay.[81] Quesnay was a remarkable figure. His origins were extremely humble: his father was a farmer and small landowner who did not tend much to the education of his thirteen children. François only learned how to read at age eleven. Despite these challenging beginnings, he eventually trained as a surgeon, before embarking on a glorious medical career that would lead him to Versailles as Mme de Pompadour's private physician and as *médecin consultant* to Louis XV. While acquitting himself of his medical duties, he also collaborated with a number of faithful "disciples," including the marquis de Mirabeau (father of the famous revolutionary), to produce the liberal economic doctrine known as Physiocracy.

Before Quesnay turned his attention to economics, however, he wrote a series of works on surgical and medical topics, including the *Essai physique sur l'œconomie animale* (1736). In a much revised and enlarged edition of this work, published in 1747, he laid out the fundamental premises of the political theory that would later underpin Physiocratic doctrine. Interestingly, in this early exposé, the economic arguments for which Quesnay and his circle would gain notoriety were mostly missing.[82] What we do find clearly expressed, however, is an affirmation of the preservation regime of natural rights.

Quesnay arrived at this topic via a lengthy reflection on epistemology, which takes up most of the third volume of the *Essai physique*. In the section entitled "La Liberté," he declared his intention to counter the misguided opinions of certain "Philosophers and Theologians" on the true meaning of freedom.[83] After redefining this concept as "the power of using reason to act or not to act" (350), he considered how the presence of others might affect the enjoyment of our freedom. This was the question that led him to assert the existence of natural rights: "[B]y natural rights, I mean those that nature herself gave us; hence, for instance, the right to sunlight enjoyed by all men to whom nature gave eyes; it is evident that one cannot prevent their use, without violating the order established by the supreme intelligence. . . ."[84] Quesnay's example may seem odd, but may have derived from Roman law: the *Digest* lists how "by natural law, the following are common to all: air, flowing water, the sea, and consequently the seashore."[85] From the rest of his discussion, it becomes apparent that these rights are primarily related to our efforts at self-preservation. An individual's natural right "is effectively limited by nature herself to the quantity of goods necessary to conserve oneself" (365). With an implicit nod to Hobbes, Quesnay recognized that in theory this right could extend to everything: "[A]ll men therefore each have a natural right to everything indiscriminately [droit à tout indistinctement]." To avoid conflicts, we must accordingly "desist" ourselves of our theoretical right to all, in order to cohabitate peacefully with others ("the [natural] order demands that each man desists himself of this general and indiscriminate right"). But for Quesnay, this reassessment of our "indiscriminate" natural right did not amount to a loss. In order to establish the proper scope of our natural rights, "intelligent beings" will necessarily acknowledge "an authority or power which subjects them sovereignly to the laws that it prescribes." This sovereign power, however, is no Leviathan and does not abridge our natural rights: "This power does not destroy the natural right of every man; on the contrary, it guarantees and regulates it in the most fitting and interesting way for society" (369). Hence, Quesnay could summarize his views with a strong preservationist statement: "In the social order [l'ordre de la Société] men always have natural and legitimate rights."[86]

Though phrased here in the collective (*les hommes*), the rights identified by Quesnay were clearly individual. Ironically, Hobbes may have played an important role in disambiguating collective and individual natural rights, through his relentless insistence on self-preservation as the supreme "right of nature." As we saw in chapter 2, self-preservation was the one natural right that even Hobbes acknowledged we preserved in political society. While objecting to Hobbes's *reductio ad bellum* of this natural right, and while rejecting his abridgment regime, Quesnay nonetheless retained the central Hobbesian claim that natural rights belong wholly to the self and are primarily exercised by individuals (to take Hobbes's examples, by resisting imprisonment or death). As the rest of this chapter shows, it was this individualistic understanding of natural rights that the Physiocrats championed and disseminated more broadly in French Enlightenment discourse. This interpretation would later intersect with the collective or corporatist conception of natural rights, which reemerged in legal circles after the 1770 Maupeou coup (see below).

If Quesnay rejected the abridgment hypothesis that our natural rights do *not* persist in society, it was because he did not recognize any ontological, moral, or juridical distinctions between the state of nature and civil society. Both are part of what he called the *ordre naturel*. Whether or not individuals have given themselves a sovereign ruler, they "cannot, without acting against the natural order and against their own reason, refuse one another the part which by natural right belongs to each of them" (365). Placing themselves under the control of government, therefore, does not alter their condition or their rights, since laws simply confirm the divisions of the natural order: "[T]he portion granted to every man will belong to him by natural and legitimate right. [ . . . ] It belongs to him by legitimate right, because it was given by laws, which men agreed to establish amongst themselves" (366).

These arguments, which Quesnay would repeat and develop in *Le droit naturel* (1765), reveal a curious and rather idiosyncratic logic of rights, one that runs counter to those historical accounts crediting an increased concern with individualism for the rise of subjective rights talk.[87] Indeed, Quesnay's affirmation of natural rights takes a fairly Aristotelian point of departure.[88] Not only does he regard the political state as the natural human condition, but he also subscribes to an Aristotelian notion of distributive justice, based on fairness.[89] The *ordre naturel* is an inherently theological concept for Quesnay ("the order established by the supreme intelligence") and determines what our fair share of goods ought to be.[90] Here Quesnay remains faithful to classical and Thomist notions of *jus naturae*, as an "objective" standard of justice. "The portion granted to each man": this phrase recalls Ulpian's famous *ius suum cuique tribuendi*, the foundational definition of justice in Roman law. But

Quesnay then shifts perspectives to assert our individual, "subjective" right to this share: our portion belongs to us "by natural right."

Despite the common linkage of the Physiocrats with Locke, it should be evident from this overview how little Quesnay's thesis resembles the arguments put forward in the *Second Treatise of Government*.[91] Labor plays as of yet no part in his theory of rights, and Quesnay does away with any social contract narrative.[92] So what were Quesnay's sources? This is a question that has bedeviled scholars for generations.[93] Quesnay owned copies of Richard Cumberland's 1672 *Traité philosophique des loix naturelles* (translated by Barbeyrac and published in 1744), as well as of Pufendorf's major works.[94] As we saw, however, none of these texts stressed the preservation of individual natural rights. What they did do was to criticize Hobbes, with whom Quesnay was clearly familiar, either directly or indirectly. Hobbes is the only modern philosopher whom Quesnay cites by name in *Le droit naturel*;[95] and various passages of the *Essai physique* (including the "droit à tout indistinctement") refer plainly to Hobbes.[96]

It appears likely, then, that Quesnay developed his ideas about natural rights in opposition to Hobbes's and arrived at the preservation regime by negating Hobbes's abridgment thesis. Hobbes functions as a key negative bridge between Quesnay and earlier theorists of the preservation regime. While it is conceivable that Quesnay stumbled across some pamphlets by, say, the French Huguenot exiles, there is no evidence that he did, nor is there any meaningful similarity in their views, beyond a basic resemblance of their conception of rights. The reemergence of the preservation regime in mid-eighteenth-century France was most likely not the result of a discovery of older historical sources, but rather the reinvention of an old idea. There is nothing particularly surprising or coincidental about this reinvention: once the stark divide between a state of nature and civil society was abolished, the rationale for denying the persistence of natural rights in society diminished as well.

The real question about Quesnay's natural right theory, then, is not where did he discover the idea of natural rights, but rather how did he come to view society as part of a natural order? Contemporaries noted a certain resemblance between Physiocracy and Stoicism, a parallel that historians have also underlined.[97] Quesnay had read Cicero at a young age and possessed a copy of *De officiis*, in French translation.[98] Here he could have learned about the Stoic belief that "the sovereign good is to live in conformity with what nature demands of us"; his translation may have further encouraged his natural rights talk, as it contained strong language about those who dared to "violate [blesser] the rights of humanity."[99] More generally, the basic Physiocratic narrative about the origins of the state closely follows Aristotle's, which similarly progresses in a natural, stadial development from the family, to the village, to the community, then to the state.[100]

But there is a more direct source for Quesnay's concept of an *ordre naturel*, which is the French priest and philosopher Malebranche. Quesnay's devotion to the latter is well-known: *De la recherche de la vérité* (1674–75) was one of his favorite books.[101] Scholars have detected the considerable influence of this work on Quesnay's epistemology.[102] But the idea of a natural order, or more specifically of an *ordre de la nature*, is also central to Malebranche.[103] Along with "l'ordre de la grâce," which perfected it ("réparer"), the natural order was a product of divine will: "[T]he order of nature [ . . . ] is nothing other than the eternal will [of God]."[104] Both orders were part of Malebranche's occasionalism, a doctrine that explained how matter and mind (inherently distinct categories in Cartesian metaphysics) "miraculously" aligned in our daily experience.[105]

Despite his own polemics against the Stoics (Seneca, in particular), Malebranche ultimately agreed that the good life was one in which we lived according to nature. Interestingly, he interpreted this Stoic principle in scientific terms. To find happiness, Malebranche argued, we must first understand the structure of the human body, and how different causes produce different effects: "[T]hen we will know how to conduct and conserve ourselves in the happiest and most perfect state that we can reach, according to the natural order [l'ordre de la nature] and the rules of the Gospel."[106] In many respects, this was precisely the program that Quesnay set himself in the revised edition of the *Essai physique*.[107] His own definition of an *ordre naturel* may have varied somewhat from Malebranche's—we no longer find a parallel "ordre de la grâce"—but he had no qualms in asserting its paternity. The epigraph to Pierre-Paul Le Mercier de La Rivière's *L'ordre naturel et essentiel des sociétés politiques* (1767), a work that Quesnay oversaw very closely, was taken from Malebranche and refers precisely to his concept of order: "The [natural] Order is the inviolable law of spirit; and whatever does not conform to it is not properly arranged [L'Ordre est la Loi inviolable des esprits; & rien n'est réglé, s'il n'y est conforme]."[108]

At a time when very few French authors even mentioned natural rights, and fewer still discussed them in the context of the preservation regime, the founder of Physiocracy placed them at the heart of his political theory. He would not write much more on the subject for the next decade: after his installment at Versailles in 1749, he largely ceased to publish under his own name; and for next fifteen years, his life and career would be largely consumed by the demands of the court, as well as by his own studies. These were the years when he developed—first on his own, then with the help of dedicated colleagues—his economic theory, which he summarized in the striking, if slightly baffling, *Tableau économique* of 1758 (the first edition of which was printed by no less than Louis XV, on his private press).[109] Only after the death of his patron, Mme de Pompadour, in 1764, did Quesnay and the Physiocrats begin to press their case to the public at large. At the time, the government had just embarked on its first experiments with liberalizing the grain trade, finally putting some of their ideas into practice: this move called for an energetic defense on the part of the Physiocrats and brought greater public interest in (and controversy over) their economic theory.[110]

An early result of this publicity campaign was Quesnay's short treatise on *Le droit naturel* (1765). This work largely recapitulates the arguments put forth nearly two decades earlier in the *Essai physique*. Once again, his principal opponent is Hobbes; *contra* the claim that man's natural right in the state of nature extends to all things, he argues that "the natural right of each man is in reality limited to that portion which he can acquire through labor" (12). This statement brings to mind Locke's labor theory of property, but the rest of Quesnay's argument is far from Lockean. Rather than having to "give up" this right when we enter into society, for Quesnay the passage from a state of "pure nature" to a state of society or "multitude" in fact extends and secures our natural rights: "When [humans] enter into society and establish contracts for their mutual advantage, they greatly enhance their enjoyment of their natural right" (15). What's more, this transition from one state to another is not conceived of as a phase change, but as a gradual progression. Since monarchy is for Quesnay the most natural form of government, deriving as it does from the family structure (24), then as more and more families establish bonds between them, society emerges naturally.[111] Accordingly, there is no transfer, exchange, or abridgment of rights that can or should occur: "[T]he natural right that is to be found in the order of nature and justice extends to all the states in which men find themselves" (13). Society is the ultimate preserve of natural rights, as it is the function of positive laws to defend them: "[M]en who place themselves under the rule, or rather the protection, of a tutelary authority's positive laws, greatly enhance their natural right, instead of restricting it [étendent beaucoup leur droit naturel, au lieu de le restreindre]" (28–29).

Unlike the American authors expounding on natural rights in 1765, Quesnay did not draw out their political implications.[112] The natural rights that he championed did not include a right to self-government or a right to freedom of expression. If natural rights were banished from French political discourse after 1610 because they were perceived as too revolutionary, their return 150 years later was assisted by the fact that they now seemed politically innocuous. Natural rights were essentially, and almost wholly, property rights.

While this economic focus underpinned the Physiocrats' liberal, free-market agenda, it also had a curious social corollary. Indeed, one issue that Quesnay confronted in the *Essai physique* was economic inequality, a problem that led him to recognize the importance and legitimacy of basic socioeconomic rights. If we all enjoy the same rights, he argued, we remain free to develop or ignore them as we wish. Those who make poor decisions ("a bad use of our liberty") have only themselves to blame, accordingly; and the government should not seek to eliminate inequality, since otherwise the "order of society" would be disturbed. But those who are unable to work through no fault of their own are due assistance from others: "[T]hose who cannot work, find aid in the assistance of caring men [des hommes bienfaisants], who recognize the rules of fairness and the precepts of religion" (372).

The social welfare that Quesnay describes here sounds a good deal like Christian charity, given that it is not the state but rather "caring men" who are charged with providing it. But Quesnay does not simply fall back onto Christian doctrine. He ties the requirement for public welfare back to the same natural social order that underpins all of Physiocratic economic thought: "[T]he natural order also prescribes duties to men, which religion and positive laws regulate in accordance with the self-evident goals of the Author of Nature, and social advantages" (372). Our duty toward others may be enshrined in religion, but it also has a basis in natural law. Quesnay comes closer here to Locke (whom he may or may not have read), for whom the law of nature did not only beseech us to preserve ourselves, but also "to preserve the rest of Mankind."[113] As I show in the following chapter, the idea that we have a natural right to social welfare was in fact an early feature of "social naturalism" in France; it also proved to be a key Physiocratic contribution to the French revolutionary discourse on rights.[114]

## 2.2. PHYSIOCRATIC EXTENSIONS OF NATURAL RIGHTS

Quesnay's authoritative statement on natural rights, *Le droit naturel*, would be reprinted a few years later in *Physiocratie* (1768), a collection of his works edited by his follower and collaborator Pierre Samuel Dupont de Nemours. Dupont de Nemours's lengthy introduction also drove home Quesnay's preservation thesis, as did another text he published that year, *De l'origine et des progrès d'une science nouvelle*.[115] This thesis in fact became a cornerstone of Physiocratic theory. It features in the Physiocratic journal the *Ephémérides du citoyen*, then edited by the abbé Nicolas Baudeau: "[Y]ou will only reassure men and their movable assets, by letting them enjoy their natural rights in total safety and complete liberty."[116] Quesnay's close collaborator, the marquis de Mirabeau, similarly insisted that individuals should retain their natural rights in society, in a 1774 work subtitled *Les droits et les devoirs de l'homme*.[117]

But it was a separate work—published by yet another of Quesnay's disciples, with considerable oversight from the master—that brought the most attention to this idea: Le Mercier de La Rivière's *L'ordre naturel et essentiel des sociétés politiques* (1767). This book won its author (a former intendant of Martinique) pan-European fame and an invitation to Saint Petersburg by the tsarina herself. Le Mercier's book was well received by some of the *philosophes*: Diderot placed the author above Montesquieu; Helvétius wrote a flattering letter to its author; Voltaire was less impressed but did deign to discuss the book in a letter to Catherine II.[118] While many (including Rousseau) objected to Le Mercier's theory of legal despotism, his readers will have found a strong endorsement of the preservation regime: "[T]he only favor that landowners demand of their government is that they not be disturbed in the peaceful enjoyment of their natural rights" (235). In accordance with Quesnay's doctrine, Le Mercier placed society and the state of nature on a continuum, uninterrupted by the intervention of a social contract. "It is not because men gathered together in society that they have reciprocal duties and rights," he argued, "but because they naturally and *necessarily* had reciprocal duties and rights that they naturally and *necessarily* live in society" (12). We can never lose our natural rights, since we always remain within the "natural and essential order of society."

What are we to make of Physiocracy's strong defense of natural rights? On the one hand, this history shows how the close connection between (neo)liberalism and human rights, which Samuel Moyn and others have highlighted for the 1970s, has deep roots.[119] It was in defense of landowners and free trade that rights talk blossomed in mid-eighteenth-century France. Quesnay and his followers do not appear to have been moved by sympathy or any humanitarian concerns when they advocated for natural rights. Their overriding objective was to increase the wealth of the nation.

On the other hand, it did not take long before others appropriated these rights for more politically liberal uses. A year after Mirabeau published *La science*, his son, the future revolutionary leader, published an *Essai sur le despotisme* (1775), in which he echoed many Physiocratic claims but put them to much different uses. "Men retain in a well-ordered society [la société bien ordonnée] the full extent of their natural rights, and acquire a much greater facility to use these rights," Mirabeau *fils* intoned, ventriloquizing Quesnay. But the rights to which this "well-ordered society" entitled us were not merely free trade—we had natural *political* rights, as well: "Our enthusiasm for our kings, our presumption, and especially the long-term ignorance of the rights

of man [droits de l'homme] has made us rush into our chains."[120] Mirabeau
would rehearse this argument fourteen years later, when he wrote that "the
ignorance, neglect, or contempt of the rights of man are the sole causes of
public calamities and of the corruption of governments." These words would
form part of the preamble to the Declaration of the Rights of Man and of the
Citizen. The theme of *ignoring* our natural rights would have a long legacy,
extending up through the UDHR, which similarly warns of the evils caused
by the "disregard and contempt for human rights."[121]

In Mirabeau, we thus find a direct link (among many others) between the
Physiocratic theory of natural rights and the Declaration's affirmation of the
preservation regime.[122] As we will see, by 1789 this argument was not only a
Physiocratic position, but had become accepted by others, including most of
the *philosophes*. But the Physiocrats—and perhaps more importantly, what
might be termed Physiocratic "fellow travelers"—played an important role in
transmitting and transforming natural rights into political entitlements. Two
key figures in this process were Anne-Robert-Jacques Turgot and the marquis
de Condorcet.[123]

While not a Physiocrat himself, Turgot shared many of their economic
principles. When as controller-general of finances (1774–76) Turgot also liber-
alized the grain trade, his attempts were widely viewed as an implementation
of Physiocratic theory.[124] But Turgot also developed Quesnay's belief that some
forms of social assistance were due to those in need. While he was the intendant of the Limousin, Turgot established *ateliers de charité* (charitable work-
shops) to hire rural workers who were unemployed; he pursued similar efforts
when he became controller-general of finances.[125] He was a harsh critic of the
favored old-regime solution of *dépôts de mendicité* and "poor hospitals."[126] In
his *Encyclopédie* article "Fondation" (1757), he attacked the permanence of the
*dépôts*, which disincentivized people from working and churned out "a vile
mob [une populace vile] of vagabond beggars who abandon themselves to
all sorts of crimes." The ideal solution, in his eyes, was to finance welfare privately and circumstantially, as in Bayeux, where "the inhabitants pooled their
resources, to fully get rid of begging from their town; and they succeeded, by
giving work to all the able beggars, and charity to those who are disabled."
Like Quesnay, however, Turgot acknowledged that society has an obligation to
assist those who cannot find employment or are too sick to work: "[H]umanity
and religion both make it our duty to assist our fellows in need."[127] He even
went so far as to frame this duty correlatively in terms of a right: "[T]he poor
have undeniable rights [des droits incontestables] on the abundance of the
rich." With the experiments in economic liberalism often resulting in mass
hunger and even starvation, this insistence on a right to social welfare became

increasingly central to Physiocratic justifications of free trade. By the time of
the French Revolution, Turgot's biographer, editor, and former collaborator,
Dupont de Nemours, enshrined this socioeconomic right in the *Cahier de
doléances* that he authored for his hometown parish of Dupont de Nemours:
"Anyone in a state of infancy, impotence, invalidity, or disability, has a right to
free assistance [des secours gratuits] from other men."[128]

Turgot was also a mentor to the younger Condorcet, who began writing
on political economy in the same year (1774) that Turgot launched his liberal economic agenda.[129] He defended the free-market reforms in the name of
natural rights.[130] In his *Lettres sur le commerce des grains*, Condorcet attacked
those who dared strip men of their rights: "And so some have thought that
in order to restore men to their natural rights, one had to show that they
were useful, as if there was ever a question of demanding the sacrifice of their
rights."[131] He returned to this theme two years later, in another publication
on the grain trade. The preservation regime was now enshrined as a political
axiom: "The Government owes to the nation a defense of the rights of all its
members." Nothing could justify abridging the natural rights of citizens: the
legislator "needs no particular reason to let each person enjoy their natural
rights." Defending the Physiocrats against "M. N." (i.e., Jacques Necker), Condorcet assured his readers that they only wanted to "invite their brothers to
share with them the only true goods of men, namely, the enjoyment and the
feeling of their rights."[132]

At this stage in his career, Condorcet remained within the liberal economic
framework of the Physiocrats. Only a few years later, however, he would re-
purpose the idea of natural rights to rail against slavery. "Political societies
can have but one goal, which is to maintain the rights of those who compose
them. Accordingly, any law that violates the right of a citizen or a stranger is
an unjust law, authorizing violence, and is a genuine crime," he wrote, repeating a Physiocratic principle. But now he added, "[I]t cannot be useful [utile]
for a man, let alone a perpetual class of men, to be deprived of the natural
rights of humanity."[133] While he does consider the economic advantages of
having free landholders cultivate the plantations instead of slaves, Condorcet's
primary objections to slavery in this work are moral and philosophical: see,
for instance, his claim that "[e]very legislator, and every single member of a
legislative body, is subject to the laws of natural morality."[134]

Condorcet's commitment to the preservation regime of natural rights in
society only hardened in the revolutionary period. Already in his 1784 academic *éloge* for César-François Cassini de Thury, Condorcet sketched out a
revolutionary narrative of a nation regaining its rights after years of tyranny—
except the nation in question was Austria, under the enlightened rule of

Joseph II.[135] By 1788 this nation was the United States, where great respect was shown "for the natural rights of humanity"; soon it would be France, now ruled by "a Prince who protects the rights of humanity."[136]

In addition to extending natural rights to slaves, Condorcet also sought to have them recognized for women. In his 1790 essay "Sur l'admission des femmes au droit de cité," he argued that "the common rights of human beings" ("les droits communs des individus de l'espèce humaine"—note the gender-neutral phrasing) were unfairly limited to men. Men enjoyed these rights because they are "sensible creatures [des êtres sensibles], capable of acquiring moral ideas, and reflecting on those ideas."[137] Since women have these same abilities, they should have the same rights. It is telling that with respect to both women's rights and the rights of slaves, Condorcet's logic does not rest on empathetic identification.[138] Instead, in both cases, he reasons on the basis of the principles of general utility and of equality.

The outbreak of revolution in America, and then in France, clearly brought greater publicity to the preservation regime of rights. Indeed, during this time, to look favorably on revolution generally meant to advocate for inalienable, individual rights. We can see this identification in Dupont de Nemours's biography (or rather, hagiography) of Turgot, in which he recalls how the former minister in charge of France's finances, which were then in particularly bad shape, acquiesced to funding the American revolutionaries, as they were fighting a war that had "as its subject and can only have as its goal the preservation [maintien] of the natural rights of all men and all states."[139] For the French, the American devotion to preserving the natural rights of men became even more evident after Benjamin Franklin and the duc de La Rochefoucauld d'Enville teamed up in 1783 to publish translations of the major documents of the American Revolution, including the Declaration of Independence, as well as the state constitutions.[140] As we will see in the following section, the *philosophes* similarly associated the political goals of the American revolutionaries with the preservation of natural rights. But this strong association in the 1780s should not blind us to the fact that the French had already put forward their own version of the preservation regime a decade *before* the Declaration of Independence was drafted. If they immediately recognized in the American revolutionary writings the salience of natural rights talk, it was because they already spoke the language. What remains to be seen is whether both groups understood this language in the same way.

### 3. Natural Rights Talk in the Late Enlightenment:
### The *Philosophes* Carry the Torch

Not all instances of natural rights talk in France after 1750 were inspired by the Physiocrats. As we saw, Rousseau's political arguments were independent from, and largely antithetical to, Physiocratic ideas about society and natural rights. What's more, many *philosophes* would turn against Physiocracy, either for a brief period (in the cases of Voltaire and Diderot), or once and for all.[141] But to focus on their attitudes toward the Physiocratic doctrine as a whole is to overlook the fact that they often accepted many aspects of the Physiocratic political framework and discourse. In what follows, therefore, I do not claim that the *philosophes* all held Physiocratic beliefs, particularly about free trade, but rather argue that their adoption of the preservation regime of natural rights in the 1760s and early 1770s can be traced back to their engagement, even critical, with Physiocracy.

While this argument can be made solely on the basis of textual evidence, it is strengthened by a brief account of the social relations between the *philosophes* and the Physiocrats (see figure 3.3). A critical link, for the purposes of this study at least, was the one between Diderot and Quesnay.[142] Diderot had praised Quesnay in a 1748 publication;[143] they first met in the early 1750s, when Diderot was fishing for contributors to the *Encyclopédie*. Quesnay would subsequently publish three articles, "Evidence," "Fermiers," and "Grains," appearing in volumes 6 and 7 (published in 1756 and 1757, respectively); he withdrew another three articles after the *privilège* for the *Encyclopédie* was revoked in 1759.[144] But this relationship was more than editorial: according to Jean-François Marmontel—another *encyclopédiste*, *philosophe*, and mainstay of the Parisian salons—Quesnay hosted Diderot, d'Alembert, Helvétius, and others in his Versailles apartment (where he had been living since 1749)—perhaps including, on occasion, Mme de Pompadour herself, who housed her doctor in a basement (*entre-sol*) beneath her own rooms.[145]

Diderot and Helvétius were also fixtures in the world of Parisian salons, including the more "philosophical" salon of the baron d'Holbach.[146] D'Holbach's gatherings brought together many of the leading Parisian *philosophes* and were known for their daring intellectual conversations on matters of religion and politics. Along with the rest of France, they also debated the raging topic of the day—the liberalization of the grain trade.[147] This meant addressing Physiocratic theories, and the Neapolitan abbé Ferdinando Galiani would try out in the baron's salon many of the arguments that appeared in his 1770 anti-Physiocratic *Dialogues sur le commerce des blés*.[148] Despite the presence of this vivacious opponent of Quesnay in their midst, many of the other habitués

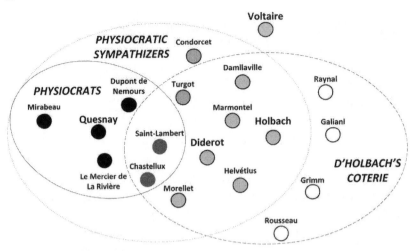

FIGURE 3.3. Overlap between major Physiocrats, Physiocratic sympathizers, and key attendees of the baron d'Holbach's salon.

viewed the Physiocratic proposals more sympathetically. These included Diderot himself, at least until 1770; the abbé André Morellet, a follower of the economist Gournay, who took the Physiocrats' defense by refuting Galiani's *Dialogues*;[149] the marquis de Saint-Lambert;[150] and Charles-Georges Le Roy, one of Diderot's close friends, who resided at Versailles (as Royal Lieutenant of the Hunt) and was one of Quesnay's collaborators in the 1750s.[151]

The influence of Physiocratic ideas on Enlightenment rights talk can potentially be traced back to the mid-1750s, when Diderot and Helvétius started frequenting Quesnay and published their own first texts discussing natural rights. By the mid-1760s, however, the direct influence of the Physiocrats became more readily apparent. An early example can be found in the famous *Encyclopédie* article "Vingtième" (about the tax that skimmed 5% off the income of commoners and nobles), written primarily by another Physiocratic sympathizer and occasional visitor *chez* d'Holbach, Étienne Noël Damilaville.[152] Damilaville was an intimate friend of Diderot and Voltaire, serving as the latter's chief correspondent in Paris from 1760 until his death in 1768; as a civil servant working in tax administration, Damilaville covered the costs of their correspondence.[153] His job experience also made him ideally suited to co-write with Diderot an article on taxation. Running over thirty double-columned pages, "Vingtième" developed a full-blown theory of political administration, including a critical assessment of Hobbes's philosophy, an attack on Colbertian mercantilism, and a brief history of government since antiquity. The authors also defended the *libre échange* of wheat, a cornerstone of Physiocracy, ascribing this doctrine to Henri IV's finance minister Sully, who

> knew very well that the source of happiness and wealth in France was to be found in the great expanse and fertility of its land. The earth, he would say, produces every treasure, both necessary and superfluous; one should only seek to multiply its products, by making their sale safe and unfettered [il ne faut qu'en rendre le commerce sûr & libre].[154]

Despite this strong defense of free trade, the authors' political arguments did not always hew to the Physiocratic line, even if in the early 1760s, this line had yet to be drawn in the sand. But they did make a strong case for the preservation of our natural rights in society. France's existing system of taxation amounted to "both a violation and an ignorance of the most sacred and inviolable natural and positive rights"; elsewhere in the article, they described consumption taxes as "contrary to liberty, safety, and all natural and civil rights."[155] As we saw, condemning the ignorance of natural rights as the root of social ills was a familiar Physiocratic theme.

The member of the *coterie holbachique* whose political views owed the most to the Physiocratic theory was arguably the baron himself.[156] Onward from the late 1760s, and under the cover of anonymity, d'Holbach churned out a series of atheistic political works that sought to refound government on natural principles. The most famous of these was the *Système de la nature* (1770), a breathless diatribe against clerical despotism that was one of the top "forbidden best-sellers" of the late eighteenth century, according to Robert Darnton.[157] A chief accusation d'Holbach leveled against priests and tyrants was that they stripped us of our natural and human rights:

> [I]t is obviously because of theological notions and the cowardly flattery of holy ministers that we have despotism, tyranny, the corruption and licence of princes, and the blindness of people who are forbidden, in the name of heaven, to love liberty [ . . . ] and to use their natural rights.

Ignorance reappears here in the more active form of blindness, now with an anti-clerical twist. The solution, according to d'Holbach, is for temporal rulers to restore their subjects in their natural rights. Princes must "always guarantee their subjects' possession of their rights, of which they are the defenders and guardians." Page after page insisted that a just society was one that ensured for all "the possession of their natural rights," and that nature taught us as much: "Nature tells man, you are free, no power on earth can legitimately deprive you of your rights." By contrast, the unbelieving baron thundered, religious precepts "legitimate or transform into duties cruelties that are absolutely contrary to the rights of humanity" and bring about "the most insulting violation of the rights of humanity."[158] Similar arguments would be repeated in d'Holbach's 1773 *La politique naturelle*; his *Système social*, published the same year; and *La morale universelle*, which appeared three years later.[159]

D'Holbach's atheism has made him an appealing candidate for Jonathan Israel's Spinoza-based "Radical Enlightenment," but his arguments about rights cannot reasonably be traced back to the Dutch philosopher.[160] As we saw in chapter 2, Spinoza was one of the first transfer theorists, claiming that we must hand over our rights when entering society, thereby forfeiting them: "[W]hoever transfers to another his power of self-defence, whether voluntarily or under compulsion, has fully ceded his natural right and has consequently resolved to obey the other absolutely in all matters."[161] D'Holbach, for his part, does not endorse the transfer regime; like the Physiocrats, if not as thoroughly, he downplays the importance of the social contract, lessens the divide between nature and society, and insists on the preservation of our natural rights in society.[162] His "radical" defense of natural rights does not appear to be inspired by a "radical" thinker at all, but by a doctor who lived out his life comfortably at the side of the French monarch.

Indeed, the preservation regime is not in the slightest dependent on an atheistic foundation; the Physiocrats, for instance, attributed the laws of nature to God.[163] Other members of d'Holbach's coterie shared his enthusiasm for inalienable natural rights but rejected his atheism.[164] In his acclaimed 1767 novel *Bélisaire*, for instance, Marmontel—a regular in d'Holbach's salon, but also a close friend of Voltaire's—preached religious toleration, alongside a belief in God, while decrying the violence of tyrants who "chop off heads that rise up above the yoke, and dare to demand the rights of nature."[165] A similar theme ran through his 1777 novelized history of the Spanish conquest of the New World, *Les Incas*: in his preface, he recalled the Spanish theologians who demanded "in the name of heaven" that the native Americans be granted "the rights of nature"; later in the work, he staged a lengthy debate featuring Bartolomé de Las Casas, who passionately defends the Indians' "natural and sacred right to freedom."[166]

Finally, further evidence of Physiocratic influence can be found in the specific rights that d'Holbach lists. They are three: liberty, security (*sûreté*), and property.[167] Along with resistance to oppression, these are the same natural rights that the 1789 Declaration of Rights would enshrine (art. 2). And they are the same three that the Physiocrats had ceaselessly emphasized. In *L'ordre naturel et essentiel des sociétés*, Le Mercier repeatedly insisted on this trinity: "PROPERTY, SAFETY, and LIBERTY [PROPRIÉTÉ, SURETÉ, et LIBERTÉ], that is what we seek."[168] Dupont de Nemours also gave them an axiomatic standing: "No property without liberty, no liberty without safety."[169] To be sure, English theorists had issued similar tripartite lists (e.g., life, liberty, and fortune); but before the Physiocrats, one finds few of such cases in France.

A last example of how the *coterie holbachique* was influential in disseminating Physiocratic ideas about natural rights can be found in a work that rattled the old regime to its core: the abbé Raynal's *Histoire des deux Indes*. Often compared to the *Encyclopédie* due to its collaborative process of composition, the *Histoire des deux Indes* was a collective effort with roots, once again, in d'Holbach's salon, where Raynal was a regular.[170] Other members of the coterie were major contributors, starting with Diderot and d'Holbach; Jacques-André Naigeon and Jean-François de Saint-Lambert also participated. The work was conceived during the same period when the *philosophes* were debating the Physiocrats' ideas (though Raynal himself does not appear to have been partial to their economic ideas).[171] The first edition of the *Histoire* appeared in 1770, but it was in its subsequent, much enlarged editions, and particularly the third edition of 1780, that the most incendiary criticisms of European colonialism, as well as the French monarchy, could be found.[172] The final volume of this edition also included a history of the American War of Independence, which would be reprinted separately as *Révolution de l'Amérique* (1781). Despite its condemnation by the French state (in 1772, then again in 1780) and inclusion on the Vatican's *Index* (in 1775), the *Histoire des deux Indes* proved immensely popular, going through thirty editions in twenty years.

A leitmotiv of its indictments of marauding colonial powers was their violations of the natural rights of peoples around the world. In the Philippines, the expulsion of the Jesuits was read as a hopeful sign that some native peoples had found "the will to recover their independence, and enough energy to regain their first rights." By contrast, the extermination of native Americans in Spanish colonies was explained by the fact that "they felt the natural right they had to freedom, because they did not want to be slaves." The Indians revealed by this stark contrast just how low the Europeans had fallen since ancient times: "Today one fights with lightning, to capture a few cities, and for the whims of a few powerful men; one used to fight with swords, to destroy or found kingdoms, or to avenge the natural rights of man [les droits naturels de l'homme]." Part of the problem lay with religion, Christianity in particular: if religion "only inspired social duties," and "only described as a crime that which violates the natural rights of humanity," then theocracy might be "the best of all governments."[173] But since there was little chance of that ever happening, tyrants and oppressors must face the threat of a legitimate resistance, as had happened in the American colonies:

If a people is content with their government, they will keep it. If they are unhappy [ . . . ] the impossibility of further suffering will lead them to change it.
The oppressor will call this salutary movement "revolt," even though it is only
the legitimate exercise of an inalienable and natural right of man [un droit
inaliénable & naturel de l'homme]. . . .[174]

Natural rights, in this reading, now extended beyond property and liberty to
include the most politically subversive right of all—what the French revolutionaries were soon to call the right of resistance to oppression.

If the *philosophes* who gathered at d'Holbach's *hôtel* latched on to the preservation regime of natural rights in the late 1760s/early 1770s, the proximate
cause for their enthusiasm can largely be found in the Physiocratic works of
this same period. Not only did most of the *philosophes* enjoy social ties with
the leading and lesser Physiocrats (as shown in fig. 3.3), but they subscribed to
many of the same ideas about agriculture, commerce, and the natural foundations of the state. To be sure, when adopting the Physiocrats' views on rights,
they could also put them to different ends. For instance, the *philosophes* were
far more anti-clerical: d'Holbach raged against religious fanatics, and Marmontel's *Incas* featured a parade of bloodthirsty priests. They also showed how
the preservation regime of rights could be used as a measure of good government. In a 1771 play, Voltaire himself, from his exile in Ferney, questioned the
legitimacy of kings who failed in this regard:

> Who placed between us and their throne
> Such immense distance, and stole from us mortals
> Our original dignity and natural rights?[175]

By the mid-1770s, Voltaire was even embellishing such arguments with revolutionary flourishes: in a dialogue on political theory, he has "C" ask "A" what
he would have done to restore liberty in modern Rome. "A" answers: "I would
have raised an altar to Cicero and Tacitus, men of ancient Rome. I would have
stood on this altar, and with Brutus' hat on my head, and his dagger in my
hand, I would have recalled to the people the natural rights they had lost."[176]
A defining feature of "natural republicanism" had been to fuse natural law
theory with classical republicanism: here we find republicanism wedded to a
theory of individual natural rights.[177]

### 4. The (Meek) Conservative Reaction

Given the politically sensitive uses to which the *philosophes* were putting the
preservation regime, at the very moment American colonists were rebelling
against their king to defend their natural rights, it is fitting that we should

find a conservative response to their assertions. It came in the form of a 1775 treatise by Jacob-Nicolas Moreau, a historian and paid propagandist for the French government.[178] Entitled *Les devoirs du prince réduits à un seul principe*, this work had originally been composed, possibly as early as 1767, for the political education of the then dauphin, the future Louis XVI, on the model of Fénelon's *Télémaque*, without the fiction (or the insubordination).[179]

In this work, dedicated to the newly crowned king, Moreau delved head-first into the natural rights debate in order to justify monarchy and counter the preservation regime. To achieve these joint ends, he leaned heavily on Hobbes, taking as his premise the belief that man in the state of nature has a right to everything: "If he had a right to that which was necessary to him in the moment, then since it is in his nature to foresee the future, he also had a right to everything he might need in the future. The whole earth was his for the taking [Toute la terre étoit à lui]" (207). If we all have a right to all things, however, others will prevent us from acquiring what we need and want: "[M]y liberty will always be impotent if, at the very moment I sought to enjoy it, everyone else had an equal right to prevent me from doing so." Accordingly, joining society involves the necessary abridgment of rights: "[T]o enjoy his freedom more safely and quietly, man was obliged to sacrifice part of his power that would otherwise degenerate into licence." The purpose of civil legislation was thus to limit natural liberty, and by extension to curtail our natural rights: "[T]here is no civil law that does not limit the primitive liberty of man" (105). Society brought us peace because the king, like God, had an executive right, which (*contra* Locke) was missing in Moreau's state of nature (see 31).

This classic restatement of the abridgment regime came with a few nods toward the arguments of the Physiocrats and the *philosophes*. Moreau claimed that our civil rights stayed true to the spirit of our natural ones and were thus basically the same (even better!): "[T]here is no civil right that is not the equivalent of a natural right, or rather that is not this natural right itself, only modified so that its enjoyment is infinitely simpler, surer, and more advantageous" (106–7). This was a twist on the transfer regime, dressed up to sound more attractive in a naturalistic age. Moreau indulged in this naturalism, agreeing with the Physiocrats (and Aristotle) that society itself was part and parcel of the natural order: "[S]ociety is the first destination and the natural state of man" (29). This claim fit neatly with his justification of royal power. "[K]ings exert over nations the authority that fathers had over the first families," he asserted (35), again in accordance with Quesnay (but also with Robert Filmer).[180] Finally, Moreau acknowledged that some rights could never be alienated: "[M]an received life; he had the right to preserve it. He was destined for happiness; he had the right to pursue it" (206). But none of these concessions affected the overarching thesis of the work, which was to insist that we need kings to save our liberty from being trampled by the madding crowd (35–36).

Published at the very moment when the grain wars and the American Revolution brought pressing relevance to natural rights talk, Moreau's treatise stood little chance of reversing this tide, notably as he was already despised by the *parti philosophique*.[181] But his text does serve as an indication that some in Versailles—most likely those who already feared the *encyclopédistes* and sought to foil Turgot's reforms—may have been alarmed by the spread of this political discourse from Physiocratic works about agriculture to philosophical texts demanding the restoration of all natural rights. Their concern can also explain the post-1771 dip in mentions of *droits naturels* (as well a *loi naturelle*) that are evident in figures 3.1 and 3.2: this period coincides with the three-year reign of the "Maupeou parlement," which replaced the traditional judicial system of *parlements* and ushered in a period of intense political censorship.[182]

### 5. Resisting Despotism: National Rights and Constitutionalism

It was in response to Maupeou's "coup" that another group of French writers latched onto the concept of natural rights. Legal professionals launched an all-out attack on the reforms, adding natural rights theory into their rhetorical arsenal. A lawyer at the Paris Parlement, the abbé Claude Mey, published a defense of the *parlementaire* position in 1772, which would be revised and expanded three years later by Gabriel-Nicolas Maultrot (also a lawyer) and other Parisian barristers.[183] The *Maximes du droit public françois*, as this work was known, was a two-volume collection of arguments for the independence of the judiciary. While historical precedents, backed up by archival sources, comprised the bulk of their evidence, the authors also synthesized works of natural law theory to buttress their case. They cited lengthy passages of Locke's *Second Treatise* and Vattel's *Droit des gens*; they referenced Grotius, Hobbes (negatively), Pufendorf, Cumberland, Sidney, Heineccius, Wolff, Montesquieu, Burlamaqui, and other authorities. For the most part, the lawyers protested against laws and political regimes that violated "objective" natural law. "Despotic government violates natural right," announced the title of chapter 2 (1:32). But they also extended this critique to the defense of individual, subjective rights: "[S]ince the individual only agreed to give up his liberty to the extent that it benefited society, his own existence, and his happiness [. . . ,] it would be harmful to deprive him of the exercise of his natural rights . . ." (1:41; the authors here were loosely translating from Christian Wolff's 1740–48 *Jus naturae methodo scientifica pertractatum*). In general, however, Mey, Maultrot, and their collaborators adhered to the abridgment regime of rights:

> [S]ince the establishment of government demanded that each member of the body politic lose [perdît] some portion of the natural enjoyment of his rights, both of liberty and property, men willingly gave this up [renoncèrent] for the common good; they abandoned [cédèrent] what was required for the good and the preservation of society. (1:40)

Despite this loss of individual rights, natural right (*le droit naturel*), understood as the system of natural laws, still retained its normative force in political society.

But where the *philosophes* appealed to natural law to condemn unjust or arbitrary positive laws, the lawyers went beyond this legal discourse to stake out a stronger political claim. Like their counterparts in the American colonies, these *patriotes* also insisted on the need for popular consent in matters of taxation, except they framed this consent somewhat differently: "[I]n every civilized kingdom, taxes can only be set, even in cases of public necessity, with the consent of the Nation" (1:136). Where American theorists made taxation dependent on individual consent, the French lawyers gave this same process a collective aspect. They justified their arguments, in part, with a long quote from Locke on legislative power (*Second Treatise*, chap. 10), as well from older, conciliarist arguments;[184] but they also appealed to a different set of rights, "les droits nationaux." These were the historic rights that the French people had retained *collectively* when they first joined together to form a political community. These "national rights" were ascribed to corporate bodies, first and foremost the Estates General, which had "the right [ ... ] to decide" (1:253–54) in situations when royal authority was in question, as well as "the right to prescribe the rules of the [French] government" (1:316).

This doctrine of national rights was by no means novel.[185] Vattel had already defined *les droits de la nation* in very similar terms in his influential *Le droit des gens*, which the *parlementaires* quoted at length.[186] For Vattel and his followers, the rights of the nation were simply an expression of the *lois fondamentales*: if royal government was bound by certain constitutional rules (e.g., Salic law), then those rules afforded correlative rights to the nation. Earlier French constitutional theorists had made the same argument, with the phrase "droits de la nation" appearing repeatedly in oppositional seventeenth-century works of political theory.[187] The authority of such rights would be tested during the controversy over the status of Louis XIV's "legitimized" sons: in his 1714 edict of Marly, the dying king had placed the duc de Maine and the comte de

Toulouse, his sons with Mme de Montespan, in the royal line of succession. Defending this edict, one pamphleteer wrote in favor of the princes, "Would it not be more reasonable to conclude that the Edict, far from violating the rights of the nation, far from harming its interests, is simply faithful to their original spirit?"[188] But another countered, on behalf of the princes of the blood, that "the Edict of 1714 violates the rights of the Nation," precisely because "it establishes [a] new line of succession to the crown, and this line deprives the Nation of its right to elect its kings."[189] The looming constitutional crisis would be averted, as Louis XIV's great-grandson survived to succeed him as Louis XV (after the deaths of his brother, father, and grandfather in 1711–12). But this dispute highlights how "national rights" belonged initially to constitutional theory, not to natural law. They would nonetheless be patched together fairly seamlessly by the *parlementaires* to produce a French version of the natural constitutionalism so common in Anglo-American political writing.[190]

But where constitutional rights were portrayed by British legal theorists (Blackstone in chief: see chapter 6) as mere extensions of universal, primeval natural rights, the relation between national and natural rights, in the French case, was not one-to-one. Instead of being an aggregate of every citizen's natural (or even constitutional) rights, the rights of the nation were collective rights, rights that "we the people" could not enjoy individually, on our own, but only as a community. Accordingly, these rights tended to be affixed, as we saw, to corporate bodies such as the Estates General or the Parlement, which also presented itself, in 1788, as a defender of the *droits de la nation*.[191] This distinction raised the specter of conflict between natural and national rights: if "the nation" could only enjoy its rights through the medium of representative bodies, then the natural rights that each citizen possessed risked being overruled by these greater corporate interests.

This collective quality of national rights is particularly evident in one of the most influential pre-revolutionary pamphlets, the comte d'Antraigues's *Mémoire sur les Etats Généraux* (1788).[192] This student of Rousseau's forcefully argued in favor of a legislative assembly composed of elected representatives: "A free people is governed by its laws; laws only deserve this august name if they express the public will" (21). As the *parlementaires* before him, d'Antraigues relied both on historical precedent and natural law theory to justify this right to self-government: "[O]thers [ ... ] have sought to establish the rights of the nation on a firm basis, by founding them on the natural rights of every human society. They strike me as having understood the issue to the fullest extent . . ." (16–17).

But here again we see how individual natural rights are transformed to become the property of a collective body. As with Rousseau's social contract, individuals who join together into political society transfer their natural rights to a sovereign legislative assembly, in exchange for laws—with the difference that, for d'Antraigues, this assembly is a representative body.[193] It is this assembly, however, that comes to enjoy and defend the rights of the nation: "[T]he rights of the Estates General are the rights of the nation itself. [ . . . ] [W]e should ask what are the rights of the nation, which expresses its will through its representatives" (20). This transfer of rights was not irreversible: if national representatives failed to express their constituents' genuine interests, they could be repudiated.[194] But so long as they faithfully conveyed the will of the people, it was in them that the national rights were to remain vested.

Where Anglo-American natural constitutionalism placed the preservation regime of rights within a legal and political tradition, its French version centered instead on the transfer regime. The French *droits de la nation* were dissimilar from "English rights and liberties" in that the latter continued to be enjoyed by individual English citizens. Parliament, in English constitutionalism, also had rights (as did the king); but these rights were not *the* national, English rights. To be sure, in neither the French nor English cases did the existence of corporate rights preclude that of individual rights; there was no intrinsic incompatibility between the two. But French champions of natural constitutionalism did not place nearly as much emphasis on individual natural rights as their English and American counterparts, who often rested their entire politico-legal edifices on this foundation. By minimizing the lasting force of natural rights in political society (in accordance with the transfer regime), and by insisting *a contrario* on corporate rights, the French promoters of this doctrine ran the risk of disenfranchising individuals of their subjective rights.

Why did the French merger of constitutionalism and natural law theory differ so substantially from its Anglo-American equivalent? Some of the difference had to do with English particularities: English common law was idiosyncratic in its affordance of rights to individuals, particularly where criminal procedure was concerned. Accordingly, when English authors combined a traditional constitutional doctrine with arguments and concepts drawn from natural law theory, the logical point of juncture was individual rights. This equation of natural and constitutional rights would be the defining feature of Anglo-American natural constitutionalism from the Levellers to the American revolutionaries.[195] While some of the early sixteenth-century French efforts to assimilate constitutionalism and natural law went in a similar direction, the widespread erasure of natural rights talk under absolutist political culture prevented the join between natural and national rights from imposing itself in the pre-revolutionary period.

But the specificities of French political culture also contributed to this difference. In particular, it is the centrality of the "nation" in this constitutional
theory that calls for explanation. As David A. Bell has observed, *la nation* was
a contested term in the eighteenth century, with multiple, often mutually exclusive definitions in circulation.[196] One feature that many of these definitions
did share, however, was that of an organically constructed community. You
were born into a nation (from the Latin *natio*, "birth"); you did not contract
into it. The *Dictionary of the French Academy* defined "nation" as "Tous les
habitants d'un mesme Estat, d'un mesme pays, qui vivent sous mesmes loix,
& usent de mesme langage, &c."[197] The Collège des Quatre-Nations, a school
in Paris, admitted students hailing from four recently acquired French territories; students at the University of Paris also divided into "nations" (such as
French, Picard, Norman, and German). In Henri de Boulainvilliers's influential *Etat de la France*, the French nation refers to the Franks, giving the term
a similar meaning to the German *Volk*.[198]

As a pre-political community, the nation did not fit easily in natural law
theory; the term is not found, for instance, in Locke's *Second Treatise*. It was
largely out of place in the social contract narratives that recounted the passage from a pre-civil state of nature to a political society, since an organic
collectivity of this sort could only be expected *after* individuals had contracted
together. It was in this posterior sense that Rousseau used the expression in
*The Social Contract* (see, e.g., 2.4).

There was a French theory of natural law, however, that facilitated the
inclusion of the nation, and that was Physiocracy. In Quesnay's Aristotelian
revision of the social contract narrative, there never was a time when we did
not live in society, and so nations could precede states. Indeed, according to
Quesnay, the formation of nations was a precondition for the development of
government: as families grew in size and came into contact,

> they grow used to seeing each other, and start trusting and helping each other.
> They form alliances through marriage, and establish particular Nations [des
> Nations particulières] of a sort, in which all are bound together for their joint
> defense, but where each remains in a state of full liberty and independence.[199]

It was only after "la constitution de ces Nations" that positive laws and sovereign government could be established, once it became clear that such mutual
defense leagues were insufficient for the safeguard of property (28).

For the Physiocrats, this precedence of the nation over the state did not
affect individual rights: they paid little heed to constitutional doctrine and embraced a philosophy of social naturalism.[200] But their insertion of the nation
into a natural law origin story of government made it much easier, conversely,

to insert natural law theory into constitutional histories of the French nation. For the *parlementaires* and d'Antraigues, natural law provided a "liberal" counterbalance to the focus, among constitutional scholars, on corporate rights. But at the hands of other theorists, natural law could in fact serve the opposite purpose, propping up collective rights at the expense of individual ones. We find precisely such an example in the most celebrated pre-revolutionary pamphlet, the abbé Sieyès's *Qu'est-ce que le tiers-état?*

To the title question of his treatise, Sieyès notoriously answered with a single word: "Everything."[201] He subsequently developed this answer by arguing that the Third Estate constituted the real French nation: "The Third Estate is a complete nation [une nation complète]" (28). The aristocracy, following this logic, was its own separate nation, which Sieyès sarcastically invited to decamp to the forests of Franconia. His pamphlet thus neatly reversed Boulainvilliers's constitutional history of France, which had retraced the origins of the nobility to the conquering Franks.

While it is this bold assertion that garnered the most attention at the time, it is Sieyès's definition of the nation that was perhaps most innovative. As he wrote in a famous passage, "[T]he nation exists before everything else, it is the origin of everything. Its will is always legal, it is the law itself. Before and above it there is only natural right" (67). This passage is often read as a Rousseauist statement about the absolute sovereignty of the collectivity.[202] But there is an important and telling chronological difference: for Sieyès, the nation *precedes* the social contract that, in Rousseau's account, is what creates political society in the first place.[203] All it takes to create a nation, according to Sieyès, is "a sizable group [un nombre plus ou moins considérable] of isolated individuals who want to join together. By this fact alone, they already constitute a nation" (65). No social contract is required; only at a *later* time ("the second epoch") does this collectivity get around to creating a body politic that can express its common will. For Rousseau, by contrast, mere cohabitation is a woefully insufficient factor for transforming isolated individuals into a body politic. As he insisted in *The Social Contract*,

> When scattered men, regardless of their number, are successively enslaved to a single man, I see in this nothing but a master and slaves, I do not see in it a people and its chief; it is, if you will, an aggregation, but not an association; there is here neither public good, nor body politic.[204]

Where Rousseau's own version of how political bodies are created stresses the "instantaneous" transformation of individuals brought together by the social contract ("At once [À l'instant], in place of the private person of each contracting party, this act of association produces a moral and collective body . . ."; 1.6),

Sieyès proposes a narrative of emergence, which is drawn out over time ("But let us jump over these historical intervals . . ."; 66). This gradual evolution into political society owes more to Physiocratic natural law theory, which similarly dispensed with a social contract, than to Rousseau.[205]

Even as a pre-political body without formal political organization, however, the nation was still the *fons et origo* of rights: "[T]hey already constitute a nation; they have all its rights; it is just a matter of exercising them" (65). Here, Sieyès parted ways with the Physiocrats, who saw the progressive development of political structures as a means of strengthening *individual* rights, not of creating national ones. To be clear, Sieyès never denies rights to individuals, quite the contrary. But not once are their rights defined as *natural* in his pamphlet. The only reference to pre-political rights is fairly dismissive: "Let us not judge [the Third Estate's] demands by the isolated observations of a few authors who are more or less knowledgeable about the rights of man [plus ou moins instruits des droits de l'homme]" (36). Individuals seemingly enjoyed rights at the pleasure of the nation, which could revoke them if it served the greater good: "The law, by protecting the common rights of every citizen, protects each citizen fully, up until he begins to threaten the common interest."[206] Only the nation is described as having any inalienable rights (66). Since the Third Estate was the genuine French nation, these rights were its particular prerogative: "[T]he Third order has its political rights, just as it has civil rights; it must exercise both on its own" (39); elsewhere Sieyès refers to "the rights of the large body of citizens [grand corps des citoyens]" (31) and "the rights of the third estates" (52).

Much has been made about Sieyès's elevation of the nation into the source of all legality and legitimacy. Hannah Arendt called attention to how his distinction between a "constituting power" ("pouvoir constituant," i.e., the nation) and a "constituted power" ("pouvoir constitué," i.e., government) gave unlimited power to the people and ushered in the tyranny of the majority.[207] But her attempt to distinguish the French *pouvoir constituant* from the American constituent people is unsatisfactory, as Jason Frank has argued: the American revolutionaries were equally committed to the principle of popular sovereignty.[208] How could this same principle be understood so differently on either side of the Atlantic? Why was *la nation* so different from "we the people"? Sieyès himself suggested that the two were identical.[209] But the American people was never understood as a pre-political, organic community. Individuals possessed rights by virtue of being humans, not by virtue of living together.[210] Most American theorists agreed with Locke that the power of the state originated in the specific rights that individuals enjoyed in the state of nature (such as the executive power), but that "it can be no more than those persons had in a state of nature before they entered into society, and gave up to the community: for no body can transfer to another more power than he has in himself."[211] All power might originally have derived from the people *qua* individuals, but the people *qua* sovereign collectivity was not all-powerful. By replacing this passage from the many (individuals) to the one (people) with a narrative that emphasized the continuity between a pre-political community and a political one (in both cases, the nation), Sieyès granted a far greater power to this collectivity, removing the checks that previous natural law theorists had placed around it to defend the rights of individuals. This theoretical difference would have vast practical ramifications during the French revolutionary Terror.

## PART II

# Social Naturalism in Early Modern France

Two decades before the National Assembly issued the Declaration of the Rights of Man and of the Citizen, and some years before the American Revolution, French writers had already outlined a theory of natural rights, even referring to them as "les droits de l'homme."[1] They had stressed the importance of preserving rights in society and had singled out liberty, security, and property—as well as, more rarely, resistance from oppression—as key inalienable rights. Emile Boutmy was justified in his response to Georg Jellinek: the Declaration's sources could just as well be found in the French Enlightenment as in American political documents.[2]

This history might also be seen as confirming the earlier accounts by Michel Villey, Leo Strauss, or (in a different vein) Richard Tuck about a shift in early modern political thought from natural law to natural rights. One could easily come away from this story thinking that, in the decades before 1789, rights talk had reached such a point of frenzied chatter that French subjects began to demand the recognition of their political rights; and, one thing leading to another, *voilà!*—the French Revolution.[3] But by focusing solely on the gradual adoption and spread of natural rights talk, we ignore the central character of the story. In reality, the uptick in appeals to *droits naturels* that we witness in the 1760s and 1780s was not particularly dramatic and may well have gone unnoticed at the time. It was dwarfed by the mass invocations of *loi naturelle* or *droit naturel* (in the singular) during this same period (see fig. 4.1). The trend lines evident on the Google Books Ngram graph below are confirmed in the ARTFL-FRANTEXT database: at their height in the 1770s, *droits naturels* were cited more than ten times less frequently than *loi naturelle*.[4] Enlightenment rights talk was real, but it was not particularly loud.

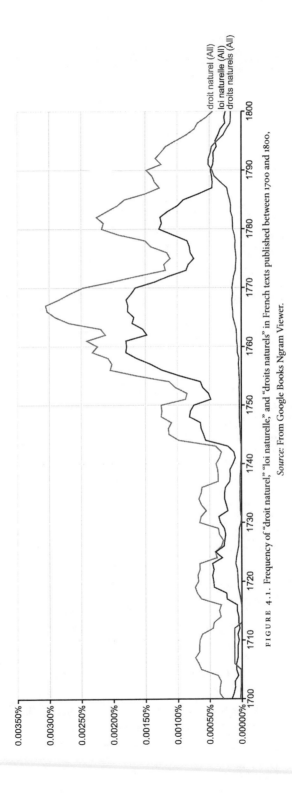

FIGURE 4.1. Frequency of "droit naturel," "loi naturelle," and "droits naturels" in French texts published between 1700 and 1800,
*Source:* From Google Books Ngram Viewer.

This empirical observation serves as an important reminder that the language of human rights, throughout the eighteenth century, was dependent on the broader grammar of natural law. The circulation of "subjective" ideas about natural rights did not dispel the "objective" concept of natural justice—far from it. Instead, as the intellectual historian Knud Haakonssen observed, "in the mainstream of natural jurisprudence in the eighteenth century, natural rights derived from natural law and natural duty. Natural rights were understood as part of a morally well-ordered universe structured and lent certainty by the law of nature."[5] The importance of Haakonssen's insight should be underlined: natural law did not just coexist alongside natural rights throughout the early modern period—it generated them. What Haakonssen's point does not explain, however, is how differing perceptions of natural law may have also contributed to changing preferences for different rights regimes.

Indeed, the success of the preservation regime in eighteenth-century France rested, as we saw in chapter 3, on a peculiarly "naturalistic" interpretation of state and society. If we wish to comprehend the appeal and ready acceptance of the preservation regime in the French Enlightenment and Revolution, we must understand not only why it became common to assume that rights should persist in society, but also why it became difficult to imagine that they could not. That is the goal of the following two chapters. The term I have adopted to describe the perception of natural law that took root around this time is "social naturalism." As the sociologists Fred Block and Margaret Somers write, apropos of free-market economists in the twentieth century:

> Social naturalism is a way of viewing the world built on the assumption that the laws governing natural phenomena also govern human society. [ ... ] Social naturalism [ ... ] insists that society is governed by those natural laws rather than by institutional rules and social rationalities. For social naturalism, society is not "like" the natural world; the social and natural worlds are one and the same and are subject to the same laws and exigencies.[6]

Block and Somers adapted this concept from their reading of Karl Polanyi and use it to criticize the "free-market utopianism" of economists such as Friedrich Hayek and Milton Friedman. But it is arguably even more fitting for the early modern period, when the assumption that the natural world was governed by universal laws first began to catch on. In the seventeenth century, the analogy between natural laws in the physical and social worlds was in fact reversed. Whereas it had long been argued that natural laws should (or did) govern human action, only with the advent of the new science was the physical world understood as law-abiding.[7] The late seventeenth and eighteenth centuries even witnessed the emergence of the first social naturalists in the economic sphere: in a loose sense, Hayek and Friedman descend from their free-market predecessors Boisguilbert, Gournay, and Quesnay.

At the heart of this social naturalism, however, is something missing from Block and Somers's definition, and without which it could never have emerged. That something was God. If the universe was "morally well-ordered," its order came from above. Modern social naturalists may seek to cut this theological root, but one may ask whether their doctrine does not continue to feed from the same metaphysical source.

Even before men of science began referring to physical laws of nature, the belief in a "morally well-ordered universe" had found expression in Stoicism. Onward from the late sixteenth century—and in response to the renewed challenge of skepticism—humanists, jurisconsults, philosophers, and theologians fell back on a number of Stoic principles. These included the pantheistic claims that "Law is the highest reason, implanted in Nature" (lex est ratio summa insita in natura) and "the entire universe is overruled by the power of God," as well as that "to live according to nature is the highest good" (ex natura vivere summum bonum sit).[8] This moral dimension of natural law privileged duties, while still recognizing rights (if at times only implicitly). This priority is evident in Grotius's first definition of the law of nature as "the Abstaining from that which is another's, and the Restitution of what we have of another's."[9] As I argued in chapter 1, Grotius's primary objective here was not to grant rights, but to determine correct moral conduct and human duties, according to natural law.[10]

Given the moral thrust of Stoic thought, it is not surprising that some of its most vocal champions in the seventeenth century were Christian apologists (see chapter 4). Even more so than the writings of the Protestant natural lawyers, it was through their popular treatises that the social naturalist vision of a "morally well-ordered universe" would be transmitted to the Enlightenment. Since the primary components of this vision were classical, it proved fairly straightforward in the eighteenth century to detach them from a Christian framework without much alteration. Hence, Stoicism would trend markedly deist and was one of the major sources for the "modern paganism" of the philosophes.[11]

The Stoic ideal of a divine, rational order received a new impetus from natural philosophy. As astronomers and physicists discovered that the universe exhibited regular patterns, some (Descartes in chief) began referring to these as "laws of nature." This appellation was initially controversial but quickly caught on. Soon moral philosophers sought to discover the laws of society, using the scientific model of empirical observation (and sometimes, mathematical proof). In both cases, these laws were seen as evidence of a divine order. This order was not always perceptible to humans, but we obeyed it all the same—we could not help but to obey it. From science, then, the idea of natural law gained a very different understanding, no longer limited to human reason, as it had been for the Stoics.

The search for the natural and divine order in society was particularly marked in jurisprudence, which is the focus of chapter 5. The Stoics had left a deep mark on jurists, as well. Cicero grounded the moral and the legal order of society in natural law; this Stoic concern was reflected in Roman law, which similarly rested on natural right (*ius naturae*). The reception of the *Corpus juris civilis*, and the manifold efforts by European jurists to remake common law in the image of Roman civil law, would constitute another important, if oft-overlooked, channel for the transmission and transformation of natural law theory. The French jurisconsult Jean Domat offered a particularly se-ductive rereading of Roman natural law, which influenced philosophers and political theorists on both sides of the Atlantic. In his Romanized interpre-tation, natural law promised salvation, and it could be felt by all. But it also governed the whole of society, from economics and law to politics and morals. A Jansenist, Domat provided the theological foundations for the early laissez-faire theories of economy.

While they embraced the Stoics' moral and legal philosophy of natural law, the *philosophes* did enact one dramatic change: rather than insisting on reason as the essential mode for discovering the laws of nature, they relied on sentiment. Their emphasis on this new emotional process led Lynn Hunt to posit that empathy might be the driving force behind the gradual exten-sion of rights to downtrodden groups, from women to African slaves. But we should not forget that empathy could have the opposite effect, as well. Indeed, its eighteenth-century theorists, Rousseau and Adam Smith in particular, in-sisted that fellow feeling only extended to those who closely resemble us. In-stead of sensibility, I show how Montesquieu's rereading of Roman natural law and the rise of Physiocracy were more important factors for the late turn to abolitionism in the French Enlightenment.

While the following sections detail each of these historical developments individually, they aim collectively to make a broader point, namely that throughout the early modern period, authors in a broad range of fields thought first about natural law, and only second about natural rights. And it was in thinking differently about natural law that they came to think differently about natural rights. It should come as no surprise, then, that the *philosophes*—like the French revolutionaries after them, but unlike their fellow Americans— would be more concerned with improving laws than with enshrining rights. These two objectives were complementary, but in a well-ordered universe it

made much more sense to start with the former. It took a great dose of pessi-
mism and disillusionment to conclude that "government even in its best state
is but a necessary evil," as Thomas Paine argued in *Common Sense*. Dreams of
a natural social order aroused many minds in the seventeenth and eighteenth
centuries; it took the nightmares of history for some to cast them aside.

Still, to shift the focus from natural rights to natural law is not to change
the subject. If we wish to understand why, by the late eighteenth century, it
had become "self-evident" to assume that natural rights must be preserved in
political society, then we must also retrace this parallel history of "the laws
of Nature and Nature's God." This history unfolds at a slower pace than the
history of natural rights and responds to different philosophical and cultural
shifts, but is nevertheless also in flux. The natural order envisaged by, say,
Aquinas or Suárez differs significantly from the one imagined by Jacques Abbadie or Jean Domat. By the time of Quesnay and Blackstone, if natural rights
seemed "naturally" to persist in political society, it was in large part because
human society itself was increasingly perceived as a quasi-natural phenome-
non. We can only tell the full story of how the preservation regime triumphed
over its rivals, particularly in France, if we recognize how it was supported by
this all-compassing vision of a divinely created, moral universe.

# The Laws of Nature in Neo-Stoicism and Science

Seventeenth-century students and scholars interested in natural law could pull from library shelves the learned works of late Scholastic theologians, such as Vitoria and Suárez; but they could also turn to classical philosophers, Cicero in chief, many of whom they had first encountered in school. Natural law was a central concept in some of his best-known works, such as *De officiis* and *De legibus*, since for Cicero, nature was the ultimate source of justice (*ex natura ortum esse ius*).[1] But not only positive laws derived from nature; so, too, should our overall moral conduct. Stoicism, in this regard, "is to be construed less as law-like than as dispositional: it offers not a fixed set of rules and class of actions that one must live by but rather a group of guidelines that are supposed to help one develop the necessary rational attitude."[2]

## 1. The Many Receptions of Stoicism

Retracing the reception of Stoic philosophy is challenging, as it permeates so many authors and ideas. It is perhaps best conceived as an intellectual ebb and flow, surging at times and in places, retreating in others. Often this movement was the result of other philosophical currents rushing in. For instance, the skeptical wave that hit Western Europe in the mid-sixteenth century only receded, for the most part, a century later, precisely around the time that Stoicism surged anew.[3] But this process was messy and by no means mechanistic. Sometimes it took place across decades; in other cases, it can be observed in the writings of a single author, as we will see with Montaigne. In the late seventeenth century, this flux of ideas briefly settled down, as a Christianized form of neo-Stoicism took root. It was from this source that the *philosophes* drew

many of their own notions about the natural and divine order of society—
though it proved surprisingly simple to strip them of any specifically Christian
wrapping.

## 1.1. "TO LIVE ACCORDING TO NATURE": STOICISM AND THE MORAL DISCOURSE OF NATURAL LAW

The Stoic revival launched by Justus Lipsius with *De constantia* (1583) did not
initially place much emphasis on natural law. Lipsius's work focused more on
Seneca (from whom the title was borrowed) than on Cicero or Marcus Aurelius.[4] With Montaigne, however, the laws of nature once again took center
stage, even if the lighting was not always clear. In the prefatory text to his
*Essais* (1580), "Au lecteur," Montaigne depicted natural law as the ideal measure of man and society: "Had I been placed among those nations which are
said to live still in the sweet freedom of nature's first laws [la douce liberté des
premieres loix de nature], I assure you I should very gladly have portrayed
myself here entire and wholly naked."[5] But throughout the *Essais*, this Stoic
ideal is tempered by skeptic caution: Montaigne calls out the verbal trickery,
for instance, of those who identify laws as "natural" when they are merely
customary, and mocks the philosophers who cannot agree on the number or
the content of the laws of nature.[6] Still, it is not the case that he rejected the
concept of natural law entirely.[7] In a later addition to the "Apologie de Raymond Sebond," Montaigne clarified his position:

> It is credible that there are natural laws, as may be seen in other creatures; but
> in us they are lost; that fine human reason butts in everywhere, domineering
> and commanding, muddling and confusing the face of things in accordance
> with its vanity and inconsistency.[8]

This statement might seem at first glance to confirm Montaigne's skepticism
about our ability to identify natural laws, but he in fact distinguishes here
between the "ontological" doubt that natural laws exist and the "epistemological" doubt that our present mental faculties (ironically dubbed "cette belle
raison humaine") are sufficient to grasp them. What Montaigne doubts, accordingly, is not the *existence* of natural laws, but rather our capacity, in our
advanced state of "civilization," to discover their content.

Montaigne's skeptical stance toward natural law was challenged by Hugo
Grotius, who opened his famed *De jure belli ac pacis* (1625) with an attack
on Carneades, a leading Greek Skeptic.[9] Grotius rebutted the skeptic view
of nature with an appeal to the "Disposition [which] the Stoicks termed

Ὀικείωσιν [oikeiôsis]."[10] Stoic themes resonate throughout Grotius's philosophy, as they would in subsequent Protestant natural law theorists, Pufendorf in particular.[11] But these theorists were not the only ones to discuss natural law during this time. There was a whole cast of Christian moralists who often steered closer to Stoic philosophy and, somewhat surprisingly, had an equally, if not greater, influence on Enlightenment writers.

Christian neo-Stoicism was culturally complex, as it incorporated strands of thought from both Greek and Roman authors and Christian natural law theorists, going back to Paul. Indeed, a commonplace reference in this literature was Romans 2:14–15, which granted a moral sense, grounded in the law of nature, to all peoples:

> 14 cum enim gentes quae legem non habent naturaliter quae legis sunt faciunt eiusmodi legem non habentes ipsi sibi sunt lex

> 15 qui ostendunt opus legis scriptum in cordibus suis testimonium reddente illis conscientia ipsorum et inter se invicem cogitationum accusantium aut etiam defendentium

> 14 Indeed, when Gentiles, who do not have the law, do by nature things required by the law, they are a law for themselves, even though they do not have the law.

> 15 They show that the requirements of the law are written on their hearts, their consciences also bearing witness, and their thoughts sometimes accusing them and at other times even defending them.[12]

While Paul does not explicitly describe the law "written on their hearts" as the law of nature, this passage has long been interpreted as a commentary (itself possibly inspired by Stoicism) on natural law.[13] It entered into the canon of Christian natural law theory with Aquinas, who offered a jusnaturalist interpretation of Paul's argument in the *Summa theologica*. Neo-Thomist authors such as Francisco Suárez would similarly return to this source.[14]

Seventeenth-century Christian moralists commonly referred to this passage as well.[15] Writing in the midst of a Stoic revival, however, they expressed greater awareness of the theological dangers in celebrating Stoic authors and often felt the need to denounce their pagan predecessors.[16] The famed Oratorian preacher Jean-François Senault, in his 1641 treatise on passions, attacked the Stoics in terms borrowed from Augustine, while acknowledging that his own arguments resembled theirs.[17] Like the Stoics, he warned that unbridled passion was "against the laws of nature."[18] However, this violation of natural laws was not juridical, as it typically was for the political theorists of natural law, but rather theological and moral: "[S]in is a real evil [ . . . ] its cause is an unhinged will, its object is a sovereign good that it offends [ . . . ] it violates all the laws of nature, it dishonors men and Angels . . ." (62).

Framed in the language of sin, Senault's injunction to obey the laws of nature had strong theological overtones ("dishonors . . . Angels"), but also gestured toward a universal, non-confessional moral code. This was a tension that had existed at the heart of Christian natural law ever since Paul. In the Thomist natural law tradition, this tension hardly registered, but by the seventeenth century, the question of whether there might be a universal moral code transcending Christian doctrine became a more pressing matter of debate. Nowhere is this clearer than in one of the most notorious Christian apologias of its day, Jacques Abbadie's *Traité de la vérité de la religion chretienne* (1684), and in its eighteenth-century reception.

Abbadie was a French Protestant theologian who spent most of his life in Berlin and London.[19] Despite his confessional identity, his *Traité* was celebrated even by Catholic readers: Mme de Sévigné praised the author in a letter to her cousin Bussy-Rabutin, exclaiming, "I don't think anyone has ever spoken about religion as he has."[20] If the Protestant preacher could make the Catholic marquise swoon with religious fervor, it was because his target in the *Traité* was not papists, but unbelievers. His defense of Christianity leaned heavily on the existence of a universal natural religion, accessible to all, even in the absence of revelation. It was this first part of his demonstration that caught the eye of his more philosophical readers in the eighteenth century, who ignored Abbadie's later conclusions: in Voltaire's sharp-tongued assessment, Abbadie "defended truth with the weapons of falsehood."[21] The Huguenot exile thus became one of those Christian apologists who unintentionally shored up his deist opponents.[22] In so doing, he also contributed to establishing natural law as a universal source of moral guidance.

Like Senault, Abbadie repeatedly criticized the "arrogant" Stoics who "claimed to rise above other thanks to their sublime morality," all the while echoing the Stoic opposition between natural law and the passions ("there is a battle between the natural law and our passions").[23] His account of natural religion also includes a very Stoic understanding of our natural moral sense:

> [W]e find within ourselves natural religion, which consists of the knowledge nature gave us of God; of the feeling of obligation we have toward him; of the principles of equity and justice that we commonly call natural law; and of the fact that we cannot violate any of those principles, without feeling pangs of guilt flare up in our hearts.[24]

Here the description of natural law is largely cordoned off from any confessional particularities. Following Paul, Abbadie is at pains to emphasize the universal and natural qualities of this intrinsic moral code. Of course, his "common consent" argument for the existence of God by necessity credits non-Christians with a finely tuned moral compass, thus leaving the door open to deism.[25] Abbadie's appeal to conscience might appear more specifically Christian: "Conscience, which incorporates and acts on the principles of natural law, is natural to man, in the same way that is our knowledge of God."[26] But Cicero, too, had warned of the "angore conscientia fraudisque cruciatu" (the anguish of remorse and the torture of a guilty conscience),[27] and Paul himself had granted a moral conscience to the Gentiles ("testimonium reddente illis conscientia ipsorum"). It required little effort, then, to extract a wholly naturalistic moral system from these Christian apologias.

### 1.2. ENLIGHTENMENT NEO-STOICISM: ONCE MORE WITH FEELING

It would be precisely in the neo-Stoic terms of Senault, Abbadie, and others that the *philosophes* developed a moral doctrine rooted in natural law, minus the Christianity.[28] Voltaire's *Poème sur la Loi naturelle* (1756), dedicated to Frederick the Great and written at his court four years earlier, offers a classic example. It takes as its premise the Stoic axiom that "Nature to man has given with bounteous hand / Whate'er his nature's cravings can demand."[29] This is a reference to our moral, not our material, needs: nature placed its bounty in "[s]ense's sure instinct, spirit's varied springs." Even our emotions cannot efface this moral guide: "Soon as our passions fierce subside and cool, / Our hearts assent to every moral rule [De nos désirs fougueux la tempête fatale / Laisse au fond de nos cœurs la règle et la morale]" (28). As the Christian apologists before him, Voltaire deploys the argument from common consent to demonstrate the universality of natural law: "Morality, unvaried and the same, / Announces to each age God's holy name" (25; trans. modified). But the ultimate evidence of this natural and universal moral code comes from its fearful enforcement mechanism, namely, our conscience:

> By nature preached, like nature it endures;
> Reason receives it, and the keen remorse
> Of conscience strengthens it, and gives it force;
> For conscience makes the obstinate repent. (25)[30]

While the theological tenor of this poem is clearly deist, it is notable how deliberately Voltaire flags the classical, and particularly Stoic, sources of his argument. Marcus Aurelius is singled out three times for his exceptional virtue (e.g., "His soul to this Aurelius still applied, / Like a philosopher he lived and died"; 29). And part 3 contains a lengthy defense of the pagans against those Christians calling for their damnation: "The Pagan virtues were but crimes at best [say some Christians], / All generous souls such maxims must detest" (33).[31] The ancients also give Voltaire fodder for his Erastian conclusion: "Aurelius, Trajan, princes of renown, / The pontiff's bonnet wore, and emperor's crown" (37). Where the English Erastian clergymen were among the strongest defenders of natural rights, however, no mention of rights is made in this poem. The demands of natural law are only expressed in terms of duty (23). The Stoic vision of a moral universe came first. It would be a separate, if complementary, matter to explicitly add rights in this order.

Voltaire's Stoic defense of natural morality was commonplace in the French Enlightenment. In the "Discours préliminaire des éditeurs" (1751) to the *Encyclopédie*, for instance, d'Alembert begins by asserting the principle that there is a "natural law which we find within us, the source of the first laws which men must of necessity have created." We find this law expressed in "the cry of Nature, resounding in all men," including "the most savage people." With the development of political thought in antiquity, natural law acquired new importance: "[N]atural law, being anterior to all particular conventions, is thus the first law of peoples," and politicians had to remember that "to be a statesman one must not cease to be a man." But its centrality lasts till this day, as natural law remains the linchpin of morality, expressing itself through conscience: "It is a result of natural law and of our conception of good and evil. One could call it evidence of the heart, for, although it differs greatly from the evidence of the mind which concerns speculative truths, it subjugates us with the same force."[32] Like Voltaire, d'Alembert insists on the perfection of moral sentiments even in the absence of a Christian faith, all the while echoing the neo-Stoic arguments of the Christian apologists.

The French philosopher who developed the fullest theory of natural morality is of course Rousseau, in *Emile*. As Christopher Brooke has observed, the educational project presented here is essentially Stoic, as it intends at all times to remain consistent with nature.[33] Accordingly, at the conclusion of his upbringing, Emile is presented as a Stoic sage: like Epictetus, he proclaims, "Rich or poor, I shall be free. [ ... ] All the chains of opinion are broken for me; I know only those of necessity. [ ... ] And why would I not know how to bear them as a free man since, if I were a slave, I would still have to bear them and those of slavery to boot?"[34] His tutor approves this speech and reminds him that freedom is not to be found in a particular government, but "in the heart of the free man." If the sage can be free even if enslaved, it is because "the eternal laws of nature and order do exist. For the wise man, they take the place of positive law. They are written in the depth of his heart by conscience and reason."[35] Thus conscience does make heroes of us all, and *Emile* is bursting with paeans to this "divine instinct," which keeps us heading down a Stoic path: "[H]e who follows conscience obeys nature and does not fear being led astray."[36] Not only the Stoic philosopher, but even "unthinking man" (in Diderot's expression, "l'homme qui n'a point réfléchi") could lead a moral life standing before "the tribunal of conscience."[37]

The reach of Stoicism in the French Enlightenment extended much further than this rapid overview can convey.[38] As its tenets were often intermingled with the Christian doctrine of natural law, it can be difficult at times to distinguish between the two.[39] Enlightened authors outside of France also inclined toward Stoicism: in Scotland, Francis Hutcheson translated Marcus Aurelius's *Meditations*, and Adam Smith echoed Stoic principles in his *Theory of Moral Sentiments*.[40] Taken together, these various examples underscore that Stoic natural law in the Enlightenment did not undergo a secularizing process, as some have assumed.[41] Neo-Stoics did not all become atheists, far from it.[42] For the most part, natural law continued to be interpreted within a theistic framework—these were still "the Laws of Nature, and Nature's God." This common framework, which the *philosophes* inherited from Christian moralists, even allowed them to claim that their philosophical musings were perfectly orthodox. Rousseau concluded the "Profession of Faith of the Savoyard Vicar" with an exhortation to accept the faith of your country.[43] But just as the deists had little difficulty in extricating Christianity from Christian neo-Stoicism, so, too, atheists could remove God from this program. Diderot makes no mention of God in his article "Droit naturel," yet this excision ultimately changes little. The directives of natural law are still to be found in the usual places—namely, universal customs and basic human passions.[44] The same holds true for d'Holbach: nature itself was sufficient to authorize our most fundamental moral laws.[45] To be sure, the question of atheism was a fraught one in the Enlightenment, but it did not greatly impinge on the authority of natural law. Even for atheists, the Stoic vision of a natural moral order continued to hold sway. Whatever claims authors made about natural rights must accordingly be read against this backdrop of natural justice, which would persist up through the French Revolution.

To the assertion that the French Enlightenment perpetuated a Stoic view of morality and law, one important modifier must be added. Where the Stoics, the Roman jurists, their commentators, and Scholastic theologians all insisted that natural laws were rational, and that we recognized their truthfulness thanks to our own faculty of reason, the *philosophes* argued instead that natural laws should be *felt*. It was not man's reason that led him to recognize natural laws, Voltaire argued in his *Poème sur la loi naturelle*, but "his judge [is] in his heart."[46] It was in part for such sentimental reasons that the *philosophes* rejected the Protestant natural lawyers: Delisle de Sales could not fathom what was "the tie that connects laws born in the human heart and the scholarly dissertations of the Cumberlands and Pufendorfs. . . ."[47] Similarly, Rousseau's fictional philosopher, in the second *Discourse*, silenced his naturally sympathetic feelings for a nearby victim by rationalizing his non-assistance.[48] Reason alone could not grant us access to natural law, he argued in *Emile*: "[B]y reason alone, independent of conscience, no natural law can be established [. . .;] the entire right of nature is only a chimera if it is not founded on a natural need in the human heart."[49] Clearly, this was not a Stoic sage speaking. Rousseau's downgrading of reason proved too extreme for most *philosophes*, but his argument that natural laws were really natural "principles" that determined our *sensibilité* was widely shared.[50] Writing on the eve of the French Revolution, Condorcet argued that our natural rights derived from our quality as "sensitive beings [êtres sensibles]."[51]

Why did the *philosophes* shift the foundations of natural law from reason to sentiment? In part, they were likely responding to the cultural craze sweeping over Western Europe at this time, oftentimes described as a "cult of sensibility."[52] This craze expressed itself mostly in literature and the arts, but also carried over into moral philosophy. Lynn Hunt has argued that this culture of sensibility was key in propagating the idea of human rights; while it is an exaggeration to suggest that it "invented" human rights, her argument is helpful for describing the *transformation* of rights talk during the Enlightenment.[53]

To some extent, however, this shift was more a matter of emphasis than of epistemic rupture. Christian neo-Stoics considered both reason and sentiment as the receptacles of natural law. As Jacques Abbadie proclaimed, "the principles of natural law" could be found "in the soundest maxims of reason," but also in "the most innocent sentiments of self-love [des sentimens les plus innocens de l'amour de nous-mêmes]."[54] This belief was often couched in Pauline terms: hence the Jansenist Pierre Nicole, a collaborator of Pascal's, wrote that self-knowledge "leads us to discover in the depths of our hearts the imprint of the natural law that prohibits us from doing to others what we would not like done to us."[55] This Pauline image remained a fixture in eighteenth-century France, as well, with even the *parlementaires* referring to it.[56] Where earlier authors had read Paul's assertion symbolically to mean that the moral law was imprinted in all humans, the *philosophes* literalized this claim and sought moral strictures in the movements of our heart.

## 2. Laws of the Natural World: The New Science

There was another place to which authors could turn, if they wished to demonstrate the existence of natural laws, and that was the natural world. Such demonstrations were not reserved for natural philosophers, or "men of science"; even theologians appealed to the cosmos as evidence of a universal natural order. Abbadie asserted, for instance, that "to know the wisdom of the Creator, so evident in his works, one must only know the general laws of nature, without needing to explain every thing in particular."[57]

To some extent, this was a familiar claim: the so-called "argument from design" had long been an arrow in the theological quiver. Only an intelligent being could have created our complex world, this line of reasoning went. But the suggestion that the physical cosmos was regulated by natural *laws* was in fact more recent, as we will see, having emerged at the time of the scientific revolution. The gradual adoption of this belief was a key factor in the development of social naturalism, which is premised on an analogy between the law-driven order of the natural world and the (presumed) lawful structure of the social sphere.

By the eighteenth century, the force of this analogy would flow from the natural to the social world. Charles Bonnet paid Montesquieu the highest compliment when he compared *The Spirit of Laws* to Newton's *Principia*, on the grounds that the Frenchman had done for "the intellectual world" what the Englishman had done for "the material world."[58] But a century earlier, it was still very much in question whether "laws" could accurately apply to anything apart from human beings. Our present-day familiarity with, say, the three laws of thermodynamics, the law of gravity, or the laws of motion can lead us to overlook the resistance that some early modern commentators expressed about extending this concept beyond its moral and rational sphere.

There was at least one classical precedent to this extension. Roman jurists had not limited the application of law to human beings alone: in their view, nature proclaimed her laws to all animals. They insisted that reason was not a prerequisite for recognizing the law: "[T]his law is not only assigned to the human race, but to all animals" (jus istud non humani generis proprium est, sed omnium animalium).[59] Evidence that natural law applied to animals could be found, for instance, in the universal urge to procreate ("maris atque feminae conjugatio"). The law of nature, for these jurists, was originally a biological law of attraction between the sexes.

But Christian theologians had limited the application of natural law to creatures endowed with rational capacities.[60] Aquinas acknowledged that "the plan of governance of the world existing in God as the ruler of the universe has the nature of law," but distinguished between rational creatures, for whom "we call their participation in the eternal law *law* in the strict sense, since law belongs to reason," and "irrational creatures," who only participate in the law "by analogy."[61] This insistence that natural law could only "belong to reason" was itself another classical legacy: Cicero had similarly defined natural law as enclosing the demands of "right reason" (recta ratio).[62]

When practitioners of the new science in the seventeenth century de-scribed the natural regularities that they discovered in terms of laws, not all accepted this designation readily. Robert Boyle, for instance, criticized "some deists" who believed that "after the first formation of the universe, all things are brought to pass by the settled laws of nature." He objected to this argument on terminological grounds: "I look upon a law, as a moral, not a physical cause [. . .;] inanimate bodies are utterly incapable of understanding what a law is, or what it enjoins, or when they act conformably, or unconformably to it."[63] Boyle was falling back here on the older Stoic-Christian position, namely that only rational beings can obey laws.

The "deists" Boyle criticized here are likely to have been Cartesians. As many scholars have noted, it was Descartes in particular who appears to have shifted the language of law from the moral and intellectual world to the physical one.[64] In his *Principles of Philosophy* (1644), Descartes very con-sciously proposed this new nomenclature to describe the regular patterns of nature:

> From this same immutability of God, we can obtain knowledge of the certain rules, *which I call* the laws of nature [que je nomme les loix de la nature], which are the secondary and particular causes of the diverse movements which we notice in individual bodies.[65]

The first law of nature, according to Descartes, was that "each thing, as far as is in its power, always remain in the same state," so that, "in accordance with the laws of nature, having once begun to move, they continue to do so until they are slowed down by encounter with other bodies."[66] The laws of nature, which came from God, allowed Descartes to explain the entirety of mechan-ical physics.[67] Descartes still recognized that these were technically laws in a merely metaphorical sense, acknowledging that what he chose to define as "laws" might otherwise be described as observable rules.[68]

The success of Descartes's terminological innovation is hard to overstate: "It is his role in bringing the idea of a law of nature from the margin of natural philosophy to its centre that makes Descartes the most important single fig-ure in the entire history of that idea."[69] Only in his aftermath did it became possible to assume that "one of the main aims—perhaps *the* main aim—of a natural philosopher should be the discovery of the laws governing the natural world."[70] By the time Newton wrote his *Principia* (1687), Boyle's concerns had been forgotten: it was only fitting that Newton should open his work with a definition of "the laws of motion" (leges motus).[71]

The adoption of this legal perspective on the natural world had major consequences for theology. Up until that point, the *inconsistency* of natural phenomena had served as an argument for God: it was precisely in the miraculous that divine intervention could be seen.[72] It might be assumed that the marginalization of the miraculous in the seventeenth century could challenge the very existence of God—yet the opposite occurred. As Alan Michael Kors has shown, the new science actually reinforced the belief in a divinely ordered world: "God manifestly had created a natural order that acted according to the laws He Himself had established."[73] Consistency now became further proof of God's existence.

The projection of laws on to the natural world was of course a necessary condition for social naturalism. The concept of law originated in the moral sphere and was applied to the natural world through analogy; but when the analogy was reversed, and scholars began once again searching for laws in "the intellectual world" (to borrow Bonnet's phrase), the idea of natural law returned transformed. First, it did not always have the character of a moral ideal. In Stoic and Christian philosophy, the law of nature retained an aspirational quality: we discovered its dictates if we followed right reason, but our judgment was often clouded by our passions. In reality, we could fall short of natural law's demands. To live according to nature was not a given; it was a prescriptive, not a descriptive, adage. Second, in its new installation, natural laws were not necessarily observable by all; they could simply define a pattern of human activity that had hitherto passed unnoticed. In other words, it did not take reason to discover these laws: we might just obey them unwittingly. One result of this new understanding of a natural order would be the Enlightenment's fondness for self-organizing systems.[74] Another example of blind obedience to natural laws would be found in the nascent field of economics, as we will see in the following chapter.

# Roman Law and Order:
# From Free-Market Ideology to Abolitionism

What is justice, asked Diderot in the *Encyclopédie* article "Droit naturel"? His answer was "the obligation to render to each person what belongs to him." If this definition sounds familiar, that is because it is: Diderot was translating Ulpian's famous maxim, "Iustitia est constans et perpetua voluntas ius suum cuique tribuens,"[1] a phrase he would undoubtedly have encountered during his short-lived legal education.[2] But Roman law was not merely a topic of study to be inflicted on long-suffering law students. It was viewed as a philosophical body of work in itself, "the best source from which one can draw a science of laws," as the jurist Antoine-Gaspard Boucher d'Argis affirmed in the *Encyclopédie*. Roman law stood above all other legal codes as "a body of principles founded on reason and equity."[3] This was the view of a legal professional, but even Montesquieu, who championed a relativistic approach to comparative law, granted that Roman law could offer "a more natural, more reasonable way of proceeding, a way more in conformity with morality, religion, public tranquility, and the security of persons and goods."[4] For others, such was the appeal of Roman law that it should be regarded as "the *true* law, the ideal law, the embodiment of reason," even when it was not the actual law of the land.[5] Its apparent rationality prompted many scholars to describe Roman law as the codification of Stoic philosophy.[6] Be that as it may, it provided a lasting framework for the transmission and interpretation of natural law up through the eighteenth century.

If Roman law captured the imagination of legal scholars and reformers during this time, it was in large part because the reality of European law differed from this orderly model. Throughout most of Western Europe, the laws in force were a mix of customary or common law (of Germanic origin), Roman law, canon law, and local edicts.[7] The rediscovery of the Justinian *Digest* in the eleventh century launched a long series of official and scholarly efforts to codify, clarify, collect, and condense these multifarious bodies of law along the simpler lines of Roman law. These efforts would persist for the next seven hundred years, culminating in England in Blackstone's *Commentaries*, in Prussia in the *Allgemeines Landrecht*, and in France in the Napoleonic Civil Code.[8]

The history of European legal reform is seldom discussed in intellectual histories of natural law, despite the fact that they were deeply intertwined.[9] It was the philosophical success of natural law theory that precipitated the scholarly move away from legal humanism, an approach epitomized by Guillaume Budé's antiquarian study of the law, toward rational jurisprudence around the turn of the seventeenth century.[10] But where philosophers, theologians, and jurists in Spain, England, the Netherlands, and the German states debated theories of natural law, in France this same interest expressed itself in attempts to rationalize (i.e., to "Romanize") the chaotic mix of civil and common law that bedeviled French jurisconsults. Sometimes this effort coincided with the moral reflection on natural law discussed in the previous chapter: a case in point is Scipion Dupleix's *L'éthique ou philosophie morale* (1610), a work primarily preoccupied with moral considerations, but which also contains a discussion of law that hews to the *Institutes'* tripartite division of law into three categories (natural law, the law of nations, and civil law).[11] Other times it took the form of arranging common law articles according to Roman principles, as with Antoine Loisel's *Institutes coutumières* (1607).[12] At the end of the seventeenth century, however, one French jurist took this effort to new heights, and in the process revolutionized not only legal thinking, but French social and economic theory as well.

### 1. The Jansenist Ethic and the Spirit of Capitalism: Jean Domat, the Natural Order, and the Origins of Free-Market Ideology

Unlike their contemporary Protestant and neo-Scholastic theorists of natural law, French legal reformers often did not discuss natural *rights* very much, perhaps for the political reasons discussed in chapter 2.[13] But their transposing of natural law theory into a more Roman key still had major repercussions for later rights theorists. One such work that resonated deeply into the follow century was Jean Domat's *Les loix civiles dans leur ordre naturel* (1689–94).[14] Domat (1625–1696) was a French legal scholar, educated at the Jesuit *collège* Louis-le-Grand. He subsequently turned to Jansenism, thanks to his friendship with Pascal. He grew very close to Pascal, two years his senior, and would serve as the latter's testamentary executor after his death. After practicing law in his native town of Clermont, he resettled in Paris in 1682, where he benefited from a royal pension and focused on his legal treatise. The king himself accepted its dedication, and the work was immediately lauded as a masterpiece.[15] It would be translated into English twice (once partially) in the early eighteenth century,[16] and its influence extended to the American colonies, where Thomas Jefferson recommended Domat to law students.[17]

Jefferson may have appreciated Domat's somewhat surprising definition of natural law, which emphasized happiness. In the Christian natural law tradition, the first law of nature was usually identified with the so-called law of the Gospel ("Do unto others as you would have them do unto you").[18] But Domat proposed an interesting alternative: "[T]he first Law of Man, is his destination to the Knowledge and Love of that Object, which is thought to be his End, and in which he is to find his Happiness [sa félicité]."[19] By happiness, he clearly did not have an Epicurean definition in mind: to be happy was to be on the road to salvation.[20] Here Domat sounded a shrill Pascalian note on the misery of man: "[F]or in himself, he will be so far from finding his Happiness there, that he will see nothing there but the Seeds of Misery and Death: And round about him, if we go over the whole Universe, we shall find nothing there that is capable of being proposed as an End either to his Mind, or to his Heart."[21] Our inability to sit alone in a room, our need for entertainment: these are symptoms of our existential insufficiency, our miserable human condition, which can only be remedied by religious devotion and genuine charity.[22]

But Domat departed from Pascal in rejecting his friend's skepticism about the human ability to grasp natural laws. As Montaigne before him, Pascal did not so much deny the existence of natural laws, as question their legibility. He pointed to the variation of laws from land to land as an indication that natural justice was out of our reach. "It is an odd kind of justice to have a river for its boundary. Truth lies on this side of the Pyrenees, error on the other," he famously mused. Legislators might counter that "justice does not reside in customs but in natural laws common to all countries." But what evidence do we have that natural laws truly exist? All sorts of horrific actions have been acceptable at different times and in different places: "Larceny, incest, infanticide, and parricide have all been accounted virtuous deeds." Accordingly, we should not expect much from natural laws: "No doubt there are natural laws, but our fine reason having been corrupted [cette belle raison corrompue], it corrupted everything," Pascal concluded, borrowing even Montaigne's sarcastic phrasing.[23]

By the late seventeenth century, however, this skeptical view of natural law was losing its bite. Pufendorf had roundly dismissed this argument, claiming: "'Tis ridiculously weak to conclude, that supposing different States to have set

up different Laws upon the Account of Profit, therefore there can be no perpetual or natural law."[24] Domat did not even consider the skeptical challenge
and simply distinguished between two types of laws, those that are "immutable" and those that are "arbitrary." The former are identical to the laws of
nature: "[T]hey are Natural, and so just at all times, and in all places, that no
Authority can either change, or abolish them." Arbitrary laws, by contrast, "are
those which may be differently established, changed, and even quite abolished,
without violating the Spirit and Intent of the Fundamental Laws [l'esprit des
premieres loix]."[25] So long as the arbitrary laws did not violate "the spirit of
the laws" of nature—an expression that Montesquieu would soon make his
own—their disparateness need not offend.

On these points, Domat was hardly original. Pufendorf had made a similar
distinction between categories of law; and Domat mainly rehearsed traditional Pauline, Thomist, and neo-Stoic arguments of Christian natural law
theory.[26] The principles of natural law, he wrote, "have a Character of Truth,
which touches and persuades more than that of the Principle of other human
Sciences."[27] In a more explicitly Pauline vein, he added, "God has engraven
on the Minds of all Men this kind of Knowledge, and Love of Justice, without which Society could not Last. And it is by the help of this Knowledge of
the Natural Laws, that even the Nations which have had no Knowledge of
Religion, have made their Societies to subsist."[28] Where Pascal had directly
challenged the Pauline argument for common consent, Domat reaffirmed this
affirmation of a universal moral code: "Ignorance of Law is to be understood
only of the Positive Law, and not of the Law of Nature, which no body can be
ignorant of."[29]

If Domat had simply brought Jansenism back in line with traditional
Christian views of natural law, his contributions would not be particularly
noteworthy. But his account of natural law introduced two important twists.
First, there was his theory of society. Again following Pufendorf, Domat insisted on natural human sociability: "God hath placed Mankind in Society,
there to unit[e] them by mutual Love." But we do not join into society in one
fell swoop: rather "God, having destined Mankind for Society, hath formed
the Ties which engage him to it [qui les y engagent]."[30] The first type of engagement was matrimony, and then, through the union of the sexes, other family
ties; social relations between non-family members formed the second type of
engagements.[31] Up until this point, Domat continued to echo Pufendorf, who
had similarly called attention to the institution of marriage as the key bond
in establishing "primary societies."[32] But then Domat abruptly broke with
the standard natural law narrative about the formation of political societies.

Where Pufendorf (along with Hobbes and Locke) insisted that a state must be created through one or more "covenants," Domat described a gradual and natural evolution from "primary societies" to government.[33] These engagements simply "demand the Use of a Government, to restrain every one within the Order of those that are peculiar to him," he affirmed. Political rulers arise naturally, since they are needed "for maintaining the Order of Society, according to the Laws which he [God] hath established in it."[34] No social contract was required to establish legitimate government.

What made it possible for Domat to abandon this key episode in natural law theory? In part, he may have been motivated by political considerations. *Les loix civiles* was dedicated to Louis XIV, and as Domat wrote in the opening line of his dedicatory epistle, "God made Kings to take his place above men."[35] Even for conservatives like Pufendorf, the first covenant, which unites individuals into a commonwealth, required the consent of all. For Domat, political power was not founded on the consent of the governed, but came directly from God. In the famous words of Paul, much loved by kings and their propagandists, "non est potestas nisi a Deo."[36]

But in addition to this absolutist claim, Domat embraced a naturalistic account of social formation.[37] The "order of society" was an *ordre naturel*, his title affirmed. Placing marriage at the heart of social formation allowed Domat to structure his account around a tie that was both natural and social, an overlap that persisted in his discussion of society as a whole. This account was also theologically grounded: we must recognize in government, Domat argued, "the Providence of God over Mankind and that Order in which he preserves Society in all times."[38] Domat's understanding of this natural order echoes that of Malebranche, for whom *l'ordre naturel* was an expression of God's eternal will (as we saw in the previous chapter). He also shared with Malebranche a more theologically inflected account of natural sociability, again in contradistinction with Pufendorf.[39]

What are we to make of these subtle changes, by a politically conservative jurist? Taken together, they are surprisingly revolutionary. Where earlier natural law philosophers had insisted that natural law remained in force in political society (even if they generally did not allow for the preservation of natural rights), they viewed government itself as a man-made, "artificial" creation.[40] When a community chose a particular kind of political rule for itself, this decision was not naturally determined, but constituted an act of will. By inscribing *all* human activity within a broader, divinely willed natural order, however, Domat opened the floodgates to a host of arguments whose common theme was that society should be (re)aligned on a natural model. This reframing also downplayed the role of the state in the organization of society.

If both society and government were natural entities, one could reform the first without the aid of the second.[41]

In his own work, Domat chiefly applied this social naturalism to legal theory: "All the Matters of the Civil Law have among themselves a simple and a natural Order, which forms them into one Body . . . ," he wrote in his conclusion to the prefatory "Traité des loix."[42] But the economic ramifications of this argument may have been the most consequential. As before, Domat arrived at economy via theology. Since the Fall, humans are no longer driven by mutual love alone but by self-love, *amour-propre*. This sinful selfishness is the source of all evil: "Whatever we see in Society that is contrary to Order, is a natural consequence of the Disobedience of Man to the first Law, which commands him to love God." As God is omnipotent, however, he must have willed the existence of evil; and since God is also benevolent, he could only have done so in order to "draw Good out of it, and a much greater Good than a pure State of Good Things would have been, without any mixture of Evil." One greater good that derived from human self-love was increased economic productivity: the Fall "hath also augmented the necessity of Labour and of Commerce, and at the same time the necessity of Engagements, and of Ties." All of this activity was beneficial to society, and ultimately forced selfish individuals to act virtuously: to obtain what it desires, self-love "complies with all Duties, and even counterfeits all Virtues."[43]

As Albert Hirschman noted, the idea that *amour-propre*, in society, could produce favorable results had already been pushed by other Jansenists, including Pascal: "We have founded upon and drawn from concupiscence admirable laws of administration, morality, and justice."[44] Pierre Nicole had similarly argued, in a famous essay, "On Greatness" ("De la grandeur"): "There is nothing that one gets more out of than human cupidity."[45] The novelty of Domat's argument came from the fact that this moral economy was now fully incorporated into a naturalistic framework.[46] It was not just that God surreptitiously transformed our private vices into public benefits, to paraphrase Mandeville; or that a system of positive laws and punishments nudged self-interest in an altruistic direction, as for Nicole.[47] Instead, the entire system of human passions, society, and even government followed the natural order willed by God and defined by natural law.

While Domat himself did not fully develop the economic consequences of his theory, his legal treatise did deal at length with a central ingredient of commercial activity, namely, contracts. Indeed, the very first book of *Les loix civiles* covers what today would be called contract law.[48] It is here that we can uncover the economic ramifications of Domat's political anthropology. Just as the social fabric is woven together by a multiplicity of individual engagements, so, too, the commercial sphere is fashioned by a multiplicity of contracts and transactions. In both cases, these exchanges are divinely ordained and part of the natural order: "[T]he Use of Covenants is a natural consequence of the Order of Civil Society, and of the Ties which God forms among Men."[49] But where Hobbes had insisted that "there must be some coërcive Power, to compell men equally to the performance of their Covenants," Domat has little to say about the conditions necessary to ensure that contracts be upheld.[50] Here as well, there does not appear to be any fundamental difference between contracting in a pre-political or a political state. Contracts create laws regardless of the political condition in which we find ourselves.[51] We may on occasion need to appeal to a judge to arbitrate our differences;[52] but the sphere of commercial activity that Domat describes is generally independent from political interference.

It is easy to see how Domat's interpretation of a natural commercial order could pave the way for the free-market ideal of allowing the economy to run its own course, without governmental meddling.[53] By minimizing, if not erasing, the ontological gulf between nature and society, social naturalism made it possible to envision the economy as a natural, self-organizing system, guided by the "invisible hand" of God.[54] By offering a providential reevaluation of sin, Domat also helped pave the way toward free-market theories that rested on "natural" pricing and the accumulation of wealth. Now, greed could be good.

One of the first economic theorists to argue that a nation's wealth would increase by "simply letting Nature act [laisser agir la Nature]" was Pierre le Pesant de Boisguilbert, a French administrator who, like Domat, had first studied with the Jesuits (in his hometown of Rouen), before entrusting himself to the Jansenists at Port-Royal.[55] The influence of Domat and Nicole on Boisguilbert has long been noted, and as a law student (then judge), he will undoubtedly have been familiar with Domat's legal work. Later laissez-faire proponents would tweak and transform Boisguilbert's insights but recognized him as an important forerunner, "the first to conceptualize the natural order on which the economic system rests."[56] In this way, Boisguilbert served as a bridge between the Jansenist school of Domat and Nicole, and the more celebrated eighteenth-century liberal economists, from Vincent de Gournay and the Physiocrats to Adam Smith.[57]

The full story of how free-market liberalism emerged out of Jansenist theology is too long and complex to relate here.[58] More relevant to the present study, and as a coda to this section, I will simply draw attention to a final feature of Domat's theory, which brings us back to rights. As part of his reflections on the natural order of society, Domat considered the plight of those who have been rendered unable to work:

Thus, the condition of those who are Members of the Society, who are destitute of the Means of Subsistence, and unable to work for their Livelihood, lays
an Obligation on all their Fellow Members to exercise towards them mutual
Love, by imparting to them a Share of those Goods which they have a right to
[un bien où ils ont droit]. For every Man being a Member of the Society has a
right to live in it [il a droit d'y vivre]: and that which is necessary to those who
have Nothing, and who are not able to gain their Livelihood, is by consequence
in the hands of the other Members; from whence it follows, that they cannot
without Injustice detain it from them.[59]

What is most striking about this passage is that Domat clearly defines the
indigent's claims on society as *rights*. Unlike Christian charity, which views
assistance to the poor as the duty of the rich, the right to public assistance here
is very clearly presented from the viewpoint of the needy. It is still justified in
theological terms: *l'amour mutuel* between humans comes from God, and if "all
men" belong to society, it is because God wants it to be so. But the welfare argument also flows directly from Domat's social naturalism: since society is the
natural order of humanity, and individuals have a right to self-preservation, it
follows that society is responsible for aiding those who cannot tend to themselves. This is the same logic that the Physiocrats would later espouse and that
would ultimately be promoted by the French revolutionaries.[60] It also reveals
how social naturalism was not only generative of those natural rights that were
the corollary of natural laws, but also introduced new socioeconomic rights.

✳

If the greatest natural law theorist of seventeenth-century France was a jurist,
not a political philosopher, this was not an accident. In the age of Louisquator-
zian absolutism, natural law theory could only have a very restricted political
application. The *philosophes* did not share his absolutist convictions, but like
Domat their engagement with natural law theory did not focus on sovereignty
(as did, say, the Jesuit and Protestant natural law traditions) and was less philosophical in style. Indeed, the clarity and elegance of Domat's style is not to be
overlooked. It would be praised in the nineteenth century by Sainte-Beuve,
who claimed that Domat had done for jurisprudence what "Boileau [did] for
verse, Corneille for tragedy, Descartes for metaphysics, Pascal for genius and
the perfection of prose, Madame de La Fayette for novels."[61] Domat did not
encumber his arguments with notes or references, thereby making them accessible to an educated, if not necessarily erudite, readership. His treatment
of natural law thus foreshadowed the worldly style of the *philosophes*, who
similarly eschewed scholarly references, addressed a broader audience, and
of course wrote in French, rather than Latin (as had Grotius and Pufendorf).[62]

The *philosophes* also followed Domat's lead in writing about natural law from more of a legal than a political perspective. To be sure, there were political elements to their discussions: they dealt with concepts—rights, laws, punishments—that traditionally fell under the purview of the state. One can further distinguish this type of discourse by means of Keith Baker's tripartite typology: as opposed to administrative or political discourses (which emphasized reason and will, respectively), Enlightenment natural law theory can be described as a judicial discourse (which, predictably, emphasized justice). But there remains a key difference, which is that the primary issues at stake in a judicial discourse remain "political": they concern the right to administer justice, or (in Baker's words) "the exercise of public power according to constitutionally prescribed legal forms."[63] In the case of the French Enlightenment, however, the central concern lay not with *who* gets to make (or to apply) the law, but rather with *what* is the nature of a good law.[64]

This decision to focus on the *what* rather than the *who* meant that writers could limit their exposure to censorship (and harassment) by challenging the content of the law, not the process through which the law is crafted. Maintaining this distinction, of course, was not always straightforward. The Physiocratic treatise on *L'ordre naturel et essentiel des sociétés politiques*, written by Le Mercier de la Rivière (under the supervision of Quesnay), sought to define "good positive laws," but ended up also proposing strict constraints on the selection and prerogatives of the legislator, constraints that were hardly compatible with absolute monarchy.[65] A previous attempt by the Physiocrats to define the relation between executive and legal authority had been scuttled due to fears of censorship.[66]

This distinction is nonetheless essential for understanding the enlightened strategy of social critique. It helps explain, for instance, why Diderot's statement, "We must speak out against senseless laws until they're reformed and, in the meanwhile, abide by them,"[67] was not just a defensive posture. In general, the *philosophes* simply did not seek to challenge the authority of those who passed laws, but rather the fairness of the laws themselves.[68] And their standard for measuring this fairness was a law's proximity to natural law: "Civil law should merely articulate the law of nature," Diderot wrote elsewhere in the *Supplément*. If this were the case, then laws would be sublimely concise and just: "How brief would be the codes of nations, if only they conformed rigorously to that of Nature!"[69] To arrive at this point, Mirabeau *père* argued in *L'ami des hommes*, "it is always necessary to uproot everything in a state that is contrary to natural right."[70] This was the rallying cry of jurists who sought to reform and standardize the law, not of political theorists who wanted to refashion government. When Voltaire insisted that "natural right is the one that nature indicates to all men,"[71] he was targeting the courts (the *parlements*), not the monarchy.

Where Domat uncovered the rational, natural, divine foundation of laws on which the French legal system was erected, the *philosophes* mostly sought to strip this edifice down to its natural studs. This was the driving force behind "natural republicanism," an apolitical theory of politics according to which sovereignty would wither away in the face of a citizenry guided entirely by natural laws and republican morals.[72] Inspired in large part by Fénelon, this tradition extended up through the young Montesquieu, Voltaire, Rousseau (in places), the Physiocrats, Diderot, d'Holbach, Sylvain Maréchal, Court de Gébelin, and, in later times, Saint-Just. As a utopian model of how a society without positive laws could be governed, however, its appeal becomes more understandable once we recognize how it reformulates, in starker terms, the canonical legal view that privileged natural, immutable laws over "arbitrary" ones.

## 2. "All Men Are Originally Born Free": Slavery, Empathy, and the Extension of Human Rights

One reason why the *philosophes* placed such faith in a natural order of society is because they believed it would preserve the natural freedom of all humans. For the Tahitian, Diderot argued, "the love of liberty is the deepest of all feelings."[73] *Liberté*, as we saw in chapter 3, was one of the specific human rights that the *philosophes*, along with their Anglo-American counterparts, identified in particular. But to insist on freedom was also to raise the question of the unfree and the enslaved. As many scholars of the Enlightenment have noted, this was a corollary that they often tactfully ignored.[74] Rousseau's "man in chains" was not an African slave on a sugar plantation, but the Frenchman who was not even aware that he was a slave (*Social Contract*, 1.1). The extension of social naturalism to actual slaves was far from automatic. Very few *philosophes* became abolitionists. Some criticized the slave trade but went no further. Others expressed misgivings but did not propose any solutions.

At the same time, the French Enlightenment was also an important source of abolitionist discourse. Montesquieu's *Spirit of Laws*, while falling short of demanding abolitionism, proved an authoritative reference for subsequent abolitionists around the Atlantic. But before we explore how and why Montesquieu leveled his attack on the institution of slavery, we must first examine why the *philosophes* resisted so long from condemning it explicitly and completely. In this next section, I explain how empathy, which Lynn Hunt suggested accounts for why slavery eventually became unpalatable to many Europeans, may on the contrary have been partially responsible for their delayed response. Instead, I suggest in the following sections that it was Montesquieu's social-naturalist interpretation of Roman law that chiefly led to the rise of abolitionist discourse.

2.1. AGAINST EMPATHY:

ROUSSEAU, SMITH, AND LYNN HUNT

In her account of Enlightenment human rights, Lynn Hunt singled out the epistolary novel as playing a particular role in their extension to all humans.[75] Because the epistolary novel trains us to empathize with characters of different (including lower) social standing, she argues, it led eighteenth-century readers to view a broader range of fellow humans as worthy of respect, dignity, and ultimately rights. But does it?

A first reason to question the expansionary powers of empathy can be found in epistolary novels themselves. While these books may on occasion make readers feel for characters who had typically been relegated to invisible, supporting roles in the past (Hunt's chief example is the servant-girl Pamela, from Samuel Richardson's eponymous novel), it is not the case that sentimental literature extends empathetic understanding to *all* characters. Indeed, some of them remain perfectly villainous in our eyes. In Montesquieu's epistolary novel *Persian Letters*, for instance, the chief eunuch (probably himself a slave) is a one-dimensional, unsympathetic character, defined by his sadistic treatment of Usbek's wives. Choderlos de Laclos's *Dangerous Liaisons* even stages the act of an audience reading letters from the novel, with an opposite effect than that predicted by Hunt. After Valmont "leaks" his correspondence with Merteuil, she is universally shunned and mocked at her last public appearance.[76] A closer consideration of eighteenth-century epistolary novels thus reveals that our capacity for empathy is highly selective.[77]

Enlightenment theorists of empathy give us a second reason to doubt its role in expanding our fellow feeling. As they remind us, some degree of identification is a precondition for empathy (which they typically called "pity" or "sympathy"). One of Rousseau's moral maxims in *Emile* expresses this precise notion: "One pities in others only those ills from which ones does not feel oneself exempt." When the differences between us become too great, we no longer experience fellow feeling: "Why does the nobility have so great a contempt for the people? It is because a noble will never be a commoner." Rousseau ultimately deplores the limitations of empathy and denounces those who forget that "Man is the same in all stations." He even extends this universal care for humanity to "the slave [who is] mistreated."[78] But by his own logic, no European, regardless of social station, could prove capable of imagining the travails of African slaves, and thus of experiencing fellow feelings toward them. In his own oeuvre, Rousseau—that most sentimental of philosophers, author of an epistolary novel, and one of the first *philosophes* to invoke *les droits de l'homme*—certainly failed to express any concern for the rights of slaves. His chapter on slavery in *The Social Contract* (1.4) deals only with political, not civil, slavery. This "republican" understanding would often eclipse the harsher reality of plantation slavery all the way up until the French Revolution.[79]

Of course, as opposed to the American colonies, most French slaves were an ocean away from the *philosophes* who ignored them.[80] The latter, to be sure, were aware of the slaves' pitiful existence. Their knowledge has led some scholars to suggest that Enlightenment authors were writing about slavery even when they weren't explicitly doing so.[81] But there may be more straightforward explanations at hand. Ironically, it is eighteenth-century theories of empathy that may best help explain why a suffering population half a world away did not capture the *philosophes'* attention. These theories are not that different from contemporary analyses: "The sympathies which really engage us are often stubbornly limited and local," observed the ethicist Jonathan Glover.[82]

In his *Theory of Moral Sentiments* (1759), Adam Smith echoes Rousseau's argument that we are naturally inclined to pity others: "We sometimes feel for another, a passion of which he himself seems to be altogether incapable; because, when we put ourselves in his case, that passion arises in our breast from the imagination, though it does not in his from the reality."[83] As with Rousseau, however, Smith insists that we can only feel sympathy when our imagination has been excited:

> Yet it may often happen, without any defect of humanity on our part, that, so far from entering into the violence of [another's] sorrow, we should scarce conceive the first movements of concern upon his account. [ . . . ] [W]e happen to be employed about other things, and do not take time to picture out in our imagination the different circumstances of distress which must occur to him.[84]

This lack of fellow feeling was all the more common when the sufferers in question are far from sight. Hunt herself brings up Smith's famous thought experiment, in which all the inhabitants of China perished in an earthquake; Smith then invited the reader to imagine the reaction of "a man of humanity in Europe, who had no sort of connexion with that part of the world." After granting that such a man would probably feel some sadness about what happened, he suggests the man would likely next move on to ponder his own self-interest (how would this disaster affect his trade?), before simply getting on with his day: "[H]e would pursue his business or his pleasure, take his repose or his diversion, with the same ease and tranquillity, as if no such accident had happened."

Hunt focuses on a later part of this hypothetical—that this same man, if it were in his power, would not sacrifice the whole of China even if it meant saving one digit of his hand. But this conclusion is only ever-so-slightly re-demptive. The more chilling takeaway from Smith's story is the fact that, "pro-vided he never saw them, he will snore with the most profound security over the ruin of a hundred millions of his brethren."[85] Smith thus highlights an even greater barrier to empathy than Rousseau had raised—namely, physical distance.[86] *Loin des yeux, loin du cœur*—this French expression, usually ap-plied to romantic attachments, also encapsulates the challenge of feeling for "distant and different people."[87] Where the formula for empathy is concerned, distance is in the denominator.

Now, these restrictions do not mean that it was impossible to empathize with the plight of African slaves, only that it was far from inevitable. There is indeed little evidence to support the claim that rights were gradually ex-tended to a growing number of social groups on the basis of increased fellow feeling and a sentimental aesthetic. In fact, it was wholly possible to express pity for the sorry fate of African slaves without militating for their rights. We find precisely this scenario in *Candide* (1759), where the hero encounters a maimed slave in Surinam; he is so moved by the slave's story and appearance that he bursts into tears and nearly abandons his optimism. While this epi-sode produces one of the most memorable lines in the novel—"It is the price we pay for the sugar you eat in Europe"—it does not lead Voltaire to accuse Europeans of violating the human rights of slaves.[88] Instead, he mainly lays the fault for this tragic scene at the feet of the Africans who sold their own people to European slavers.

To sum up, then, the Enlightenment accent on sensibility did not translate into universal feelings of empathy, in particular for the suffering of slaves. And where such expressions of empathy are found, they do not automatically translate into the recognition of rights. Rather than explain why the *philo-sophes* ultimately came out against slavery in the name of natural and human rights, the limited scope of empathy may explain, at least in part, why it took them so long to do so. Reframing the history of abolitionism in this fashion thus begs a different question: Why *did* some Europeans come to denounce slavery as a rights violation in the late eighteenth century? As we will see, the reason may have had less to do with sentimentality than with the growing influence of social naturalism.

## 2.2.  MONTESQUIEU, SLAVERY, AND ROMAN LAW

It was indeed in the name of objective natural justice that slavery was first de-nounced in the French Enlightenment. In *The Spirit of Laws*, Montesquieu re-jected slavery as being "as opposed to civil right as to natural right."[89] Tellingly, he did not attack slavery on the grounds that it violated individual human *rights*; that version of the argument would only come later in the century. Montesquieu's claim was rather that the institution of slavery itself was un-natural ("contre la nature"; 15.7). By extension, one might deduce that every human had a singular right not to be enslaved or, more positively, a right to freedom. But these two perspectives, objective vs. subjective, were not iden-tical. First, to declare slavery unnatural was to recognize a universal moral order underpinning all the different expressions of human culture. It is in the passages on slavery in particular that one can appreciate the naturalistic foun-dations of Montesquieu's legal relativism.[90] This objective framework exceeds the more narrow affirmation of individual rights.

However, and second, framing the institution of slavery as unnatural, rather than affirming a universal right to be free, left open a loophole for Montesquieu to justify slavery under specific "natural" conditions.[91] In some climates (which just so happened to fall in the equatorial location of the French Caribbean colonies), slavery appeared less unnatural: when "the heat enervates the body and weakens the courage so much that men come to per-form an arduous duty only from fear of chastisement," then "slavery there runs less counter to reason." This argument allowed Montesquieu, conveniently, to insist on the unnaturalness of slavery in general, but on its naturalness in very particular circumstances: "[A]s all men are born equal, one must say that slavery is against nature, although in certain countries it may be founded on a natural reason."[92]

Montesquieu's opposition to slavery thus stopped short of a call for total abolition. That said, to his arguments from natural law theory, he did add a further economic rationale for abolishing slavery, even in hotter climates. Paid laborers are simply more efficient than slaves; and so, "there is no climate on earth where one could not engage freemen to work."[93] This combination of natural law theory and economics would become standard in later denuncia-tions of slavery, particularly by the Physiocrats.

While Montesquieu avows that he cannot tell whether his "spirit or [his] heart" dictated his belief in the superiority of paid laborers over slaves, his condemnation of slavery was largely unsentimental. He even draws attention to the limitations of sentimentality in an ambiguous chapter that serves up commonly held pro-slavery arguments. Some found it acceptable to enslave

Africans, he relates here, since no one felt sorry for them: "These creatures are all over black, and with such a flat nose that they can scarcely be pitied."[94] While presumably not expressing Montesquieu's own views, this passage would often be misread, notably in the American South, as a justification of the African slave trade.[95]

Montesquieu's arguments against slavery thus raise a curious question, which highlights the challenges of understanding how a philosophical tradition—natural law theory—that stretches back into antiquity could be used to bring about change in the Enlightenment. Indeed, as far back as Justinian's *Institutes*, slavery had been described as "contra naturam." In fact, Montesquieu's strongest statement about the unnaturalness of slavery ("as all men are born equal, one must say that slavery is against nature") largely translates and combines two key passages on slavery, one from the *Institutes*, the other from the *Digest*:[96]

> [I]ure enim naturali ab initio omnes homines liberi nascebantur. [ . . . ] Servitus autem est constitutio iuris gentium, qua quis dominio alieno contra naturam subicitur. (*Institutes*, 1.2–3)

> Indeed, according to natural law, all men are originally born free. [ . . . ] Slavery is only established by the law of nations, since it is against nature to be dominated by another.

> Quod attinet ad ius civile, servi pro nullis habentur: non tamen et iure naturali, quia, quod ad ius naturale attinet, omnes homines aequales sunt. (*Digest*, 50.17.32)[97]

> Where civil law is concerned, slaves are not persons; but this is not the case for natural law, since, according to the law of nature, all men are equal.

How could these age-old claims gain sudden thrust and urgency in the eighteenth century? Here we find, in a nutshell, the conundrum of natural law, which has served to legitimate such a range of different and often contradictory positions over time. To understand this specific shift, we must recall how the ancients had justified slavery. For the Romans, all men were born free, according to natural law (*Institutes*, 1.2). But human societies developed various practices and conventions over time, many of which arose through war. Taken together, these time-honored traditions coalesced into the law of nations (*ius gentium*). It was this body of law that was used to justify slavery. If military victors could kill their defeated captives, then surely enslaving them was also legitimate, as it was a less cruel fate. Hence, even though slavery was originally unlawful, it became accepted in time through the conduct of war. As the *Institutes* summarized, "Slavery is a creation of the law of nations [Servitus autem est constitutio iuris gentium]" (1.3).

This distinction between natural law and the law of nations persisted throughout the early modern period.[98] But by the eighteenth century, it was beginning to break down. In his 1724 translation, Jean Barbeyrac dismissed Grotius's claim that "the *Right of Nations* [ . . . ] derives its Authority from the Will of all, or at least of many, Nations," countering: "This Positive *Law of Nations*, distinct from the *Law of Nature*, is a mere Chimera."[99] In the *Persian Letters* (1721), Montesquieu had similarly described peace treaties between peoples as "so sacred [ . . . ] that it seems they are the voice of nature, reclaiming its rights." He went on to equate the law of nations (*le droit des gens*) as "that of reason."[100] It would be for this very reason that he rejected the Roman justification for slavery in terms of *droit des gens* in *The Spirit of Laws*.[101] By the mid-eighteenth century, this opinion was indeed becoming standard. The major Enlightenment theorist of the law of nations, Emmerich de Vattel, allowed that the application of natural law to nations could lead to "very different obligations and rights" and "cannot produce exactly the same decisions," yet still defined the law of nations as the "application" of natural law.[102] In his *Encyclopédie* entry "Droit des gens," the jurist Boucher d'Argis argued more forcefully that there was simply no difference between the two: "[O]ne must recognize that [ . . . ] natural right is identical to the law of nations, both being based on the natural light of reason."[103]

In fact, the identification between these two categories of law had been a long time coming. Boucher d'Argis pointed to Pufendorf's *Of the Laws of Nature and Nations* (1672), as evidence of their assimilation. Here Pufendorf rejects the supposition that there might be substantial differences between the two and simply defines the law of nations as the law of nature extended to different peoples.[104] Pufendorf himself attributed this line of reasoning to Hobbes, who in *De Cive* had argued that "the precepts of both are the same: but because commonwealths once instituted take on the personal qualities of men, what we call a *natural law* in speaking of the duties of individual men is called the *right of Nations*, when applied to whole commonwealths."[105] Just as the new science was revealing the existence of immutable natural laws in the physical world, it became increasingly difficult to imagine a separate set of human laws that could violate the moral laws of nature.

Reconnecting the law of nations to the law of nature did not mean that the two concepts were now wholly identical, but rather that the law of nations could no longer be understood as authorizing any actions forbidden by the law of nature. Most eighteenth-century authors accordingly used the "law of nations" to describe the laws of war, or what today we would call international law; but they no longer considered *ius gentium* as the historical corrective of *ius naturae*, as the Romans had. Once the laws of nations' distinct and independent basis in history was replaced by an unchanging, natural foundation, the well-trodden Roman claim that slavery was *contra naturam* (echoed everywhere in classical, medieval, and early modern texts) was now powerfully relevant. The Roman case for slavery was demolished, leaving only the Romans' own case for abolition.


### 2.3. SLAVERY IN THE *ENCYCLOPÉDIE*

Despite his ambiguities and reservations, Montesquieu's criticism of slavery proved highly influential throughout the Atlantic world. But abolitionism would not garner much steam for another few decades. Once again, we hit upon here the historical problem of why it took so long for the *philosophes* (but also British and American writers) to come out against slavery. Montesquieu's arguments were extremely well-known and couched in a natural law discourse familiar to all. If so many resisted the logical abolitionist conclusion of this argument (as did Montesquieu himself), it may have been in part because empathy was so hard to come by for beings not fully considered human.

As David Brion Davis has shown, another important source for later abolitionists was the *Encyclopédie*. Most historians, Davis included, have focused on the chevalier de Jaucourt's later article "Traite des nègres," which appeared in 1765.[106] But Jaucourt's earlier article "Esclavage," largely inspired by his idol Montesquieu, is also worth a closer look, as the student here already sought to surpass the shortcomings of the master. This lengthy piece, published in 1755, insisted that slavery "damages the liberty of man and that it is contrary to natural and civil law [droit naturel & civil], that it offends the structures of the best governments, and that finally it is useless in and of itself."[107] Much of this article condensed and summarized book 15 of *The Spirit of Laws*;[108] Jaucourt did not add any sentimental accounts but rather surveyed in great detail "the history of *slavery*, from its origin to our days." As in Montesquieu, no mention was made of natural rights, but slavery's incompatibility with natural law was repeatedly stressed: "[I]t was a very unusual nation, according to M. de Montesquieu, where civil law loosened natural law." Jaucourt also drew on the traditional Pauline injunction that the "principle of nature and of religion that should be deeply engraved in the hearts of all men."[109]

But Montesquieu was not the only author from whom Jaucourt borrowed in this article. He also lifted a number of passages from a 1738 judicial memoir defending the right to freedom of a slave brought to France from Saint-Domingue.[110] Written by a lawyer named Jean Mallet, the *Mémoire pour Jean Boucaux* had already deployed the language of natural law theory to denounce slavery; more importantly for Jaucourt, Mallet also laid out a historical narrative according to which slavery had been banished from France in the twelfth and thirteenth centuries.[111] One of the French kings who starred in this uplifting story was Louis X, whom Mallet claimed had abolished the seignorial privilege of mortmain. Jaucourt pursued this lead, citing the edict in question (of July 3, 1315) to even greater effect.[112] The edict, whose actual legal value was demythologized by Marc Bloch nearly a century ago, famously asserted that "according to the law of nature, everyone should be born free."[113] Jaucourt had pulled this quote from yet another work, the *Nouvel abrégé chronologique de l'histoire de France* (1744) by the *président* Charles-Jean-François Hénault, Voltaire's and Montesquieu's friend.[114]

In truth, this notorious line merely translated the well-known passage from the *Institutes* cited above. But by adding a medieval layer to Montesquieu's modern claims, Jaucourt could present the natural law argument against slavery as having demonstrated pragmatic force. The Romans had recognized the unnaturalness of slavery but accepted the practice; Louis X had appealed to its unnaturalness precisely in order to abolish it (or so it was alleged). Jaucourt further underscored the force of this claim by equating serfs and slaves: "our sovereigns, determined to weaken the lords and to free the common people from the yoke of their power, took the side of freeing the slaves [les esclaves]." If natural law had been invoked in medieval times to free slaves, it followed that it could be used again in his own day for a similar end.[115]

Despite his extensive reliance on Montesquieu, Jaucourt thus managed to come down even harder against slavery. "Nothing in the world can render *slavery* legitimate," he affirms, a line that one does not read in *The Spirit of Laws*. It is true that Jaucourt does repeat Montesquieu's infamous assertion that slavery might be acceptable in excessively warm climates, yet even when he hews closer to his master, he manages to introduce some critical distance. After raising the question, "Are there no cases or locations where *slavery* derives from the nature of things?," he starts off by answering firmly in the negative: "I respond 1) to this question, there are none." Only after this blunt assertion does he defer to Montesquieu: "I respond next, with M. de Montesquieu, that if there are countries where *slavery* appears founded on a natural cause, it is those where heat enervates the body. . . ." He goes on to paste the relevant passages from *The Spirit of Laws* (15.1, 6–7) but very clearly—and, for Jaucourt, unusually—marks out these opinions as not his own: "These last reflections are from *de l'Esprit des lois*." As we say today, retweets are not endorsements, and the overall thrust of his article was thus more abolitionist than his source had been.[116]

Where it was once viewed as a pivotal intervention in the march toward abolition, scholars have since discovered that Jaucourt's later article on the slave trade was similarly cribbed from another source, in this case George Wallace's *A System of the Principles of the Law of Scotland*.[117] Accordingly, many historians now credit Wallace with having enabled "one of the first real denunciations of the colonial project in French thought."[118] But in addition to minimizing Jaucourt's earlier entry "Esclavage," this assessment does not consider his own additions to Wallace.[119] The opening paragraph, for instance, set a thundering tone: "This purchase of Negroes to reduce them into slavery is a trade that violates all religion, morals, natural law, and the rights of human nature."[120] This line was not pulled from Wallace. While the Scottish author also challenged slavery in the name of individual rights, he did not specifically emphasize natural or even human rights.[121] That is, however, how Jaucourt now phrased the issue: "Is it legitimate to strip the human species of its most sacred rights?" he asks rhetorically, after denouncing those who accept unjust laws that legitimate slavery: "[T]his results in deciding the rights of humanity by despicable civil laws [les lois civiles d'une gouttière], as Cicero said" (a line he borrows from Montesquieu).[122]

It is not entirely wrong, then, to describe this article as providing "one of the earliest and most lucid applications to slavery of the natural rights philosophy."[123] But one can question the extent to which this reframing of abolitionism in terms of natural rights, as opposed to natural law, was really a game changer. While it is true that this distinction had left some wiggle room for Montesquieu to accommodate slavery in hotter climates, Jaucourt had already firmly condemned the practice in the name of natural law ten years earlier. The appeals to natural rights found in the 1765 article may have added a rhetorical twist of the knife, but they do not appear to have accomplished any new major conceptual work. As we saw in chapter 3, natural rights talk was more prevalent in the 1760s than it had been a decade before. The insertion of that language here may simply reflect more the discourse of the day than any new philosophy.

For intermingled with these affirmations of subjective natural rights are the usual invocations to objective concepts of natural right. The opening paragraph refers to both, as if interchangeably ("les lois naturelles, & tous les droits de la nature humaine"). Slavery continues to be denounced here as a violation of the "laws of humanity and equity." If anything, it is natural law that constitutes the fundamental bulwark against slavery, since "the law of nature [ ... ]

obligates all men in all times and places." One finds the same insistence on "the Law of Nature" and "the Laws of Humanity" in Wallace.[124] So, even if the 1765 article offers a more full-throated defense of abolitionism, it is ultimately artificial to separate out a "natural rights philosophy" from natural law theory more broadly. It was still the old Roman claim, made new in a social naturalist context, that all men were born free and slavery was unnatural, that drove the *philosophes* and their Atlantic fellow travelers to slowly push for abolition. Conversely, it was the denunciation of slavery as contrary to natural law that generated the claim that slaves had a natural right to freedom.

## 2.4. PHYSIOCRACY AND ABOLITIONISM

Even in 1765, few voices were being raised to condemn slavery. So how did abolitionism finally get off the ground? In France, one key factor was the success of Physiocracy. While critics of slavery had been making economic arguments for abolition ever since Montesquieu, the Physiocrats welded together the moral and the economic in an inseparable fashion.[125] The earliest popular example of this line of attack was Jean-François de Saint-Lambert's short tale *Ziméo* (1769).[126] Saint-Lambert was best known for his poem *Les Saisons*, which brought him much renown and celebrity in French salons. *Ziméo* was published in the same edition as this poem and proved extremely popular as well. It recounts the travails of its title character, a slave in Jamaica, and concludes with a forceful call for abolition. It is also notorious for depicting the horrors of the Middle Passage, in what was perhaps the first such description in French.

At a surface level, this tale might seem to confirm Hunt's thesis. Ziméo's story is highly melodramatic: it involves kidnapping, cannibalism, sex on a slave ship, tragic separation, furious revenge, and fortuitous reunion. The hero is no "ordinary" slave, either, but a dashing Beninese prince. These features would all seem to contribute to facilitating European fellow feeling for a star-struck, aristocratic black Apollo. But if Saint-Lambert wielded the rhetoric of empathy strategically, it was not out of sentimentality that he denounced slavery. Saint-Lambert was a Physiocrat, though commentators have tended to overlook the overwhelmingly Physiocratic tone of this story.[127] An early clue can be found in Ziméo's account of his upbringing in Benin: "I was taught the details of agriculture, the source of all our wealth" (56). Quesnay's philosophy had apparently reached the coasts of Africa in the space of a few years. But it is in the concluding "Reflections" that the author flies his Physiocratic colors. The reason why slavery is so abominable is because it violates "the principle of natural right." Tellingly, Saint-Lambert does not speak out against the violation of the individual subjective rights of African slaves, but rather argues that the institution of slavery itself is at odds with objective natural right:

> Civilized peoples, learned peoples, beware, you will only have morality, good governments and customs, when the principles of natural right are known to all men; and when you and your legislators apply them consistently in your actions and laws. (259)

This final appeal to a system of government and morals closely aligned with natural law is precisely what Quesnay had advocated in *Le droit naturel* (1765), and what Mercier de la Rivière developed in more detail in *L'ordre naturel et essentiel des sociétés politiques* (see chapter 3). While Saint-Lambert put sentiment to the service of his argument, it seems far more likely that it was these theoretical works, which had contributed to make "the principles of natural right [ ... ] *known* to all men," that led him to frame the cause of abolitionism in terms of natural law. To be sure, others had sketched these principles out before. Saint-Lambert mentions Locke, Burlamaqui, and Montesquieu by name. But he questions whether their works had gone far enough: "[E]ven in these books, are [the principles of natural right] clearly based on the common interest of all nations and all men?" This focus on *interest* points again to the Physiocratic logic of his thesis: as Dupont de Nemours would observe, in his review of Saint-Lambert's tale, slavery is a costly and inefficient method for cultivating land.[128]

There were undoubtedly other factors contributing to the success of abolitionist discourse in the name of natural human rights, but the popularity of Physiocracy seems to have played an important role, not in the least because many of the leading Enlightenment critics of slavery were associated with, or partial to, this group. They typically expressed their attacks in terms of economic benefit, but they readily spoke the language of moral outrage, as well. "[W]e will use all our natural reason and strength to destroy, if possible, the chains of a large portion of humanity," Dupont de Nemours proclaimed.[129] One finds a similar blend of economic and moral arguments in Condorcet's slightly later (1781) call for abolition.[130] Ultimately, it is impossible to fully separate out these two strands: the logic of a natural social order encompassed both. Natural laws applied to all areas of human activity, from government and economy to morals and daily conduct. The Physiocrats emphasized the economic sphere alongside the others.[131]

### 3. Conclusion

The return of rights talk in eighteenth-century France should certainly be counted among the major events in the history of French natural law theory, from the Reformation to the Revolution. But equally important as identifying the twists and turns of this history is recognizing what only changed more modestly. Throughout this period, natural law continued to serve as a foundation for moral, legal, political, and economic thought. The *philosophes* may have given new sentimental expression to this foundation, but its role in structuring society as a whole remained largely the same. Accordingly, we should not zoom in on rights talk during the Enlightenment without keeping the larger backdrop of natural law in our sights. What's more, we must be cautious not to be tricked by our own historical perspective. Before the 1780s, it is doubtful that many French readers would have even been aware of the rise in rights claims. It is only retrospectively that we can uncover this prehistory to the Declaration of Rights, and human rights more generally.

The French treatment of natural law as a legal, more than political, discourse may have been exacerbated by a tradition of absolutist political culture, but this focus was in no way a French anomaly, some sort of hereditary *légicentrisme*, as a number of French scholars have suggested.[132] Perfecting positive law had always been the *telos* of natural law theory, and this ambition was only slightly more accentuated in those territories where Roman law remained in force and offered a model for reform-minded jurisconsults. The goal of "uproot[ing] everything in a state that is contrary to natural right" (Mirabeau) was not antithetical to asserting individual subjective rights—as we saw in chapter 3, the Physiocrats eagerly stressed both. But in continental Europe, priority was always given to the first. It was simply more logical to start off by seeking to ameliorate existing laws. To proceed the other way around, and to demand the recognition of rights up front, would be viewed as an avowal of defeat and an abandonment of the belief in a "morally well-ordered universe" expressed in law.

Of course, the French Revolution began in precisely this "backward" way. The reasons for this about-turn are complex, and I examine them at greater length in chapter 7. One obvious reason why the French kicked off their legislative revolution with a declaration of rights had to do with American precedents. It is typically the contrast between the American state declarations and the Bill of Rights, on the one hand, and the French Declaration of Rights, on the other, that leads scholars to criticize the French version for its excessive *légicentrisme*. But as I argue in Part III, one should not take the Anglo-American conception of rights as the norm and the French as the exception.

If anything, it should be the other way around. If the Americans were more forceful about rights and had less faith in laws, it was for reasons having little to do with natural law theory and more with the development of English common law. It was the strange and atypical history of common law and constitutionalism in England and its colonies that led the American revolutionaries to prioritize rights. Accordingly, it is their rights-centrism that is anomalous and demands greater explanation (as I show in chapter 6).

To fully grasp the history of human rights in Enlightenment France, then, one cannot proceed as if the Declaration of Rights constituted its climax. Rather, one must approach this document as a hybrid between a homegrown French tradition, which was more in keeping with European natural law theory, and an imported American model, which owed more to English common law. In many respects, it is this Anglo-American model, with its emphasis on basic rights, rather than better laws, that has since imposed itself, in part because it was better suited to survive the positivist turn in legal thinking that followed the Age of Revolutions.[133] Emerging out of common law practices, it could shed its jusnaturalist flourishes with few consequences. And yet we should not forget that pre-revolutionary French liberalism, particularly (but not only) as formulated by the Physiocrats, was not only a rights-based economic doctrine, as many today would portray (neo)liberalism, but in fact depended on a much broader naturalistic worldview, with moral, theological, legal, and political ramifications.[134] If we forget how widespread and prevalent this vision of society was before the Revolution, we will misread the appeals to, and the understanding of, rights throughout this time. Nor should we assume that it disappeared after 1789: indeed, the shadow of this natural moral order still stretches across the Universal Declaration of 1948.[135] Its legacy is complex: if it lived on in the liberal economic theories of the twentieth century, it also played a critical intellectual role in bringing about the abolition of slavery in the Western Hemisphere.

## PART III

# Rights and Revolutions

By the time the deputies of the National Assembly were circulating and debating drafts for a declaration of rights, they had multiple examples to draw on from the newly minted United States. Benjamin Franklin and the duc de La Rochefoucauld d'Enville (himself a future member of the Assembly) had published a translation, in 1783, of the major political documents of the American Revolution, including the thirteen state constitutions or colonial charters, six of which were preceded by declarations of rights.[1] Shortly thereafter, in 1788, the revolutionary enthusiast Filippo Mazzei came out with a very popular history of the American Revolution, which dealt at length with the Virginia Declaration of Rights (included there in translation as well).[2] Some transatlantic connections were even more direct: the marquis de Lafayette began collaborating with Thomas Jefferson on drafts for a French declaration in January 1789 and would continue to consult with his American friend up through July.[3]

The great interest that the French paid to the events of the American Revolution, and in particular to their political statements, has been interpreted in a variety of ways. One approach has been to reduce the 1789 Declaration to a pale imitation of its American precedents. The foremost defender of this thesis, the German historian Georg Jellinek, asserted back in 1899, "The French Declaration of Rights is for the most part copied from the American declarations or 'bills of rights.'"[4] A contrario, the American examples raise the question of what the French Enlightenment's own contributions may have been.[5] This perspective has led other historians to focus on the differences between American and French declarations, with some French scholars expressing a certain degree of "rights envy": where the Americans asserted rights in no uncertain terms, the French tempered their claims with the higher authority of

civil laws. Accordingly, these historians have deplored the seemingly congen-
ital French mania for laws—in their words, a *légicentrisme*—that stemmed,
they suggest, from centuries of rule under a centralized, absolutist-minded
monarchy.[6]

I offer in the following two chapters a different take on the Franco-
American declarations, one that encourages us to view the rights of man and
*les droits de l'homme* less as fraternal twins than as *faux amis*. While both
nations enshrined the natural rights of liberty, property, safety (*sécurité*), and
"resistance to oppression," their understanding of the relation between these
rights and constitutional government differed greatly. In the account offered
here, the French did not abnormally cling to laws like a security blanket. Their
conception of rights was rather what one would expect from historical actors
steeped in the continental natural law tradition. It is the Americans who were
atypical, as they interpreted natural rights through the peculiar lens of English
common law and constitutionalism—a hybrid tradition I have been calling
"natural constitutionalism."[7] The French can hardly be faulted for not having
access to this politico-legal discourse and practice. All the same, this contrast
in legal systems may help explain why the French Revolution was ultimately
more vulnerable to political violence.

# Natural Constitutionalism and American Rights

When Jefferson wrote that "all men . . . are endowed by their Creator with certain unalienable Rights," and that "whenever any Form of Government becomes destructive of these ends, it is the Right of the People to alter or to abolish it, and to institute new Government," it seemed fairly clear to later historians that he was drawing on social contract and natural law theory. The fact that another line of the Declaration of Independence reproduces nearly verbatim a sentence from Locke's *Second Treatise* would appear to confirm this impression.[1] And Jefferson's text is not the only instance of Lockean influence on American authors: Elisha Williams's *The Essential Rights and Liberties of Protestants* (1744) and James Otis's *The Rights of British Colonies Asserted and Proved* (1764), to name but two famous pre-revolutionary works, both cite the *Second Treatise* at length. A long-standing historiographical tradition has accordingly credited natural law theorists, and Locke in particular, with supplying the American revolutionaries with their philosophical premises.[2]

But this reading of American rights talk has been challenged by another set of historians, who have questioned whether such philosophical premises actually existed. Instead, they suggest that the American colonists had a much more elastic notion of rights. Drawing on Villey's distinction between an objective and a subjective right, James Hutson cast doubts on the old assumption that Americans were always rights loving, pointing out that this term was employed far less pervasively than is commonly believed. Tracking the usage of rights talk up through the eighteenth century, Hutson found that it was not at all systematic, and often intermingled with more traditional English constitutional claims to liberties and privileges. On the eve of the 1760s crisis, American readers faced a "bewildering jumble of usages," such that "the concept of a right [would have been] incoherent and even incomprehensible" to many of them.[3] A similar assessment was reached by Knud Haakonssen, who concluded that "there was considerable confusion concerning the term 'natural rights'" in eighteenth-century America;[4] and by Daniel Rodgers, who chose "Natural Rights" as one of his contested concepts in American political discourse, on the grounds that "there was nothing static or consensual about the language of Natural Rights in America."[5] This reassessment of the older "liberal" interpretation of the American Revolution was also buoyed by the "republican" turn in historiography—a turn that pivoted around downplaying Locke's importance on the road to 1776.[6]

Amidst this apparent confusion about the meaning of rights, however, other historians have insisted that there was in fact one privileged lens for reading rights in eighteenth-century America. The jurist Roscoe Pound observed back in the 1930s how "one of the stabilizing factors in the formative era in America was the identification of the natural rights of man, as declared by the Continental jurists, with the immemorial common-law rights of Englishmen as declared by Coke and Blackstone."[7] This perspective on American rights talk, which also finds support in the "republican" historiography, has been particularly developed by John Phillip Reid, who argued that for the American colonists, natural rights "were not abstract rights received by the authority of nature, but specific rights, grounded in constitutional legislation."[8] The rise of a natural rights vocabulary in the 1760s, in this perspective, can be seen as strategic. Eric Slauter, for instance, noted how budding American revolutionaries "shift[ed] the rhetorical grounds of their claims from history and national legal precedent (the rights of Englishmen) to philosophy and universal nature (natural rights and the rights of man)."[9]

While these three takes on American rights talk might appear mutually exclusive, they may also describe the same reality. Eighteenth-century Americans wrote and spoke frequently about rights, sometimes invoking nature, sometimes the English constitution as their source. Different groups of historians have understandably privileged one source over the other or questioned the consistency (and highlighted the opportunism) of such talk more broadly. With few exceptions, however, historians of American rights have focused predominantly on Anglo-American texts from the 1760s and '70s, without placing this corpus within a broader chronological and geographical scope. Resituating these American examples in the longer Atlantic history of rights— including their earlier American history—can provide welcome contrasts and clear up confusions. It also points to how the different accounts of American rights talk are all, to an extent, correct. Most American authors did believe that natural rights lay at the origin of their political freedoms, yet when it came to defining these freedoms in practice, they fell back on the "liberties and privileges" of the English constitution and common law. They adhered, in sum, to the doctrine of natural constitutionalism, a political theory that had first emerged in England during the Civil War and had remained in favor among marginal Protestant groups such as the Quakers and Puritans.[10] It is not that surprising, then, that it would take root and flourish in the American colonies (even if not all Americans were conversant in it). Natural constitutionalism differed from social naturalism in that, while similarly placing government on a natural foundation, it also took on board the historical precedents that had accumulated over time within a specific constitutional tradition; and it linked rights provisions up with constitutionally mandated institutions (in particular, the justice system). In the American case, the political and legal jurisprudence that made up English common law provided a lens through which Americans interpreted the perceived natural elements in their government and, in particular, their rights.

This synthetic, perhaps more charitable, reading of American rights talk is buttressed by three comparative findings. First, the American usage of "natural rights" was not significantly vaguer than it was, say, in the French Enlightenment. The *philosophes* similarly identified *liberté, propriété,* and *sûreté* as cardinal rights, often without specifying how they should or would be protected.[11] The important point here is not to compare apples and oranges: political pamphlets, sermons, novels, and essays will not use terms with the same theoretical precision as philosophical treatises.

Despite the occasional flexibility in definitions, second, there is little evidence that "natural rights" really was a particularly contested term. Most Americans would have nodded in agreement with Otis's claim that they "had a natural right to be *free*,"[12] even if they may have entertained slightly different ideas about what freedom meant. "Natural rights" on both sides of the Atlantic were foundational rights that underpinned more specific ones. If there was some vagueness to them, it was because they were purposefully broad. In fact, American rights talk was arguably *more* consensual than its English equivalent, since Americans overwhelmingly embraced the preservation regime of rights. I was only able to identify a single author who defended the transfer regime of rights before 1765.[13] All others insisted that natural rights must be preserved in society. As we saw in chapter 2, English authors disputed this point bitterly.

Third, it is misleading to view the choice between a "liberal" and a constitutionalist reading of American rights as an either/or. To repeat, there was a long tradition, stretching back to the English Civil War, of amalgamating natural and constitutional rights. The Levellers conflated "the natural rights, freedoms and properties of the free Commoners of England (confirmed to them by Magna Charta, the Petition of Right, and the Act for the abolishment of the Star-chamber)."[14] During the Restoration, William Penn perpetuated this natural constitutionalism, arguing: "*There can be nothing more unreasonable* [ ... ] but to take away the LIBERTY and PROPERTY of any (which are natural Rights) without breaking the Law of *nature* (and not of Will and Power). [ ... ] We shall proceed to make it appear that *Magna Charta* (as recited by us) imports nothing less then [*sic*] their preservation."[15] Curiously, in his American publications, Penn downplayed the jusnaturalist dimension of his rights talk, which became almost purely constitutional.[16] But many other authors continued to view these arguments as two sides of the same coin. In an anonymous letter published by Benjamin Franklin in 1739, for instance, we read that "no Government can be legally established in any of the Plantations but on the Basis of an *English Constitution*; otherwise our natural Rights could not be preserved."[17] In other words, the Americans had no need to "*assimilate* the English constitution into the traditional natural law framework"; this assimilation had already occurred in seventeenth-century England.[18]

So how important was natural law theory, if the Americans ultimately adopted an English perspective on rights? I argue that it still played an essential role, as it allowed American authors to weave other elements of social contract theory into their constitutional arguments.[19] When it came to justifying rebellion and independence, for instance, natural law offered arguments that English constitutionalism lacked—nowhere in the Magna Carta or the 1689 Bill of Rights was it written that "a government of our own is our natural right" or that the people could "institute new Government."[20] Hence, as we will see, Otis clung dearly to the "rights of the British colonies" and colonists, but turned to Locke to justify resistance to oppression, when necessary. What's more, the fact that English liberties were perceived, first and foremost, as natural rights, also made it easier—though it was never easy—to cut the umbilical cord with Britain. The English constitution was a privileged form of government, but only so long as it did not veer into tyranny; at that point, it lost its exceptionality and could be replaced.

Most studies of American rights talk were conducted before the advent of mass book digitization and of archival databases. Today, we can explore the corpus of eighteenth-century American writing in far greater detail and depth than would have been possible a mere ten or fifteen years ago.[21] Retracing the history of natural rights across colonial texts highlights the extent to which Americans adopted a natural constitutional understanding of rights; but it also reveals how the early history of rights in America was a localized story, centered around one town: Boston.

## 1. Boston, Locke, and Natural Rights (1715–64)

In the first half of the eighteenth century, the language of natural and constitutional rights would be heard in Boston more than in any other American city.
In 1717 the Roxbury-born, Harvard-educated Reverend John Wise, who had
led the 1687 Ipswich tax rebellion against Governor Edmund Andros in the
name of the English constitution, offered an elaborate summary of Pufendorf's
arguments on natural sociability and the origins of the state.[22] While echoing
Pufendorf's insistence that "[man must] resig[n] himself with all his [natural]
Rights for the sake of a Civil State," Wise brought the preservation regime back
in, arguing that "[t]he End of all good Government is to Cultivate Humanity,
and Promote the happiness of all, and the good of every Man in all his Rights,
his Life, Liberty, Estate, Honour, without injury or abuse done to any."[23] The
emphasis in this work was clearly on natural law, though the "Great Charter of
*English Liberties*" (85) was never far from Wise's mind (a concern foregrounded
in Wise's slightly earlier work, *The Churches Quarrel Espoused*).[24] With Wise,
then, we already find the three strands of American natural constitutionalism
woven together: the older Puritan language of natural law (with typical emphasis on Romans 2:14); more recent jurisprudential sources of natural law
and natural rights theory (in this case, Pufendorf, though Locke would soon
replace him); and English constitutionalism, which had enjoyed a renaissance
in the colonies after the Glorious Revolution.[25] With varying degrees of emphasis, these strands would remain interwoven up until the Revolution; each
played a critical role in enriching American rights talk; none can be dismissed
as irrelevant or, *a contrario*, singled out as uniquely determinant.

This combination of political traditions was of course not new. What we
observe with Wise is how this discourse had already been reconstituted by
the early eighteenth century, with minor adjustments, in the American colonies—or at least in Massachusetts Bay. But it remained a distinctly English
discourse, with near-identical vocabulary and arguments used on both sides
of the Atlantic. A 1750 Boston publication neatly highlights this resemblance:
originally published a year earlier in London by an anonymous English author
(possibly the free-thinker Peter Annet), it defended "the natural and reasonable right of mankind" against tyranny, in precisely the same terms that New
England authors were pressing their own claims.[26] This similarity also helps
explain why Blackstone's *Commentaries* would be so quickly assimilated by
the American colonists (see below). Perhaps the greatest difference between
American and English versions of natural constitutionalism was that, until
Blackstone, it remained more marginal in England.

Curiously, however, this pre-1760 enthusiasm was not spread out evenly across the American colonies. Only in Boston did nearly every discussion or controversy lead authors to invoke their natural and constitutional rights. In a 1732 essay on "ecclesiastical government," the Reverend William Homes noted that "tho' every freeholder has a natural right to sit in parliament, yet they [the English] look upon it as more prudent to deligate [sic] a certain number of the most capable persons among them to manage the affairs of the government for them."[27] Other authors insisted on the inalienability of "the natural Rights of Mankind, which it is the End of all Government to preserve."[28] And they worried about tyrants who "have born down all regard to the Law of Nations, or the natural Rights and Properties of Men."[29] If they generally recognized that the English constitution uniquely safeguarded their rights, they invariably claimed that these rights preceded the establishment of government: "Every Man has a natural Right to some things in common with all Men, as being of one Blood, made and preserved by one God . . . ," wrote one author (arguing against smallpox inoculation).[30] And another: "For surely Men have a natural Right to worship God, in that Way which their own Conscience stimulate them to, as most pleasing and acceptable to Him."[31] The natural right to religious conscience would be a touchstone in the decades to come.

To be sure, Boston did not have a monopoly on natural rights talk in the early eighteenth century; in Philadelphia, Chief Justice James Logan declared in a court hearing:

> Of all the Worldly Blessings Mankind can enjoy in Society, to live under a Regular Government is certainly the greatest. It is by This alone, that every Man is secured in the Enjoyment of his Life, his Liberty, his Possessions, and of all he can account dear to him: Every of which, without This, would be constantly exposed to the Insults and Attacks of all, whose Avarice, Ambition, Lust, or Cruelty might prompt them to invade the Natural Rights of their Neighbours.[32]

Logan, who had been William Penn's secretary, was famous for his vast library, which included books by Grotius, Locke, and Hutcheson.[33] He was also a close friend of Benjamin Franklin.[34] Franklin himself would start using natural rights talk around this time, encouraging his readers in an anonymous letter against the "pretensions" of the Clergy to "heartily and unanimously join in asserting our own natural Rights and Liberties in Opposition to their unrighteous Claims."[35] But if these scattered instances of natural constitutionalism demonstrate that this political language was available to colonists elsewhere on the eastern seaboard,[36] one does not find anything in other colonies like the frequency with which such claims were made in Boston (where Franklin himself, of course, was born and bred). Which raises the question: Why Boston?

## 1.1. THE GREAT AWAKENING

A first answer is Puritanism. As we saw in previous chapters, the preservation regime of natural rights was closely intertwined with the Calvinist revolutionary tradition, first among French Huguenots, then with English Levellers, many of whom were themselves Puritans. The New England Puritans inherited a natural law tradition that had been central to these earlier political movements.[37]

A second answer may have less to do with Boston than with Cambridge. Indeed, most of the authors cited above (and below) were Harvard graduates. By at least 1723, the Harvard College Library contained many notable works on natural law, including Grotius's *De jure belli ac pacis*, Pufendorf's *De jure naturae et gentium*, and Locke's *Two Treatises*.[38] Colleges were the obvious place to learn about natural law. When Franklin published his own thoughts on education, which would soon inform the curriculum at the "Academy of Philadelphia" (later the University of Pennsylvania), he seconded Locke's proposal that students acquaint themselves with Pufendorf and Grotius in order to "be instructed in the natural Rights of Men."[39]

Boston also had many occasions in pre-revolutionary times to put natural rights talk into practice. The first major crisis that produced a spike in rights claims was the Great Awakening.[40] The rise of popular itinerant preachers (most famously, George Whitefield) led established clergymen to seek restrictions on unofficial ministering. The response by the revivalists was forceful: every man has "a natural Right of private Judgement in Matters of Religion," wrote Elisha Williams, a minister, Harvard graduate, and former rector of Yale College.[41] Williams, like his predecessors, adhered to the natural constitutional doctrine, arguing: "The Rights of *Magna Charta* depend not on the Will of the Prince or the Will of the Legislature; but they are the *inherent* natural Rights of *Englishmen*" (65). At the same time, similarly to Wise before him, he drew heavily on natural law theory, in this case on "the celebrated Mr. *Lock*" and "his *Treatise of Government*" (5).

But the Locke we encounter in this text has undergone a curious Americanization. Williams invokes him as the author who had best clarified "the natural Rights of Mankind" (5), yet he proceeds to quote from the very chapter in which Locke describes those rights we must *give up* upon entering into civil society.[42] After detailing Locke's transfer thesis, Williams then makes the crucial move, one that seeks to transform Locke into a preservation theorist.

Where Locke had been mostly silent in the *Second Treatise* on the question of whether we retained any natural rights after joining society, Williams reaches a different conclusion: "no more is parted with; and therefore *all the rest* is ours still [ . . . ] *no more natural Liberty or Power is given up than is necessary for the Preservation of Person and Property*" (6). Here we find a foreshadowing of the Ninth Amendment's logic, which Locke had not spelled out.[43] Indeed, the rest of Williams's treatise concerns those rights that we retain, most importantly the right of religious conscience, but also freedom of speech ("the *Right* that *everyone* has *to speak his sentiments openly* concerning *such Matters as affect the good of the whole*"; 6). By shifting the emphasis from what we give up to what we preserve, Williams helped turn Locke into an American-friendly theorist of natural rights.[44]

The specific rights that Williams defended were also those recognized by English constitutionalism. But this did not mean that natural law theory merely served as rhetorical window dressing for his arguments. Rather, it grounded these rights in a supra-national, universal foundation. The English constitution was exceptional, unique even, but not because it was the work of a great lawgiver, in the classical republican sense. Its uniqueness came from the fact that England alone had preserved natural liberty, at least as much of it as possible. This was another common theme in the "New Light" (i.e., pro–Great Awakening) literature. The Bostonian, Harvard-educated Reverend Ebenezer Pemberton, who welcomed Whitefield in New York City, praised "the liberties of *England*" with a jab toward "neighbouring nations": "we shall find them in subjection to lawless *tyrants*, who have establish'd their power, by invading the *natural rights* of a free people."[45] This unfavorable comparison (likely to France) had been a commonplace of English constitutional discourse as well. The introduction to Penn's *Excellent Priviledge* begins with a terrifying portrait of how "[i]n France, and other nations, the meer Will of the Prince is Law, his Word takes off any mans Head, imposeth Taxes, or seizes any mans Estate. . . ." Since the exceptionality of the English constitution derived from its preservation of natural rights, any infringement of such rights was regarded as "tyrannical." Even anti-revivalist, rationalist theologians made this same point. The Boston Reverend Charles Chauncy (also Harvard educated) lashed out against "the tyranny of inferiour offices, who may treat those under their power, as tho' they had no *natural* rights, not to say a just claim to the invaluable priviledges of *Englishmen*."[46] And his younger friend Jonathan Mayhew, who graduated from Harvard in 1744, thundered in a 1749 sermon that "all who any ways discourage freedom of inquiry and judgment in religious matters, are, so far forth as they are guilty of this, encroachers upon the natural rights of mankind."[47]

While it was in "religious matters" that New England authors were most likely to see the specter of tyranny, they also rang the alarm for political reasons. The year 1749 marked the centennial anniversary of Charles I's execution, which provided Mayhew with the topic of a notorious sermon. He offered a full-throated defense of Parliament's actions as necessary "to vindicate their natural and legal rights: to break the yoke of tyranny, and free themselves and posterity from inglorious servitude and ruin."[48] John Adams would later point to this sermon as one of the earliest expressions of "the principles and feelings which produce[d] the Revolution."[49] Indeed, the political moral of this tale was not of mere historical interest, and soon Bostonians would be denouncing tyranny themselves. But ten years before the tax crisis that precipitated the move toward independence, fears of tyranny overflowed regarding taxes on a substance more valuable than tea or stamps—liquor.

## 1.2. CONTRABAND RUM AND NATURAL RIGHTS

A 1754 Massachusetts excise bill on liquor required individual households to pay duties on wine and spirits, based on a sworn statement of what they consumed privately.[50] The bill was extremely unpopular in the coastal townships of Massachusetts, which benefited the most from alcohol smuggling. While the main source of disgruntlement was of course monetary, the provision that drew the most ire in the pamphlet literature opposing the bill concerned its execution. Tax collectors, it was alleged, would be permitted to search houses for contraband liquor. The governor of the province, William Shirley, expressed his own discomfort with this measure, in his declaration postponing its enactment: "I shall ill discharge the trust repos'd in me by his Majesty, if I should join in imposing a Burthen upon the People, which would be inconsistent with the natural Rights of every private Family in the Community."[51] This was the argument that opponents of the bill would also hammer away at. "Who would not chuse any other Way of paying the same Subsidy, than that which forces upon them perhaps at inconvenient Hours and Seasons, a *petulent Invader* against whom his natural Rights are no Security?" demanded the author of one pamphlet.[52] The Reverend Samuel Cooper warned of a "*State Inquisition*" that would extend "beyond our natural Rights."[53] And in an indication of how Bostonian natural rights talk had developed into a self-aware political tradition, the printer Daniel Fowle—who had been imprisoned for publishing another oppositional pamphlet, *The Monster of Monsters*—quoted the passage from Williams's 1744 *Essential Rights and Liberties* about "the *inherent* natural Rights of *Englishmen*" (cited above) in his own attack.[54]

The controversy over the excise bill (which would eventually be authorized, after an appeal to England, in August 1755) highlights once again the complex relation between Lockean natural law and New Englander rights talk. Fowle has been described as "in general follow[ing] John Locke in his *Appendix*."[55] In fact, there is no mention of Locke in the pamphlet, nor was I able to trace any of its multiple citations back to any of his works. Fowle's text is, by his own admission, largely a collage of quotes, most of them unattributed.[56] But nearly all of those pertaining to natural law theory come from Francis Hutcheson's *Short Introduction to Moral Philosophy* (1747).[57] Fowle in fact had little to say about natural rights per se; the expression itself only appears in the quote from Williams. While natural law provides the political foundation for his claims about "the End and Design of Civil Government," it is English constitutionalism, particularly as laid out by Edward Coke (one of the few authors to be cited by name), that concerns him most.

Locke does, however, feature prominently in the one extant pamphlet published in favor of the excise bill. Written under a pseudonym ("Rusticus") by William Fletcher, an assemblyman representing Cambridge at the General Court, *The Good of the Community Impartially Considered* carefully considered the objections to the bill and sought to rebut them.[58] Locke came up in Fletcher's justification of the government's right to tax property. The actual passage he cites is taken from the second chapter, on the state of nature (§ 6). But Fletcher follows this quote with a discussion of what occurs when we "quit *the State of Nature*"—the topic of the ninth chapter of the *Second Treatise*. He mainly paraphrases Locke's argument that "mankind" must "give up a certain Part of that Liberty, in order to enjoy themselves in Society," but, like Williams before him, Fletcher emphasizes what we preserve: "[E]very particular Society enjoy more or less of their *natural Rights*, according to their Agreement, and as they apprehend to be for their greatest Good" (32). The good of society requires that each individual "give up a certain Portion of his Property" (34). But Fletcher is at pains to insist that we retain other natural rights. When it comes to the warrantless searches by tax collectors, for instance, Fletcher adopts a position close to the one laid out by Governor Shirley and appeals to natural rights:

> I say, when this comes to be the Case, that our Dwelling-Houses are to be exposed to a Search, I hope every true Friend to Liberty will oppose it to the utmost of his Power; this would indeed be striking at the *natural rights* of Mankind, when the internal State of their Familys should come to be exposed to the View of others.[59]

Fletcher's response to this concern was simply to insist that no such powers were authorized by the bill. He thus accepts the premise that warrantless searches violate our natural rights, but argues that it does not apply in this particular instance.[60]

If Fletcher, as Williams before him, needs to "Americanize" Locke to make him more palatable to New England readers, it is difficult to claim that Locke lies at the source of American rights talk. But if this is the case, why then invoke his authority, particularly if Locke's more careful readers were aware that the *Second Treatise* did not advocate for the preservation of natural rights? For both Fletcher and Williams—and, as we will see momentarily, James Otis— Locke offered a way to step back from English constitutionalism and discuss the foundation and origins of all governments. In this regard, while his own account of rights was something of an obstacle, Locke helped the colonists frame their constitutional rights within a broader theory of government. He provided them with the concepts and vocabulary requisite for describing the formation—and re-formation—of political authority, even if, in the 1750s, this was not yet a looming problem.

### 1.3. PAYING FOR WAR AND ARGUING FOR RIGHTS: JAMES OTIS

Indeed, New Englanders not only reached for natural rights talk in moments of crisis, but also to hit more patriotic notes. This trend was on display during the Seven Years' War. Mayhew, who had defended freedom of conscience as a natural right in 1749, praised George II a decade later as "a friend of the natural rights of mankind, especially to those of his own subjects," and, after the monarch's death in 1760, as "a friend to toleration, and religious liberty; which cannot indeed be violated without violating the natural rights of mankind."[61] Another author celebrated the British victory over the French in Canada as salvation from "arbitrary Power, Popish Caprice and Superstition," which would have "deprived" the Americans of "our natural Rights, civil and religious."[62]

But the war also brought new challenges. New Englanders bristled at the requirement that they billet British soldiers, prefiguring the much greater dispute that would arise with the Quartering Act of 1765. The Massachusetts Assembly protested this point in a 1757 address to Governor Thomas Pownall, couched in the now-familiar language of natural constitutionalism:

> We beg Leave further to observe, and we doubt not your Excellency will think it a proper Occasion, That the Inhabitants of this Province are intitled to *the natural Rights of English-born Subjects*; that by the Royal Charter, the Powers and Privileges of civil Government are granted to them, that the Enjoyment

of these Rights, these Powers and Privileges, is their Support under all their Burdens and Pressures.[63]

The specific problem of quartering soldiers that winter would be resolved by the Assembly's passing their own bill authorizing this practice. A showdown between royal prerogative and provincial self-determination was thus narrowly avoided. But toward the end of the war, another issue drove a wedge between these two conflicting views of American colonial governance: taxes.

While the Sugar and Stamp Acts of 1764 and 1765 (respectively) would set the scene for the great drama of independence, a dress rehearsal of sorts was played out in Massachusetts in 1762. This conflict was notable because it saw the participation of James Otis, who would occupy a starring role in pre-revolutionary disputes. Otis first shot to provincial notoriety in 1761, when he defended a group of Boston merchants against the "writs of assistance," a type of general warrant that custom officials used to search vessels for contraband.[64] In a speech that a young and spellbound John Adams witnessed, copied down (in parts), and summarized fifty-seven years later, Otis gave "a dissertation on the rights of man in a state of nature. He asserted that every man, merely natural, was an independent sovereign, subject to no law, but the law written on his heart." But these were not only rights that men enjoyed in the state of nature: Otis further "asserted that these rights were inherent and inalienable. [ . . . ] [T]hey never could be surrendered or alienated but by idiots or madmen." Finally, English subjects were fortunate above all others because "[t]hese principles and these rights were wrought into the English constitution as fundamental laws."[65]

Whether or not Adams accurately recalled the details of this speech is, to some extent, irrelevant, as Otis would make these same claims in a series of subsequent pamphlets (including on abolitionism, a point that particularly struck Adams: "Nor were the poor negroes forgotten").[66] Adams heralded Otis's speech as marking a new departure in American colonial discourse. "Here [ . . . ] began the revolution in the principles, views, opinions, and feelings of the American people," he asserted in an 1815 letter; "American independence was then and there born," he wrote in another letter, two years later; or finally, "I shall only say, and I do say in the most solemn manner, that Mr. Otis's oration against writs of assistance breathed into this nation the breath of life."[67] To varying degrees, historians of rights have echoed his general claim that Otis introduced a language of rights and liberty that became the *lingua franca* of the colonists in the run-up to independence.[68] But in fact, none of the three fundamental tenets of Otis's speech—(1) that all men have natural rights; (2) that these rights are inalienable; and (3) that the English constitution uniquely safeguards these rights—were new. By 1761 these were all well-worn political commonplaces, at least in New England. They may have sounded original to a twenty-six-year-old John Adams, but the same natural constitutional ideas (with the exception of the abolitionist claim) had been defended by Wise, Williams, Fletcher, Mayhew, and many others before him.

Otis is nonetheless a crucial figure in this story, as he bridges the earlier New England rights tradition with the broader revolutionary-era discourse of rights. What's more, the political struggles in which Otis found himself bore a striking resemblance to the coming showdown between the colonies and Parliament. One such struggle, in 1762, revolved around the right of the Massachusetts legislature "of originating all Taxes."[69] This right had seemingly been called into question when Governor Francis Bernard equipped a warship without first appropriating the requisite funds.[70] Writing for the House, Otis issued a stern remonstrance, which included the daring statement: "[I]t would be of little consequence to the people whether they were subject to George or Lewis, the King of Great Britain or the French King, if both were arbitrary, as both would be if both could levy Taxes without Parliament" (15). This line infuriated Bernard, who responded that "the King's name, dignity, and cause, are so improperly treated" (16) in the remonstrance, that the offending comparison should be expunged. It was, but Otis justified its initial inclusion in *A Vindication of the Conduct of the House of Representatives of the Province of Massachusetts-Bay* (1762). After laying out the facts and documents in the case, Otis proceeded to argue from natural law theory why the right to originate all taxes could only lie in the legislature.

To back up his arguments, including the premise that "God made all men naturally equal" (17–18), Otis included passages from Locke's *Second Treatise* in a long footnote that ran across four pages.[71] Most notable about his usage of Locke was, first, that it included the famous passage in chapter 14 ("Of Prerogative") on the "appeal to heaven," when the legislature and executive were at odds ("The people have no other remedy in this, as in all other cases where they have no judge on earth, but to appeal to heaven"; qtd. 19). The specter of revolution here reared its angry head; Otis had "weaponized" rights talk, as had happened during earlier political struggles (see chapter 2).

A second feature of Otis's Locke is that he was both Americanized and Anglicized. He was Americanized, since Otis, as Williams and other New Englanders had before him, turned Locke into a preservationist. Otis did so, not through a creative reading of chapter 9, but simply by quoting the preface of the *Two Treatises*, which celebrated William for protecting "the people of England" and "their just and natural rights, with their resolution to preserve them . . ." (qtd. 20). As we saw in chapter 2, this was one of the few places where Locke did endorse a preservation regime of rights. Otis thus played on an existing ambiguity in the Lockean theory of rights to present him as their staunch defender. At the same time, and again very much in line with his predecessors, he Anglicized Locke by fusing his natural law theory with English constitutionalism. The "two or three data" advanced by Otis to justify his position segue seamlessly from natural law principles to the statement that "[t]he British constitution of government as now established in his Majesty's person and family, is the wisest and best in the world" (17, 20). Otis thus placed natural constitutionalism on a more robust jusnaturalist foundation, while remaining a devotee of "the rights of the British Colonies" (the title of his later pamphlet). This dual allegiance—which he clearly viewed as complementary and unified—allowed him to conclude this pamphlet by swearing that "the Liberty of his country, and the Rights of mankind, he will ever vindicate to the utmost of his capacity and power" (53).

When the Sugar Act lurched the colonies into full-blown constitutional crisis, Otis had a ready-made arsenal of arguments and references to draw on. His famous pamphlet on *The Rights of the British Colonies Asserted and Proved* (1764) systematized the claims he had already leveled against the colonial administration, but now redirected them toward the British Parliament. All the usual ingredients of New England natural constitutionalism were thrown in:

1. The philosophical premise of his dissertation was that political and moral conduct should be guided and evaluated by means of a universal natural law, authored by God, and the source of all pre-political rights: "There can be no prescription old enough to supersede the law of nature, and the grant of almighty; who has given to all men a natural right to be *free*, and they have it ordinarily in their power to make themselves so, if they please."[72] We can recognize in this premise the philosophical foundation common to both the Catholic/neo-Stoic and Calvinist/Puritan traditions.

2. As before, Locke serves as Otis's touchstone for questions of natural law; and as before, Otis highlights the more revolutionary passages in Locke, namely, those dealing with the people's right of resistance.[73] But he also exhibits familiarity with contemporary Enlightenment authors such as Emmerich de Vattel, the marquis d'Argenson, and Rousseau, even echoing Rousseau's disdain for Grotius and Pufendorf.[74] In keeping with this Enlightenment spirit, Otis extends some of these natural law principles to their more daring conclusions, challenging slavery and gender inequality: "Is not every man born as free by nature as his father? Has he not the same natural right to think and act and contract for himself? Is it possible for a man to have a natural right to make a slave of himself or of his posterity? [ . . . ] Are not women born as free as men?" (4).

3. But Otis's general commitment to natural constitutionalism stayed unchanged. English common law still provided the surest ground of liberty:
"The common law is received and practiced upon here, and in the rest of
the colonies; and all antient and modern acts of parliament that can be
considered as part of, or in amendment of the common law, together with
all such acts of parliament as expressly name the plantations; so that the
power of the British parliament is held as sacred and as uncontroulable in
the colonies as in England" (71–72). The ties between natural rights and
English liberties were unbreakable, as the latter merely codified the former:
"In order to form an idea of the natural rights of the Colonists, I presume
it will be granted that they are men, the common children of the same
Creator with their brethren of Great-Britain" (28).

Looking back on Otis's speeches and pamphlets some forty years after
the Declaration of Independence, John Adams would claim that not only the
American revolutionary declarations, but also "all the French constitutions of
government" and the most notorious pamphlets of that age—"Mr. Thomas
Paine's *Common Sense, Crisis,* and *Rights of Man*"—were all prefigured by
this Boston lawyer. There is more to this thesis than a fellow New Englander's
boast: Otis's pamphlet was very widely read, both in the American colonies
and in England (it was reprinted in London); and Boston did, after all, lead the
way in protesting Parliament's new taxes and, later, in outright rebellion.[75] But
for Adams to be right, Otis would have to have been the only author voicing
these principles. And by the 1760s there was another, even more influential
source for natural constitutionalism: Sir William Blackstone.

## 2. Blackstone and English Common Law

The striking similarities between natural constitutionalism, as it had been developed by New Englanders in the early eighteenth century, and the political
and legal theory of Sir William Blackstone was observed by none other than
Otis himself. "Blackstone's Commentaries would have saved [me] seven years'
labor," he complained to his brother.[76] Otis was one of the first American
authors to quote Blackstone in print, citing an earlier work, *An Analysis of
the Laws of England* (1756), in his *Vindication of the British Colonies*.[77] Otis
would not be the only one to lean on Blackstone to support his claims: Samuel
Adams, John Dickinson, and Alexander Hamilton all read and praised "the
judicious Blackstone" (as Hamilton dubbed him). Others, such as Thomas
Jefferson and James Wilson, criticized aspects of his work, but still appreciated
and recognized its descriptive value.[78] The contributions of Blackstone to the

cause of American independence have indeed long been recognized: already in 1775, Edmund Burke remarked, "I hear that they have sold nearly as many of Blackstone's *Commentaries* in America as in England."[79]

If the *Commentaries* enjoyed such success on both sides of the Atlantic, it was for different reasons. At the time they were published, natural constitutionalism had become a very marginal political theory in England. It did not feature at all, for instance, in the Wilkesite reform movement, which drew inspiration instead from the 1689 Bill of Rights.[80] The belief that the "rights of Englishmen" were also "natural rights" had largely faded from view in mid-eighteenth-century England. Tellingly, it was only faintly present in Blackstone's first codification of his Oxford lectures, *An Analysis of the Laws of England*. One of the central concepts of his account here was the "absolute rights [ . . . ] [of] Englishmen." This was not a common term in English political thought, but Blackstone did not yet identify them with "natural rights."[81] He defined them as "consist[ing] in Political or Civil LIBERTY," which he in turn glosses as "the natural Liberty of Mankind."[82] But the *Analysis* draws very little on natural law theory: if he mentions "natural law" or the "law of nature" on a few occasions, it is mainly in the Roman spirit of distinguishing between natural law, civil law, and the law of nations.[83] Indeed, both the *Analysis* and the *Commentaries* belong to the long line of legal treatises seeking to apply the clear principles of Roman law to the murky perplexity of common law.[84]

But the decade in which Blackstone published his *Analysis* also witnessed a resurgence in natural law theory: major works by Burlamaqui, Rousseau, Hutcheson, and Vattel all came out to international acclaim. As Blackstone settled into the academic profession, becoming Vinerian Professor of Common Law at Oxford in 1758, he, too, sought to express his legal thought in the political language du jour.[85] When volume 1 of the *Commentaries* appeared in November 1765, it bristled with overwhelmingly positive references to Locke's *Second Treatise*, Grotius's *De jure belli ac pacis*, and Pufendorf's *De jure naturae et gentium*.[86] These were not exactly cutting-edge authors in the 1760s, and Blackstone does not cite any of the more recent work on natural law, with the partial exception of Montesquieu.[87] Indeed, judging by citation volume alone, Blackstone remained more indebted to Roman jurisconsults (Cicero in chief) and the *Corpus juris civilis* than to any modern authors. But the net result was the same. The claims about "absolute rights" made in the *Analysis* now received the imprimatur of natural law. These rights, Blackstone argued in the *Commentaries*, are "those which are so in their primary and strictest sense; such as would belong to their persons merely in a state of nature, and which every man is intitled [*sic*] to enjoy *whether out of society or in it*."[88] By reformulating his theory of rights in a natural law framework, Blackstone emerged as a fierce defender of the preservation regime: "[T]he principal aim of society is to protect individuals in the enjoyment of those absolute rights, which were vested in them by the immutable laws of nature. [ . . . ] [T]he first and primary end of human laws is to maintain and regulate these *absolute* rights of individuals."[89] American politicians would soon be enshrining these very principles in official declarations.

While it is easy to comprehend why American authors would have readily approved such passages, there is an element of irony to this meeting of minds. What we find with Blackstone is not so much the retransmission of a natural constitutional doctrine, passed down from religious dissenters of old. Rather, we are witnessing its reconstitution in a wholly different context, by an author with entirely different political (Tory) and religious (Anglican) sympathies. If Blackstone could reassert, with such forceful language, the credo of natural constitutionalism, it could only be because its older associations with marginal religious groups had, in 1760s England, been obscured. They had not completely disappeared: the rational dissenter Joseph Priestley would soon tussle with Blackstone about the natural rights of religious conscience in a series of letters, and would himself revive this political discourse in the 1770s.[90] But Blackstone's situation was ultimately similar to Quesnay's in France: both formulated theories of natural rights with radical implications precisely because those implications were so far from their minds.

Unlike the Physiocrats, however, Blackstone brought rights into sharp constitutional focus. Though he insisted that governments should, above all, seek to preserve our natural rights, not all succeeded or even sought to do so: "These [rights] therefore were formerly, either by inheritance or purchase, the rights of all mankind; but, in most other countries of the world being now more or less debased and destroyed, they at present may be said to remain, in a peculiar and emphatic manner, the rights of the people of England."[91] This nationalist account of the English constitution was hardly original, even if Blackstone could now harness the authority of a "learned French author" (i.e., Montesquieu) who had recently declared "that the English is the only nation in the world, where political or civil liberty is the direct end of it's [sic] constitution."[92] The particular rights that Blackstone singled out were also familiar: "personal security, personal liberty, and [ . . . ] private property." What made his retelling more significant and original was the role he granted to the English legal system and the common law more broadly. In addition to the specific role of the English Parliament and to the limits on royal prerogative, Blackstone singled out the "right of every Englishman [ . . . ] of applying to the courts of justice for redress of injuries" as one of the constitutional safeguards of English rights.[93] This right to judicial appeal also extended to judicial forms: "Not only the substantial part, or judicial decisions, of the law, but also the formal part, or method of proceeding, cannot be altered but by parliament." Books 2–4 of the *Commentaries* were dedicated to such judicial matters;[94] only the first book dealt with the political structure of the English constitution. With Blackstone, accordingly, English common law became the essential bulwark against the loss of natural rights: "[T]o vindicate [their] rights, when actually violated or attacked, the subjects of England are entitled, in the first place, to the regular administration and free course of justice in the courts of law."[95] While always implicit in earlier American defenses of natural constitutionalism, this judicial component would grow increasingly central in the aftermath of independence. As the Americans lost faith in the other constitutional safeguards provided by Blackstone—Parliament and limited royal sovereignty—they held on ever tighter to this common law tradition.

But it would be a mistake to view Blackstone's role in this story as redirecting English rights from a natural to a constitutional basis. Natural law not only featured on the distant historical horizon of the English constitution. It remained an active legal principle, to which Blackstone would refer repeatedly, particularly in his examination of property. Indeed, the foundation of property, for Blackstone, lay in first occupancy: "[B]y the law of nature and reason, he who first began to use it, acquired therein a kind of transient property," which "industry, art, and labor" made permanent.[96] While arable land is rapidly divvied up, thus necessitating civil laws to regulate the transmission of property, some physical objects always remain under the rule of natural law: for instance, "water is a moveable, wandering thing, and must continue common by the law of nature."[97] Likewise, hunting wild animals remained in most cases a "natural right."[98]

As important as water and hunting rights would be for American colonists, however, there was another element of natural law that they would soon cling to far more fervently. Once English subjects had exhausted all other forms of redress, including "the right of petitioning the king, or either house of parliament," there remained, according to Blackstone, one "last auxiliary right of the subject," namely "that of having arms for their defence, suitable to their condition and degree, and such as are allowed by law." Blackstone's source here was the 1689 Bill of Rights, which indeed stated that "the subjects which are protestants, may have arms for their defence suitable to their conditions, and as allowed by law." But Blackstone interpreted this statute in a more radical, Lockean vein, as "a public allowance, under due restrictions, of *the natural right of resistance and self-preservation*, when the sanctions of society and laws are found insufficient to restrain the violence of oppression."[99] This is certainly not what the "right to bear arms" had been intended to mean in 1689, when popular resistance to James II was expressly denied as a cause of revolution.[100] The theme of "resistance" had also been missing from Blackstone's earlier *Analysis*; as the language used in the *Commentaries* suggests, it most likely came from his reading of Locke's *Second Treatise*.[101]

This hypothesis finds further confirmation in a subsequent discussion of resistance, where Blackstone distinguishes between "the *ordinary* course of law" and "those *extraordinary* recourses to first principles, which are necessary when the contracts of society are in danger of dissolution, and the law proves too weak a defence against the violence of fraud or oppression." In these "extraordinary" situations, "resistance is justifiable to the person of the prince" if and only if "the being of the state is endangered, and the public voice proclaims such resistance necessary."[102] Blackstone follows this assertion with a reference to Locke on the purpose—and dangers—of royal prerogative, citing a paragraph where Locke considered the instances when improper use of prerogative led to "public disorders, before the people could recover their original right, and get that to be declared not to be prerogative, which truly was never so."[103] As Blackstone's own comments on resistance similarly arose in the context of "those branches of royal prerogative," and as he, too, insisted that legitimate resistance can only occur if it has broad public support, his indebtedness to Locke on this topic appears convincing.

The *Commentaries* thus present a very similar combination of political and legal traditions as we found in the earlier New England pamphlets (though this similarity is not an indication of influence). They all ground civil rights in natural law, which they also draw on to defend a revolutionary doctrine of legitimate resistance, if and when widespread violations of rights occur. Despite Locke's own adherence to the transfer regime of rights, he nonetheless features in these works as the primary theorist of revolution. Barring such extreme measures, rights are otherwise defended and defined through the historical process that produced constitutionalism and common law. One accordingly finds in natural constitutionalism a mixture of political and judicial traditions, a characteristic that would persist in the American declarations of rights. For Blackstone, the political uniqueness of the English constitution took symbolic precedence over its judicial system, but in practice the *Commentaries on the Laws of England* lived up to their title and dwelt more lengthily on legal matters. Soon the Americans would discover that these two entwined pieces could be pulled apart, and the common law extracted from its constitutional setting. But they would retain this combination of natural and common law justification and interpretation of rights.

## 3. Natural Rights and Revolution

The year that volume 1 of Blackstone's *Commentaries* was published also saw the passage of the infamous Stamp Act (1765). This piece of legislation elicited massive opposition throughout the American colonies and spurred the colonists to develop a shared political consciousness and to adopt similar arguments, which would largely be drawn from natural constitutionalism.[104] To some extent, the Stamp Act was an occasion for "the peculiarly New England view of American origins [to] spread to the colonies as a whole, entering deeply into the formation of American nationality."[105] Regardless of where this liberal doctrine originated, by the late 1760s it would become the American language of political resistance par excellence. In an oft-reprinted and much-admired pamphlet, Daniel Dulany, then mayor of Annapolis, deplored how "British Americans" could soon "be reduced to the unhappy necessity of giving up their natural rights, and their civil privileges."[106] This same equation of natural and civil rights was echoed up and down the eastern seaboard. In Virginia, Thomas Jefferson's older cousin Richard Bland hammered away on this theme in *An Inquiry into the Rights of the British Colonies* (1766). "Great is the Power of Parliament," he observed, "but, great as it is, it cannot, constitutionally, deprive the People of their *natural* Rights; nor, in Virtue of the same Principles, can it deprive them of their civil Rights, which are founded in Compact, without their own Consent."[107] Even after the Stamp Act was repealed (in 1766), writers continued to drive this point home: the pastor John Joachim Zubly (a Swiss immigrant) insisted in South Carolina that "[n]o tax can be laid, or revenue be raised, on the *Americans*, but where they are represented, and in a manner which they think consistent with the natural rights as men, and with their civil and constitutional liberties as *Britons*."[108] The great circulation of pamphlets and newspapers in the aftermath of the Stamp Act buttressed public opinion and provided a common language of resistance.[109]

The adoption of natural constitutionalism to counter the crown's revenue-exacting efforts was also evident in the provincial assemblies, where it slowly entered the official genre of declarations.[110] It did not take hold immediately: the Virginia resolutions put forward by Patrick Henry (in May 1765) did not appeal to natural rights, but were grounded solely in English constitutionalism. The same was true for the Rhode Island and Connecticut resolves.[111] But in Pennsylvania, the House of Representatives reminded George III that "[t]he Inhabitants of his Province are entitled to all the Liberties, Rights and Privileges of His Majesty's Subjects in *Great-Britain*, or elsewhere, and that the Constitution of Government in this Province is founded on the natural Rights of Mankind, and the noble Principles of *English* Liberty, and therefore is, or ought to be perfectly free."[112] British officials noticed this claim, with William Knox singling it out for criticism: "[T]hat *the natural rights of mankind* should give any people a right to all the liberties and privileges of Englishmen, is, I believe, a doctrine unknown to all civilians, except the assembly of Pennsylvania."[113] But other assemblies came to the same conclusion: unsurprisingly, the Massachusetts House of Representatives passed a near-identical resolution, asserting that "there are certain essential rights of the British Constitution of government, which are founded in the law of God and nature, and are the common rights of mankind," and that "the inhabitants of this Province are unalienably entitled to those essential rights in common with all men." Accordingly, "imposing taxes on the inhabitants, are infringements of our inherent and unalienable rights as men and British subjects."[114] James Otis would bring some of this New England spirit to the Stamp Act Congress in New York, whose Declaration of Rights and Grievances (October 1765) demanded that Parliament "respec[t] the most Essential Rights and Liberties of the colonists."[115] Following the Townshend Acts (1767–68), and in response to the Massachusetts circular letter of February 1768, the Virginians framed their opposition in these terms as well: the House of Burgess sent their own circular letter (dated May 9, 1768, and signed by the Speaker Peyton Randolph, cousin to both Bland and Jefferson) to other colonial assemblies, in which they stated that they "do not aspire to more than the natural Rights of British Subjects."[116]

It is hard to argue that natural rights, in these documents, were a contested concept. There was, on the contrary, no disagreement among American authors and politicians that natural rights entailed all men (and British subjects more particularly) to preserve their property, unless they had agreed to part with some portion of it. The only voices contesting this claim came from the British government. In Massachusetts, a fascinating exchange took place between Governor Thomas Hutchinson and the Assembly on this very question. In a speech delivered on January 6, 1773, Hutchinson cut straight to the heart of the New England rights regime, challenging its core assumption that we can preserve our natural rights in society:

> They who claim Exemption [from acts of Parliament], should consider that every Restraint which Men are laid under by a State of Government is a Privation of Part of their natural rights, and of all the different Forms of Government which exist, there can be no two of them in which the Departure from Natural Rights is exactly the same.

Having established (in accordance with the abridgment regime) that natural rights cannot be preserved in any form of government, Hutchinson went further, countering the very line of attack that the colonists had been repeating

for the past eight years: no taxation without representation. But just what did
they expect to achieve with representation, he asked.

> Even in Case of Representations by Election, do they not give up Part of their
> natural Rights when they consent to be represented by such Person as shall be
> chosen by the Majority of the Electors, although their own Voices may be for
> some other Person? And is it not contrary to their natural Rights to be obliged
> to submit to a Representative for seven Years, or even one Year, after they are
> dissatisfied with his Conduct?[117]

This was a smart and forceful counter-offensive that tried to upend the logic
of American resistance. Hutchinson essentially made the same point, if in a
more favorable light, as Rousseau had in *The Social Contract*—that the English
are only free on the day they go to the polls.[118] But instead of serving to criticize political representation, as it did for Rousseau, this observation allowed
Hutchinson to deny the possibility of a full-blown preservation regime of
rights. In any system of representative government, individual citizens had to
"give up" some of their political rights to let others act on their behalf.

The Assembly countered this objection by means of the argument that
their New England predecessors had honed vis-à-vis Locke. They granted that
entry into political society entailed the loss of *some* rights, but that these were
only given up in order to retain other, more essential ones:

> It is true, that every Restraint of Government is a Privation of natural Right.
> [ ... ] But as they arise from the Nature of Society and Government; and as
> Government is necessary *to secure other natural Rights infinitely more valuable,*
> they cannot therefore be considered as an Objection either "against a State of
> Government" ... Life, Liberty, Property, and the Disposal of that Property with
> our own Consent, are natural Rights. [ ... ] The Preservation of these Rights
> is the great End of Government.[119]

The Assembly thus found a way to shift the emphasis from abridgment back
to preservation. Hutchison could well point out, in a further rebuttal, that
their attempts to "distinguis[h] some natural Rights as more peculiarly exempt
from [sovereign] Authority than the rest, rather tend to evince the Impracti-
cability of drawing such a Line. . . ."[120] But the New England rights regime was
impressively impervious to such critiques. Indirectly, the Americans may have
had Locke to thank for its robustness: precisely because he himself was not a
preservationist, his American readers had learned to recast the "giving up" of
some secondary rights (such as the "executive" right of punishing) as a mere
technicality for securing the rest.

The debate between Hutchinson and the Massachusetts Assembly highlights the real theoretical importance of natural law theory in the run-up to the revolution. To be sure, defending natural rights would not necessarily translate into endorsing independence: Dulany, for instance, ended up a Loyalist.[121] But the basic argument that animated the colonial opposition from 1765 onward—"no taxation without representation"—depended on natural law theory to be persuasive. Indeed, this was not a claim that flowed from English constitutionalism. The 1689 Bill of Rights insisted that "levying money for or to the use of the Crown by pretence of prerogative, *without grant of Parliament*, for longer time, or in other manner than the same is or shall be granted, is illegal" (emphasis added). On the face of things, neither the Stamp Act nor the Townshend Acts contravened this principle: both were approved by Parliament. Indeed, Parliament even reminded the American colonists of this principle in the Declaratory Act of 1766, which reasserted the "full power and authority" of Parliament "to bind the colonies and people of *America* [ . . . ] in all cases whatsoever."[122] Now, Parliament had originally acquired such power because it was itself a representative body; the power to "levy money for the Crown" was thus at least indirectly based on a principle of representation. But British officials argued that this representation was only "virtual": not everyone had a vote in parliamentary elections, yet they still had to pay their taxes.[123] Some in Britain (most famously, Edmund Burke) challenged this idea of representation, yet it proved difficult to dislodge on constitutional grounds alone.

From a natural law and social contract perspective, however, a clearer case could be made against virtual representation. If property was acknowledged as a personal, natural right, then "the Disposal of [ . . . ] Property with our own Consent" had to be one as well. The right of levying taxes could thus only come from the *individual* acceptance by each and every member of society; or, as Otis wrote in 1764, "the supreme power cannot take from any man any part of his property, *without his consent* in person, or by representation" (note the use here of the third-person singular). The same argument formed the crux of the influential Massachusetts circular letter of February 11, 1768, penned by Otis and Samuel Adams:

> [I]t is an essential, unalterable right, in nature, engrafted into the British constitution, as a fundamental law, and ever held sacred and irrevocable by the subjects within the realm, that what a man has honestly acquired is absolutely his own, which he may freely give, but cannot be taken from him without his consent.[124]

In this social contract narrative, every single individual (including, for Otis, women) had to consent to share sovereignty. Virtual representation, on the

British model, was not a legitimate solution.[125] Viewed through the lens of natural rights, the British imperialist defense of parliamentary representation seemed a sham.

Natural law theory thus made a crucial contribution to the colonists' criticism of Parliament and helped push the colonies toward war and independence. But the old liberal doctrine that credits this contribution to Locke is flawed, as well. Locke was certainly important for the colonists; he was often cited as an authority (particularly in New England) and offered the most sophisticated theory of legitimate resistance. While it's true that Loyalists also referred to Locke, they typically did so *because* he was so strongly associated with the patriot cause. As William Knox observed, he rested his own counter-arguments to the colonists' claims on Locke's authority, because "his opinions in this [second] treatise have been principally relied on as the foundation of many extravagant and absurd propositions which he never meant to encourage."[126] But if Loyalists could use Locke in this fashion, it was because Locke's views on rights did not align with those of his New England, and later American, readers. In this respect, Locke cannot accurately be described as a source of American natural rights theory. His own thoughts on rights had to be tweaked and revised in order to make him a fitting authority.

### 4. Declaring Rights: From Natural Law Back to English Common Law

Natural law theory was rarely wielded in isolation in the American objections to British taxation and was almost always encased within the traditions and practices of English constitutionalism and common law. In this regard, Blackstone was more representative of American rights thinking than Locke. But while natural and constitutional law were not perceived as distinct entities, in practice they tended to separate. This distillation is particularly visible in the declarations that the Continental Congress, and the states themselves, passed from 1774 onward.

The Declaration and Resolves of the First Continental Congress, issued on October 14, 1774, set the pattern that subsequent declarations would follow.[127] After laying out a series of grievances, Congress asserted that "the inhabitants of the English colonies in North-America, by the immutable laws of nature, the principles of the English constitution, and the several charters or compacts, have the following RIGHTS." Here we find a typical formulation of natural constitutionalism, in which the natural and constitutional sources of authority are simply juxtaposed. But the list of resolves pulls these twin sources apart. The first resolve—"That they are entitled to life, liberty and property: and they have never ceded to any foreign power whatever, a right to dispose of either without their consent"—draws only from natural law: these are not specific rights of English subjects, but universal rights of all individuals. The specificity of English subjects becomes clear in the second resolve, which explicitly introduces constitutional rights: "That our ancestors, who first settled these colonies, were at the time of their emigration from the mother country, entitled to all the rights, liberties, and immunities of free and natural-born subjects, within the realm of England."

In the subsequent resolves, natural and constitutional rights are on occasion mixed (see, e.g., "the foundation of English liberty, *and of all free government*, is a right in the people to participate in their legislative council"; emphasis added). But most of the other rights affirmed in the declaration stem distinctly and uniquely from English constitutionalism and common law. This attachment to the common law en bloc is underscored in the fifth resolve: "That the respective colonies are entitled to the common law of England, and more especially to the great and inestimable privilege of being tried by their peers of the vicinage, according to the course of that law." Even the wording of the declaration draws on the English constitutional tradition: the ninth resolve—"That the keeping a standing army in these colonies, in times of peace, without the consent of the legislature of that colony, in which such army is kept, is against law"—echoes the 1689 Bill of Rights ("raising and keeping a standing army within this kingdom in time of peace without consent of Parliament, and quartering soldiers [is] contrary to law").

The pattern that the 1774 Declaration put into place, then, is both temporal and categorical. Rights drawn from natural law come first, both in a historical sense and in the structure of the declaration. But these rights are also categorically distinct from those derived from the constitution and common law. Natural rights are primarily political; they are used to define and judge "free government." Constitutional rights tend to be more civil and procedural; they concern such rights as a trial by jury ("being tried by their peers of the vicinage") or the "right peaceably to assemble, consider of their grievances, and petition the king" (eighth resolve).

Even after the Second Continental Congress declared independence, this pattern of asserting political/natural rights first, and procedural/English constitutional rights second, persisted. Though its style differed significantly from the other declarations of its day, the Declaration of Independence followed suit: the famous second paragraph lists the natural, political rights necessary to institute good government; but the long list of grievances insists on the constitutional rights that George III violated. These include "[keeping] among us, in times of peace, Standing Armies without the Consent of our legislatures," "quartering large bodies of armed troops among us," and "depriving

us in many cases, of the benefits of Trial by Jury." The document with which
the American colonies overthrew English rule still managed to find room to
celebrate "the free System of English Laws."

After independence, the new state declarations would attempt a delicate
operation: to surgically extract English common law from the English imperial constitution. Natural rights provided the scalpel for this maneuver: it was
in the lofty terms of natural law that the states asserted their independence.
The Virginia Declaration of Rights, drafted by George Mason and adopted
June 12, 1776, began with a ringing endorsement of the preservation regime:
"That all men are by nature equally free and independent, and have certain
inherent rights, of which, when they enter into a state of society, they cannot,
by any compact, deprive or divest their posterity." It then detailed these "inherent rights," which were the natural entitlements of all men, and not just of
(former) British subjects: "the enjoyment of life and liberty, with the means
of acquiring and possessing property, and pursuing and obtaining happiness
and safety." This list would prove greatly influential, both for the other state
declarations, as well as for the Declaration of Independence itself.[128] Pennsylvania, Vermont (which declared statehood in 1777), and Massachusetts
followed Virginia's lead in singling out these same rights in their opening
articles; Delaware, Maryland, and North Carolina departed from this norm
by insisting instead that "all government of right originates from the people"
(Delaware, Maryland; Virginia placed this right in its second article). In both
cases, however, natural rights served to establish the political foundations
of government and, implicitly, to further justify independence from Great
Britain.

Once these natural foundations had been laid, the declarations then pivoted to their secondary, yet equally essential objective, retaining "the free
System of English Laws." Some declarations took a blunt approach to this
endeavor, simply importing this system wholesale. For instance, the Maryland
Declaration unambiguously announced:

> That the inhabitants of Maryland are entitled to the common law of England,
> and the trial by Jury, according to the course of that law, and to the benefit
> of such of the English statutes, as existed at the time of their first emigration,
> [ . . . ] and of such others as have been since made in England, or Great Britain,
> and have been introduced, used and practiced by the courts of law or equity.[129]

As this passage highlights, what the Americans wished to preserve above all
were the common law rules of criminal procedure, chief amongst which was
the trial by jury.[130] American revolutionaries could wax lyrical over this right.
The Delaware Declaration affirmed, "[T]rial by jury of facts where they arise

is one of the greatest securities of the lives, liberties and estates of the people"
(§ 13). Similarly lofty language filled the North Carolina Declaration: "[I]n all
controversies at law, respecting property, the ancient mode of trial, by jury,
is one of the best securities of the rights of the people, and ought to remain
sacred and inviolable" (§ 14). Indeed, every state declaration secured this right
by name.[131]

The American obsession with juries was not surprising: the 1689 Bill of
Rights had enshrined the trial by jury as an essential right of Englishmen
(art. 11); and Blackstone had described the trial by jury as "the principal
bulwark of our liberties" and "a privilege of the highest and most beneficial
nature."[132] More generally, however, the importance granted to juries points to
the way in which Americans understood liberty (a natural right) to depend
on the justice system (and common law). This, too, had been Blackstone's
argument: "Since the law is in England the supreme arbiter of every man's
life, liberty, and property [the three natural rights], courts of justice must at
all times be open to the subject, and the law be duly administered therein."[133]
At a more practical level, the Americans had recently experienced the loss
of this right: the vice-admiralty courts, established during the crisis, passed
down judgments without a jury, thus strengthening American attachment to
them even more.[134]

While trial by jury was the centerpiece of this system, it was not the only
part. The state declarations overflowed with other criminal procedural rights,
again all taken from English common law. They forbade warrantless searches;[135]
they came down against excessive bail;[136] and they insisted on the quintessen-
tial English right of *habeas corpus*.[137] Even the refrain against retrospective
laws expressed a judicial concern.[138]

Once the Americans had finished the messy business of severing ties with
England, then, they scrambled to regain the legal benefits of their old association. Their argumentative two-step can come across as schizophrenic:
Gordon Wood has described the state declarations as "a jarring but exciting
combination of ringing declarations of universal principles with a motley collection of common law procedures."[139] But there was a logic to this apparent
jumble of rights: the logic of natural constitutionalism. The juxtaposition of
natural law and English constitutionalism, which had characterized so many
pre-revolutionary claims, was now drawn out over separate articles, lend-
ing the appearance of distinct traditions. But the declaration genre, and the
political necessities caused by independence, merely pulled apart the common
thread uniting the two. Americans, and particularly New Englanders, had
long understood English common law and constitutionalism as institutional
solutions for the preservation of natural rights.

The American state declarations have received far less attention than their later, more famous successor, the Bill of Rights. Still, it is helpful to situate the Bill of Rights in the broader context of these earlier declarations, not simply to track which specific rights were already featured, but to see what disappears. Perhaps the most striking absence in the Bill of Rights are the natural rights with which all the state declarations had begun. This is not to say that Americans did not view the rights enshrined in the Bill of Rights as lacking a natural foundation: the anti-Federalists in particular insisted that these rights were, for the most part at least, derived from natural law.[140] But missing from the Bill of Rights are the rights on which the revolutionaries of '76 sought to found a new government. Of course, when Congress submitted the articles of amendment to the Constitution, in 1789, government had, by definition, already been founded. There was no longer any need for the "ringing declarations of universal principles" contained in the state declarations. Unlike the French Declaration of the Rights of Man and of the Citizen, the Bill of Rights did not precede the Constitution. Rather than a statement of first principles, it was a placating measure to ensure the Constitution's ratification.

Had the Constitutional Convention approved any of the motions to join a bill of rights to the new Constitution, its language may have ended up resembling that of the earlier declarations that preceded the state constitutions.[141] In fact, one of the proposals circulating in 1788 for the Bill of Rights was a draft by George Mason, which recycled much of his 1776 Virginia Declaration, including the first articles on natural rights.[142] The erasure of natural rights talk from the Bill of Rights may in part be viewed as accidental.

At the same time, and despite the fact that many Americans did perceive these rights as grounded in natural law, the Bill of Rights ended up consolidating legal entitlements that came almost solely from the English common law tradition.[143] The criminal procedural rights that had already featured prominently in the state declarations reappeared here as well: indeed the Fourth, Fifth, Sixth, and Eighth Amendments all deal with the criminal justice system. If one adds in the Seventh Amendment, which deals with civil trials, then a full half of the original ten amendments concern "judicial" rights and criminal procedure.

While not substantially distinct in content from the earlier declarations, the Bill of Rights nonetheless marks a shift in the history of natural constitutionalism. "The Laws of Nature and Nature's God," so often invoked to authorize rights, had disappeared. Whether intentional or not, this erasure would make the Bill of Rights far more susceptible, in subsequent generations, to positivist interpretations. This dominant approach to constitutional law today raises the hackles of natural law admirers.[144] But if references to natural law were omitted from the Bill of Rights, it was also because they could be. Natural rights had primarily allowed Americans to justify resistance, then revolution, to the British, and the establishment of new government. Once this work had been done, the more relevant rights for enjoying civil society were those that had been elaborated within English common law.

By the time the Americans were discussing the Bill of Rights, natural constitutionalism had thus lost much of its urgency as a political philosophy. But this also means that at least half of the Bill of Rights belonged to a legal tradition that, from a continental European perspective, was an eccentricity. No other common law countries, let alone civil law ones, enjoyed such detailed criminal procedural rights, or the precedent of an earlier (English) Bill of Rights. The American Bill of Rights thus stands out as an anomaly in the longer history of early modern rights: its jusnaturalist casing had disappeared, and its contents had been sourced from a different legal tradition. Congress discussed Madison's draft amendments during the same summer months that the National Assembly was debating its Declaration. But apart from this temporal coincidence, the two documents would remain continents apart.

# From Nature to Nation: French Revolutionary Rights

Only when the rights of the nation had been secured did the revolutionaries claim the rights of man.

KEITH M. BAKER, *Inventing the French Revolution*[1]

Where most contemporary observers considered the American and French declarations of rights to be cut from the same cloth, Edmund Burke famously disagreed. The "rights of men" that the French affirmed had no foundation in history, he claimed, but rather emerged fully armed from "the clumsy subtilty of their political metaphysics." To these fictional rights, Burke opposed the "wise, sober, and considerate [ . . . ] *Declaration of Right*," or what we more commonly call the English Bill of Rights, passed by the Convention Parliament in 1689. These were (in his eyes, at least) the same constitutional rights that the American colonists would later invoke in their own conflict against Parliament and, ultimately, against the British crown.[2] Burke's defense of the American colonists, and his attack on the French revolutionaries, largely boiled down to this fundamental distinction. The French Declaration of Rights was little more than "a mere rant of adulatory freedom," whereas Anglo-American rights were grounded in the long constitutional history of the English monarchy, stretching from the *Magna Carta* to the Glorious Revolution.[3]

Burke's specific account of how the French and American rights regimes differed is grossly incomplete, but remains noteworthy for its insight that people thought differently about rights in Philadelphia and in Paris. Others have pursued a similar line of thought. Writing at the time of the bicentenary, Marcel Gauchet called attention to the different political projects of American and French revolutionaries, noting how "the primary American concern with preserving individual independence clashes with the Continental obsession over the collective appropriation of power."[4] For Gauchet, this French "obsession" had been fashioned by the absolutist tendencies of the French monarchy.[5] Where the Americans supposedly dreamed of free, independent individuals, the French tried to channel power into a rational, unitary nation and sought to achieve social perfection through laws. Following Tocqueville, Gauchet argued that the Revolution did not disrupt this "legicentric" ideal, but simply perpetuated it in a republican guise. Accordingly, the French Declaration of Rights only mildly defended "the rights of each" (les droits de chacun), leaving individuals vulnerable against "the rights of all" (les droits de tous).[6]

If Gauchet, unlike Burke, resituated the French doctrine of rights within a longer political history, he paid little attention to the Americans' own cultural heritage. In his story, the French emerge as the odd people out, atavistically drawn to centralized government. But as Burke reminds us, it was in fact the English and their American cousins who were arguably more unusual. No continental Europeans enjoyed the same degree of criminal procedural rights as the English, whose common law tradition provided uncommon bulwarks against arbitrary state coercion.[7] The declaration of these rights, along with others, by individual American states, then by the nation as a whole, did not reflect the "normal" vision of a society committed to freedom and equality, but rather the idiosyncrasies of the British justice system. In other words, it wasn't the French who were unnaturally "obsessed" with the law, but the English and Americans who were eccentrically attached to rights.

To fully grasp the differences between the American and French rights regimes, we must accordingly be more attentive to the intricacies of *both* politico-legal cultures. In the case of France, this culture extended well beyond absolutism, which was always more of an aspiration than a reality, and encompassed the efforts at legal reform that the monarchy had pursued since at least Louis IX (1214–1270).[8] Indeed, the *légicentrisme* that Gauchet and others have imputed to the French was less a distinctive feature of the Bourbon monarchy than a political ideal that had animated European rulers and jurists since the rediscovery of the *Corpus juris civilis*.[9] In this civil law perspective, the pressing problem was thought to be the conflicting jumble of customary and written laws that held in different (sometimes the same) parts of the country. This lack of legal coherence was blamed for a host of social and political issues. Solving these issues thus demanded legal reform, which was typically imagined as standardizing existing law according to the more "rational" model of Roman law.[10]

When the French sought to redress governmental abuses in 1789, they retained this assumption that good laws, above all, provided the best protections against injustice. As I discuss below, it is likely for this reason that half the articles of the French Declaration of Rights provide legal guidelines, rather than rights provisions. While this emphasis on the law may strike us as anomalous today, when citizenship is so closely tied to rights, it followed clear

Enlightenment logic. Justice would be served, and progress made, when the law and legal procedures became more rational, uniform, and complementary. The Physiocrats propounded this vision most vocally, but it was a common aspiration of the *philosophes* and their allies across Europe.[11]

Misplaced or not, this faith in legal perfectionism as means of political reform had the merit of appearing relatively straightforward: fix the law and the rest will follow. Once again, it is the Anglo-American premise that government and society will always be in conflict that was more atypical. Famously voiced by Thomas Paine, and already gestured at by Locke, the idea that individuals should be armed with rights *against* their government rests on a disillusioned view of the state: "[G]overnment, even in its best state, is but a necessary evil."[12] This was an opinion that one would be hard-pressed to find on the Continent.[13] Of course, the European trust in good government was no less constructed than the "artificial" Anglo-American concept of the state.[14] The social naturalism that infused French Enlightenment thought was simply a better disguised ideology, masking its artificiality beneath the appearance of naturalness.[15]

The French reliance on the law to construct a more perfect nation was still somewhat idiosyncratic, even by continental standards. In particular, it was the French concept of the *nation* that stood out for its rigidly cohesive and unitary features. For Gauchet, these features were a legacy of absolutism, according to which sovereignty must be exercised and expressed by a single individual or institution. In this reading, the National Assembly simply filled the empty space left by the king.[16] But Gauchet overlooks how the concept of the nation also served as a touchstone of "patriotic" political discourse. Invocations of the nation were nothing new: it was in the name of *la nation* that *parlementaires* had long defended their opposition to royal will; and it was their theory of national rights that the revolutionaries would perpetuate. This theory was wholly distinct from absolutist doctrines; indeed, it predated them.[17] And it was particularly appreciated by the professional group most broadly represented in the National Assembly—namely, lawyers.

But where the national "rights and privileges" of the English were entitlements to be enjoyed by individual subjects, the *droits nationaux* defended by French patriots were to be exercised collectively. Individual citizens could decry their violation, but only a representative body such as the Estates General or the National Assembly could enforce them. They were constitutional rights yet did not owe their existence to a historical document, even one lost in the mists of time. Rather, they were the birthrights of the French people—or, for aristocratic theorists such as Boulainvilliers, of the Frankish aristocrats who alone had been free (*francs*).[18]

As the Physiocratic account of natural sociability gained ground over more traditional social contract narratives, the nation became increasingly perceived as an organic entity, one that did not owe its existence to an act of will but was closer to a fact of nature. National rights thus acquired the same status as natural rights, as we saw with Sieyès's famous pamphlet.[19] At that point, however, there loomed a potential conflict between the rights of the nation and those of the citizen. Where Gauchet and his fellow revisionist historians explained this confrontation of each versus all as a consequence of the revolutionaries' efforts to impose the general will on the nation, I show instead that it took the form of dueling rights claims. Both individual and national claims could be recognized as valid, which explains why the Jacobins remained committed, even at the height of the Terror, to the Declaration of Rights. But national rights typically trumped individual ones. Moreover, given that the criminal procedural rights afforded to French citizens were less robust than those enshrined in the U.S. Bill of Rights, the French government had less trouble stripping away due process for individuals suspected of harming the nation.

## 1. Whose Rights Are They, Anyway?
### Rights Talk in the *Cahiers de Doléances*

There has been an attempt of late to credit the idea of the Declaration of the Rights of Man and of the Citizen to the "radical principles" of a small group of "philosophe-révolutionnaires."[20] Leaving aside the American examples that had already widely publicized this idea, there is plentiful evidence in the *Cahiers de doléances* that French citizens across the country and from different social classes were advocating for a declaration long before the National Assembly even formed, with some groups even drawing up their own draft declarations. At least 24 *Cahiers* explicitly demanded a "Déclaration des droits"; some even called for a "Déclaration des droits de l'homme et du citoyen."[21] Most of these demands came from the Third Estate (17 *Cahiers*), though the nobility also pressed the case (5 *Cahiers*).[22]

To be sure, not all of this interest was spontaneous: some of the drafts included in the *Cahiers* contained near-identical language, often modeled on the *Instruction donnée par S.A.S. Monseigneur le duc d'Orléans*. This influential pamphlet, published in January 1789, and likely written by Pierre Choderlos de Laclos, contained a set of seventeen articles, the first of which began, "Individual liberty will be guaranteed to all the French"; it also included a provision against the *lettres de cachet* ("no-one can be arrested, or made a prisoner, without a warrant [un décret], issued by regular judges").[23] It was followed by a series of *Délibérations à prendre pour les assemblées de bailliages* written by Sieyès, which encouraged the Estates General to "present to the people the list of their essential rights, under the heading of *Declaration of Rights*."[24] Widely distributed and carefully mapped out, this text hints at a more concerted effort to have the Estates General issue a declaration.

If there was an influential group of revolutionaries who were pushing and plotting for a declaration of rights, it was not a shadowy network of "philosophe-révolutionnaires," but the very public members of the Société des Trente, who gathered at the home of the parliamentarian Adrien Duport starting in November 1788.[25] This group included the marquis de Lafayette, who shared a first draft for a declaration of rights with Thomas Jefferson in January 1789 and would present one of the first proposals of a declaration (his third draft) to the National Assembly on July 11, 1789;[26] Dupont de Nemours, who penned part of the *Cahier* for the Third Estate of Nemours (his hometown), asking the Estates General to "declare [ ... ] the rights of men and of citizens";[27] Condorcet, who published a draft declaration in February 1789 and composed most of the *Cahier* for the nobility of Mantes, which similarly demanded that "a declaration of rights be immediately issued";[28] Alexandre de Lameth, whose speech to the assembly of the three estates in Péronne called for "a constitution grounded in natural rights";[29] the comte de Mirabeau, who would take a leading role in the drafting of the final Declaration; the duc de La Rochefoucauld d'Enville, who had translated the American state declarations with Franklin; as well as Sieyès, Lepeletier de Saint-Fargeau, Dominique Garat, Destutt de Tracy, the comte de Volney, and others.

The Société des Trente lay at the intersection of multiple influential social and intellectual networks. Most members hailed from the liberal nobility, and many would go on to have illustrious careers in the Revolution. At least three members had close ties to American revolutionaries: Lafayette, La Rochefoucauld d'Enville, and Dupont de Nemours, who was also friends with Jefferson.[30] A number were intimately connected to the *philosophes*: Dupont de Nemours, Condorcet, and La Rochefoucauld d'Enville all corresponded with Voltaire; Garat (future minister of justice), with d'Alembert; Volney, Garat, Condorcet, and Mirabeau attended the cercle d'Auteil, Mme Helvétius's salon, which d'Alembert, Diderot, and d'Holbach also frequented.[31] The Société included Freemasons: Dupont de Nemours, Destutt de Tracy, Garat, Sieyès, and Volney all belonged to the prestigious lodge of the Neuf Sœurs.[32] But with respect to their role in promoting a declaration of rights, perhaps the most relevant connection that many members shared was a direct or close engagement with Physiocracy. Dupont de Nemours was a key Physiocratic impresario; Condorcet had been one of the first to adapt the Physiocratic defense of free trade to the defense of political rights and the abolition of slavery; Mirabeau's father was Quesnay's closest collaborator and would publicly honor their contribution to the Declaration;[33] and Sieyès, as we saw, was well versed in Physiocratic tenets.

Given the earlier role played by the Physiocrats in disseminating the preservation regime of rights (see chapter 3), it seems reasonable to grant them a special place in the genealogy of the Declaration. But it would still be a gross overstatement of their influence to suggest that the Declaration was the sole result of Physiocratic ideas (or any other "radical" ideas, for that matter). If only a fraction of the *Cahiers* explicitly requested that the Estates General produce a declaration of rights, the vast majority sought to enshrine basic political rights. As Gilbert Shapiro and John Markoff demonstrated in their quantitative study of the *Cahiers*, the demand that the *lettres de cachet* be abolished was found in 71% of Third Estate *Cahiers*, and 67% of those from the nobility. The plea that personal liberties be protected was equally widespread (contained in 66% of Third Estate and 75% of the noble *Cahiers*).[34] These requests, moreover, were often expressed in the language of natural rights: the assemblies asked the Estates General to "conserve," "consecrate," "recognize," "assure," "guarantee," and "re-establish" their rights.[35] The terms they used were still in flux: "droits naturels," "droits des hommes," and "droits de l'homme" were used interchangeably.[36]

All three estates adopted this language, with the Third Estate employing it most commonly.[37] But the First Estate could be just as strident. The clergy's embrace of natural rights talk was already evident during the Assembly of the Clergy, held in the summer of 1788. At the closing ceremony, the archbishop of Narbonne, Arthur Richard Dillon, celebrated the king for having granted civil and legal rights to Protestants, with the Edict of Versailles (1787): "[W]e will bless Your Majesty with having put an end to the shocking contradiction that fortified laws against the rights of nature," he asserted.[38] This edict continued to be celebrated as a milestone in the *Cahiers* of the clergy. "[W]e are far from ignoring the imprescriptible rights of nature that our errant brothers possess," wrote the First Estate of Beauvais.[39] The clergy also invoked natural rights in support of other reforms. Their *Cahier* from Caen lambasted the excessive taxes that "violate all the rights of men at once," and the clergy of Clermont-en-Beauvoisis denounced *lettres de cachet* as violating "the most sacred of natural rights."[40] Underpinning some of these assertions was the old doctrine of conciliarism. "The clergy also wish to see the return of synods, provincial councils, and a national council," wrote the First Estate of Caen, a demand that many other clerical *Cahiers* would echo.[41] But the clergy's backing of natural rights, in the *Cahiers*, reminds us that until Pius VI attacked the

Declaration of the Rights of Man in his 1791 encyclical *Adeo nota*, the French
Church remained committed to a doctrine that had long been, after all, the
purview of theology.[42]

From the perspective of the *Cahiers*, it thus appears overdetermined that
the National Assembly would take up the question of a declaration of rights.
But *whose* rights were being defended, exactly? A deep ambiguity ran through
the demands in the *Cahiers*. Precisely half of the 24 explicit pleas (identified
above) for a declaration of rights framed this request in terms of *individual*
rights, while the other half wanted the Estates General to affirm *national*
rights. "Do not let the Estates General disband without having written, in the
clearest and most exact manner, the declaration of the rights of the nation and
the laws of its constitution," affirmed the nobility of Etain, in a typical statement.[43] This directive often coexisted with assertions in favor of individual
rights, as well: the nobility of Château-Thierry asked the Estates to "obtain
from the King a declaration of the rights of the nation and of the individual
rights of the French."[44] But the declaration that many *Cahiers* sought was often
limited to the assertion of national rights: "the bill decreeing the declaration
of the rights of the nation will be solemnly passed according to form by the
assembly of the Estates"; "a declaration of national rights shall be written."[45]

The difference between calling for a declaration of the rights of man and
a declaration of the rights of the nation may, in some cases, have been merely
terminological; though as Stéphane Rials has observed, "[W]e should note
that most often the expression 'declaration of the rights of the nation' does
not refer to the fundamental rights of individuals, but to the requisite political
balances."[46] What's most interesting about this terminological and conceptual
confusion is that it points to how, in the run-up to the meeting of the Estates
General in May 1789, French political actors were beginning to combine the
two rival rights discourses then circulating in France. A revealing instance of
this combination can be found in Sieyès's *Délibérations* that were appended
to the duc d'Orléans' *Instruction donnée*. Many of the passages here paraphrase the arguments that Sieyès had made earlier in *Qu'est-ce que le Tiers
Etat?* We read, for instance, that "to the Nation belongs all powers, all rights,
since the Nation is identical to an individual in the state of nature, who has
no trouble looking after himself." But now this argument was made to support the proclamation of a declaration of rights: "present to the people the
list of their essential rights, under the heading of *Declaration of Rights*." Even
though these rights are clearly identified as individual and pre-political ("the
universal rights of Man and of the Citizen"), the nation's ability to grant—and
by implication, to deny—rights meant that they did not have the inalienable
quality that the preservation regime of rights guaranteed.[47]

## 2. Debating Rights at the National Assembly

Histories of the French Declaration of Rights that only dwell on the finalized version, passed on August 26, 1789, will likely miss the tension between individual and national rights that pervaded revolutionary political discourse. With one interesting exception (article 3, discussed below), this document largely reflects, at least in its final form, the more liberal, Enlightenment commitment to those individual rights that are "engraved in our hearts." But if we broaden our scope of inquiry to consider the debates running up to the final acceptance of the Declaration, we discover that national rights were never far from the deputies' minds.

These debates began shortly after the Estates General had renamed itself the National Assembly. On June 19, the Jansenist lawyer Guy-Jean-Baptiste Target moved that the different bureaux into which the Assembly had divided itself now turn to the "great work of the declaration of rights." He presented his proposal as a matter of fact; it was not seen as a radical suggestion but rather as a response to the *Cahiers*. Indeed, a deputy who spoke in support of Target's proposal added, "[I]t is from there [the *Cahiers*] that we must draw, that we must consult the national genius to produce the declaration of rights."[48] That the Assembly should pursue this effort was simply taken as a given: it had been requested by the people, as Clermont-Tonnerre would reiterate a month later.[49] When the topic of the Declaration came up in subsequent discussions, its future existence was usually taken for granted.[50] The *Cahiers* would remain a source of inspiration throughout the coming weeks.[51]

The first steps toward the Declaration did not involve the full Assembly but were taken by three consecutive committees.[52] On July 9, the first of these committees presented its report, delivered by Jean-Joseph Mounier, a moderate deputy from Grenoble who had risen to prominence at the 1788 meeting of Dauphiné Estates General.[53] His report was favorably received; the deputies even applauded the minutes the following day.[54] Mounier laid down the principles to which the Assembly would remain committed for the duration of the debates. The first point that he made was stylistic: "This declaration should be short, simple, and precise."[55] By extension, this definition excluded more "philosophical" and "metaphysical" drafts, such as those of the abbé Sieyès (see below).[56] It was a definition that enjoyed broad support over the coming weeks. Lafayette would echo his appeal to "simple" and "common principles";[57] Mounier himself would reiterate the view that the Declaration "should not be metaphysical, but clear and simple,"[58] and others would emphasize this goal as well.[59] It was ultimately enshrined in the Declaration's Preamble, which describes the articles as outlining "simple and incontestable principles."

Equally important, however, was Mounier's second point, which clarified the role of the Declaration vis-à-vis the Constitution: "For a constitution to be good, it must be based on the rights of men [les droits des hommes], which it must obviously protect [. . . ;] each article of the constitution must be the consequence of a principle." This relation between a general theoretical set of first principles and a more specific list of constitutional laws would characterize how the deputies would understand the purpose of the Declaration, both during the debates and throughout the Revolution.[60] As Lafayette would put it, two days later, the Declaration must "express those eternal truths from which all the institutions [of government] are derived."[61] While apparently straightforward and logical, this was nonetheless a conception that had drastic and wide-ranging consequences.

At a basic level, the dependence between the Declaration and the Constitution meant that they should be proclaimed jointly, a point that Mounier underscored.[62] Other deputies would voice similar concerns about issuing the Declaration too far in advance of the Constitution, for fear that unnamed "slanderers" might falsely extrapolate from its very general principles. Instead, the natural rights that the Assembly sought to declare must be "immediately tied to positive rights" so that the deputies' intent could be clearly read.[63]

But this desire to deduce the specific structures of government spelled out in the Constitution from the lofty principles of the Declaration also reveals the gap between French and American understandings of rights. Both sides insisted that rights should be preserved in a political society. In Anglo-American political culture, however, government was intended to preserve rights, but there was always a tension between the two. Both the English and American Bills of Rights detailed provisions to protect citizens from governmental overreach. They provided a check on governmental power and marked out a separate, sometimes antagonistic sphere (to use Locke and Paine's term, "society"). In the French case, by contrast, the Declaration was more like an Ur-constitution, or the stem cell of all legitimate regimes; later French revolutionaries would go so far as to describe it as "the constitution of all peoples."[64] Accordingly, where the American Bill of Rights defined the kinds of laws Congress should *not* pass, the French Declaration of Rights mostly insisted on what the legislative should do.

There were a number of cultural, political, and legal reasons why the French took this opposing view of the Declaration's function, but it bears noting that Mounier himself drew attention to the differences between the French and the American situations: "We are aware that the French are not a new people, who have recently left the woods to form an association, but a large society of twenty-four million people who seek to tighten the ties that unite them."

What this "longer" French history entailed, according to Mounier, was that no social contract was needed to assemble or constitute the French people into a political society: this society had long existed and merely sought to redefine and "tighten its ties."[65] Despite the iconography and rhetoric of a dawning golden age, the French deputies in July 1789 did not proceed under the aegis of a *novus ordo seclorum*, nor did they portray themselves as in a political state of nature.[66] But this longevity of French society implied that some of its old properties could be preserved under the new regime. Those in particular that Mounier had in mind were the "rights of the French people [droits du peuple Français]." Indeed, at this early stage of the debates, Mounier in fact imagined that the Assembly could issue a series of declarations: after taking care of "the declaration of the natural and imprescriptible rights of man," it should turn next to "the rights of the French nation" (followed by "the rights of the King," "the rights of citizens," and "the rights of representatives").[67] The Assembly would not get around to declaring these other rights but did not express any objections to them. While they did not make it into the final Declaration, national rights were clearly lurking in the wings.

The Assembly heard a first full draft of a declaration of rights on July 11, when the marquis de Lafayette presented his proposal. He added an enlightened twist to Mounier's insistence on stylistic simplicity: the Declaration, he observed, should "recall the feelings that nature engraved in the hearts of every individual."[68] While echoing the Physiocratic emphasis on "recalling" rights, Lafayette drew attention here to their sentimental foundation, reviving the *philosophes'* literal interpretation of Romans 2:15. Other deputies would strike this sentimental chord in the following weeks: the archbishop of Bordeaux, Champion de Cicé, described the "fundamental truths" contained in the Declaration as deriving from nature, "which placed them in every heart next to the spark of life";[69] Jean-Baptiste Crénière argued that if the natural rights demanded by the French people "are not issued in a Charter [une Charte], they are engraved in the heart of citizens";[70] and Jean-Nicolas Démeunier claimed that the Declaration should only reaffirm "the purest truths, the most certain principles [that] are engraved in the greatest number of hearts."[71] The same sentimental impulse that presided over the mass abandonment of privileges on August 4 thus also drove the (chronologically overlapping) discussion of the Declaration of Rights.[72]

Lafayette's declaration was a solid expression of liberal principles: unrestrained freedom of opinion and expression, untrammeled personal liberty. In various places, it echoes the Virginia Declaration of Rights, starting with the first sentence, "nature made men free and equal" (la nature a fait les hommes libres et égaux): compare with "all men are by nature equally free."[73]

Other passages suggest the influence of his friend and collaborator Jefferson: for the first time in a French declaration, resistance to oppression featured as a natural right;[74] and Lafayette insisted on the people's right to periodically revise the Constitution (another pet idea of Jefferson's). But the Declaration also included this more typically French statement: "[T]he principle of all sovereignty resides in the nation. No body nor individual can exercise any authority which does not proceed directly from it."[75] With very slight emendations, this phrasing would become article 3 of the final Declaration. Thus the nation made its appearance in the Declaration of the Rights of Man.[76]

It would be another two weeks before the Assembly took up the subject of the Declaration in earnest, on July 27. This time, the deputies were asked to compare two draft declarations, one by Sieyès, the other by Mounier (whose draft largely incorporated Lafayette's, including the above wording about national sovereignty).[77] The debate followed a report from the new constitutional committee by Champion de Cicé, who tipped his hat in favor of Mounier. If Sieyès's proposal was clear and "precise," its flaw lay in its overly abstract formulations: "[E]veryone must be able to read and understand it," and few could follow the abbé's "wisdom which is as profound as it is rare." By contrast, most people "will easily read" Mounier's draft.[78] The most notable difference between these drafts, again, was stylistic. The age of the erudite treatise on rights had passed.

There were of course a number of conceptual differences between the drafts as well, but it is a commonality that is most striking. Both drafts placed almost equal importance on laws as on rights. Out of the 32 articles in Sieyès's proposal (excluding the lengthy preliminary observations), 12 articles mention rights explicitly, with another 3 articles alluding to them implicitly; but a full 10 articles address only the law, including the one article that would make its way into the final Declaration: "[A]ny citizen summoned or arrested in the name of the law must immediately obey. He becomes guilty by resisting."[79] In Mounier's case, the proportions are very similar, with 8 out of 23 articles concerning the rights of citizens, and 12 dealing with the law. Both proposals define the law as the "expression of the general will" (art. 26 and art. 11, respectively), a definition that would be included in article 6 of the final Declaration. More significant, perhaps, than the debated influence of this Rousseauist principle on revolutionary politics is the fact that a declaration of rights should even be defining the law in the first place.

The relative importance of laws and rights would furnish the topic of a subsequent debate, on August 4. Members of the clergy, led by the abbé Henri Grégoire, urged the Assembly to add duties to the Declaration of Rights.[80] This demand has sometimes been viewed as an attempt to derail the process entirely.[81] But for anyone schooled in continental natural law theory, it was not at all out of the ordinary. Samuel von Pufendorf's abridged textbook on natural law, in which many deputies at the National Assembly would have studied the subject, was entitled *De officio hominis et civis juxta legem naturalem* (1673), or *On the Duty of Man and of the Citizen According to the Natural Law.*[82] This title echoed Cicero's *De officiis*, a text that was required reading for every schoolboy, and which tied respect for, and knowledge of, natural law with religious ceremonies and legal obligations.

More broadly, though, many deputies were merely calling attention to the correlative nature of rights and duties, one of the principles of rights theory today.[83] Grégoire made this very point in his initial plea: "Rights and duties are correlative; they exist in parallel; we cannot speak of the first without speaking of the second; just as they cannot exist without each other, they express ideas which contain each other."[84] Of course, this same argument could be used against Grégoire's proposal, as it was by the marquis de Clermont-Lodève: if rights and duties are joined at the hip, then it would be redundant to list both ("the word 'citizen' entails a correlation with other citizens, and this correlation implies duties"). The Assembly ended up voting to exclude duties in the Declaration, not because deputies opposed them, but because they already considered them to be in it.[85]

This episode is indicative, however, of how stormy and unpredictable the debates could be at the National Assembly over the Declaration. There was a contingent of deputies who did seek to kill the entire process, or at least postpone it until the Constitution was complete. It was also an incredibly difficult process to manage, with nearly 1,200 deputies in attendance.[86] And the deputies had many other crises to manage at the same time. After a third committee, led by Mirabeau, failed yet again to produce a satisfactory draft (though it would provide the Preamble that ultimately crowned the Declaration), the deputies started to lose confidence. Finally, on August 19, they voted to select a draft that could serve as the "canvas" for future discussions.[87] Rather than settling on those of Sieyès, Lafayette, or Mounier, they chose the fairly undistinguished draft produced by the group of deputies from the Sixth Bureau (one of the thirty bureaux into which the Assembly had divided itself to facilitate discussions).[88] This draft would undergo drastic transformations over the following week, with only its last five articles (20–24) finding their way into the Declaration (as articles 12–16). But it offered the deputies a conceptual blueprint that guided their subsequent deliberations about rights.

Over the next week, from August 20 to 27, the Assembly argued, applauded, decried, criticized, and ultimately approved the seventeen articles that made up the final Declaration of Rights. The process could be chaotic and the results unpredictable. Often the deliberations reached their conclusion less by conviction than by exhaustion. The deputies had already been debating the topic for over a month, and rights fatigue had set in. They spent hours squabbling over the first three articles of the Declaration, on August 20, without coming to an agreement; finally, as evening set in ("the hour was very late"), Mounier took the floor and proposed the wording that would carry the day. His winning proposal recycled his own well-received draft, as well as Lafayette's, but the Assembly may also just have approved it out of weariness.

Indeed, on a number of occasions, the Assembly spent a long time wordsmithing proposals, only to fall back on an initial phrasing. For instance, Alexandre de Lameth proposed the wording for articles 4 and 5 at the onset of the debates on August 21; the Assembly considered a half dozen other proposals, before eventually reverting back to his. The following day, Target and Duport proposed the wording for articles 7–9 early on in the debate, but it took the Assembly a full day to circle back to their proposals. On August 24, the duc de la Rochefoucauld was the second speaker of the day and hit upon the final phrasing of article 11; the Assembly considered a number of other proposals and ultimately fell back on his. Toward the end of the debates, the Assembly simply stopped trying to improve on the Sixth Bureau's draft: the deputies wasted a day trying to revise article 20, then acknowledged that "the only flaw of article 20 is that it was written by the Sixth Bureau"[89] and passed it as article 12. A similar story can be told for articles 13–16: as Lally-Tollendal observed, apropos article 16, "after many debates, which will lead nowhere, we will return to the article of the Sixth Bureau."[90]

In the case of some articles, however, the debates extended far beyond particular wording. For article 6, the Assembly's point of departure was a fairly conservative statement by the Sixth Bureau: "The first duty of every citizen being to serve society according to his capacity and talents, he has the right to be called upon for any public function." Having expressly shunned "duties talk," the Assembly did not care for this statement. It did keep the following article, that "As the law is the expression of the general will, every citizen must directly collaborate in the creation of the law," though it would take more than a dozen proposals before Charles Maurice de Talleyrand-Périgord came up with the winning prose.[91]

No doubt the most contentious debates occurred over article 10, on religious liberty. On this occasion, the deliberative process led to a vastly different result than what had been on the table. As was the case with many other drafts before it, the Sixth Bureau had proposed declaring a national religion ("To maintain religion, a public cult is required"; art. 17). But it also sought to preserve a special moral jurisdiction for religion and morality ("Since the law cannot reach secret crimes, it must be supplemented by religion and morality"; art. 16). This last claim was strongly supported by the clergy and challenged by others in the Second and Third Estates. Some even wanted to remove any reference to religion altogether, not on secularist grounds, but because they thought the proper place to discuss this topic was in the Constitution: as Talleyrand, the irreligious bishop of Autun, argued, "It is there [in the Constitution] that the sacred and saintly words of Catholic religion should be pronounced."[92] And yet this discussion inevitably raised the question of religious freedom, which caused the Assembly to erupt in discord. It took a very pragmatic speech by the comte de Mirabeau, and the impassioned (and long) plea by the Protestant minister Rabaut de Saint-Etienne, to convince the Assembly to affirm the freedom of conscience, if only in implicit terms: "No one shall be disquieted on account of his opinions, *including* his religious views, provided their manifestation does not disturb the public order established by law" (art. 10; emphasis added).[93] This was not, of course, the Assembly's final word on religion, and it would revive the idea of a "culte public" with the Civil Constitution of the Clergy.

### 3. The Legal Spirit of the French Declaration of Rights

When the Assembly finished revising the Sixth Bureau's draft, the deputies passed a final article, proposed by Adrien Duport. It defined property as "an inviolable and sacred right," adding that "no one shall be deprived thereof except where public necessity, legally determined, shall clearly demand it, and then only on condition that the owner shall have been previously and equitably indemnified" (art. 17). The founder of the Société des Trente, which as we saw included many leading Physiocrats, ensured that the Declaration concluded on a Physiocratic statement of faith.[94] Interestingly, there might have been an article 18 that also made social welfare a political right: the Assembly briefly entertained a proposal by Dupont de Nemours affirming, "All members of society, whether they are indigent or disabled, have a right to free assistance [ont droit aux secours gratuits] from their fellow citizens."[95] The deputies decided instead to end discussions of the Declaration, though this last proposal marks one of the earliest expressions of "social rights," which would later make their way into the Declaration of Rights of 1793.[96]

In fact, a Physiocratic spirit extended over many articles in the Declaration. This spirit was not just the narrowly economic one of Quesnay, who had little interest in political rights, but the looser and more extensive spirit of Physiocratic fellow travelers such as Condorcet and Mirabeau *fils*. At a basic level, this was the spirit that found expression in article 2, which offered one of the most straightforward and uncompromising statements of the preservation regime of rights: "The aim of all political association is the preservation [conservation] of the natural and imprescriptible rights of man. These rights are liberty, property, security, and resistance to oppression." With the exception of the right of resistance (a largely American import, probably courtesy of Thomas Jefferson), these lines could have been copied straight out of any Physiocratic work. The comte de Mirabeau affirmed as much during the debates: praising an idea from Sieyès (or so he claimed) that "since men who join together in society do not renounce any of their natural liberty [ . . . ] they could not have alienated any of the rights they received from God and from nature, as they are inalienable," Mirabeau marveled how "this paragraph is in itself a declaration of rights," before adding, "Everything is to be found in this elevated, liberal, and fruitful principle that my father and his illustrious friend, M. Quesnay, established thirty years ago."[97]

But the Physiocratic spirit can also be observed in the equal attention paid to laws and rights. Ten articles in the Declaration outline individual rights;[98] an almost equal number (eight) call attention to the proper usage of the law.[99] Two of those articles placed limitations on the extent of the law, in a vein similar to the First Amendment of the U.S. Bill of Rights ("Congress shall make no law . . ."; arts. 5 and 8). But the rest empowered the law to define the limits of rights, including liberty (art. 4), justice (art. 7), religious worship (art. 10), and freedom of expression (art. 11). This is the *légicentrisme* that Gauchet and others have denounced; but it is entirely in keeping with the Physiocratic—and, more broadly, social naturalist—emphasis on aligning natural and positive laws, and not viewing rights in an adversarial relation with laws.

As a consequence of this perspective, rights are formulated less absolutely in the French Declaration than in any American equivalents. Freedom of press was described in the Virginia Declaration of Rights as "one of the greatest bulwarks of liberty [which] can never be restrained but by despotic governments" (§ 12). The French similarly call it "one of the most precious of the rights of man," according to which "every citizen may, accordingly, speak, write, and print with freedom," but did not hesitate to restrain it "as shall be defined by law" (art. 11). Similarly, where the Virginians insisted that "all men are equally entitled to the free exercise of religion" (§ 16), the French added a qualifier that this freedom was contingent on not disturbing "the public order established by law" (art. 10).

The most telling contrast between American and French rights talk concerns criminal procedure. As elsewhere, the French did not place their confidence in ironclad rights but rather in the law: "No person shall be accused, arrested, or imprisoned except in the cases and according to the forms prescribed by law," they averred (art. 7). While the intended goal of this article was the abolition of *lettres de cachet*, it did not provide much detail about which specific "forms" the law could, or could not, prescribe. If the laws imposed draconian forms, as they would during the Terror, they would be no less legitimate, and citizens could not claim that their rights had been violated.

This is not to say that the French were in any way opposed to the criminal procedural rights so cherished by the Americans. On the contrary, they espoused similar principles of legal protection, including the presumption of innocence (art. 9). Other features, such as trial by jury, would be adopted at a later date.[100] This temporal difference reflects the very different positions of the American and French declarations. The Americans were largely conservative, enshrining legal principles that long formed part of established criminal procedure. The French did not have this same tradition to draw on; their reforms lay in the future.

But these differing attitudes to existing judicial forms only tell half the story. The French impulse was to defend citizens against state overreach by pursuing legal perfection, rather than strengthening rights protections. Article 8 is an illuminating example of this approach: it affirms that "The law shall provide for such punishments only as are strictly and obviously necessary, and no one shall suffer punishment except it be legally inflicted in virtue of a law passed and promulgated before the commission of the offense." Again, some of these sentiments could be found in the American state declarations, which similarly banned *ex post facto* laws.[101] But the French chose to express them in terms of the penalties that the law could or should impose, and not in terms of the judicial rights that individuals ought to enjoy, no matter what the law said.

In one respect, the French Declaration did resemble its American counterparts: it made no mention of national rights, despite the demands found in the *Cahiers*. This omission, however, may not be as telling as it seems. A few drafts considered by the Assembly contained references to the *droits de la nation*.[102] And during the parliamentary debates, deputies occasionally referred to the object of their efforts under this other name.[103] Even after the Declaration was passed, it could be referred to in such terms.[104]

As we saw, moreover, there is at least one article that points in the direction of the national constitutional doctrine of rights: "The principle of all sovereignty resides essentially in the nation. No body nor individual may exercise any authority which does not proceed directly from the nation," declares article 3.[105] Read solely within the context of the Declaration, this claim does not appear very threatening. All of the American state declarations had included comparable statements. Section 2 of the Virginia Declaration of Rights, for instance, affirms "[t]hat all power is vested in, and consequently derived from, the people; that magistrates are their trustees and servants and at all times amenable to them." As an assertion of popular sovereignty, then, article 3 was simply a set piece of revolutionary constitutional doctrine.

And yet, let us not forget that "the people" and "the nation" are dissimilar concepts.[106] The people are a collectivity who compact together and pool their individual natural rights to produce a political state. In its common French acceptance, the nation was understood as a singular entity, which preexists government and does not require any kind of social contract to acquire rights.[107] How the nation could exercise its collective rights was not always clear; but its rights existed independently from those of its individual members. In the Declaration of Rights itself, none of this was spelled out. But the tension between national and individual rights would grow problematic as the Revolution wore on.

### 4. The Revenge of National Rights

The Declaration of the Rights of Man and of the Citizen is generally viewed as antithetical to the political violence that reached a climax in France in 1793–94.[108] And yet, at the very height of this repression, its agents repeatedly and enthusiastically proclaimed their adherence to this Declaration and to human rights. *Représentants en mission* traveling through Charente-Maritime replaced religious icons with copies of the Declaration and the Constitution in a local church.[109] A popular opera composed in November 1793 opened with this song:

> How lovely is the age in which we live!
> This age, when I have seen
> The empire of liberty established
> On the rights of humanity![110]

One way to justify the repression of counterrevolutionaries was to argue that they were denatured and had forfeited their rights. "The Declaration of the Rights of Man will never be understood by the enemies of the fatherland," the *conventionnel* Antoine Thibaudeau warned ominously on May 7, 1794, "but men who have not been debauched by false pleasures, or stultified by prejudice, who, remaining close to nature, have always retained in their heart the seeds of liberty and equality, will easily understand it without any commentary."[111] This argument, as I've shown elsewhere, could be supported with natural law theory, which was particularly harsh toward "enemies of the human race" who violate the laws of nature and must be destroyed.[112] In this respect, celebrating the rights of man was not opposed to denying them to some. Robespierre insisted that the Vendéen rebels be exterminated precisely *because* they "will eternally conspire against the rights of man and the happiness of all peoples."[113]

But this privatory logic—that certain individuals could be deprived of rights—was reinforced and complemented by the assertive logic of national rights. If the nation had rights, it could press to have them recognized and upheld. During the first year of the Revolution, this argument was mainly levied against government bodies that overstepped their authority. Hence, in November 1789, Antoine Barnave accused the Metz Parlement of issuing a ruling that was "offensive to the rights of the nation, by the accusations it contains; seditious in its call to arms; insulting to the King and the National Assembly. . . ."[114] Even the Assembly's own decrees could be criticized in this manner. A month later, Mirabeau warned that the Assembly did not have the right to exclude one of its own deputies, since to do so would be to "propose a humiliating bill for the Assembly, offensive to its liberty and contrary to the rights of the nation, which alone can judge, in the final instance, the conduct of its representatives."[115]

By spring 1790, however, it was more common to find deputies asserting the Assembly's power to exercise the rights of the nation on its behalf.[116] During a debate over how to fund parish priests, following the abolition of the *dîme*, Jacques Guillaume Thouret asked, "[A]re the rights of the nation on [Church] goods [ . . . ] to defray the costs of religious service acknowledged?" before responding in the affirmative, "Yes, these rights are acknowledged. . . ."[117] A few months later, Isaac-René-Guy Le Chapelier raised a troubling prospect: "What would become the rights of the nation, if it were possible, in moments of turmoil and disorder, when each of us [representatives to the National Assembly] is subject to hatred, revenge, and factions, to drag us away from our duties, and force us to stand before a judge?"[118] To exercise the rights of the nation, members of the National Assembly should be inviolate. And in an attempt to ingratiate himself with the National Assembly, a certain Arnauld, leading a delegation of representatives from Saint-Domingue, denounced his island's colonial assembly for assuming "the rights and powers of the National Assembly: as if the attributes of sovereign power could belong to any others than those who fully exercise the rights of the nation."[119]

This claim that the National Assembly, and only it, could "fully exercise the rights of the nation" found its most vocal supporter in Maximilien Robespierre. When discussing the establishment of a high court to try "crimes of *lèse-nation*," which he defined as "attacks committed directly against the rights of the nation," Robespierre argued that "a court defending the rights of the nation" could only be placed in Paris, under the surveillance of the Assembly.[120] Among the powers of government, he reasoned, only the "legislative body" could enforce national rights.[121] Indeed, this was its very purpose. "We have been sent to defend the rights of the nation," the Incorruptible pronounced on the eve of the Assembly's dissolution.[122] At times, he even appropriated this role for himself in particular: "I call on [je réclame] the rights of the nation against a system that I find opposed to them [qui m'y paraît contraire]."[123]

It was during the first months of the National Convention that the punitive and repressive potential of these appeals to national rights became evident. As the Convention tried Louis, numerous deputies intoned against the king for having "violated," "erased," "impaled," "undermined," and "invaded" the rights of the people.[124] Robespierre again made the most effective use of this argument, claiming that even the defenders of Louis's constitutional inviolability acknowledged that "those who, on August 10, might have destroyed Louis XVI would have committed a virtuous action." And yet, he deftly observed, "the only basis for this opinion could be Louis XVI's crimes and the rights of the people." So, he concluded, "has an interval of three months changed either his crimes, or the rights of the people?"[125] In this speech, as in those by other deputies, the rights of the nation were nearly synonymous with natural rights. The natural constitutionalism theorized by Sieyès had become, in the eyes of many deputies, a political reality: with the dissolution of the monarchy, the nation had returned under the jurisdiction of natural law.[126]

Tellingly, deputies increasingly referred to the rights of the *people* (*droits du peuple*) rather than those of the nation.[127] This terminological shift mirrored the abrupt rise of a new criminal category, the enemy of the people. Rarely used during the first three years of the Revolution (though in fact an older expression than *droits de la nation*), it rose to prominence in 1792, before becoming a cornerstone of the Terror legislation in 1793–94.[128] Whoever violated the rights of the people became their enemy; and it was to prosecute such offenses against the collectivity that the individual rights of the accused would be peeled away.

To be sure, this process was not inevitable, and in some circumstances, the rights of the nation could cohabitate with individual rights. Early in the Revolution, when the National Assembly charged the Châtelet court with trying crimes of *lèse-nation*, it had insisted that it respect the new procedural rights that the Assembly had just established, in accordance with "the rights of man."[129] But as political turmoil increased, the rights of man and those of the nation clashed with increasing prevalence. When Georges Couthon introduced the Law of 22 Prairial, which stripped the *ennemis du peuple* of most procedural rights, one of his justifications was that "the rights of the republic have been far less respected in the prosecution of crimes against liberty."[130]

## 5. Conclusion

The observation that French revolutionaries, during the Terror, suppressed individual liberties in the name of collectivity is hardly new. Revisionist historians, following the lead of François Furet and Keith Baker, made similar claims. But the argument I am presenting here differs in key respects. First, from a methodological perspective, I am not suggesting that the logic of national rights invariably led to the suppression of individual rights, but rather, and more weakly, that it could push in that direction. Other political practices, theories, and institutions pushed in other ways, and the outcome of these conflicts cannot be determined by looking at political ideas alone. As justifications for, and incitements to, action, however, ideas can gain broad support at critical junctures and significantly influence events.

Second, at a conceptual level, there are important differences between appeals to the nation or people and to the general will. As we saw with Sieyès, the concept of the nation could adopt certain qualities of the Rousseauist body politic, but it retained its own defining features. In addition to being pre-political and not contractually constituted, the nation or people had rights that could be defended without the people themselves voicing their demands. In other words, the rights of the nation or people were not the product of will; they owed their existence to constitutional precedent and (especially after August 1792) the laws of nature. This distinction explains why the Jacobins, in 1793, could explicitly reject voluntaristic conceptions of the body politic, while continuing to pose as defenders of the people's rights.[131]

Revisionist historians also pursued the Tocquevillian thesis of a continuity between the political projects of the old and new regimes. Drawing on Claude Lefort, Furet argued that the French revolutionaries rushed to fill in the gap left by absolute sovereignty, replacing the royal *bon plaisir* with popular will.[132] Marcel Gauchet and Lucien Jaume also faulted the National Assembly for perpetuating an absolutist political culture that laid excessive emphasis on laws rather than rights.[133] But the account I offer above suggests that at least one critical legacy of the old regime did not originate in Versailles but rather in the Paris Parlement. It was the *parlementaires* who first portrayed themselves as the staunch defenders of national rights. Even the term *lèse-nation* can be traced back to the *patriote* literature attacking the "despotic" Maupeou ministry.[134] In his anonymously published *Mémoires de l'abbé Terrai* (1776), one of the "forbidden best-sellers" of the old regime, the lawyer Jean-Baptiste-

Louis Coquereau thundered: "[The public] could not be satisfied with such light punishments for a monster guilty of the worst crime, the crime of *Leze-Nation*, a crime as superior to that of *Leze-Majesty*, as the nation is to its sovereign."[135] A similar warning would resurface in the *Cahier* of the Third Estate of Paris: "Any person convicted of acting in a way that sought to prevent the holding of the Estates General will be declared a traitor to the fatherland, guilty of the crime of *lèse-nation*. . . ."[136] The first two signatories of this *Cahier* were the president of the Assembly, Guy-Baptiste Target, and its vice president, Armand-Gaston Camus, two of the most famous lawyers in Paris at the time, both close to the *parlementaires*.[137] While obviously modeled, in name at least, on the monarchic crime of *lèse-majesté*, this new offense of high treason, which the revolutionaries sought to prosecute as early as July 1789, was still a product of the *parlementaire* pursuit of national collective rights. If the revisionist continuity thesis was essentially formal, resting as it did on a *parallel* between the understanding and exercise of sovereignty before and after 1789, the lasting commitment to national rights, by contrast, constitutes a direct and concrete instance of political continuity.

One might ask, in closing, how central the French Revolution is to this history of rights. The thesis that all humans derive rights from nature, which they should continue to enjoy in political society, had been common since at least the sixteenth century and was revived during the Enlightenment; the doctrine of national rights similarly predated 1789. Did the Revolution significantly affect these ideas? At a theoretical level, this question is debatable: revolutionaries may have introduced new rights (most notably social rights), but they largely perpetuated earlier rights regimes. At a more practical level, however, the Revolution marked a turning point in French history, as the moment when rights became the foundation of politics. The Declaration of Rights—which in August 1789 had only been passed as a temporary measure, to be revisited when the Assembly came closer to completing its work on the Constitution— rapidly transformed the language of politics and had immediate ramifications for the justice system and religious toleration.[138] Rights went from constituting a political theory to becoming a political practice. But the rights of the nation had, in fact, already featured in old regime political culture. Transferred from the Parlement to the National Assembly, these rights now entered the same political arena as the *droits de l'homme*. Just as the *parlementaires* had invoked the rights of the nation to defend against royal "despotism," so, too, did the deputies call upon these rights to fend off the king and later anyone they identified with royalism. In practicing a politics of rights, the Revolution thus became a stage where conflicts between these rival conceptions of rights could play out. In the process, both doctrines were pressed to their logical conclusions. The enlightened theory of individual rights revealed itself to be less than universal, its protections vanishing for those deemed "unnatural"; while the constitutionalist theory of national rights became, in the troubled years of 1792–94, a judicial and political instrument of repression. The Declaration of Rights may have been heralded as a new set of divine commandments, but it was a god whose time had not yet come.

# Conclusion: A Stand-in for the Universal Declaration, 1789–1948

As a chapter in the intellectual history of human rights, the Enlightenment cannot lay claim to many titles of originality. Human rights were not invented in the eighteenth century, nor did they then become universalized for the first time. The *philosophes* and their allies may have popularized rights, by incorporating them into new genres. They offered a more intimate and sentimental access to rights. And they insisted (not for the first time, but with particular vigor) that the universal dimension of human rights include all humans, male and female, free and enslaved. For the history of the Enlightenment, these are all essential and decisive measures. But for the history of human rights, they do not constitute major ruptures or innovations. The evolution of human rights talk in the eighteenth century was just that—an evolution. The Enlightenment was not the birthplace of modern human rights, but rather the culmination of an early modern debate over the purposes of political society, the balance of power between individuals and the state, and the principles of universal justice. Parts of this debate had been going on since antiquity.

From the perspective of the nineteenth and early twentieth centuries, however, the Enlightenment and Atlantic Revolutions appeared to many as an epochal disruption. The early modern history of rights was completely overshadowed by the massively publicized achievements of the American and French revolutionaries. This idolatry of the eighteenth-century declarations can make for poor intellectual history. But it also played a crucial role in shaping how jurists, politicians, and others thought about human rights after 1789. For some, these declarations offered a model of what a future universal declaration of human rights might resemble. The French Declaration of 1789 in particular (as well as the subsequent Declaration of 1793) functioned as a stand-in for a more exhaustive, more explicitly international declaration to come.

The long and wide reverberations of the 1789 and 1793 Declarations also ensured a degree of continuity in how people thought about human rights up until 1948. This continuity is all the more remarkable given how much the world changed after 1789. Industrialization, colonization, and technological innovations transformed social and economic life. International law emerged as a legal discipline and began exerting its effect on geopolitics. International treaties, such as the Geneva Convention of 1864, established norms for humanitarian aid and conduct. And the first international organization, the League of Nations, was created.[1] How could documents produced by a predominantly agricultural society, documents that hardly took their own colonies into account, serve as a blueprint for a far more complex and intertwined global situation?

Some lawyers and politicians solved this problem by imagining a declaration that differed substantially from the actual Declaration of 1789. For Spanish American political founders, writing in the aftermath of independence, this reimagined declaration said nothing about freedom of religion, and sometimes did not even apply to non-citizens. By contrast, for constitutional lawyers at the turn of the twentieth century, it was a declaration without a nationalist context.[2] The 1789 and 1793 Declarations became symbols, meaning that they could be interpreted in many ways, from a sign of national sovereignty to that of an international order.

But the Declarations were not an empty space to be filled with whatever one wished to find there. They were a set of statements, of speech acts, that could obstruct or encourage particular actions.[3] In this respect, the Declarations did make a very significant intervention in the longer history of rights that I have retraced in this book: they consolidated the preservation regime of rights as the dominant, and eventually sole acceptable, framework for thinking about rights. They did not achieve this result thanks to any conceptual innovations, but rather through their vast publicity and the simplicity of the Declaration genre. The basic statement that "[t]he aim of every political association is the preservation of the natural and imprescriptible rights of man" (art. 2) put a conclusive stop to two centuries of polemics over the fate of natural rights in political society.

Many subsequent constitutional framers and legal scholars read the Declarations as an affirmation of basic protections owed to all individuals by all states. For this reason, the rights that they afforded were often incorporated into constitutions, rather than enunciated in prefatory declarations. While differing in format, the constitutionalization of human rights was very much in keeping with the French revolutionary spirit (and ultimately with the American Bill of Rights). As we saw, the French themselves understood their

Declarations as the generic, universal foundation from which the specific contents of their Constitution should be drawn.

There were other rights that political progressives—and, more surprisingly, conservatives—also wished to see in the Declaration, social and economic rights that were missing from the 1789 Declaration.[4] As many were quick to point out, however, these rights, too, had a revolutionary pedigree, one that could be traced back to the 1793 Declaration. By the early twentieth century, various lawyers and legal organizations were coming up with models for an international declaration that would combine the basic protections afforded in 1789 with the social and economic promises of 1793, as well as other, more contemporary needs.

The "cult" of the 1789 Declaration was only of the tributaries flowing into the interwar surge of interest in international human rights.[5] Other cultural, legal, and philosophical movements also made important contributions, and my focus in this conclusion on the legacy of the French Declarations is not intended to downplay their importance. But I do wish to push back against the argument that to trace a continuity between 1789 and 1948 is to engage in a Whiggish, "textbook history" of human rights.[6] The French Declarations are not central to this history because they *actually are* the most important modern documents leading up to the Universal Declaration of Human Rights (UDHR). They are central because generations of lawyers and politicians repeatedly returned to these Declarations and represented them as the drafts of a future declaration. This mythology became part of their history.

I also wish to challenge a trend in the recent historiography of human rights, which is to look to the Catholic Church, and interwar Christianity more broadly, as a driving force behind the push toward the UDHR. While the scholarship on the Church and human rights has brought to light a number of fascinating networks and concepts, it rests on an important misconception, which is the novelty of the Church's position. As I show in the following section, the Church did not turn to human rights in the 1930s. It had long favored them—even during the French Revolution.

## 1. The Catholic Church, Natural Law, and Human Rights

If the contributions of Catholic philosopher Jacques Maritain to the drafting process of the UDHR are well recognized, historians have only recently begun to explore the broader role of the Catholic Church.[7] The Church's claim to the spotlight stems largely from wartime statements by Pius XI and his successor, Pius XII, who threw the Vatican's weight behind "the unforgettable rights of man."[8] This embrace of human rights by the papacy has been described as a

"critical turning point," given that "the Catholic Church had previously rejected the hitherto secular and liberal language of human rights."[9]

The fact that subsequent popes gave their blessing to human rights may
well have accelerated their widespread adoption, and elements of Christian
doctrine, such as "personalism," may have influenced the language of the
UDHR. But there are a number of misconceptions about the Church's historical position on human rights. First, as we saw in chapters 1 and 2, Catholic
thinkers had long engaged in human rights talk. Francisco de Vitoria defended the natural property rights of native Americans. Domingo de Soto
considered self-preservation the "most fundamental right" of all humans. And
for Francisco Suárez, property was a subjective *ius ad rem* (right to an object).[10]
When Maritain retraced the genealogy of human rights not "to the philosophy
of the eighteenth century," but rather "to Grotius, and before him to Suárez
and Francisco de Vitoria; and further back to St. Thomas Aquinas," this was
not an invented tradition, nor did it require "a sleight of hand," as Samuel
Moyn suggests in *Christian Human Rights*.[11] To be sure, some of the rights that
we might consider today to be fundamental human rights were missing from
these neo-Thomist (or, for that matter, Protestant) theories of natural law. But
with respect to the concept of human rights per se, the Church had no hostility
toward them. On the contrary, Christian theologians had done a great deal to
develop and promote them.

A second confusion concerns the Church's attitude toward human rights
during the French Revolution. It is near universally assumed that the papacy came out against human rights in 1791, and that this opposition colored
Church dogma for a century or more. No less than a Pontifical commission
recognized, in 1975, that the Church had not always "defended and promoted
the rights of the human person with enough clarity of energy," in reference to
the revolutionary age.[12] But as I show in this section, Pius VI, who was pope
at the time, did not reject human rights *in toto*, only their manifestation in
the Declaration of the Rights of Man and of the Citizen (DRMC). What's
more, the Church remained committed to human rights throughout the nineteenth century, offering a full-throated defense in the 1891 encyclical *Rerum
novarum*. Rather than an agent of change and renewal, the Church was mainly
a source of continuity for the neo-Scholastic tradition of human rights.

It was in April 1791 that Pius VI, in the encyclical *Adeo nota*, described
the human rights (*jura hominis*) proclaimed by the French as "contrary to
religion and to society."[13] The primary target of this encyclical was not the
DRMC, which had been approved by the National Assembly a year and half
earlier (in August 1789), but the political disturbances in the papal states of
Avignon and the Comtat Venaissin, where revolutionary sympathizers wished

to impose the French Civil Constitution of the Clergy.[14] They also agitated to place their territory under French sovereignty. The Assembly in Carpentras signaled its desire to join the French state by voting to adopt the Declaration of Rights in June 1790.[15]

It was in reference to this particular vote that Pius expressed his disfavor of the French Declaration. The characterization of its contents as contrary to religion and society comes as an aside in his broader attack of this Assembly's vote as illegitimate. But the topic of the Declaration does not resurface anywhere else in the encyclical. It is accordingly difficult to know exactly what to make of Pius's comment. While clearly negative, it does not betray a hostility to the idea of human rights in general. Indeed, elsewhere in the text, he alludes favorably to "the most sacred rights of nations" (sanctiora gentium jura).[16] This appeal to *ius gentium*, the law of nations, suggests that the pope was comfortable with the natural law framework out of which the concept of human rights itself evolved. It also suggests that he did not view this framework as antithetical to rights, even if the rights in question here do not belong to the individual, but to a community.

The thrust of Pius's criticism of human rights becomes clearer when we consider a statement he had made a month prior, in the encyclical *Quod aliquantum* (March 10, 1791). Addressed to Cardinal Dominique de la Rochefoucauld and the archbishops and bishops in the National Assembly, this letter sought to offer some guidance on how they should react to the Civil Constitution of the Clergy (approved by the Assembly on July 12, 1790). Pius was deeply disturbed by the Civil Constitution, yet hesitated to condemn it fully—after all, it had received royal sanction.[17] But the pope could not accept that a temporal power claimed authority over the Church's spiritual sovereignty. Such drastic overreach could only stem, he reasoned, from the Assembly's insistence that it was a right "of a man in society to enjoy any kind of liberty [omnimoda libertate]" in religious matters. Pius was referring here to articles 10 and 11 of the Declaration of Rights, which guaranteed, respectively, that "No one shall be bothered on account of his opinions, including his religious views . . ." and "The free communication of ideas and opinions is one of the most precious of the rights of man. Every citizen may, accordingly, speak, write, and print with freedom, but shall be responsible for such abuses of this freedom as shall be defined by law."[18] From the Church's perspective, however, it was totally "insane" (inanius) to proclaim liberty "without any consideration of reason" (ut nihil rationi tribuatur). Liberty was not license and could only be genuine if it was reasonable. This was particularly true of rights we preserved in society, though Pius took the Aristotelian (and Thomist) view that nature destined humans for social life ("naturare inductione in societatem communionemque coierunt"). To determine human rights, he concluded, one cannot start from the principle of total liberty, but rather from the Stoic-Thomist rule to live life in accordance with reason ("vitamque suam ad rationis").[19]

As this rapid summary of *Quod aliquantum* makes clear, Pius was not opposed per se to human rights, only to the manner in which the French had interpreted and declared them. No doubt there were other aspects of the Revolution that disturbed him as well. He rejected the revolutionary theory of national sovereignty, for instance, repeating many times (on Paul's authority) that all power comes from God, and so kings must be obeyed. But the pontiff did not oppose the French Revolution en bloc and insisted that he did not want a return to the old regime.[20] In its beginnings, he even found things to praise, such as the Revolution's initial efforts to "reduce the burdens of the people" (populorum levanda onera).[21] The DRMC only drew his ire to the extent that he saw its scope extend to spiritual matters over which the National Assembly should have no say.

The best evidence that Pius remained favorably inclined toward human rights, at least in a more rational expression, can be found in his involvement in, and praise of, another publication, Nicola Spedalieri's *De' diritti dell'uomo* (*The Rights of Man*, 1791). Spedalieri, a priest and professor, had received a benefice in St. Peter's from the pope in 1784.[22] He does not appear to have undertaken his study of human rights coincidentally. Both the timing of this work and Spedalieri's position make it likely to have been the Vatican's semi-official response to the DRMC.[23] It proved to be a risky gamble: Spedalieri's book set off a firestorm of criticism. But it was not his defense of human rights that raised ecclesiastic eyebrows, rather it was his justification of tyrannicide. "[I]t is lawful for anyone to kill a Prince" (E' lecito a chiunque di uccidere un Principe), Spedalieri affirmed, drawing on the authority of none other than the infamous Jesuit Juan de Mariana (who had justified the assassination of Henri III as lawful tyrannicide).[24] Despite this controversy, Pius himself celebrated the work, allegedly asserting, "For a long while rulers have been asking *quid est papa*. Your book will teach them *quid est populus*."[25]

Indeed, in Spedalieri's work, the pope would have found a discussion of human rights more to his liking. The first right that Spedalieri defended, following the Thomist tradition, was that of self-preservation; the second was a right to self-perfection, in accordance with reason; and the third, a right to property (16). Against Hobbes, he insisted that a right is only a power "conforming to reason" (18), and so ended up endorsing a fairly Lockean theory of natural property rights based on labor. He further affirmed a right to liberty, defined as "doing everything that concerns the rights to self-preservation, self-perfection, and property" (19), and the liberty "to think, or be the judge of what is said" (libertà anche in pensare, o sia in giudicare circa ciò, di che si è parlato; 20). And critically, he endorsed a right to self-defense (20). These were the human rights we enjoyed in accordance to reason; and due to the "natural equality of the human condition" (la naturale egualianza della condizione degli uomini; 17), they were universal. Spedalieri joined to this list of rights a number of duties (obbligazioni), insisting that the two go hand in hand (la idea della obbligazione è relativa a quella del diritto; 22). Here he explicitly followed Pufendorf (25), whose natural law textbook similarly emphasized our duties (*De officio hominis et civis juxta legem naturalem*, [*On the Duty of Man and of the Citizen According to the Natural Law*]; 1673).

Spedalieri also took pains to distinguish the rights he had in mind from those proclaimed by the French. He criticized article 10 of the Declaration of Rights as "insane" (insensate), since it granted "unlimited toleration" in religious matters—precisely the same objection Pius had made in *Quod aliquantum*.[26] And Spedalieri did not stop there, pointing out how, bewitched by the *philosophes*, the French revolutionaries had placed their Declaration under the aegis of the Supreme Being, rather than Jesus Christ (328). Clearly, they had abandoned Christianity and were promoting deism, perhaps atheism (188)! By contrast, Spedalieri argued, the surest safeguard of human rights lay not in such dubious state declarations, but in the teachings of Christianity. And what did the doctors of the Church teach, other than that "the measure of a right should always be reason" (la misura del diritto debb' esser sempre la ragione; 12)? While Spedalieri also embraced Enlightenment concepts of happiness and sensationalism, his understanding of human rights and natural law remained firmly rooted in a Thomist framework.[27]

A more detailed reconstruction of the Vatican's views on human rights thus contradicts the received wisdom that the Church opposed them in 1789–91, and hints instead at a much greater and longer continuity in Catholic doctrine. To be sure, the pope was in a delicate position at the time. Given the widespread identification of *les droits de l'homme* with the French Revolution, it was difficult to wrestle this doctrine away from the French while also protesting their reorganization of the clergy. It is easy to see how historians could have missed the subtlety of Pius VI's position. But even if the Church did not loudly promote human rights during the revolutionary decades, it certainly did not turn against the idea.

What this means for the longer history of Christian human rights is that Pius's successor and namesake in the 1930s did not need to steer Catholic doctrine 180 degrees around. In fact, as Mary Elsbernd demonstrated, nineteenth-century popes perpetuated the Church's commitment to natural rights. Under Gregory XVI (in office, 1831–46), "a vocabulary of right began to enter the papal encyclical language," whereas under Pius IX (1846–78), "the vocabulary of *jus* increased and diversified in the encyclicals."[28] In his encyclical *Respicientes* (1870), the pontiff even referred to "the sacred and inviolable rights of so many" (iura tot titulis sacra atque inviolabilia), which "for centuries had been investigated and settled in disputes, unchanged" (per saecula semper explorata et inconcussa habita in controversiam).[29] This emphasis on rights reached a high point under Leo XIII (1878–1903), whose 1891 encyclical *Rerum novarum* made a strong case for social rights. This encyclical also sought to wrestle the defense of the poor away from socialists, whose doctrine, Leo claimed, was "contrary to the natural rights of mankind" (naturalibus singulorum iuribus repugnat), since "the State has for its office to protect natural rights, not to destroy them" (est autem ad praesidium iuris naturalis instituta civitas, non ad interitum).[30]

The central place of *Rerum novarum* in twentieth-century Church doctrine has long been acknowledged: Pius XI hailed it has an "immortal document," and his successor, Pius XII, celebrated its fiftieth anniversary.[31] If one wishes to recount the modern history of human rights and the papacy, then, the logical place to start is not in the 1930s, but in 1891. But even substituting Leo XIII for Pius XI is insufficient, since it implies that modern popes had to break with past doctrine in order to reconcile the Church with human rights. In reality, no significant break had to occur. The papacy had consistently asserted a neo-Thomist tradition that it would continue to defend in the decades leading up to 1948.

## 2. From National Constitutions to an International Declaration

A year before Leo XIII issued his defense of "the natural rights of mankind," another Italian, Pasquale Fiore (1837–1914), also took up his pen in their favor. Fiore was not a theologian, but a professor of constitutional and international law, and in 1890 he published a massive work: *International Law Codified and Its Legal Sanction*.[32] Here he made a case for "the international rights of man," understood as "those which belong to him as a man" and defined "in opposition to sovereignty."[33] Rather than turning to Roman law or Christian doctrine for his argument, he looked to the eighteenth century, celebrating the authors who "had all defended the rights of mankind" and assisted in "the development of the eminently just principles of the international community." Three authors in particular—"Hume, Quesnay, and Turgot"—drew extensive praise for having discovered "the great truth that liberty is the principal condition of commercial prosperity" (§ 2). This Physiocratic principle undergirded the true object of his admiration, namely, the DRMC. It was this document that would serve as a template for Fiore's own enumeration of the "international rights and duties of man" (title XXIII). The DRMC was not a perfect or final document, but it pointed the way forward: "To-day the work goes on; the effort is to perfect the principle already secured, and to better determine the rights of the individual, of society, and of the collectivity as opposed to the rights of sovereignty" (§ 10). The French Revolution had opened up a space for reflecting on, codifying, and ultimately instituting "the declaration of the rights that everyone expects [la dichiarazione dei diritti spettanti a ciascuno]" (§ 15/§ 11 for Italian).

How did it come to pass that an Italian law professor would be rhapsodizing over the DRMC in 1890 and gesturing toward a perfected declaration to come? Some of his countrymen, such as Giuseppe Mazzini, had expressed similar enthusiasm in the past.[34] But it was not just an Italian infatuation. Similarly to the American Declaration of Independence, news of the DRMC had spread around the world.[35] And the echo chamber where it resonated loudest was precisely the area that Fiore knew best: constitutional law. It was in the great explosion of constitution writing following the French Revolution that the DRMC found a political afterlife.[36]

From an early modern perspective, the ease with which various national constitutions absorbed elements of the DRMC is unsurprising. As we saw in preceding chapters, the historical moments when the preservation regime had flared up largely corresponded to frantic episodes of constitutional thought and practice. Both claims drew on the potent brew of conciliarism and neo-Thomistic natural law theory that John Major and his student Jacques Almain had propounded in early sixteenth-century Paris.[37] To take some examples from previous chapters, the French Huguenots, who invoked "droits humains" against a tyrannical king, wrote constitutions for their confessional strongholds; the rights-pushing Levellers demanded a written English constitution; and both the American and French revolutionaries combined constitution making and rights pronouncements. By the later eighteenth century, these twin efforts were increasingly viewed as two sides of the same coin. Vicenzo Ferrone has shown how *settecento* Italian reformers made human rights the foundation of their constitutional theories;[38] one of them, Gaetano Filangieri, was widely hailed across Europe and the United States for his new "science of legislation."[39]

But how compatible were *national* constitutions with *universal* human rights? For Lynn Hunt, the rise of nationalism in nineteenth-century Europe obstructed the spread of human rights, since "by definition, the rights of 'man' repudiated any idea that rights depended on nationality."[40] From a constitutionalist perspective, however, there is no inherent contradiction between framing the government of a nation and asserting universal human rights. Both the American and French revolutionaries offer examples of how these endeavors could proceed in parallel. Inscribing natural rights within a national constitution did not mean that these rights *only* existed by virtue of the nation.[41] As I argued in chapter 1, that is not at all how rights were understood or used throughout the early modern period. Much as Blackstone saw the English constitution as a kind of scaffolding wrapped around the natural rights of all humanity, subsequent constitutional thinkers, from Filangieri to Fiore, defined the national constitution as the proper place to ensure that governments preserved universal human rights. Their focus on preservation at a national level did not conflict with the *a priori* universal and international quality of these rights. For these thinkers, the national constitution was simply the first and usually best defense for the preservation of human rights, since it was where (what contemporary constitutional scholars would call) "rights provisions" could be included and guaranteed.[42] When the constitution failed to defend these rights, one could appeal to them above and beyond the constitution: this was the logic that propelled the American colonists toward independence. This imbrication of supranational rights in a national constitution does not differ substantially from current structures. Article 1 of the European Convention on Human Rights (1950), for instance, insists that "[t]he High Contracting Parties shall secure to everyone within their jurisdiction the rights and freedoms defined in Section I of this Convention."[43] The first obligation of European states, in other words, is to see that their constitutions (and by extension, their judicial systems) do not violate the European Convention on Human Rights. To be sure, no international conventions of this sort existed in the nineteenth century, but constitutional and international legal theorists had begun to imagine, with the help of the DRMC, what they might contain.

The human rights regimes embedded in nineteenth-century constitutions could differ considerably from our contemporary regimes. As Moyn points out, today we place the emphasis on individual protection, whereas nationalist liberators such as Giuseppe Mazzini focused on collective emancipation.[44] In so doing, they accepted a ready recourse to violent means, which we might no longer view as legitimate. As I showed in the previous chapter, the conflict between national (collective) rights and individual ones contributed to the political repressions of the Terror. It would be a gross overstatement, however, to say that the DRMC (or subsequent constitutions) paid no heed to individual protections. The attention to judicial rights—which greatly increased in post-independence Spanish America and post-Napoleonic Europe—clearly benefited individuals. Even during the French Revolution, as Charles Walton reminds us, individual journalists appealed in court to article 11 of the DRMC to defend their right to publish freely.[45] Many of the criminal procedural rights that would be incorporated in nineteenth-century constitutions, and which resurfaced in the UDHR (esp. arts. 6–12), protected individuals. Human rights NGOs today still militate for fair trials around the world.[46]

Even if we acknowledge that collective emancipation can conflict with individual protections, this does not mean that the DRMC's insistence on individual rights is irrelevant to the longer history of human rights and that our modern regime has a completely separate source. It is far more helpful to think of this longer history in terms of both additions and subtractions. Yes, new concepts and practices of human rights came along that modified our understanding of them. But sometimes "new" understandings were brought about by other concepts dropping out of the picture. Even when older understandings of human rights are entwined with objectives we no longer recognize, they can still lie upstream from our own. The demand for individual protections was central to rights thinking long before the nineteenth century. If these protections appear more prominent today than in the past, it is not because our ancestors judged them unimportant, but because they now enjoy our undivided attention.

## 2.1. CONSTITUTIONS AND RIGHTS IN HAITI AND IN SPANISH AMERICA

It will come as no surprise that the DRMC was also very well-known throughout the Francophone world. The founders of Haiti, for instance, were intimately familiar with its language. Echoes are not so much to be heard in the Haitian Declaration of Independence, but rather in constitutional texts. For instance, the 1801 Constitution that installed Toussaint Louverture as president for life may not have been prefaced by a Declaration of Rights, but it did contain a number of articles directly inspired by the DRMC.[47] Article 3 affirmed that, on that island, "all men are born, live, and die free and French" (Tous les hommes y naissent, vivent et meurent libres et Français), a modification of article 1 in the DRMC ("Les hommes naissent et demeurent libres et égaux en droits"). Article 5 insisted: "No other distinctions exist than those of virtues and talents. [ ... ] The law is the same for all, whether it punishes or protects," echoing article 6 of the DRMC ("Elle [la loi] doit être la même pour tous, soit qu'elle protège, soit qu'elle punisse [ ... ] sans autre distinction que celle de leurs vertus et de leurs talents"). And article 13 declared property "sacrée et inviolable," the same adjectives that the French deputies had used in their article 17 ("La propriété étant un droit inviolable et sacré ...."). Most of these rights would be reiterated in the 1805 Constitution (notably those in arts. 5 and 13, found here as arts. 4 and 6).

But the most abundant source of human rights claims in the aftermath of the American and French Revolutions is to be found in the many constitutions penned in Central and South America. As with the Haitian Constitution, many of the post-independence Spanish American republics incorporated rights provisions directly in their constitutions, rather than calling them out in separate prefatory declarations.[48] The earliest instance of this practice can be found in the former Spanish province of New Granada. Revolutionary ideas had begun circulating in this province very early on. Already in 1793, in Bogotá, the future president of Cundinamarca (now part of Columbia) Antonio Nariño had printed a Spanish translation of the DRMC, which led to his arrest and prosecution.[49] It was only after the abdication of the Spanish kings in 1808 that these rights entered into Spanish American constitutional discourse. The Venezuelan Declaration of Independence of July 5, 1811, for instance, appealed to "the imprescriptible rights that belong to all peoples," adding that their people had "been deprived of [these rights] for more than three centuries."[50] Precisely what these rights consisted of was not said in the Declaration; but the Constitution, issued that same year, was more explicit.

There was no prefatory declaration to this Constitution of "the United States of Venezuela," but its eighth chapter detailed the "[r]ights of man [derechos del hombre], which are to be acknowledged and respected throughout the whole extent of the State."[51] A certain ambiguity characterized this section. Despite referring to these rights as "derechos del hombre," the constitutional framers portrayed them as the product of civil society, and not as pre-political rights to be preserved (art. 142):

> After men have been constituted into society, they have renounced that unlimited and licentious liberty to which they were easily led by their passions, it being only adapted to a savage state. The establishment of society pre-supposes the renunciation of these fatal rights, the acquisition of others more sweet and pacific, as well as a subjection to certain mutual duties. (art. 141)

One of the reasons why the Venezuelan framers may have hedged on describing the "rights of man" in more openly universal, natural terms is that the French Revolution was widely viewed in Spanish America as a cautionary tale.[52] The distaste for the excesses of the Jacobin republic, however, did not prevent them from copying language from the DRMC, even though the latter had insisted that "the establishment of society" served to *preserve* natural rights. The Venezuelans followed the French in defining law as "the free expression of the general will . . ." (art. 149; cf. art. 6 of the DRMC). They proclaimed: "It shall not be lawful to hinder any thing not prohibited by law, and no one shall be obliged to do any thing, that is not thereby prescribed" (art. 157; cf. DRMC, art. 5: "Tout ce qui n'est pas défendu par la Loi ne peut être empêché, et nul ne peut être contraint à faire ce qu'elle n'ordonne pas"). They announced: "Every person shall be presumed innocent, till he has been declared guilty in conformity to the laws . . ." (art. 159; cf. DRMC, art. 9, identical phrasing). And, regarding criminal procedure, they affirmed that "[n]o person shall be judged, or condemned, to the sufferance of any punishment in criminal matters, till after he has been legally heard" (art. 160; cf. the very similar art. 7: "Nul homme ne peut être accusé, arrêté ni détenu que dans les cas déterminés par la Loi, et selon les formes qu'elle a prescrites").

One of the most important departures from the DRMC concerned criminal procedural rights. Here the Venezuelan framers looked to the U.S. Constitution and Bill of Rights.[53] Article 160 allowed defendants "the right of demanding the motive of the accusation attempted against [them]" (cf. art. 1, § 9, of the U.S. Constitution). It also insisted that "no person shall be compelled or forced in any cause, to give testimony against himself" (cf. the Fifth Amendment). The following article (161) established trial by jury (cf. the Sixth Amendment). Others (162–63) forbade warrantless searches (cf. the Fourth Amendment). The American influence extended to an article outlawing the quartering of soldiers during peacetime (art. 177; cf. the Third Amendment), and to the establishment of a "a well-regulated and trained militia" (una milicia bien reglada, é instruida) as the most secure defense of a free state ("la defensa [ . . . ] mas segura á un Estado libre": see art. 178; cf. the Second Amendment). This adoption of the Anglo-American emphasis on rights in the judicial sphere marked a notable step toward the eventual convergence of continental natural law theory and Anglo-American common law jurisprudence in the UDHR.

Not all Spanish American revolutionaries looked favorably upon this Constitution, which lasted for a mere year. Simón Bolívar, in his *Cartagena Manifesto* (1812), expressed skepticism about its "exaggerated notion of the rights of man" or, more specifically, the people's preparedness for them: "Generally speaking, our fellow-citizens are not yet ready to take on the full and independent exercise of their rights, because they lack the political virtues marking the true citizen of a republic. Such virtues are impossible to attain in absolutist governments, where there is no training in the rights or duties of citizenship."[54] Accordingly, in the 1821 Constitution of Cúcuta, which established Bolívar as president, there is almost no mention of individual rights.[55]

In other Spanish American constitutions, however, rights stayed front and center, and concerns about their pre-political nature diminished. The never-enacted Argentine Constitution of 1819 (officially known as the Constitution of the United Provinces of South America) embedded a "declaration of rights" as its fifth section.[56] It began with five articles on the "rights of the nation," and then listed twenty-one articles on "particular rights." The framers of this Constitution left the question of the natural versus social origins of these rights unsettled, though the implication is clearly that they preexisted the Constitution. The first article on particular rights reads, "Members of the State should be protected in their enjoyment of the rights of life, reputation, liberty, security, and property" (art. CIX). Although these rights are not ascribed to "all men" but only to "members of the state," the fact that they are referred to as "*the* rights" suggests that they had been recognized as such prior to the Constitution's enactment. The article on "freedom of publication" also describes this as "a right *as appreciable to man* as it is essential to the preservation of civil liberty" (art. CXI; emphasis added), again pointing to its universal application.

Much like the Venezuelan Constitution of 1811, the Argentine Constitution combined American and French approaches. It included a similar laundry list of criminal procedural rights: trial by jury, no warrantless searches, *habeas corpus*, and so on. But it also provided considerable leeway to the legislature in determining the extent and form of those rights. The article outlining the five basic rights that all citizens can enjoy contains a second sentence: "No one can be deprived of any of them except in accordance with law" (art. CIX). And this Constitution also incorporates the same articles from the DRMC on obligations toward the law (art. CXIII; cf. art. 5) and the sacredness of property (art. CXXIII; cf. art. 17).

While the phrasing and tenor of the many constitutions issued in post-independence Spanish America varied considerably, the initial hesitancy about *naming* rights and their possessors seems to have dissipated over time. The 1824 Acta Constitutiva of the United Mexican States, while largely modeled on the U.S. Constitution, included among its "General Provisions" an article instructing the nation "to protect by wise and just laws the rights of man [derechos del hombre] and of the citizens."[57] The Uruguayan Constitution of 1830 had a similar section on "General provisions" (§ XI), where one reads that "[a]ll men [Los hombres] are equal before the law" (art. 132).[58] And the 1857 Mexican Constitution opened with an article stating: "The Mexican people recognize that the rights of man [los derechos del hombre] are the basis and the object of social institutions."[59] One could multiply the examples, but the basic point is clear: constitutionalism was a vehicle for promoting and defending human rights during the Spanish American struggles for independence and nationhood.

## 2.2. CONSTITUTIONALISM IN
## NINETEENTH-CENTURY EUROPE

But it was not only in Spanish America that constitution making provided an opportunity for asserting human rights. Back on the Continent, the wave of successive constitutions that were issued on the Iberian peninsula and in France, Italy, Germany, and elsewhere served very much the same purpose. The Spanish Constitution of 1812, itself a model for many of the Spanish American constitutions, affirmed: "The nation is obliged to preserve and protect with sagacious and just laws civil liberty, property, and the legitimate rights [derechos legítimos] of all individuals who compose it" (art. 4).[60] This phrasing, again, was somewhat ambiguous, though the placement of this article toward the head of the Constitution, among other general statements about the Spanish nation, hinted at a pre-constitutional origin for these rights. The fact that the previous article directly echoed the DRMC ("sovereignty resides essentially in the nation . . .") reinforces this impression.[61] Ten years later, by contrast, the Portuguese had no qualms about celebrating the "most precious rights of man" (mais preciosos direitos do homem; art. 7).[62] Their Constitution echoed the French Declaration even more explicitly, opening as it did with a section on "the individual rights and duties of the Portuguese" (title 1). Article 1 defined the object of the Constitution as guaranteeing the "liberty, security, and property of all Portuguese." As with the Spanish American declarations discussed above, the framers of the 1822 Portuguese Constitution also adopted the DRMC's articles 5, 6, and 17 (here, articles 2, 12, and 6), as well as the legislative authority to define the scope of rights (see, e.g., the second clause of art. 6, "segundo as leis").

The revolutions of 1848 ushered in a second wave of constitution writing, further consolidating the place of human rights in European constitutional law. As before, different countries embraced the universal nature of these rights to varying degrees. The Frankfurt Constitution of March 28, 1849, contained a lengthy section on the "fundamental rights of German people" (§ 6), without clarifying whether these rights were "fundamentally" those of all people or only of Germans. As was increasingly the trend in nineteenth-century constitutions, many of these rights concerned the criminal justice system (e.g., §§ 137–40, 175–83). In Italy, the constitution granted by King Charles Albert of Sardinia in March 1848, known as the Statuto Albertino, included a long list of the "rights and duties of citizens" (arts. 24–32), also highlighting criminal procedure (e.g., arts. 26–27). The more liberal Constitution of the Roman Republic passed a year later, dedicating its first section to "the rights and duties of citizens."[63] Despite Mazzini's own role in drafting this Constitution, it did not specify where these rights came from. But many of the rights it proclaimed were identical to those considered human rights at the time: individuals (le persone) and property were deemed inviolable (art. 3). Freedom of thought (manifestazione del pensiero) was decreed (art. 7, paraphrasing art. 11 of the DRMC), and the death penalty was abolished (art. 5). In this and other measures, the Roman Constitution followed the model of the recent 1848 French Constitution (which similarly did away with capital punishment and slavery).

Predictably, the French offered a more full-throated embrace of human rights in their Constitution of 1848. While it did not contain a prefatory Declaration, article 3 of its Preamble asserted that the French Republic "recognizes the rights and duties that are anterior and superior to positive laws." This choice of terms is revealing: these rights both temporally precede the Constitution (and other positive laws) and legally supersede any legislation. They did not come into being through an act of constitutional founding, but were universal in application. Tellingly, the subsequent article pivoted toward international matters: the Republic "respects foreign nationalities, as it intends others to respect its own; will not engage in wars of conquest, and will not use its forces against the liberty of any people" (art. 4).[64] A legacy of the first French Revolution, this declaration of pacific intent was here linked to a supranational rights framework.

These few examples underscore why nineteenth-century constitutionalism should not be reduced to nationalism, and that, on the contrary, there was a republican tradition that carved out a place for individual human rights within national contexts. Not everyone was willing to identify these rights as universally applicable, and the precise relation between supranational rights and positive law was still under negotiation. Nor is there any reason to assume that the outcome of these negotiations would be the human rights regimes that followed a century later. But it is undeniable that, within this constitutional tradition, some framers viewed human rights as supranational restraints on governmental action, and that, regardless of where one came down on this claim, the constitutional tradition kept this debate alive. And it was in these documents that the legacy of the DRMC lived on.

### 2.3. COMPLEMENTING THE 1789 DECLARATION: SOCIAL AND ECONOMIC RIGHTS

One of the most noticeable differences between the DRMC and the UDHR are the social and economic rights included in the latter. As some of these rights are largely aspirational, outlining a social ideal rather than a reality, some have argued that they affected the very status of the UDHR. Where eighteenth-century declarations primarily sought to preserve basic pre-political rights in a political order, establishing civil rights where necessary to further this goal, the social and economic rights found in the UDHR were not in any meaningful sense "natural" or pre-political. Only a state can provide social security, health care, or education. If the revolutionaries sought to guarantee a minimum amount of protection, the UDHR drafters thus took a maximal approach, looking ahead to a more just society by holding up "a common standard of achievement for all peoples and all nations" (Preamble). The 1948 Declaration has accordingly been described as "a template for national welfarism."[65]

On this point as well, however, the differences between the Declarations of 1789 and 1948 are not as great as they seem. As we saw, there were socioeconomic rights lurking just beneath the surface of the 1789 Declaration. More important is the fact that social and economic rights did not so much emerge as a logical extension of political and judicial rights, but emerged out of a different source entirely—namely, social naturalism.[66] Indeed, it was in keeping with the ideal of natural, distributive justice that these rights first entered into political discourse; and their entrance even predated the French Revolution.

It is often assumed that social and economic rights only made their official debut in the Declaration of 1793.[67] But historians then forget the French Constitution of 1791, which already endorsed welfare ideals. Its very first section mandates, "A general bureau of public assistance [secours publics] will be created and organized, to raise abandoned children, aid the sick poor, and provide work to the able poor who cannot find any." The same section also insisted on free primary education.[68]

The adoption of social and economic rights in the 1793 Declaration, then, cannot be chalked up to pressure by the *sans-culottes* or to a more "progressive" Jacobin agenda. As we saw, concerns about public assistance, or "secours publics," had been regularly voiced for over a century.[69] During the eighteenth century, enlightened reformers sought to improve the inhumane conditions that prevailed in these places, with some genuine efforts toward free health care for the poor appearing on the eve of the French Revolution.[70] The Physiocrats and fellow free-market proponents were particularly active on this front, as they sought to maximize economic productivity and counterbalance the fluctuations of the grain trade.

It was thus more as a social duty, than as a natural right, that the objectives of public welfare were originally imposed.[71] This observation holds true both for the Constitution of 1791, and the Declaration of 1793: public assistance is there described as "a sacred debt. Society owes subsistence to unfortunate citizens, either by providing them with work, or by providing those who cannot work with the means to survive" (art. 21). To be sure, this phrasing could easily be reversed: if society has a duty to provide such assistance, unfortunate citizens have a right to it. It's revealing, however, that this right was initially, and for a long while, thought of first and foremost in terms of an obligation.

As with other rights claims, it was in the context of national constitutions that social and economic rights continued to be recognized in the nineteenth century. Article 8 of the French 1848 Constitution, ratified in November of that year, affirmed that "the Republic must [ . . . ] through fraternal assistance, provide for citizens in need, either by finding them work to the extent that it can, or by giving [ . . . ] assistance to those who can no longer work." Although the conservative-leaning Assembly had rejected the "right to work" dear to Louis Blanc and other members of the Provisional Government, and had shut down the *ateliers nationaux* in May, it retained this more traditional welfare clause.[72] The Roman Constitution of 1849 would proclaim free public education (art. 8). The Frankfurt Constitution similarly asserted that "[s]cience and teaching are free" (§ 152). The Mexican Constitution of 1917 enshrined a "right of education" (art. 3) and also guaranteed social welfare (arts. 27.20, 123.29).

As conservatives trembled before the specter of socialism, however, they, too, began to promise social rights. Bismarck passed a series of social ordinances in the 1880s, one of which established social insurance for workers.[73] And in the encyclical *Rerum novarum* (1891), written in reaction to "refute false teaching" (i.e., socialism), Pope Leo XIII also defended social welfare:

> It would be irrational to neglect one portion of the citizens and favor another, and therefore the public administration must duly and solicitously provide for the welfare and the comfort of the working classes; otherwise, that law of justice will be violated which ordains that each man shall have his due [suum cuique tribuere].[74]

This is a striking passage, as it draws upon Ulpian's founding definition of justice in Roman law to justify social welfare.[75] Inadvertently, the pontiff uncovers here the hidden origins of this right to public assistance: rather than one more right among others, it emerged as a corollary of natural law.

By the turn of the twentieth century, this distinction between an individual right and a social duty was rapidly fading, perhaps as a consequence of a new, more systematic approach to social welfare in the industrial age.[76] As a result, human rights defenders in the ensuing decades would seek to "complement" eighteenth-century declarations with a new set of rights. This effort started off in academic circles, where it was spearheaded by law professors, before gaining steam thanks to the human rights leagues that took off in the early twentieth century.

## 2.4. LAWYERS AND LEAGUES:
### GREAT EXPECTATIONS FOR A UNIVERSAL DECLARATION

Given the importance of constitutions in foregrounding human rights during the nineteenth century, it is not surprising that constitutional lawyers also played a central role in this story.[77] I have already mentioned Pasquale Fiore, the Italian professor of constitutional and international law who developed a theory of international human rights in the late nineteenth century. It was a theory that showed some teeth, as Fiore laid down a principle of state intervention in cases of human rights violations:

> No state can, by virtue of its independence, claim the right to reject the collective intervention of states which agree unanimously that the exercise of its sovereign powers constitutes a palpable violation of international law, an offense against the rights of humanity and an evident violation of common law. [ ... ] When, in the course of civil war, massacres, spoliations, torture and other atrocities occur, provided these acts as a whole are in the nature of an evident violation of international law and the sovereign of the state has neither the power nor the means to prevent offenses against the rights of humanity [diritti della personalità umana], the intervention of great powers, which agree upon the necessity of ending such abnormal conditions and of restoring the authority of common law, cannot be contested on a claim of the right of independence.[78]

Fiore's argument for a right-to-protect fell back on the more traditional "society of nations" ideal (here, "great powers"), of the kind found in earlier works on the law of nations, such as Vattel's *Droit des gens*.[79] But where these traditional defenses of *ius gladii* (the right to punish) typically rested on violations of natural *laws*, Fiore reversed the logic and made them dependent on violations of human *rights*.[80] Great powers were no longer called upon to punish offenders, but to protect victims.

As we saw, Fiore inscribed his theory of international human rights within the French revolutionary tradition, and even chose as a kind of motto Mirabeau's famous pronouncement "le droit est le souverain du monde" (law is the ruler of the world).[81] However, he revealingly misquoted Mirabeau, writing instead that "le droit *sera un jour* le souverain du monde."[82] This slip nicely captures the relation in Fiore's mind between the DRMC and the future international convention on human rights he awaited.

One of Fiore's admirers was another professor of international law, the Russian André Mandelstam (1869–1949).[83] After receiving a doctorate in law at Saint Petersburg University, he had pursued a diplomatic career, spending sixteen years at the Russian embassy in Constantinople. His public service came to a halt with the Bolshevik Revolution, which led him into exile in Paris, where he lived out the rest of his life. He became a member of the Institut de droit international (IDI), a distinguished association of international lawyers (it won the Nobel Peace Prize in 1904), and taught at the Academy of International Law in The Hague.[84]

His first book, *Le sort de l'empire Ottoman*, appeared in 1917. It was a long, complex work that delved into the history of the late Ottoman Empire, with particular attention to the Armenian Genocide of 1915. These massacres prodded Mandelstam to consider international law in the book's final chapter, which is where he enthusiastically endorsed and summarized Fiore.[85] Like his Italian predecessor, he defended humanitarian intervention ("l'intervention d'humanité") in cases of human rights violations. He even imagined the creation of a future "league" and called upon the victors of the Great War to found it. This league would rest on various principles, including "the supremacy of the common law of humanity (human law [droit humain]) and international law over the law of the state" and "the right to intervention, in the name of human law and international law, against those states that violate human rights [les droits de l'homme]."[86] Despite the dismal topic matter of his book, *Le Sort de l'empire Ottoman* retained a somewhat hopeful outlook. Mandelstam chose as an epigraph the same (misquoted) phrase by Mirabeau as Fiore: "Le Droit sera un jour le souverain du monde."

During his Paris years, Mandelstam was very active in the IDI, as well as in other networks of international lawyers, many of whom were foreigners or refugees like himself. At a session of the IDI in New York, in October 1929, he presented a Declaration of the International Rights of Man (La Déclaration des Droits Internationaux de l'Homme), which the group approved, with minor changes.[87] It was a short document, consisting of six articles and a preamble, very self-aware that its own genealogy stretched back to the revolutionary era: "The Declarations of Rights inscribed in a large number of constitutions, and in particular the American and French constitutions of the late eighteenth century, hold not only for citizens, but for man [n'ont pas seulement statut pour le citoyen, mais pour l'homme]."[88] The articles combined French-style affirmations of the right to life, liberty, and property (art. 1) with an American insistence on due process and equal protection (referring explicitly to the Fourteenth Amendment). It was well publicized in the early 1930s (see below), and still remembered in 1941, when the American jurist George Finch described it as a precursor to Roosevelt's "Four Freedoms."[89] It would be one of the declarations considered by John P. Humphrey when he prepared the first draft of the UDHR.[90]

Mandelstam was also involved in the Russian League for human rights. He was joined there by a younger Russian Jewish colleague, Boris Mirkine-Guetzévitch (1892–1955), also in exile in Paris after 1920, and like Mandelstam a professor of international law, as well as a member of the IDI.[91] Mirkine-Guetzévitch was the secretary general of the Russian league and often wrote for the *Cahiers des droits de l'homme* (*CDH*), the publication of the French Ligue des droits de l'Homme (LDH).[92] In a series of works published between 1925 and 1933, Mirkine-Guetzévitch gave the French eighteenth-century declarations greater international legitimacy, as he tracked their influence through the national constitutions written around the world after 1789.

An expert in Soviet law, Mirkine-Guetzévitch had shown an early interest in human rights in a 1925 article for the *CDH* denouncing the conditions of political prisoners in the Soviet Union. Describing the Soviet penal system as "organized sadism," he ended with an appeal to his Western readers: "[T]he horror of Soviet prisons cannot fail to deeply upset democratic consciences."[93] "Questions de conscience" were a growing issue in the interwar period, driving both Mandelstam (apropos the Armenian Genocide) and Mirkine-Guetzévitch to clamor more loudly for international human rights.[94]

The following year (1926), Mirkine-Guetzévitch published a short study of the Soviet constitution, and more particularly of its lack of human rights safeguards. After analyzing Lenin's 1918 Declaration of Rights of the Working and Exploited People, and comparing it with the DRMC, he summarily concluded that "the Rights of Man and of the Citizen [tous les Droits de l'Homme et du Citoyen] are unknown in Soviet Russia." What is most interesting about this article, however, is how Mirkine-Guetzévitch here conceptualized human rights. "[T]he Rights of Man and of the Citizen, following the French Declarations of 1789 and 1793," he wrote, "can be divided into two groups: individual rights [ ... ] and political rights."[95] This is a telling definition, as it suggests that for Mirkine-Guetzévitch the French eighteenth-century Declarations pointed toward a set of rights whose existence and legal standing were largely independent of their (historically contextual) Declaration. The fact that the DRMC was a French document, in this regard, was irrelevant. The rights it had announced were of all times and all places. Accordingly, all states must accept them, regardless of whether they recognized the DRMC per se. As we will see, this was also the understanding of the LDH: the motto it chose for its publication (the *CDH*) was

Have human rights been proclaimed?—Yes.
Have they been applied?—No!

But even Mirkine-Guetzévitch recognized that the 1789 and 1793 Declarations were incomplete. In a study of the European constitutions issued after 1918, he observed:

> In 1789 and 1793, it was those Rights of Man and of the Citizen that corresponded to the age that were inscribed. Clearly none of them are obsolete, but the list itself is incomplete in the twentieth century. Life today requires not only the preservation of all the rights found in the 1789 Declaration, but also that of the new rights that emerged with the evolution of society. The new European constitutions, in this respect, have kept up with this evolution.[96]

It was in the manifold constitutions issued since 1789, and more particularly after 1918, that Mirkine-Guetzévitch discovered the necessary complements to the French Declarations. He published a number of volumes in the field of comparative constitutional law, a field he helped to establish, often with French translations of constitutions from around the world.[97] In the post-WWI constitutions, Mirkine-Guetzévitch identified a tendency that he called "the rationalization of power," which he again traced back to the French Revolution.[98] One element in this rationalization was the inclusion of human rights provisions in the constitutions themselves.[99] Indeed, for Mirkine-Guetzévitch, national constitutions were the logical place for such provisions to be located, since it was typically at the national level that violations could most readily be prosecuted.[100] It was through constitutions—not only those issued post-1918, but all constitutions written in the aftermath of the French Revolution—that the spirit of the DRMC had survived and grown, adding new social and economic rights.[101]

This was also the take-away of his 1929 collection of world constitutions. His coeditor was Alphonse Aulard, who had held the chair for the History of the French Revolution at the Sorbonne until 1922 (he died in 1928). At the head of their volume, they placed the 1789 Declaration. Since, from a chronological standpoint, it was not actually the first, they felt the need to justify their decision: "Although the American declarations are the oldest, it is the French declarations, in particular of 1789, whose influence was greater, as the following texts will show."[102] Their collection included a thorough index, allowing readers to see how rights originally announced in the DRMC were repeated, often word for word, in constitutions the world over.

Given his admiration for the DRMC, it is unsurprising that Mirkine-Guetzévitch was so closely associated with the LDH. This organization had been founded in 1898 under the presidency of Ludovic Trarieux—a lawyer, senator, and former Justice minister, who testified in favor of Emile Zola at his trial during the Dreyfus Affair.[103] It was in response to this affair that Trarieux and some Dreyfusard colleagues established the LDH, which remains in existence today and is one of the oldest human rights NGOs. For its founding charter, they did not draw up a new document, but simply chose the DRMC.[104] The full title of this organization highlights its revolutionary genealogy even more clearly: it is officially known as the French League of the Defense of the Rights of Man and of the Citizen (Ligue française pour la défense des droits de l'Homme et du citoyen).

During the Third Republic, the LDH enjoyed remarkable success: in 1933 it boasted 180,000 members throughout France, including many politicians and ministers.[105] It would inspire over a dozen similar leagues, mainly in other European nations, but also in Egypt, Turkey, and China.[106] Though the Third Republic famously did not adopt the DRMC or any other declaration as part of its 1875 constitutional laws, the LDH participated in the promulgation of a "national catechism" based on a "cult" of *les droits de l'homme*.[107]

The relevance of LDH to the history of human rights has been disputed by Samuel Moyn, who argued that such groups, to which he added the American Civil Liberties Union (ACLU), "rooted their claims not in universal law but in allegedly deep national traditions of freedom. [ . . . ] For many years, civil libertarians mostly gazed within, rather than toward the suffering around the world. And so they did not spark the creation of international human rights as an idea or as a movement."[108] In a more recent work, Moyn further argued that "1789 and the liberal secular values for which that date stood in European and world history were not popular in the 1930s or even 1940s and may not have survived the coming of dignity unscathed"; and he faulted Mirkine-Guetzévitch for having "been blind to the era's true breakthrough," which in his view was the recognition of human dignity as the foundation of rights.[109] It is the inscription of "the dignity and worth of the human person" (la dignité et la valeur de la personne humaine) in the Preamble to the UDHR, that for Moyn should instead tip off historians that they need to look at Christian doctrines.

Taken together, these arguments present a very lopsided account of the LDH and of its role in the development of international human rights, as well as of the importance of "liberal secular values" during this period. To begin with, it is not the case that the LDH "mostly gazed within." While the group did choose a national document as its founding charter, it saw this document as a universal, not a national, model. Already in 1901, the LDH was proclaiming: "The spirit [of the 1789 Declaration] should be the charter for our *international* relations."[110] Moyn's lumping together of the LDH with the ACLU is misleading: while the LDH served as a model for the ACLU, the two organizations had vastly different profiles.[111] Where the ACLU focused on domestic issues (e.g., the Scopes Trial, in 1925), the LDH was equally, if not more, preoccupied with global concerns.[112] As we saw, it was in the journal of the French LDH that Mirkine-Guetzévitch published his account of human rights violations in Soviet prisons; the same issue contained an article on war in Morocco.

It was precisely such attention to "the suffering around the world" that inspired the LDH to take the lead in "the creation of international human rights as an idea" and "as a movement." Moyn omits to mention that in 1922 members of the LDH and other affiliated groups founded an umbrella group, the Fédération internationale des ligues des droits de l'Homme, known today by its French acronym, FIDH. This organization also found its governing spirit in the French Revolution. Article 3 of its founding charter proclaimed, "The goal of the Federation is to propagate and realize *in all countries* the principles of justice, liberty, equality, and popular sovereignty derived from the French Declarations of the Rights of Man of 1789 and 1793."[113]

In an "appeal to all peoples," issued at the time of its creation, the Federation insisted on "the sacred and inviolable character of the human person [la personne humaine] and of the natural union of persons known as a people."[114] This reference to the human person highlights another problem with Moyn's criticism and counternarrative: Christian thinkers were not alone in adopting the concept of personhood.[115] Moyn acknowledged that "the essential indeterminacy of the concept itself made personalism highly ambiguous," though he held that it could in fact be defined negatively, as "a repudiation of the rival materialisms of liberalism and communism."[116] In the FIDH's *appel*, however, we find a liberal, republican discourse rooted in the French Revolution (the expression "sacred and inviolable" is also taken from the DRMC: see art. 17). In fact, liberals and communists could invoke "the human person" just as well. Pasquale Fiore uses the expression regularly in his 1890 *International Law Codified*.[117] To consider a few other examples, a 1921 article by a communist militant referred to the "sacred rights of every human person"; the concept was incorporated into a well-known academic treatise on international law; and a feminist publication noted that "woman, like man, equally to man, is a human person."[118] This last example is perhaps the most instructive: in the age of suffragism, it was unfashionable to speak only of "droits de *l'homme*," and "the human person" was conveniently gender neutral.[119] It did not necessarily convey a Thomistic, anti-individualist conception.

Together, the European leagues for the defense of human rights played a central role in demanding a new universal declaration of human rights and continually invoked the Declarations of 1789 and 1793 as their point of departure. To be sure, the *ligueurs*, as they were known, did not always recognize human rights violations where we see them today. Many members accepted, and even encouraged, European colonialism as a way of extending human rights to "backwards" countries.[120] But it was in the context of this international movement that the different efforts discussed above merged and surged in an institutional groundswell.

Indeed, by 1930, numerous national leagues were calling for a new and extended declaration of human rights, ideally to be "guaranteed" by the League of Nations. At a meeting of the FIDH's executive council in 1930, Victor Basch (then president of the French LDH) offered a rationale for such a revision. "The old Declaration of 1789 no longer satisfies national and international needs," he observed. Accordingly, he approved his Austrian colleague Rudolf Goldschied's proposal to assemble "a Congress to issue a new declaration which would add articles dealing with contemporary questions (female suffrage, trade unions, etc.)." Other delegates noted similar calls made by the Swiss and Serbian leagues.[121]

The following year, in 1931, the same council discussed a motion by the German league to place "the revision of the Declaration of the Rights of Man" on the agenda for their upcoming Congress.[122] The council dithered, but the 1932 Congress in Paris indeed addressed the *"revision of the 'Declarations of Right.'"*[123] The first speaker was Mandelstam, who encouraged deputies by assuring them that "since the Great War, the modern science of international law evolves, at a rapid pace, toward the primacy of international and human law [la primauté du droit international et du droit humain] over state law" (34). He also shared his own proposal for a Declaration of International Human Rights, adopted by the IDI three years prior, whose contents he described article by article.[124] Mirkine-Guetzévitch spoke next, underscoring how current efforts should emphasize the "expansion [élargissement] of the content of the Declarations [of 1789 and 1793]" (35–36), as opposed to any fundamentally new ideas. The revolutionary declarations were still seen as foundational; the goal now was to elaborate on their principles. Basch drove this point home, suggesting that the first nine articles of the 1789 Declaration be left in place, as a basis for a new declaration (36). Ultimately, the Congress agreed to recognize the existence of international human rights, though punted on the contents of the revised declaration (37).

Four years later, the executive council of the FIDH finally placed the "Nouvelle Déclaration des Droits de l'Homme et du Citoyen" on the agenda for its Luxembourg Congress in March 1936.[125] A commission including Basch and Mandelstam drew up a draft proposal, and the international Congress ultimately approved this "Project for a Complement to the Declaration of the Rights of Man." As its title suggests, this proposal was presented and understood as an addendum to the Declarations of 1789 and 1793, a point made abundantly clear in its preface: "Human rights [les Droits de l'Homme], 'natural, inalienable, and sacred rights,' were inscribed in the Declaration of 1789," reads its first sentence. The "Complement" insists on a number of aspects that had not been stressed in the French revolutionary Declarations. For instance, article 1 emphasizes that rights are afforded regardless of sex, race, nationality, or religion (precisely the claim found in article 2 of the UDHR); article 3 details the rights of mothers; and articles 5–7 outline the social rights of workers. But none of these additions were presented as departures.

The draft for this "Complement" was described by René Georges-Etienne, who presented it to the LDH in July, as the spiritual legacy of Aulard, a *ligueur* and (as we saw above) leading historian of the French Revolution who had collaborated with Mirkine-Guetzévitch on a comparative volume of revolutionary declarations.[126] Aulard had also presided over the inaugural meeting of the FIDH in 1922.[127] Inspired by Aulard's teachings, Georges-Etienne again depicted the drafting committee's proposal as a literal complement: it was not intended to replace the "magnificent" Declarations of 1789 and 1793, which were still idealized around the world, but merely to bring them up-to-date.[128] As the LDH's vice president Albert Bayet put it, "just as the Declaration of '93 respected the Declaration of '89, the Declaration of 1936 must, I believe, respect those of '89 and '93."[129]

The international Congress had encouraged all the national leagues to discuss and refine its proposal. Conveniently, the French league was meeting four months later in Dijon. The Central Committee of the French LDH made a few minor modifications to the Luxembourg proposal, before submitting it to its membership, alongside a number of alternative proposals.[130] After a lengthy debate, the LDH members approved the "Complement."[131] The action of the LDH has at times been portrayed as *sui generis* but was obviously related to the FIDH's prior work.[132] Basch himself participated in both the Luxembourg and Dijon Congresses, as did the LDH's *rapporteur*, Georges-Etienne. In presenting the Central Committee's draft proposal, Georges-Etienne noted that the FIDH had considered various approaches—they could have started from scratch and scrapped the earlier revolutionary Declarations.[133] This would be the approach mostly favored by the drafters of the UDHR. But the LDH's approach shows how these earlier efforts to produce a new, universal declaration of human rights were very much conducted in the long shadow of the French Revolution.[134]

## 3. The Archaeology of the Universal Declaration of Human Rights

One of the LDH members present at the 1936 Dijon Congress was René Cassin. Cassin (1887–1976) had been a member of the LDH since 1921.[135] Educated during the Third Republic in its *écoles laïques*, trained as a lawyer and jurist (specializing in civil law), and born into a Jewish family, he embodied the republican, secular tradition of human rights that the LDH championed. During the 1930s, he met Mirkine-Guetzévitch, whose classes and writings he lauded after the latter's death.[136] One of the first lawyers to rally to the Free French government in London, Cassin would go on to play a celebrated role in the drafting of the UDHR, a role for which he (and, controversially, he alone) received the Nobel Peace Prize in 1968.

While Cassin contributed in many ways to the UDHR, including proposing its name, one of his primary achievements seems to have been editorial.[137] The principal first draft of the UDHR was prepared by the director of the Human Rights Division of the UN Secretariat, the Canadian jurist John P. Humphrey. He put together a "Draft Outline of International Bill of Rights," while his division produced a 410-page "Documented Outline," a dossier of primary sources, providing examples taken from national constitutions for each of the articles in the Humphrey draft.[138] Cassin then translated this draft into French and added some new material (including most of the Preamble), though not a great amount. In one estimation, "three-quarters of the Cassin draft was taken from Humphrey's first draft."[139] While this revelation has led some historians to minimize Cassin's role in the drafting process, he did undertake one important step, which was to reorganize the articles in the "Secretariat Outline."[140] In so doing, he produced a draft declaration that was more coherent and that also laid bare its genealogy.

Indeed, Cassin's draft neatly reflects the different layers of human rights history. He organized the articles into nine chapters, whose titles would disappear in the final declaration, but whose ordering principle would remain. They were

General Principles
Right to Life and to Physical Integrity
Personal Freedoms
Legal Status
Public Freedoms
Political Rights
Nationality and Protection of Aliens (Etrangers)
Social, Economic, and Cultural Rights
Final Dispositions

This structure brought articles that had been scattered throughout Humphrey's draft into logical groupings. For instance, where Humphrey dealt with criminal procedure in articles 4, 6, 7, and 11, Cassin collected them all into his fourth chapter. This editorial work should not be undersold: as Pascal observed, "Let no one say that I have said nothing new: the arrangement of the material is new."[141] In reorganizing the articles, moreover, Cassin teased apart the different tributaries that flowed into the UDHR.

The final version of the UDHR would depart in some areas from Cassin's draft, but it followed his basic structure. Articles 1–5 merge the first three of Cassin's categories, laying down general principles (arts. 1 and 2), the right to life and physical integrity (i.e., abolition of torture; see arts. 3 and 5), and personal liberty (i.e., abolition of slavery: art. 4). If the terminology in these articles partially reflects more recent developments in human rights talk (e.g., the reference to "dignity" in article 1, and the explicit enumeration of ethnic, sexual, and religious difference in article 2), these are still the rights one could already find in eighteenth-century declarations and that stem from the continental natural law tradition.

With article 6, the Declaration moves on to Cassin's list of juridical rights, including some of the articles he had placed in the chapter on personal liberty. These rights were conspicuously missing from the DRMC and originate in the Anglo-American common law tradition. They had been detailed in the U.S. Bill of Rights, as well as in numerous nineteenth- and twentieth-century constitutions.[142] They are discussed in seven articles (6–12) and make up the longest section in the UDHR.

Cassin's chapter on nationality and foreigners comes next, consisting of articles 13–15, followed by a section that combines his "personal liberties" and "political rights." These articles (16–21) address the right to marry, the right to own property, freedoms of thought, expression, and religion, freedom of association, and the right to participate in government through free elections. With the exception of the right to marry (which earlier theorists had not deemed necessary to make explicit), these are also rights that were typically present in eighteenth-century declarations. They appear "later," both in the declarations and time, as they are rights that become manifest in political society.

Article 22 marks the turn to "economic, social, and cultural rights," rights that already appeared in the French Constitution of 1791 and Declaration of 1793, and that attracted increasing interest after 1848. This section contains six articles (22–27), including rights that had only recently been formulated (e.g., the right to "periodic holidays with pay"; art. 24). Finally, the UDHR closes with a series of "Final Dispositions" (arts. 28–30), which lay out a framework for interpreting the Declaration itself.

Breaking down the articles of the Declaration in this manner thus reveals both its historical layers and manifold sources. That these layers are stacked in an almost geological fashion, according to their moments of historical importance, is unsurprising given what we know about the drafting process. The committee primarily sought inspiration in the French Declarations of 1789 and 1793, in the U.S. Bill of Rights, and in the fifty-five national constitutions listed in Humphrey's "Documented Outline," along with some more recent attempts by Jacques Maritain and H. G. Wells.[143] Both Cassin and Humphrey before him borrowed liberally from previous declarations, constitutions, and other statements (such as the Atlantic Charter). It is only to be expected, then, that the UDHR's different sections and articles would echo different chapters in the history of human rights.

By calling attention to the historical strata of the UDHR, I do not mean to suggest that certain sections merely copy earlier rights claims. Many scholars have drawn comparisons between the UDHR and the DRMC, but the differences are just as striking.[144] Most notable, perhaps, is the disappearance of the "legalistic" insistence that rights be curbed, where necessary, by laws—a desire, as we saw in chapter 6, that derived from the broader faith in social naturalism. A century later, the idea that all of society could be reformed according to the laws of nature would seem quaint. As Martti Koskenniemi notes, natural law had become "an outdated concept [ ... ] that had little intellectual credibility."[145] But the DRMC can also not be reduced to this one dimension, and many of its articles transcended this limitation.

The vocal championing of human rights by Christian thinkers should of course be inserted into this excavation of the UDHR. For instance, the three references to the "dignity" of all human beings (twice in the Preamble, once in article 1) were probably influenced by the success that this concept enjoyed Christian circles.[146] But it is hard to see why Christian doctrines of the 1930s and '40s should be granted a privileged status in the UDHR's genealogy.[147] As we saw, one did not have to be Christian to celebrate "the human person," nor was dignity an essentially theological category.[148] As Charles Beitz has noted, dignity in the UDHR mainly does the foundational work that natural law had previously done in the eighteenth century.[149] If anything, it allowed the drafters to sidestep any explicit theological or metaphysical reference.[150] In any case, given that the drafters discovered most of the UDHR's articles in national constitutions, and that republican, secular groups and individuals had been pushing for an international declaration since WWI, it did not take the endorsement of the Church or of Christian thinkers to realize the idea of an international declaration of human rights.

At the same time, there is no reason to present this history as an either/or choice. Christian thinkers such as Maritain, after all, became very close to the secular jurists like Cassin or Mirkine-Guetzévitch (who eventually converted to Catholicism).[151] And why shouldn't they have? The constitutional and Thomist branches of human rights had grown out of the same trunk. If they moved apart during the French Revolution, they became close again in the twentieth century, sometimes to the secularists' surprise.[152] In between, both branches extended in unpredictable directions, the revolutionary Declarations nourishing a thicket of national constitutions, and the Church recasting its social ministry in terms of social rights. While neither of these developments was preordained, a lengthy historical perspective suggests that the antagonism between Christian and constitutional traditions was more accidental than profound. The Church had not objected per se to the French Declaration of 1789; it was only in response to the Civil Constitution of the Clergy, and the annexation of papal lands in France, that the Vatican lashed out at the revolutionaries. But that political skirmish did not rest on any fundamental disagreement about the existence of human rights or the need to preserve them in political society. Four centuries after a neo-Thomist and constitutional revival of natural rights theory got under way at the University of Paris, these twin traditions merged together again under the auspices of the United Nations. This merger would have important ramifications for the postwar period, particularly for the embrace of the UDHR by the papacy.[153] But it was only one among multiple factors leading to its promulgation. An arguably more critical role was played by the Declaration of 1789, whose universal spirit inspired generations of politicians and lawyers to continue pushing for rights guarantees around the world.

# Acknowledgments

This book started out life, eight years ago, as a review of Lynn Hunt's *Inventing Human Rights* (2007) and Samuel Moyn's *The Last Utopia* (2010). Despite our disagreements, Lynn and Sam have been model interlocutors throughout the book's gestation, and their ideas and comments have spurred me on at many junctures. I am deeply grateful for their insights, encouragement, and example. Thanks also to Joël Castonguay-Bélanger for the invitation to the University of British Columbia that set this project in motion.

It was at Princeton's University Center for Human Values, where I spent a happy year as Laurance S. Rockefeller Visiting Professor, that this book really took shape. Conversations and lunches with Chuck Beitz, Peter Brooks, Melissa Lane, Jan-Werner Mueller, Philip Pettit, and Annie Stilz proved invaluable for the book's genesis, as were discussions with UCHV fellows, in particular Alison McQueen, David Plunkett, Amy Dru Stanley, and Alec Walen. I also benefited greatly from interactions with the wider Princeton community, including David Bellos, Göran Blix, Linda Colley, Anthony Grafton, Yair Mintzker, Phil Nord, Sophie Rosenfeld (then at IAS), Mira Siegelberg, and Steve Vincent (also at IAS). As always, David A. Bell was a cherished interlocutor, dear friend, mentor, and happy hour companion.

I greatly benefited from the feedback of colleagues who took the time to read or listen to sections of this work. At the Université Paris-Sorbonne (Paris IV), thanks to Pierre Serna; at the University of California, Berkeley, to Carla Hesse and Jonathan Sheehan; at Washington University in Saint Louis, to Tili Boon Cuillé and Rebecca Messbarger; in Turin, and then again in Venice, to Patrizia Delpiano, Vicenzo Ferrone, Franco Motta, and Gerardo Tocchini; at Columbia, to Charly Coleman, Madeleine Dobie, and Pierre Force; at Cornell, to Elizabeth Anker, Jason Frank, Paul Friedland, and Camille Robcis;

at Trinity College, Dublin, to James Hanrahan; at Johns Hopkins, to Wilda Anderson, Michael Kwass, Laura Mason, Jacques Neefs, and Elena Russo; at Bryn Mawr, Rudy Le Menthéour and Jennifer Tamas; at Dartmouth, Larry Kritzman and Darrin McMahon; and at Wesleyan, Andrew Curran, Ethan Kleinberg, and Matthew Specter; and at the Institute for Historical Research, in London, to Richard Bourke and Quentin Skinner.

I am fortunate to rub elbows with intimidating colleagues here at Stanford, who also provide me with exceptional guidance: thanks especially to Jonathan Gienapp, Robert P. Harrison, Josh Landy, Glory Liu, Alison McQueen (again), Bernadette Meyler, Josiah Ober, Jack Rakove, Debra Satz, Matthew Smith, Norm Spaulding, and Caroline Winterer. This book would never have seen the light of day without the friendship, mentorship, and generosity of Keith M. Baker, to whom it is dedicated.

I'm equally grateful to friends and colleagues at other institutions: special thanks to David Armitage, Stefanos Geroulanos, David Grewal, Stefan-Ludwig Hoffmann, Daniel Lee, Antoine Lilti, Anton Matytsin, Robert Morrissey, Emmanuel Naquet, Arnaud Orain, Emma Rothschild, Quentin Skinner, Eric Slauter, Mark Somos, Céline Spector, Benjamin Straumann, and Charles Walton. Not for the first time, this book was written in parallel with a book by Jacob Soll—*merci, mon vieux*. And many thanks to Gerardo Tocchini for suggesting the image on the book cover.

At the University of Chicago Press, I have enjoyed the expert stewardship of a phenomenal editorial crew: special thanks to Alan Thomas, Priya Nelson, and Dylan Montanari. They chose ideal reviewers for this book, whose reports were amazingly helpful. Since both of them outed themselves, I can thank Paul Friedland and Kent Wright for their reviews. Thanks as well to my eagle-eyed copy editor, Erin DeWitt.

I am grateful to my research assistants for this project: thanks to Phoebus Cotsapas, Biliana Kassabova, Dhara Yu, and Lena Zlock.

I tried not to inconvenience my family too much while writing this book. Thanks to *Frozen*, my daughters, Anaïs and Eloise, learned about behavior "that's a little outside of nature's laws." If my prose is at all legible, my wife, Zoë, should take the credit (death to semicolons!). My parents and sister Jenny have been a constant source of encouragement and support. Teddy Bear, our beloved Keeshond, lay beside me as I wrote some of the earliest chapters; I wish he lay beside me still.

As one leaves an empty place setting for Elijah, I would also like to recognize the many colleagues and students who nudged this book on at different times, and whose contributions I have failed to record here.

*

An early version of this book's thesis appeared in the *Journal of Modern History* ("Enlightenment Rights Talk"). Thanks to Jan Goldstein for her comments and help in ushering it into press, as well as to the three anonymous reviewers. I worked out some of the more theoretical parts of the project in an article for *Humanity* ("Is There a 'Modern' Natural Law Theory? Notes on the History of Human Rights"), which Sam Moyn was generous to solicit. A summary of the first few chapters came out as "Early-Modern Rights Regimes: A Genealogy of Revolutionary Rights," in *Critical Analysis of Law*—thanks to Norm Spaulding for inviting me to participate in that issue. Parts of chapter 7 feature in *Rethinking the Age of Revolutions: France and the Birth of the Modern World*, edited by David A. Bell and Yair Mintzker. And my arguments about the Catholic Church and human rights are drawn from two fora on Moyn's recent book, *Christian Human Rights*: "Not Church History?" in *The Immanent Frame*, and "Christian Human Rights in the French Revolution," in the *Journal of the History of Ideas*. Thanks to Daniel Steinmetz-Jenkins and Udi Greenberg for organizing these.

# *Notes*

## Chapter I

1. See notably Quentin Skinner, *The Foundations of Modern Political Thought* (Cambridge: Cambridge University Press, 1978), vol. 2, chap. 5; Richard Tuck, *Natural Rights Theories: Their Origins and Development* (Cambridge: Cambridge University Press, 1979); Brian Tierney, *The Idea of Natural Rights: Studies on Natural Rights, Natural Law, and Church Law, 1150–1625* (Atlanta: Scholars Press, 1997); and Annabel Brett, *Liberty, Right and Nature: Individual Rights in Later Scholastic Thought* (Cambridge: Cambridge University Press, 1997).

2. See the speech by Governor Hutchinson to the Massachusetts Assembly, discussed in chapter 6.

3. The term is fairly common in the literature: see notably Jack Donnelly, *Universal Human Rights in Theory and Practice* (Ithaca, NY: Cornell University Press, 2002), chap. 8.

4. In *Leviathan*, this right is takes three forms: "the right of resisting them, that assault him by force, to take away his life," and the rights of refusing to be wounded or imprisoned: *Leviathan*, in *The Clarendon Edition of the Works of Thomas Hobbes*, ed. Noel Malcolm (Oxford: Clarendon Press, 2012), vol. 4, 1.14, p. 202. I return to Hobbes in chapter 2.

5. "Individual rights are political trumps held by individuals. [ . . . ] Individuals have rights when, for some reason, a collective goal is not a sufficient justification for denying them what they wish, as individuals, to have or to do . . .": Ronald Dworkin, *Taking Rights Seriously* (Cambridge, MA: Harvard University Press, 1977), 6.

6. See, respectively, the Virginia Declaration of Rights (1776), § 1; and the French Declaration of the Rights of Man and of the Citizen (1789), art. 2.

7. See Lorraine Daston and Fernando Vidal, eds., *The Moral Authority of Nature* (Chicago: University of Chicago Press, 2004).

8. See, e.g., Francisco Suárez, *De legibus ac deo legislatore* (1612): "the precepts of the *ius gentium* were introduced by the free will and consent of mankind [ . . . ] therefore they are a part of the human, and not of the natural law." In *On the Laws and God the Lawgiver*, 2.17.8, in *Selections from Three Works of Francisco Suárez*, trans. Gwladys L. Williams et al., ed. Henry Davis (Oxford: Clarendon Press/Carnegie Endowment, 1944), 332.

9. See chapter 5.

10. Rousseau, *The Social Contract*, 1.6, in *The Social Contract and Other Later Political Writings*, ed. Victor Gourevitch (Cambridge: Cambridge University Press, 1997), 50. More generally, see Joshua Cohen, *Rousseau: A Free Community of Equals* (Oxford: Oxford University Press, 2010), 82–83.

11. See Robert Derathé, *Jean-Jacques Rousseau et la science politique de son temps* (1950; Paris: Vrin, 1995).

12. See Quentin Skinner, *Hobbes and Republican Liberty* (Cambridge: Cambridge University Press, 2008), 152–54.

13. Samuel Moyn, *The Last Utopia: Human Rights in History* (Cambridge, MA: Belknap Press of Harvard University Press, 2010), 12, 14.

14. See Quentin Skinner, "Meaning and Understanding in the History of Ideas," *History and Theory* 8, no. 1 (1969): 3–53.

15. See, e.g., John Pocock, "Virtue, Rights, and Manners: A Model for Historians of Political Thought," in *Virtue, Commerce, and History* (Cambridge: Cambridge University Press, 1976).

16. See Samuel Moyn, "The Continuing Perplexities of Human Rights," *Qui Parle* 22, no. 1 (2013): 95–115.

17. For a recent exposition of the staying power of Roman law in early modern European political thought, see Benjamin Straumann, *Roman Law in the State of Nature: The Classical Foundations of Hugo Grotius' Natural Law* (Cambridge: Cambridge University Press, 2015).

18. See Paolo Grossi, *A History of European Law*, trans. Laurence Hooper (Chichester, UK: Wiley-Blackwell, 2010).

19. For instance, Ulpian's famous definition of justice, "Iustitia est constans et perpetua voluntas ius suum cuique tribuendi" (*Digest* 1.1.10), draws on Cicero: "the Greek name for law (νομος), which is derived from νεμω, to distribute, implies the very nature of the thing, that is, to give every man his due (suum cuique tribuendo)." Cicero, *De legibus*, trans. Clinton Walker Keyes (Cambridge, MA: Harvard University Press/Loeb, 1928), 1.5. Cicero may have had Plato's *Republic* in mind, more specifically the definition of justice attributed there to Simonides: "it is just to give to each what is owed to him" (τὸ τὰ ὀφειλόμενα ἑκάστῳ ἀποδιδόναι δίκαιόν ἐστι). *The Republic*, in *Plato Complete Works*, ed. John M. Cooper and D. S. Hutchinson (Indianapolis: Hackett Publishing Company, 1997), 331e. See Aldo Schiavone, *The Invention of Law in the West*, trans. Jeremy Carden and Antony Shugaar (Cambridge, MA: Harvard University Press, 2012); and Andrew Riggsby, *Roman Law and the Legal World of the Romans* (Cambridge: Cambridge University Press, 2010).

20. See Harold Berman, *Law and Revolution: The Formation of the Western Legal Tradition* (Cambridge, MA: Harvard University Press, 1983). William Blackstone's 1756 *An Analysis of the Laws of England* (the precursor to his better-known *Commentaries on the Laws of England*) was merely one in a long series of works that sought to codify common law within the structures of civil (i.e., Roman) law: see chapter 5.

21. *Institutes*, 1.2.1.

22. See, for instance, preface to *The Classical Tradition*, ed. Anthony Grafton, Glenn W. Most, and Salvatore Settis (Cambridge, MA: Harvard University Press, 2010), vii–xi.

23. Aristotle, *The Art of Rhetoric*, trans. H. C. Lawson-Tancred (London: Penguin, 1991), 1.13, p. 125. The *Rhetoric* was translated into French on at least seven different occasions, most of which were published in multiple editions. Two further editions appeared in 1718 and 1733. In his *Encyclopédie* article on "Esprit," Voltaire wrote, "Aristotle taught perfectly in his *Rhetoric* how to say things wittily [avec esprit]." In Denis Diderot and Jean le Rond d'Alembert, eds., *Encyclopédie, ou dictionnaire raisonné des sciences, des arts et des métiers, etc.*, ed. Robert Morrissey and Glenn

Roe (University of Chicago: ARTFL Encyclopédie Project, 2016), 5:974. More broadly, see my chapter on "The Aristotelian Enlightenment," in *Let There be Enlightenment*, ed. Anton Matytsin and Dan Edelstein (Baltimore: Johns Hopkins University Press, 2018).

24. In French, this is still the meaning of *le droit*, as in the phrase, *le droit civil*. I develop some of the arguments in this section in "Is There a 'Modern' Natural Law Theory? Notes on the History of Human Rights," *Humanity* 7, no. 3 (2016): 345–64.

25. See *Institutes*, 1.1; and Michel Villey, "La genèse du droit subjectif chez Guillaume d'Occam," *Archives de philosophie du droit* 9 (1964): 97–127 (esp. 103). Villey glosses *ius suum* as "son juste partage."

26. For Michel Villey, see in particular *Leçons d'histoire de la philosophie du droit* (Paris: Dalloz, 1962); "La genèse du droit subjectif"; and *Le Droit et les droits de l'homme* (Paris: PUF, 1983). On Villey, see Tierney, *Idea of Natural Rights*; Stéphane Rials, *Villey et les idoles* (Paris: PUF, 2000); Norbert Campagna, *Michel Villey, le droit ou les droits?* (Paris: Michalon, 2004); Francis Oakley, *Natural Law, Laws of Nature, Natural Rights: Continuity and Discontinuity in the History of Ideas* (New York: Continuum, 2005), 95–106; and Pierre-Yves Quiviger, *Le Secret du droit naturel, ou Après Villey* (Paris: Garnier, 2012).

27. Villey, *Le Droit et les droits de l'homme*.

28. Tuck, *Natural Rights Theories*. Tuck discusses Villey extensively at 7–13, 19–23.

29. Tuck, *Natural Rights Theories*, 13.

30. Leo Strauss, *Natural Right and History* (Chicago: University of Chicago Press, 1953), 181, 183.

31. Tuck references Strauss's *The Political Philosophy of Hobbes* (Oxford: Clarendon Press, 1936), in *Natural Rights Theories*, 125n17.

32. Richard Tuck, *The Rights of War and Peace* (Oxford: Oxford University Press, 1999), 5. The discussion of Strauss in this work prefaces his explanation of why he abandoned the claim, in *Natural Rights Theories*, that the Protestant natural lawyers had rejected Renaissance humanism: "in fact the 'modern' school of natural law arose not out of a critique or repudiation of the Renaissance, but out of a profound sympathy with some of the fundamental themes of Renaissance political and moral thought" (5). This had of course been a major element of Strauss's own theory of modern natural right, namely, the debt that Hobbes owed to Machiavelli.

33. See Anthony Pagden's introduction to Francisco de Vitoria, *Political Writings*, ed. and trans. Anthony Pagden and Jeremy Lawrance (Cambridge: Cambridge University Press, 1991), xvi. There is no reference substantiating this claim, but its debt to Tuck's thesis (which had been restated in an earlier volume of essays edited by Pagden) is evident. See also Anthony Pagden, "Human Rights, Natural Rights, and Europe's Imperial Legacy," *Political Theory* 31, no. 2 (April 2003): 171–99.

34. See Jerome Schneewind, *The Invention of Autonomy: A History of Modern Moral Philosophy* (Cambridge: Cambridge University Press, 1998).

35. See J. H. Burns, "Conclusion," in *The Cambridge History of Political Thought, 1450–1700*, ed. J. H. Burns and Mark Goldie (Cambridge: Cambridge University Press, 1991), 654. While this narrative of a "radical break with the received ideas of long past" cannot be attributed to Tuck alone, his account of Protestant natural law theories clearly sustained it. Tuck's own contribution to this volume, which revisits his earlier claims, appears in the part entitled "The End of Aristotelianism."

36. Tierney himself would propose a different, but chronologically similar, genealogy, situating the flourishing of subjective rights during "the great age of creative jurisprudence that, in the twelfth and thirteenth centuries, established the foundations of the Western legal tradition":

*Idea of Natural Rights*, 42. Tierney is drawing here on Berman, *Law and Revolution*. Brett makes similar points in *Liberty, Right and Nature*; see also her chapter "Individual and Community in the 'Second Scholastic': Subjective Rights in Domingo de Soto and Francisco Suárez," in *Philosophy in the Sixteenth and Seventeenth Centuries: Conversations with Aristotle*, ed. Constance Blackwell and Sachiko Kusukawa (London: Routledge, 1999).

37. See notably Fred D. Miller, *Nature, Justice, and Rights in Aristotle's "Politics"* (Oxford: Oxford University Press, 1995); Phillip Mitsis, "The Stoic Origin of Natural Rights," in *Topics in Stoic Philosophy*, ed. Katerina Ierodiakonou (Oxford: Clarendon Press, 1999), 153–57; Benjamin Straumann, "Is Modern Liberty Ancient? Roman Remedies and Natural Rights in Hugo Grotius's Early Works on Natural Law," *Law and History Review* 27, no. 1 (2009): 55–85; and Straumann, *Roman Law*.

38. Tierney, *Idea of Natural Rights*, 31, 33.

39. Hugo Grotius, *The Rights of War and Peace* (1625), 3 vols., ed. Richard Tuck, trans. John Morrice et al. (Indianapolis: Liberty Fund, 2005), Prolegomena, §VIII, p. 86.

40. There is a lengthy literature in legal and ethical philosophy on the correlation of rights and duties that underpins this debate: see notably Wesley Hohfeld, *Fundamental Legal Concepts* (New Haven, CT: Yale University Press, 1919); H. L. A. Hart, "Are There Any Natural Rights?" *Philosophical Review* 64 (1955): 175–91; and David Lyons, "The Correlativity of Rights and Duties," *Noûs* 4 (1970): 45–55.

41. See also Brett, who argues that "objective right in later mediaeval scholasticism cannot be seen as a direct 'opposite' of subjective right": *Liberty, Right and Nature*, 124.

42. For an account that takes Tierney's criticism even further, see Gladden Pappin, "Rights, Moral Theology and Politics in Jean Gerson," *History of Political Thought* 36, no. 2 (2015): 234–61.

43. Strauss, *Natural Right and History*, 182. For a more recent restatement of this claim, see Perez Zagorin, *Hobbes and the Law of Nature* (Princeton, NJ: Princeton University Press, 2009), 21.

44. See Tim Hochstrasser, *Natural Law Theories in the Early Enlightenment* (Cambridge: Cambridge University Press, 2000).

45. Word frequency counts were produced using the ECCO-TCP database, a subset of the ECCO (Eighteenth-Century Collections Online) database, which contains 2,387 works published in Britain in the eighteenth century. Each text was double-keyed, and thus is much more accurate than the larger database (which was produced by OCR). It is also available on Philologic, through the ARTFL Project: http://artfl-project.uchicago.edu/content/ecco-tcp. These findings align with Peter de Bolla's conclusion, also reached through quantitative measures: "we need to attenuate the common interpretation that, over the course of the Anglophone eighteenth century, rights were increasingly understood as subjective": *The Architecture of Concepts: The Historical Formation of Human Rights* (New York: Fordham University Press, 2013), 82.

46. James Otis, *The Rights of the British Colonists, Asserted and Proved* (London: Almon, 1764), 42–43. See also: "The law of nature, was not of man's making, nor is it in his power to mend it, or alter its course. He can only perform and keep, or disobey and break it" (46). On this point, to which I return in chapter 6, see James H. Hutson, "The Emergence of the Modern Concept of a Right in America: The Contribution of Michel Villey," in *The Nature of Rights at the American Founding and Beyond*, ed. Barry Alan Shain (Charlottesville: University of Virginia Press, 2007), 25–63.

47. Data taken from my "Enlightenment Rights Talk." Frequency counts are from the ARTFL Project's FRANTEXT database: http://artfl-project.uchicago.edu. The graph from the Google books Ngram Viewer corroborates these results.

48. See notably Johannes Morsink, *The Universal Declaration of Human Rights: Origins,*

*Drafting, and Intent* (Philadelphia: University of Pennsylvania Press, 1999); Guðmundur S. Al-freðsson and Asbjørn Eide, eds., *The Universal Declaration of Human Rights: A Common Standard of Achievement* (The Hague: Kluwer Law, 1999); Mary Ann Glendon, *A World Made New: Eleanor Roosevelt and the Universal Declaration of Human Rights* (New York: Random House, 2001), esp. 77; Moyn, *Last Utopia*; Stefan-Ludwig Hoffmann, ed., *Human Rights in the Twentieth Century* (New York: Cambridge University Press, 2011); Moyn, "The Universal Declaration of Human Rights of 1948 in the History of Cosmopolitanism," *Critical Inquiry* 40, no. 4 (2014): 365–84; and Stefan-Ludwig Hoffman, "Human Rights and History," *Past & Present* 232, no. 1 (2016): 279–310. On the lasting importance of the natural law tradition at this time, see especially Jacques Maritain: "natural law and the light of moral conscience within us do not prescribe merely things to be done and not to be done; they also recognize rights, in particular, rights linked to the very nature of man": *The Rights of Man and Natural Law* (original French edition 1942; San Francisco: Ignatius Press, 1986), 106; Maritain's role in the drafting of the UDHR is discussed in Moyn, "Personalism, Community, and the Origins of Human Rights," in *Human Rights in the Twentieth Century*, ed. Hoffman, 85–106. I return to this question in the conclusion.

49. As Morsink notes, an early draft of article 1 included a reference to nature ("endowed *by nature . . ."*), the authors of which intended "as a reference to Christian natural law theory": *Universal Declaration of Human Rights*, 284–91. See also Tore Lindholm, "Article 1," in *Universal Declaration of Human Rights*, ed. Alfreðsson and Eide, 41–74.

50. Morsink suggests that "conscience" features in Confucian philosophy and should not be read "as simply a Western construct:" see his *Universal Declaration of Human Rights*, 299. As he himself acknowledges, however, this language was proposed by the French drafter René Cassin. On Cassin, see notably Glenda Sluga, "René Cassin: *Les droits de l'homme* and the Universality of Human Rights, 1945–1966," in *Human Rights in the Twentieth Century*, ed. Hoffmann, 107–24. See also the conclusion.

51. Moyn, *Last Utopia*, 13, 21.

52. Tuck, *The Rights of War and Peace*, 11–12.

53. See notably Skinner, *Foundations of Modern Political Thought*, vol. 2; Tierney, *Idea of Natural Rights*, esp. chap. 9; also by Tierney, *Foundations of the Conciliar Theory: The Contribution of the Medieval Canonists from Gratian to the Great Schism*, new ed. (Leiden: Brill, 1998); Dale Van Kley, *The Religious Origins of the French Revolution: From Calvin to the Civil Constitution, 1560–1791* (New Haven, CT: Yale University Press, 1996); and Francis Oakley, *The Conciliarist Tradition: Constitutionalism in the Catholic Church, 1300–1870* (Oxford: Oxford University Press, 2003). In *Natural Rights Theories*, Tuck himself had pointed to Jean Gerson as having established "the first rights theory" (25).

54. Gerson, *De Vita spirituali animae* (1402); quoted in Tuck, *Natural Rights Theories*, 27. It is Tierney, *contra* Tuck, who insists on the importance of conciliarism for interpreting Gerson's argument: see his *Idea of Natural Rights*, 220.

55. Jacques Almain, "A Book Concerning the Authority of the Church," in *Conciliarism and Papalism*, ed. J. H. Burns and Thomas M. Izbicki (Cambridge: Cambridge University Press, 1997), 134–200 (135–36 for quote). Original in Jean Gerson [Joannes Gersonii], *Opera omnia, novo ordine digesta et in V tomos distributa*, 5 vols., ed. Louis-Ellies Du Pin (Antwerp: sumptibus Societatis, 1706), 2:977. On Almain, conciliarism, and Gerson, see also Francis Oakley, *The Watershed of Modern Politics: Law, Virtue, Kingship, and Consent (1300–1650)* (New Haven, CT: Yale University Press, 2015), chap. 8.

56. Almain, "A Book Concerning the Authority of the Church," 137.

57. In his discussion of Stoicism, Cicero noted, "it is love of self which supplies the primary

impulse to action": *De finibus*, trans. H. Harris Rackham (Cambridge, MA: Harvard University Press/Loeb, 1931), 3.5.16. Aquinas similarly observed, "every substance by nature seeks to preserve itself"; "[to] preserve our human life and prevent the contrary belong to the natural law": *Summa theologica*, I–II, Q. 94, Art. 2; English translation in Aquinas, *Treatise on Law*, trans. Richard J. Reagan (Indianapolis: Hackett, 2000), 36.

58. On Vitoria, see notably Anthony Pagden, "Dispossessing the Barbarian: The Language of Spanish Thomism and the Debate over the Property Rights of the American Indians," in *The Languages of Political Theory in Early-Modern Europe*, ed. Anthony Pagden (Cambridge: Cambridge University Press, 1987); also Pagden's introduction to Vitoria, *Political Writings*; Tierney, *Idea of Natural Rights*; and Brett, *Liberty, Right and Nature*. I have preferred the Carnegie to the Cambridge translation, as the former is more literal and also complete: see *De Indis et de iure belli relectiones*, ed. Ernest Nys, trans. John Pawley Bate (Washington, DC: Carnegie Institution of Washington, 1917).

59. The Indians "have polities, which are orderly arranged" (habent civitates, quae ordine constant): Vitoria, *De Indis*, 1.23, p. 127 (English), p. 231 (Latin) [page numbers for both languages are to the Carnegie edition].

60. "But then, when we hear of so many massacres, so many plunderings of otherwise innocent men, so many princes evicted from their possessions and stripped of their rule, there is certainly ground for doubting whether this is rightly or wrongly done." Vitoria, *De Indis*, p. 119.

61. Vitoria, *De Indis*, p. 122; "habet enim peccator ius defendendi propriam vitam" (p. 225).

62. See chapter 3.

63. This expression occurs repeatedly in Bodin's *Six livres de la république* (1576), notably in the following section: "But as for divine and natural laws [loix divines et naturelles] every prince on earth is subject to them, and it is not in their power to contravene them unless they wish to be guilty of treason against God. . . . Indeed he (Innocent IV) who best understood what absolute power is . . . said that it is nothing but the power of overriding ordinary law. He did not say the laws of God and of nature." Jean Bodin, *On Sovereignty*, ed. and trans. Julian H. Franklin (Cambridge: Cambridge University Press, 1992), 1.8, p. 13.

64. See *Leviathan*, 2.26. More generally, see Kinch Hoekstra, "Hobbes on Law, Nature, and Reason," *Journal of the History of Philosophy* 41, no. 1 (2003): 111–20; and Zagorin, *Hobbes and the Law of Nature*.

65. See Grotius: "We must also know, that Kings, and those who are invested with a Power equal to that of Kings, have a Right to exact Punishments, not only for Injuries committed against themselves, or their Subjects, but likewise, for those which do not peculiarly concern them, but which are, in any Persons whatsoever, grievous Violations of the Law of Nature or Nations": *Rights of War and Peace*, 2.20.40.1, 2:1021. On Grotius and "R2P," see notably Luke Glanville, *Sovereignty and the Responsibility to Protect: A New History* (Chicago: University of Chicago Press, 2014). Tuck, in fact, acknowledged the interventionist dimension of Grotius's thought in *Rights of War and Peace* (81), though it arguably had an imperialist intent.

66. See, e.g., Joseph Raz, "Human Rights without Foundations," *Oxford Legal Studies Research Paper* 14 (2007). Available at SSRN: http://ssrn.com/abstract=999874.

67. Moyn, *Last Utopia*, 27; emphasis added.

68. See Ernst Kantorowicz, *The King's Two Bodies: A Study in Medieval Political Theology* (1957; Princeton, NJ: Princeton University Press, 1997), 166–67. See also Peter Riesenberg, *Inalienability of Sovereignty in Medieval Political Thought* (New York: AMS Press, 1970).

69. Voltaire traced the history of "inaliénation" from Roman emperors up to François I. Predictably, the article strikes a mocking tone: "the domain of Roman emperors used to be

inalienable, it was the sacred domain; then the barbarians came, and it was very much alienated [il fut très aliéné]." See "Inaliénation, Inaliénable," in *Questions sur l'Encyclopédie*, in *Œuvres complètes de Voltaire*, ed. Nicholas Cronk and Christiane Mervaud (Oxford: Voltaire Foundation, 2011), 42A:399–400. See also Montesquieu on the Roman origins of inalienability: *The Spirit of the Laws*, trans. and ed. Anne M. Cohler, Basia Carolyn Miller, and Harold Samuel Stone (Cambridge: Cambridge University Press, 1989), 30.14. On sovereign inalienability in France, see Rafe Blaufarb, *The Great Demarcation: The French Revolution and the Invention of Modern Property* (Oxford: Oxford University Press, 2016), chap. 1.

70. "Our rights that are, as it is said, dominial, & patrimonial, & inalienable of our crown": "Sur le faict des Notaires & Tabellions du Royaulme de France & des gardes des seaulx," in *Ordonnances, loix, statutz, et edictz royaulx, de tous les Roys de France . . .*, ed. Pierre Rebuffi (Lyon, 1547), feuille L.

71. Bodin, *Six livres de la République*, 1.10; English translation in Bodin, *On Sovereignty*, 49.

72. For some typical French seventeenth-century examples, see Pierre Dupuy, *Traitez touchant les droits du roi tres-chretien sur plusieurs états . . .* (Rouen: Laurens Maurry, 1670), 221; and Pierre Bayle, *Commentaire philosophique sur ces paroles de Jésus-Christ*, in *Œuvres diverses* (The Hague: P. Husson, 1727), vol. 2, part 1, chap 5, p. 412 [ARTFL]. On the English side, see, for instance, Robert Dallington: "For in all other cases, all Lawyers and Historiens of France agree, that it [the domain of the French king] is inalienable, and many Arrests haue beene made of late yeeres to confirme it": *The View of Fraunce* (London: Symon Stafford, 1604), n.p. Tellingly, the term "inalienable" appears fairly commonly in the first half of the seventeenth century in English translations of French works, which, moreover, identify inalienability with sovereign rights. See, for instance, the translation of Innocent Gentillet's *Discours sur les moyens de bien gouverner* (1576): "The like may we say of the Law, whereby the lands and provinces united to the Crowne of Fraunce, are inalienable: For a king of France cannot abolish that Law, because it is the third piller upon which the realme and his estate is founded." Gentillet, *A Discourse Vpon the Meanes of Wel Governing . . .*, trans. Simon Patericke (London: Adam Islip, 1602), 22; and Jean de Serres, *A General Inuentorie of the History of France* (London, 1607); as well as Pierre Matthieu, *The History of Lewis the Eleuenth* (London, 1614).

73. Richard Kingston, *Tyranny Detected and the Late Revolution Justify'd . . .* (London, 1699), 67, 29 [EEBO]. Biographical details from the Oxford DNB entry.

74. See, respectively, Francis Hutcheson, *An Inquiry into the Original of Our Ideas of Beauty and Virtue* (London, 1726), 294; and Richard Fiddes, *Theologia speculativa*, 2 vols. (London, 1718), 1:645. In English, "unalienable" would be the preferred form (over "inalienable") until the mid-nineteenth century: see James Schmidt, "Rights, "Unalienable" or "Inalienable"?: A Concluding Philological Postscript," *Persistent Enlightenment* (2014): https://persistentenlightenment .wordpress.com/2014/07/07/rights-unalienable-or-inalienable-a-concluding-philological -postscript/.

75. The first illustration of the term "inaliénable" found in the 1694, 1762, and even 1798 editions of the *Dictionaire de l'Académie française* is "Le Domaine de la Couronne est inaliénable" (The Crown's Domain is inalienable).

76. One of the first was Daniel Dulany, *Considerations on the Propriety of Imposing Taxes in the British Colonies . . .* (Annapolis: Jonas Green, 1765) [EVANS], 30.

77. Diderot, s.v. "Droit naturel," *Encyclopédie*, 5:116. Nearly all the other uses of the term "inaliénable" in the *Encyclopédie* refer to the crown, a point underscored by Boucher d'Argis's short article "Inaliénable": "said of objects whose possession cannot validly be given to another. The crown's domain is by nature inalienable" (8:641). Diderot may have been inspired by Hutcheson:

see chapter 3. But he would not refer to inalienable rights again until 1769, in a short text on John Dickinson's *Letters from a Farmer in Pennsylvania*: see "Sur les Lettres d'un Fermier de Pensylvanie," in *Œuvres complètes de Diderot*, ed. Jules Assézat (Paris: Garnier, 1875), 4:88.

78. Baron d'Holbach, *Système social ou principes naturels de la morale et de la politique . . .* (Chicago: ARTFL Electronic Edition, 2009), 168; though even in this instance, d'Holbach remained aware that he was appropriating this qualifier from sovereign rights: "Sovereigns established the maxim that their rights are imprescriptible, inalienable, and sacred" (169). On both of these authors, see chapter 3.

79. *Vindiciae contra tyrannos* (1579), ed. George Garnett (Cambridge: Cambridge University Press, 1994), 7–8.

80. See Skinner, *Foundations of Modern Political Thought*, 2:330; emphasis added.

81. See Skinner, *Foundations of Modern Political Thought*, 2:130–33; see also David Johnston, "The Jurists," in *The Cambridge History of Greek and Roman Political Thought*, ed. C. J. Rowe and Malcolm Schofield (Cambridge: Cambridge University Press, 2000); Magnus Ryan, "Political Thought," in *The Oxford Companion to Roman Law*, ed. D. Johnston (Oxford: Oxford University Press, 2015), 423–51; and Daniel Lee, *Popular Sovereignty in Early Modern Constitutional Thought* (Oxford: Oxford University Press, 2016), chap. 1.

82. *The Digest of Justinian*, trans. Charles Henry Monro (Cambridge: Cambridge University Press, 1904), 1.4.1, 1:23; translation modified.

83. See Lee, *Popular Sovereignty in Early Modern Constitutional Thought*; see also Ryan, "Political Thought."

84. See notably Brian Tierney, *Religion, Law, and the Growth of Constitutional Thought, 1150–1650* (Cambridge: Cambridge University Press, 1982); and Lee, *Popular Sovereignty in Early Modern Constitutional Thought* (on "residual dormant right," 63).

85. See, e.g., Kathleen Ann Parrow, *From Defense to Resistance: Justification of Violence during the French Wars of Religion* (Philadelphia: American Philosophical Society, 1993); and Lee, *Popular Sovereignty in Early Modern Constitutional Thought*, 45.

86. Grotius, *Rights of War and Peace*, bk. 1, chap. 3, § 8, p. 261; for the original Latin, see the reproduction of the 1646 edition in *De jure belli ac pacis*, ed. James Brown Scott (Washington, DC: Carnegie Institution, 1913), 53. On the *lex regia* in Grotius, see Straumann, *Roman Law*, 197; and Lee, *Popular Sovereignty in Early Modern Constitutional Thought*, chap. 8.

87. See *Leviathan*, 2.17, p. 260.

88. Almain, "A Book Concerning the Authority of the Church," 137.

89. Daniel Defoe, *Jure Divino* (London, 1706), bk. II, 1:17.

90. On republican liberty, see notably Skinner, *Hobbes and Republican Liberty*; on the relation between natural rights and libertarianism, see Robert Nozick, *Anarchy, State, and Utopia* (New York: Basic Books, 1974). I return to Nozick in my discussion of Locke in chapter 2.

91. I discuss this approach in *The Terror of Natural Right* (Chicago: University of Chicago Press, 2009), esp. 5–6. In a slightly different context, this narrative focus also informs *The Enlightenment: A Genealogy* (Chicago: University of Chicago Press, 2010), 14–18. With Keith Baker, I explored the concept of political "scripts" in the introduction to our coedited volume, *Scripting Revolution* (Stanford, CA: Stanford University Press, 2016).

92. See, e.g., Skinner, "Meaning and Understanding"; and John Pocock, "The Concept of a Language and the *Métier d'Historien*: Some Considerations on Practice," in *Languages of Political Theory in Early-Modern Europe*, 19–38.

93. See Pagden on the "four languages" of early modern political thought in his introduction to *Languages of Political Theory in Early-Modern Europe*, 3–6.

94. I develop this argument in "Intellectual History and Digital Humanities," *Modern Intellectual History* 13, no. 1 (2015): 237-46; and, with Paula Findlen, Giovanna Ceserani, Caroline Winterer, and Nicole Coleman, in "Historical Research in a Digital Age: Reflections from the Mapping the Republic of Letters Project," *American Historical Review* 122, no. 2 (2017): 400-424.

95. See Lynn Hunt, *Inventing Human Rights: A History* (New York: Norton, 2007), 23.

96. See especially Vicenzo Ferrone, *Storia dei diritti dell'uomo: L'Illuminismo e la costruzione del linguaggio politico dei moderni* (Rome: Laterza, 2014).

## Chapter II

1. *Mémoires de l'estat de France, sous Charles neufiesme . . .* , 3 vols., ed. Simon Goulart (Meidelbourg [Geneva]: Heinrich Wolf, 1577). The first edition is extremely rare; no copy seems to be available at the BnF. La Boétie's text appears in vol. 3, 160-91. Fragments of his work had already appeared in *Le Reveille-matin des François, et de leurs voisins* (Edinburgh, 1574) [GALLICA]. On these publication details, see J. H. M. Salmon, *The French Religious Wars in English Political Thought* (Oxford: Clarendon Press, 1959); see also Paul Bonnefon, *Montaigne et ses amis* (Paris: Armand Colin, 1898), 163-66.

2. La Boétie, *Discours de la servitude volontaire* (Paris: Bossard, 1922), 57, 62. See Nannerl Keohane, "The Radical Humanism of Étienne de La Boétie," *Journal of the History of Ideas* 38, no. 1 (1977): 119-30.

3. Montaigne, "On Friendship," in *The Complete Essays of Montaigne*, trans. Donald M. Frame (Stanford, CA: Stanford University Press, 1957), 1.28, p. 144.

4. As Montaigne acknowledged: "this work [by La Boétie] has since been brought to light, and with evil intent, by those who seek to disturb and change the state of our government." Montaigne, "On Friendship," p. 144.

5. See, for instance, Fulgenzio Micanzio, *The Life of the Most Learned Father Paul . . .* (1651) [EEBO], translated from the Italian: "the Parliaments of *France*, and the Sorbon it selfe have maintained these liberties, as the naturall rights of all the churches, but in *France* they have beene better defended then elsewhere from the usurpations of others . . ." (154); and for a similar claim, Peter Heylyn, *Cosmographie in Four Bookes* (London: Henry Seile, 1652) [EEBO]: "the *Gallican Clergy* stands more stoutly to their naturall rights against the usurpations and encroachments of the See of *Rome*, than any other that live under the Popes Autoritie" (148).

6. For example, see Edward Symmons, *A Vindication of King Charles* (1648) [EEBO]: "truly what is it but a *Scruple,* a needlesse *Scruple,* for any to question, whether a *Protestant* Prince, should use the helpe of *Papists* in case of necessity, to defend himself in his naturall rights, and Royalties?" (181). See also, on the "natural rights of Princes," Samuel Parker, *A Discourse of Ecclesiastical Politie . . .* (London: John Martyn, 1671) [EEBO].

7. Sir John Hayward, *An Answer to the First Part of a Certaine Conference, Concerning Succession . . .* (1603), 6 [EEBO].

8. A Latin version of this work also appeared the same year: *Dialogi ab Eusebio Philadelpho cosmopolita* (Edimburgi [Edinburgh]: J. Jammaei, 1574). On this work, see Skinner, *The Foundations of Modern Political Thought* (Cambridge: Cambridge University Press, 1978), 2:326-27.

9. *Le Reveille-matin des François*, 1:81.

10. *Le Reveille-matin des François*, 2:126. The author also defended "the right of peoples [le droit des peuples]" (2:88), insisting that "there is no statute of limitations against the rights of peoples [la prescription contre les droits du peuple est invalide]" (2:89).

11. *Le Reveille-matin des François*, 1:90; emphasis added.

12. *Le Reveille-matin des François*, 2:186.

13. Théodore de Bèze, *Du droit des magistrats sur leurs subjets: traitté tres necessaire en ce temps pour advertir de leur devoir, tant les magistrats que les subjets* (1575; Paris: EDHIS, 1977), 87 [GALLICA]. For a similar line, see also 11–12. See John Witte, *The Reformation of Rights: Law, Religion and Human Rights in Early Modern Calvinism* (Cambridge: Cambridge University Press, 2007), 122–50.

14. Bèze, *Du droit des magistrats sur leurs subjets*, 100.

15. Cf. Samuel Moyn, *The Last Utopia: Human Rights in History* (Cambridge, MA: Belknap Press of Harvard University Press, 2010) (see discussion in chapter 1).

16. Bèze, *Du droit des magistrats sur leurs subjets*, 105–6.

17. See notably Julian Franklin, introduction to *Constitutionalism and Resistance in the Sixteenth Century: Three Treaties* (New York: Pegasus, 1969); J. H. M. Salmon, *Society in Crisis: France in the Sixteenth Century* (London: Methuen, 1979); Skinner, *Foundations of Modern Political Thought*; Nannerl O. Keohane, *Philosophy and the State in France: The Renaissance to the Enlightenment* (Princeton, NJ: Princeton University Press, 1980); and Perez Zagorin, *Rebels and Rulers, 1500–1660*, vol. 2: *Provincial Rebellion* (Cambridge: Cambridge University Press, 1982), 59–71.

18. For a collection of these texts, see Gordon Griffiths, ed., *Representative Government in Western Europe in the Sixteenth Century* (Oxford: Clarendon, 1968). See also Henry Heller, *Iron and Blood: Civil Wars in Sixteenth-Century France* (Montreal: McGill-Queen's University Press, 1991); and Mack P. Holt, *The French Wars of Religion, 1562–1629* (Cambridge: Cambridge University Press, 1995), esp. 99–102.

19. See the declaration of the Assembly at Nîmes in January–February 1575, in Griffiths, *Representative Government in Western Europe*, 285.

20. This ambiguity between corporatist and individualistic natural rights can already be found in Gerson: see Brian Tierney, *The Idea of Natural Rights: Studies on Natural Rights, Natural Law, and Church Law, 1150–1625* (Atlanta: Scholars Press, 1997), chap. 9.

21. Bèze, *Du droit des magistrats sur leurs subjets*, 19, 105–6.

22. François de Vérone Constantin [Jean Boucher], *Apologie pour Iehan Chastel Parisien, execute a mort, et pour les peres & escholliers, de la Societé de Iesus, bannis du Royaume de France* (1595), 81; emphasis added. Skinner does not mention this work but does discuss Boucher and other *ligueurs* in passing: *Foundations of Modern Political Thought*, 2:345–47. See also Holt, *French Wars of Religion*, 131–32; and Monique Cottret, "La justification catholique du tyrannicide," *Parlement[s], Revue d'histoire politique* 3, no. hors série 6 (2010): 107–17.

23. This was the conclusion that Skinner reached *contra* Michael Walzer in *Foundations of Modern Political Thought* (2:322–24). This paragraph largely summarizes the history that Skinner provides in volume 2 of the *Foundations*, albeit without the focus on rights.

24. See Skinner, *Foundations of Modern Political Thought*, 2:135–36.

25. John Major, *Historia Majoris Brittaniae tam Angliae quam Scotiae* (1521); *A History of Greater Britain as Well England as Scotland*, trans. Archibald Constable (Edinburgh: University Press, for the Scottish History Society, 1892), bk. 2, chap. 6, p. 82.

26. See Francisco de Vitoria, *De Indis et de iure belli relectiones*, ed. Ernest Nys, trans. John Pawley Bate (Washington, DC: Carnegie Institution of Washington, 1917) (and chapter 1); more generally, see Annabel Brett, *Liberty, Right and Nature: Individual Rights in Later Scholastic Thought* (Cambridge: Cambridge University Press, 1997).

27. See Franklin L. Ford, *Political Murder: From Tyrannicide to Terrorism* (Cambridge, MA: Harvard University Press, 1985); and Mario Turchetti, *Tyrannie et tyrannicide de l'Antiquité à nos jours* (Paris: PUF, 2001); see also Cottret, "La justification catholique du tyrannicide."

28. See Eric Nelson, *The Jesuits and the Monarchy: Catholic Reform and Political Authority in France (1590–1615)* (Aldershot, UK: Ashgate, 2005).

29. See Harro Höpfl, *Jesuit Political Thought: The Society of Jesus and the State, c. 1540–1630* (Cambridge: Cambridge University Press, 2004), chap. 13; and Harald Braun, *Juan de Mariana and Early Modern Spanish Political Thought* (Aldershot, UK: Ashgate, 2007).

30. See Laurence Brockliss, *French Higher Education in the Seventeenth and Eighteenth Centuries: A Cultural History* (Oxford: Clarendon Press 1987), 298–300; and Höpfl, *Jesuit Political Thought*, 321.

31. See Tierney, *The Idea of Natural Rights*, 316.

32. "It is lawful for any Man to engage himself as a Slave to whom he pleases. [ … ] Why should it not therefore be as lawful for a People that are at their own Disposal, to deliver up themselves to any one or more Persons, and transfer the Right of governing them upon him or them, without reserving any Share of that Right to themselves?" Hugo Grotius, *The Rights of War and Peace* (1625), 3 vols., ed. Richard Tuck, trans. John Morrice et al. (Indianapolis: Liberty Fund, 2005), 1.3.8, 1:261. On Grotius's rights theory and the relevant scholarship, see chapter 1. Rousseau would attack this argument in the *Social Contract* (1.4).

33. Auger de Moléon de Granier, *Recueil de divers mémoires, harangues, remonstrances, et lettres servans à l'histoire de nostre temps* (Paris: Chevalieer [sic], 1623), 380 [G'BOOKS].

34. Agrippa d'Aubigné, *Histoire universelle … : comprise en trois tomes …* (Amsterdam, 1626), 1:117–18 [G'BOOKS].

35. Philippe de Béthune, *Le conseiller d'estat ou Recueil des plus générales considérations servant au maniment des affaires publiques* (1633; Paris: Compagnie des libraires du Palais, 1665), 73 [GALLICA]. An English translation of this text, *The Counsellor of Estate*, was published in 1634 (and is available on ECCO).

36. Jean Claude, *Les Plaintes des protestants cruellement opprimés dans le royaume de France* (1686; Paris: Fischenbacher, 1885), 120. This text would be republished in 1713; an English translation appeared the same year as the French (a second edition followed in 1707). Similar arguments can be found in English texts of this period, also on this topic: see, e.g., John Quick, *Synodicon in Gallia reformata, or the Acts, decisions, decrees and canons of those famous national councils of the reformed churches in France* (London: T. Parkhurst and J. Robinson, 1692), cxxvi. On Claude, see Hubert Bost and Didier Poton, "La voie est ouverte à la renaissance des idées monarchomaques." In "Le rapport des réformés au pouvoir au XVIIe siècle: Elie Merlat ou la fin du monde," in *Genèse et enjeux de la laïcité: christianismes et laïcité* (Geneva: Labor et Fides, 1990), 31–55 (52 for quote).

37. Jean Claude, *Les Œuvres posthumes de Mr. Claude* (Amsterdam, 1688), 553 [G'BOOKS].

38. Jean Tronchin du Breuil, *Lettres sur les matières du temps*, 3e année (Amsterdam, 1690), 94 [G'BOOKS]. On this historical incident, see John A. Lynn, *The Wars of Louis XIV, 1667–1714* (London: Longman, 1999), 179–81.

39. Louis Moréri, *Le Grand dictionnaire historique sur le mélange curieux de l'histoire sacrée et profane*, 6th ed., ed. Jean Le Clerc (Utrecht-Leiden-Amsterdam, 1692), 2:27 [G'BOOKS]. On Le Clerc, see notably S. J. Savonius, "The Role of Huguenot Tutors in John Locke's Programme of Social Reform," in *The Religious Culture of the Huguenots, 1660–1750*, ed. Anne Dunan-Page (Aldershot, UK: Ashgate, 2006), 137–62.

40. This was clearly the case with Pierre Jurieu, who advanced similar claims in his *Lettres pastorales adressées aux fidèles de France qui gémissent* (Rotterdam, 1686); on his Calvinist sources, see Jean Hubac, "Tyrannie et tyrannicide selon Pierre Jurieu," *Bulletin de la Société de l'histoire du protestantisme français* 152 (2006): 583–609.

41. William of Orange, *A supplication to the Kings Maiestie of Spayne, made by the Prince of*

*Orange, the states of Holland and Zeland, with all other his faithfull subiectes of the low Countreys, presently suppressed by the tyranny of the Duke of Alba and Spaniards* . . . (1573), 12 [EEBO]. On the rather limited invocations of natural rights during the Dutch Revolt, see Martin van Gelderen, *The Political Thought of the Dutch Revolt, 1555–1590* (Cambridge: Cambridge University Press, 2002).

42. Pieter de la Court, *Memoires de Jean de Wit, grand pensionnaire de Hollande*, trans. Johanna Dorotheâ von Lindener Zoutelandt (Ratisbonne: Erase Kinkius, 1709), 330. An English translation appeared in 1702. On Dutch republicanism at the turn of the eighteenth century, see Margaret Jacob, *Radical Enlightenment: Pantheists, Freemasons, and Republicans* (London: Allen & Unwin, 1981).

43. Jean Jennet, *Histoire de la république des Provinces-Unies des Païs-Bas, depuis son établissement jusques à la mort de Guillaume III, roi de la Grande-Bretagne*, 4 vols. (The Hague: Jean van Millinge, 1704), 1:19–20 [G'BOOKS]. See also the English translation, *The History of the Republick of Holland, from Its First Foundation to the Death of King William*, 2 vols. (London, 1705).

44. On the (disputed) attribution of this work, see Pierre Bayle, *Avis aux réfugiés, Réponse d'un nouveau converti*, ed. Gianluca Mori (Paris: Honoré Champion, 2007). See also Jean Delvolvé, *Essai sur Pierre Bayle: religion, critique et philosophie positive* (Paris: Alcan, 1906), 177–210.

45. Quotes from a slightly later edition: Pierre Bayle, *Avis important aux refugiez sur leur prochain retour en France* (Paris: Gabriel Martin, 1692), 66, 82, 249.

46. Jacques Abbadie, *Défense de la nation britannique, ou Les droits de Dieu, de la Nature, & de la Société clairement établis au sujet de la revolution d'Angleterre* . . . (The Hague, 1693), 261. There is apparently an earlier edition that appeared in 1692 in London. On this work, see notably John Marshall, *John Locke, Toleration and Early Enlightenment Culture* (Cambridge: Cambridge University Press, 2006), 89–90.

47. With the publication of *Les Droits de Dieu, de la nature et des gens, tirés d'un livre de M. Abbadie intitulé: "Défense de la nation britannique . . ." On y a ajouté un discours de M. Noodt sur les droits des souverains (traduit du latin par Barbeyrac)* (Amsterdam, 1775).

48. See Salmon, *French Religious Wars in English Political Thought*; see also Skinner, *Foundations of Modern Political Thought*, vol. 2.

49. See Richard H. Helmholz, "Natural Law and Human Rights in English Law: From Bracton to Blackstone," *Ave Maria Law Review* 3, no. 1 (2005): 1–22.

50. An exception can be found in the works of the Anglican theologian and bishop Godfrey Goodman, who argued that "[t]he kingdome of grace doth not overthrow our naturall rights, and therfore God shal still leave unto us, whole, sound, and entire, without violence or coaction, the free choice, and election of our owne wils": *The Fall of Man, or the Corruption of Nature, Proved by the Light of our Naturall Reason* (1616), 264; see also 274, as well as his later book, *The Creatures Praysing God: or, The religion of Dumbe Creatures* (1622) [both in EEBO]. Far from being a Low Church radical, Goodman was suspected of Catholic sympathies (see his entry in the DNB).

51. See W. J. Torrance Kirby, "Richard Hooker's Theory of Natural Law in the Context of Reformation Theology," *Sixteenth Century Journal* 30, no. 3 (1999): 681–703.

52. See in general Perez Zagorin, *The Court and the Country: The Beginning of the English Revolution* (New York: Atheneum, 1970); Lawrence Stone, *The Causes of the English Revolution* (1972; London: Routledge, 2002); John Morrill, *The Nature of the English Revolution* (London: Routledge, 1994); and more recently, Clive Holmes, *Why Was Charles I Executed?* (London: Contiuum, 2006).

53. See Parliament's "Declaration to Justify Their Proceedings and Resolutions to Take Up Arms": "we the Lords and Commons, are resolved to expose our Lives and Fortunes for the De-

fence and Maintenance of the true Religion, *the King's Person, Honour and Estate . . .*" (emphasis added).

54. See David Underdown, *Pride's Purge: Politics in the Puritan Revolution* (Oxford: Clarendon Press, 1971).

55. See notably G. E. Aylmer, ed., *The Levellers in the English Revolution* (Ithaca, NY: Cornell University Press, 1975); and Rachel Foxley, *The Levellers: Radical Political Thought in the English Revolution* (Manchester: Manchester University Press, 2013); on the Puritan roots of this movement, see David Como, "Radical Puritanism, c. 1558–1660," in *The Cambridge Companion to Puritanism*, ed. J. Coffey and P. Lim (Cambridge: Cambridge University Press, 2008), 241–58.

56. See John Lilburne, *The Charters of London; or, The second part of Londons liberty in chaines discovered* (1646), 1 [EEBO].

57. Richard Overton, *An Arrow against all Tyrants* (1646) [EEBO]; reprinted in *The English Levellers*, ed. Andrew Sharp (Cambridge: Cambridge University Press, 1998), 69. See also the subtitle of this pamphlet, which announces its subject: "Wherein the originall rise, extent, and end of magisterial power, the natural and national rights, freedoms and properties of mankind are discovered, and undeniably maintained" (54). By the same author, see also *To the High and Mighty States, the Knights and Burgesses in Parliament Assembled . . .* (1646) [EEBO].

58. John Lilburne, William Walwyn, Thomas Prince, and Richard Overton, *An Agreement of the Free People of England* (1649), art. 1; in Sharp, *English Levellers*, 170.

59. Sharp, *English Levellers*, 54–56.

60. On this ambiguity in Leveller natural rights talk, see Foxley, *The Levellers*, 27–30.

61. Sharp, *English Levellers*, 103.

62. See notably Victoria Kahn, "The Metaphorical Contract in Milton's *Tenure of Kings and Magistrates*," in *Milton and Republicanism*, ed. David Armitage, Armand Himy, and Quentin Skinner (Cambridge: Cambridge University Press, 1995), 82–105.

63. See John Milton, *The Tenure of Kings and Magistrates*, ed. William Talbot Allison (New York: Henry Holt, 1911), 9. Cf. *Institutes*, 1.2.

64. Cf.: "it is unreasonable for men to be judges in their own cases, [as] self-love will make men partial to themselves and their friends. [ . . . ] I easily grant, that civil government is the proper remedy for the inconveniencies of the state of nature [ . . . ] where men may be judges in their own case." Locke, *Second Treatise*, § 13. On the transfer of rights in Locke, see below.

65. It would appear elsewhere in the text: see ". . . our Ancestors who were not ignorant with what rights either Nature or ancient Constitution had endowd them, when Oaths both at Coronation, and renewd in Parlament would not serve, thought it no way illegal to depose and put to death their tyrannous Kings." Milton, *Tenure of Kings*, 26.

66. Henry Vane, *A Healing Question* (1656), 3. This argument is criticized by John Rogers in *Diapoliteia* (1659), 42 [EEBO].

67. Ruth E. Mayers, *1659: The Crisis of the Commonwealth* (London: Boydell Press, 2004), 219.

68. William Penn, *The Peoples Ancient and Just Liberties Asserted in the Tryal of William Penn, and William Mead . . .* (1670), 58, 49.

69. See Edwin B. Bronner, "First Printing of Magna Charta in America, 1687," *American Journal of Legal History* 7 (1963): 189–97. I pick up the American storyline in chapter 5.

70. See, for instance, Edward Stephens, *A Caveat against Flattery, and Profanation of Sacred Things to Secular Ends* (London, 1689), 23; A.B., *Some Remarks upon Government* (London, 1689); and Slingsby Bethel, *The Providences of God, Observed through Several Ages, towards this Nation* (1691), 35. Stephens was a strident moral reformer who attacked nonconformism but also the Church of England: see Tony Claydon, *William III and the Godly Revolution* (Cambridge:

Cambridge University Press, 2004), 112–14. Bethel was a commonwealthman, suspected of re-
publican sympathies: see Gary S. De Krey, *London and the Restoration, 1659–1683* (Cambridge:
Cambridge University Press, 2005). More generally, see Steve Pincus, *1688: The First Modern
Revolution* (New Haven, CT: Yale University Press, 2009).

71. John Tutchin, for instance, argued in a short (two-page) pamphlet that the English "shall
bravely stand up in the defence of our natural Rights, our Religion and Liberties, against all
Opposers," in *Reflections upon the French Kings Declaration for the Restauration of the Late King
James, to the Kingdom of England* (London: Langley Curtiss . . . , 1690), 2. On Tutchin, see Me-
linda S. Zook, *Radical Whigs and Conspiratorial Politics in Late Stuart England* (University Park:
Penn State Press, 2010), and his entry in the *DNB*.

72. William Hopkins, *Animadversions on Mr Johnson's answer to Jovian in three letters to a
country-friend* (London: Walter Kettilby, 1691), 3 [EEBO]. "Jovian" here refers to George Hickes,
an Anglican clergyman whose Stuart loyalties led him to refuse to take the oath of allegiance
to William and Mary. Johnson had argued in his pamphlet that "Christianity destroys no mans
Natural or Civil Rights, but confirms them": *Julian the Apostate Being a Short Account of his Life*
(1682), 59 [EEBO]. For a similar criticism to Hopkins's, see Lewes Sharp, *The Church of England's
doctrine of Non-Resistance, Justified and Vindicated as Truly Rational and Christian; and the
Damnable Nature of Rebellious Resistance Represented* (1689), 30, 34, 39. Biographical information about Johnson, Hickes, and Hopkins is from the *DNB*; see also Zook, *Radical Whigs and
Conspiratorial Politics*.

73. John Toland, *A Letter to a Member of Parliament, Shewing, That a Restraint on the Press is
Inconsistent with the Protestant Religion . . .* (London: J. Darby . . . , 1698), 7. This letter is sometimes
attributed to Matthew Tindal, though as I argue in a following section, Tindal's views on rights
differed significantly. Toland, for his part, remained committed to the argument presented here:
see his *Letters from the Right Honourable the late Earl of Shaftesbury, to Robert Molesworth, Esq. . . .*
(London, 1721), xvii. For another example of Whig literature at the close of the seventeenth century,
see John Edwards, *Sermons on Special Occasions and Subjects* (London, 1698), 178–79.

74. See, for instance, "All those *Natural* Rights we are invested with, we derive from him who
is the Author of our Nature; who by creating us what we are, and uniting us by Natural Ligaments
to one another, hath endowed us with all those Rights, which we claim as Rational Creatures
dwelling in Mortal Bodies, and joyned together by *Natural Relations* and *Society*. So that to deal
*justly* by one another, or with respect to our Natural Rights, is only to allow one another what God
hath entailed upon our Natures." John Scott, *The Christian Life, Part III* (1696), 112. For another
Tory example, see Charles Davenant, *An Essay upon the Probable Methods of Making a People
Gainers in the Ballance of Trade* (London: James Knapton . . . , 1699), 110.

75. See Daniel Defoe, *Four Letters to a Friend in North Britain* (London, 1710), first letter, 19;
and Joseph Addison, "Of his Majesty's Character," Monday, December 26, 1715; in *The Free-holder,
or, Political Essays* (1716), 7.

76. See, respectively, Daniel Defoe, *A Letter to a Member of Parliament* (1699), 58; and Joseph
Addison, *The Evidences of the Christian Religion* (London: Tonson, 1733), 264. On rights more
generally, for Defoe, see *Jure divino* (London, 1706), esp. 16–22; see also chapter 1.

77. See, for instance, the anonymous essay on "Tyranny, Anarchy, and Free-Governments,"
collected in *London Magazine* (1733): "*Tyrannies* are *Powers* built upon the *Destruction* all the
*natural Rights* of Mankind. *Free Governments* are only *Recognitions, Establishments, Enforcements*
and *Securities* of all those Rights. [ . . . ] The Government of *England* comes the nearest to *this Plan*
of any Government now in the World." In *London Journal*, January 6, no. 706, 7 [ECCO]. See also
Thomas Stackhouse, *A Complete Body of Divinity: Consisting of Five Parts* (London, 1729), 903.

78. This discussion draws on Noel Malcolm, *Aspects of Hobbes* (Oxford: Oxford University Press 2002); Kinch Hoekstra, "Hobbes on Law, Nature, and Reason," *Journal of the History of Philosophy* 41, no. 1 (2003): 111–20; Quentin Skinner, *Hobbes and Republican Liberty* (Cambridge: Cambridge University Press, 2008); Philip Pettit, *Made with Words: Hobbes on Language, Mind, and Politics* (Princeton, NJ: Princeton University Press, 2008); and Perez Zagorin, *Hobbes and the Law of Nature* (Princeton, NJ: Princeton University Press, 2009).

79. Thomas Hobbes, *On the Citizen*, ed. and trans. Richard Tuck and Michael Silverthorne (Cambridge: Cambridge University Press, 1998), 2.3, p. 34.

80. See *Leviathan*, in *The Clarendon Edition of the Works of Thomas Hobbes*, ed. Noel Malcolm (Oxford: Clarendon Press, 2012), vol. 4, 1.14, p. 200; emphasis added.

81. For an analysis of this frontispiece and discussion of the different editions of *De Cive*, see Ioannis D. Evrigenis, *Images of Anarchy: The Rhetoric and Science in Hobbes's State of Nature* (Cambridge: Cambridge University Press, 2014), 81–87; and Quentin Skinner, "Hobbes and the Humanist Frontispiece," in *From Humanism to Hobbes* (Cambridge: Cambridge University Press, 2018), 222–315.

82. Höpfl, *Jesuit Political Thought*, 231. See also Benjamin Straumann, *Roman Law in the State of Nature: The Classical Foundations of Hugo Grotius' Natural Law* (Cambridge: Cambridge University Press, 2015), esp. chap. 6.

83. Aristotle, *Politics*, 1.2, 1252b9.

84. For quotes, see *Leviathan*, 4.46, 5:1082; and 1.13, 4:195. On anti-Aristotelianism more broadly, see Craig Martin, *Subverting Aristotle: Religion, History, and Philosophy in Early Modern Science* (Baltimore: Johns Hopkins University Press, 2014). Montaigne had already claimed that the "cannibals" of Brazil had no government ("no name for a magistrate or for political superiority"): see "Of Cannibals," *Complete Essays*, 153. There were, of course, other classical sources that also imagined a pre-political human state (e.g., Cicero, Ovid, Lucretius).

85. On the artificiality of the Hobbesian state, see *Leviathan*, 1.16 (on "artificiall persons"; 4:244); and 1.17 (the agreement "of men, is by Covenant only which is Artificiall"; 4:260). On this point more generally, see Quentin Skinner, "Hobbes and the Purely Artificial Person of the State," in *Visions of Politics: Hobbes and Civil Science* (Cambridge: Cambridge University Press, 2012), 3:177–208; and David Bates, *States of War: Enlightenment Origins of the Political* (New York: Columbia University Press, 2012), 77. For an excellent summary of early modern theories of the body politic as an organic entity, see Paul Friedland, *Political Actors: Representative Bodies and Theatricality in the Age of the French Revolution* (Ithaca, NY: Cornell University Press, 2002), chap. 1.

86. Here as well, Hobbes departed from Grotius, for whom natural laws applied equally in both states (and who retained the Aristotelian theory of natural sociability): see Straumann, *Roman Law in the State of Nature*, chap. 6.

87. See *Leviathan*, 1.14, p. 200; see also Hoekstra, "Hobbes on Law, Nature, and Reason"; and Zagorin, *Hobbes and the Law of Nature*.

88. *Leviathan*, 2.26, 4:419. See the rest of this paragraph for Hobbes's theory of how natural and civil law are imbricated.

89. In *De Cive*, for instance, the examples that Hobbes provides of a rights transfer deal primarily with private property: *On the Citizen*, 2.4–7, pp. 34–35.

90. *Leviathan*, 1.14, 4:201–2. See also the following paragraph, "Whensoever a man Transferreth his Right, or Renounceth it . . ."

91. See also the passage in *Leviathan*, 2.26, cited above.

92. *Leviathan*, 1.14, 4:210; and 2.17, 4:260.

93. John Bramhall, *The Catching of Leviathan*, in *The Works of the Most Reverend Father*

445

*in God, John Bramhall* . . . (Oxford: John Henry Parker, 1844), 4:583–84. My thanks to Alison McQueen for bringing this work to my attention.

94. Malcolm, *Aspects of Hobbes*, 437.

95. *Leviathan*, 1.14, 4:210.

96. Of course, with one very important exception (discussed in chapter 1): the natural right to preserve our lives, bodies, or physical liberty could never be transferred or renounced.

97. See especially Jon Parkin, *Taming the Leviathan: The Reception of the Political and Religious Ideas of Thomas Hobbes in England, 1640–1700* (Cambridge: Cambridge University Press, 2007).

98. On Edward Stillingfleet, and more specifically his debt to Hobbes, see Jon Parkin, *Science, Religion, and Politics in Restoration England: Richard Cumberland's 'De Legibus Naturae'* (Woodbridge, UK: Boydell, 1999), 19–21; and also by Parkin, *Taming the Leviathan*, 207–8. See also Richard H. Popkin, "The Philosophy of Bishop Stillingfleet," *Journal of the History of Philosophy* 9, no. 3 (1971): 303–19. Stillingfleet denounced Hobbes's epicureanism in another work, the *Origines sacrae* (1662).

99. Edward Stillingfleet, *Irenicum* (1659; n.p., 1662), 426, 132–33.

100. Edward Stillingfleet, *A Sermon Preached before the Queen at White-Hall* . . . (London: Henry Mortlock . . . , 1691), 7. See also Stillingfleet, *Thirteen Sermons Preached on Several Occasions Three of Which Never Before Printed* . . . (London: Henry Mortlock . . . , 1698), 261.

101. See notably Gilbert Rule, *An Answer to Dr. Stillingfleet's Irenicum by a Learned Pen* (London: Richard Janeway . . . , 1680); John Barret, *The Rector of Sutton Committed with the Dean of St. Paul's* (1680); Vincent Alsop, *A Reply to the Reverend Dean of St. Pauls's Reflections on the Rector of Sutton, &c.* (1681); and William Atwood, *The Fundamental Constitution of the English Government Proving King William and Queen Mary our Lawful and Rightful King and Queen* (London, 1690), 4 and *passim*.

102. Jeremy Taylor, *Ductor dubitantium, or, The Rule of Conscience in all her Generall Measures Serving as a Great Instrument for the Determination of Cases of Conscience* (London, 1660), 221, 369, 387.

103. Samuel Parker, *Discourse of Ecclesiastical Politie*, 122, 92.

104. William Sherlock, *The Case of Resistance of the Supreme Powers Stated and Resolved according to the Doctrine of the Holy Scriptures* (London: Fincham Gardiner, 1684), 205, 77, 174.

105. John Kettlewell, *Christianity, a Doctrine of the Cross, or, Passive Obedience, Under any Pretended Invasion of Legal Rights and Liberties* (1691), 76.

106. Richard Cumberland, *A Treatise of the Laws of Nature* (1727), trans. John Maxwell, ed. Jon Parkin (Indianapolis: Liberty Fund, 2005), 677. I return to Cumberland below.

107. "Whoever enters into a *Community*, divests himself of his natural Freedom, and puts himself under Government, which, amongst other things, comprehends the Power of Life and Death over him, together with Authority to enjoin him some things to which he has an utter Aversion, and to prohibit others, for which he may have as strong an Inclination; so that 'tis possible he may often, in obedience to this Authority, be oblig'd to sacrifice his private Good to that of the publick": Samuel von Pufendorf, *Of the Law of Nature and Nations*, trans. Basil Kennett, ed. Jean Barbeyrac (London: Walthoe et al., 1729), 7.4.1, p. 626. See also Samuel von Pufendorf, *The Whole Duty of Man According to the Law of Nature*, trans. Andrew Tooke (London, 1705), 2.13. I return to Pufendorf in chapters 3 and 5.

108. See Algernon Sidney, *Discourses Concerning Government* (1698), ed. Thomas G. West (Indianapolis: Liberty Fund, 1996). More generally, see Alan C. Houston, *Algernon Sidney and the Republican Heritage in England and America* (Princeton, NJ: Princeton University Press, 1991).

109. "The Apology of Algernone [sic] Sidney in the Day of his Death," in *Discourses Concerning Government* (London: A. Millar, 1751) [ECCO], 34.

110. See John Trenchard and Thomas Gordon, *Cato's Letters*, cited below starting at n. 177.

111. Sidney, *Discourses Concerning Government*, 1.7, p. 18; see also 2.9, p. 100.

112. Sidney, *Discourses Concerning Government*, 1.9, p. 22.

113. Sidney, *Discourses Concerning Government*, 2.5, p. 81.

114. Sidney, *Discourses Concerning Government*, 2.9, p. 101. On this point in particular, see Quentin Skinner, *Liberty Before Liberalism* (Cambridge: Cambridge University Press, 1998).

115. See Andrew Starkie, *Church of England and the Bangorian Controversy, 1716–1721* (Woodbridge, UK: Boydell Press, 2007).

116. Richard Fiddes, *Theologia speculativa*, 2 vols. (London, 1718), 2:55, p. 60.

117. See "natural Rights might be, and are in Fact, in many respects, superseded by positive and humane Laws," in Richard Fiddes, *The Life of Cardinal Wolsey* (1724), 292; and "It is impossible to form any Scheme of Government, or legal Constitution, wherein Men shall not be obliged to depart from their natural rights," in Fiddes, *A General Treatise of Morality, Form'd Upon the Principles of Natural Reason Only* (London, Billingsley, 1724), 438.

118. William Wollaston, *The Religion of Nature Delineated* (London, 1724), 7.6, p. 150. A French translation followed shortly after: *Ébauche de la religion naturelle*, trans. Garrigue (The Hague: J. Swart, 1726); a German translation appeared two years later. Like Hobbes (whom he does not cite), Wollaston recognizes that we cannot renounce all our natural rights, as "some things are *essential* to our beings, and some it is not in our power to part with." On Wollaston, see Diego Lucci, "William Wollaston's Religion of Nature," in *Atheism and Deism Revalued: Heterodox Religious Identities in Britain, 1650–1800*, ed. Wayne Hudson, Diego Lucci, and Jeffrey R. Wigelsworth (Farnham, UK: Ashgate, 2014), 119–38.

119. Heineccius, *A Methodical System of Universal Law: Or, the Laws of Nature and Nations*, trans. George Turnbull (London, 1763), § CCCLXXXIV. On Heineccius, see Knud Haakonssen, *Natural Law and Moral Philosophy: From Grotius to the Scottish Enlightenment* (Cambridge: Cambridge University Press, 1996), 85–90.

120. The bibliography on Spinoza's political thought is vast: I have helpfully drawn on Alexandre Matheron, *Individu et communauté chez Spinoza* (Paris: Minuit, 1969); Douglas J. Den Uyl, *Power, State and Freedom: An Interpretation of Spinoza's Political Philosophy* (Assen: Van Gorcum, 1983); Etienne Balibar, *Spinoza and Politics*, trans. Peter Snowdon (London: Verso, 1998); Steven Barbone and Lee Rice, introduction to Spinoza, *Political Treatise*, trans. Samuel Shirley (Indianapolis: Hackett, 2000), 1–30 (hereafter abbreviated *TP*); and Steven Nadler, *A Book Forged in Hell: Spinoza's Scandalous Treatise and the Birth of the Secular Age* (Princeton, NJ: Princeton University Press, 2011). See also the more specific references cited below.

121. Letter 50, Spinoza to Jarig Jelles, June 5, 1764; in *Complete Works*, trans. Samuel Shirley, ed. Michael L. Morgan (Indianapolis: Hackett, 2002), 891.

122. Jonathan Israel: "in place of Hobbes' assigning a contracted overriding power to the sovereign, Spinoza leaves the citizen with his natural right intact, according to an automatic and inevitable 'right of resistance.'" *Radical Enlightenment* (Oxford: Oxford University Press, 2001), 259. As we will see, both of these claims are mistaken: Spinoza does not leave the individual citizen with *his* natural right intact, nor is there in Spinoza a positive right of resistance. See also Nadler: "Spinoza believes that through the social contract citizens confer on the sovereign only their power, preserving their natural rights even in the state." *Book Forged in Hell*, 194; and Arthur P. Monahan, who claims that Spinoza "rejected the Hobbesian emphasis on the sacredness and inviolability of sovereign power over individual subjects, preferring to opt plainly for

certain inalienable rights in the individual citizen": *The Circle of Rights Expands: Modern Political Thought after the Reformation, 1521 (Luther) to 1762 (Rousseau)* (Montreal: McGill-Queen's Press, 2007), 193.

123. See also the use of *right* in the following passage: "Nature's right and her established order [Jus & Institutum naturae], under which all men are born and for the most part live, forbids only those things that no one desires and no one can do": Spinoza, *Theological-Political Treatise*, trans. Samuel Shirley (Indianapolis: Hackett, 2011), chap. 16, p. 174. For the Latin, see *Tractatus theologico-politicus* (Hamburg: Henricum Künrath, 1670), 176. Hereafter abridged *TTP*.

124. *TTP*, 173 (Latin, 175).

125. See, e.g., Robert J. McShea, *The Political Philosophy of Spinoza* (New York: Columbia University Press, 1968), 57–59 and *passim*; see also Den Uyl, *Power, State and Freedom*, 6–14.

126. See Spinoza: "Everyone has the natural right to act deceitfully and is not bound to keep his engagements except through hope of greater good or fear of greater evil." *TTP*, 177. Compare Hobbes: "Covenants, without the Sword, are but Words." *Leviathan*, 1:14. On Spinoza's contractarianism, see notably Matheron, *Individu et communauté*, 307–29; Edwin Curley, "Kissinger, Spinoza, and Genghis Khan," *Cambridge Companion to Spinoza*, ed. Don Garrett (Cambridge: Cambridge University Press, 1996), 315–42; and Barbone and Rice, introduction to Spinoza, *Political Treatise*, 1–30.

127. *Leviathan*, 2.18, 4:264.

128. Spinoza considers other governments but views democracy as the "most natural form of state" (*TTP*, 179).

129. See McShea, *Political Philosophy of Spinoza*, 86–87.

130. Spinoza is even more forceful in the *Political Treatise*: an individual in society, he states, "has in reality no right over Nature except that which is granted him by the communal right" (2.16).

131. See Matheron, *Individu et communauté*, 290–300; and Den Uyl, *Power, State and Freedom*, 14–19.

132. See Skinner, *Hobbes and Republican Liberty*.

133. See Balibar, *Spinoza and Politics*, 35–36; and Erik H. Stephenson, *Spinoza and the Ethics of Political Resistance* (PhD diss., McGill University, 2010). As Stephenson notes, there is little in the *TTP* or *TP* affording individuals a positive right to resistance (again, contrary to what Israel asserts in *Radical Enlightenment*). Stephenson suggests that such a right can, however, be reconstructed from the *Ethics*.

134. James Craufurd (sometimes spelled Crawford), *A Serious Expostulation with that Party in Scotland, Commonly Known by the Name of Whigs, Wherein is Modestly and Plainly Laid Open the Inconsistency of their Practices* (London: Richard Chiswell, 1682). The only secondary source I could find that mentions Craufurd is Clare Jackson, *Restoration Scotland, 1660–1690: Royalist Politics, Religion and Ideas* (Woodbridge, UK: Boydell, 2003). Locke's friend Anthony Collins owned a copy of this book: see Giovanni Tarantino, *Lo scrittoio di Anthony Collins (1676–1729): i libri e i tempi di un libero pensatore* (Milan: FrancoAngeli, 2007), 495.

135. *Scottish Notes and Queries* 6, no. 4 (1891): 49.

136. "*Who shall be judge,* whether the prince or legislative act contrary to their trust?" Locke, *Second Treatise*, § 240. As Locke notes elsewhere, however, this was "an old question" (§ 168); this italicized phrase does turn up in dozens of earlier texts.

137. "The Government of the worst of Princes is infinitely preferable to Anarchy and Confusion, where Guilty and Innocent are equally obnoxious to Danger" (9); "To be short, the Supream Power falling sometimes into no good hands, doth not frustrate the chief ends of Government;

but if discontented spirits may find ways lawfully to make opposition, nothing can keep it from being dissolved" (8).

138. Craufurd's "Lives, Liberties, and Fortunes" may sound to the modern ear strikingly Lockean (cf. *Second Treatise*, § 137), but the expression was in fact widespread in early modern English (as a string search on EEBO quickly reveals).

139. Wim Klever lists a great deal of evidence that Locke was familiar with a number of Spinoza's works (including the *TTP* and the *Ethics*), though his attempt to reduce all of Locke's thought to Spinoza is not convincing: see his "Locke's Disguised Spinozism [Part 1]," *Revista Conatus: Filosofia de Spinoza* 6, no. 11 (2012): 61–82, and "Locke's Disguised Spinozism [Part 2]," in the following issue (53–74). Klever does not discuss the similarities between Locke's and Spinoza's arguments about the transfer of natural rights.

140. See esp. A. John Simmons, *The Lockean Theory of Rights* (Princeton, NJ: Princeton University Press, 1992); and Jeremy Waldron, *The Right to Private Property* (Oxford: Oxford University Press, 1988); as well as the references listed below.

141. The classic libertarian interpretation is Robert Nozick, *Anarchy, State, and Utopia* (New York: Basic Books, 1974), notably chap. 3. Tellingly, Nozick argues for a quasi-identity between the state of nature and civil society in Locke (133). For an overview of his argument and other libertarian views on Locke, see Ellen Frankel Paul, Fred D. Miller, and Jeffrey Paul, eds., *Natural Rights Liberalism from Locke to Nozick* (Cambridge: Cambridge University Press, 2005). For a typical expression of this interpretation, see Michael Zuckert: "the institution of government" for Locke is designed for "the securing of rights." *Natural Rights and the New Republicanism* (Princeton, NJ: Princeton University Press, 1994), 302.

142. One could multiply examples: A. John Simmons provides a list of scholars who share this view in *On the Edge of Anarchy: Locke, Consent, and the Limits of Society* (Princeton, NJ: Princeton University Press, 1993), 101.

143. See, for instance, Willmoore Kendall, *John Locke and the Doctrine of Majority-Rule* (Urbana: University of Illinois Press, 1965); James Tully, *A Discourse on Property: John Locke and His Adversaries* (Cambridge: Cambridge University Press, 1980), esp. 165; and Kirstie M. McClure, *Judging Rights: Lockean Politics and the Limits of Consent* (Ithaca, NY: Cornell University Press, 1996). See also Alex Tuckness, who questions the libertarian claim that "the public good consists only in the protection of persons from rights violations (injuries to life, liberty, and property)," arguing instead that "the fundamental law [of nature] allows governments a wider activity than a libertarian theory would": *Locke and the Legislative Point of View* (Princeton, NJ: Princeton University Press, 2002), 183.

144. On the dating of Locke's composition (likely 1679–83), see Peter Laslett, introduction to Locke, *Two Treatises of Government*, ed. Laslett (Cambridge: Cambridge University Press, 1988), 123–36.

145. See also, "every Man has a *Property* in his own person. This no Body has any Right to but himself" (§ 27); but again, he is discussing "Man" in the state of nature.

146. See Simmons, *On the Edge of Anarchy*, 61–63. One exception (curiously not mentioned in the *Second Treatise*) is the right to freedom of conscience, which is beyond the scope of civil government: "Liberty of Conscience is every mans natural Right," Locke writes in *A Letter Concerning Toleration and Other Writings*, ed. Mark Goldie (Indianapolis: Liberty Fund, 2010), 53.

147. For a similar discussion of this passage, see Tully, *Discourse on Property*, chap. 7; and McClure, *Judging Rights*, chap. 7. Locke even recognizes that we may need to give up some of our innocent delights: "he is to part also with as much of his natural liberty, in providing for himself, as the good, prosperity, and safety of the society shall require" (§ 130).

148. See, e.g., §§ 8–11. As Simmons notes, "Locke never gives us anything like a definition of a right in his works," adding that "power" is one of the synonyms he uses on occasion: *Lockean Theory of Rights*, 70.

149. Hence, it is incorrect to equate "wholly giving up" with *alienating*, as Zuckert does: see *Natural Rights*, 83.

150. As Skinner noted, this is not a novel argument but can already be found in Jacques Almain: *Foundations of Modern Political Thought*, 2:119.

151. Locke also introduces a "fundamental law of property," on which more anon, but even that is not framed as an individual right (and I offer an argument for why it cannot be said to correlate with certain rights below).

152. See chapter 5. The Ninth Amendment reads, "The enumeration in the Constitution, of certain rights, shall not be construed to deny or disparage others retained by the people." There is considerable disagreement in Locke scholarship on this point: see Simmons, *On the Edge of Anarchy*, 65–66.

153. Here I disagree with Waldron, for whom preserving the property we owned in the state of nature is the same as preserving the property *rights* we enjoyed in the state of nature: *Right to Private Property*, 138, 232–41.

154. See also, "the law of nature being unwritten [ . . . ] it serves not, as it ought, to determine the rights, and *fence the properties* of those that live under it" (§ 136; emphasis added); and "The reason why men enter into society, is the preservation of their property; and the end why they chuse and authorize a legislative, is, that there may be laws made, and rules set, as guards and fences to the properties of all the members of the society" (§ 222).

155. Zuckert tries to get around this problem by arguing that "Locke mostly, but not entirely, renames rights as 'property'; he uses the language of rights more less interchangeably with the language of property": *Natural Rights*, 18. I find this argument unconvincing, for the reasons advanced in this paragraph.

156. See Tuckness, *Locke and the Legislative Point of View*; and McClure, *Judging Rights*: "Locke's theoretical transfer of natural rights to civil determination [ . . . ] invests particular governments with such jurisdiction over propriety as the necessity of the case shall require for the good, prosperity, and safety of the commonwealth as a whole" (257).

157. It makes even less sense to consider natural rights as our titles to property in society, given the effects of money on Locke's labor theory of property in the state of nature. If I bought the field next to my own, could I claim a natural right to it?

158. Waldron acknowledges that government can regulate property, but distinguishes that "from its confiscation or redistribution": *Right to Private Property*, 238. He does not, as far as I can tell, address the fact that Locke explicitly grants a legislative majority the power to do just that, in the form of taxation.

159. Interestingly, we find a similar point in Robert Filmer: "by politic human constitutions it is oft ordained that the voices of the most shall overrule the rest": *Patriarcha*, in *"Patriarcha" and Other Writings*, ed. Johann P. Sommerville (Cambridge: Cambridge University Press, 1991), 20.

160. See more broadly, Locke, *Second Treatise*, chap. 18, "On Tyranny"; and see esp. John Dunn, *The Political Thought of John Locke: An Historical Account of the Argument of the 'Two Treatises of Government'* (Cambridge: Cambridge University Press, 1982), on this point.

161. Again, I leave aside the *Preface* (which is not technically part of the *Second Treatise*), for the chronological reason stated above.

162. See Stephen Lalor, *Matthew Tindal, Freethinker: An Eighteenth-Century Assault on Religion* (London: Continuum, 2006). Tindal seemingly first entered into contact with Locke in 1697.

163. On Locke and Tindal, see notably Marshall, *John Locke, Toleration and Early Enlightenment Culture*, 565–66.

164. Matthew Tindal, *An Essay Concerning Obedience to the Supreme Powers, and the Duty of Subjects in All Revolutions with Some Considerations Touching the Present Juncture of Affairs* (London: Richard Baldwin . . . , 1694), 8, 33, 10–11 for quotes.

165. See Tindal to Locke, January 20, 1697, in *Electronic Enlightenment Scholarly Edition of Correspondence*, letter editor E. S. de Beer, http://dx.doi.org/10.13051/ee:doc/lockjoOU0050749a1c.

166. Tindal, *An Essay Concerning the Power of the Magistrate* (1697), 10; emphasis added.

167. [Tindal, anonymously,] *The Rights of the Christian Church Asserted* (1706), 11, 7; emphasis added. Like Locke, Tindal also insists that freedom of religious conscience is one of "those Natural Rights of Mankind which can't be made over to Prince or Priest" (lxxxiii–iv).

168. George Hickes, "A Preliminary Discourse to the Following Treatise," in William Carroll, *Spinoza Reviv'd, or a Treatise Proving the Book Entitled: The Rights of the Christian Church, &c [ . . . ] is the Same with Spinoza's Rights of the Christian Clergy . . .* (1709). Hickes's "Discourse" is not paginated, but the quotes appear on page images 7 and 5, respectively, of the ECCO edition. On Hickes, Carroll, and this particular work, see Stuart Brown, " 'Locke as Secret Spinozist': The Perspective of William Carroll," in *Disguised and Overt Spinozism around 1700*, ed. Wiep Van Bunge and Wim Klever (Leiden: Brill, 1996), 213–34; see also Israel, *Radical Enlightenment*, 468–69 and *passim*.

169. Benjamin Hoadly, *The Foundation of the Present Government Defended* (London, 1710), 3, 12.

170. See Starkie, *Church of England and the Bangorian Controversy*. The work that set off this controversy was Hickes's *The Constitution of the Catholick Church, and the Nature and Consequences of Schism* (London, 1716).

171. See John Jackson, *The Grounds of Civil and Ecclesiastical Government Briefly Consider'd* (1714; London, 1718).

172. Zuckert, *Natural Rights and the New Republicanism*, 302; more generally, see 297–319. See also the classic works by Caroline Robbins, *The Eighteenth-Century Commonwealthman* (Cambridge, MA: Harvard University Press, 1959); and Bernard Bailyn, *The Ideological Origins of the American Revolution* (1967; Cambridge, MA: Harvard University Press, 1992).

173. *Cato's Letters: Or, Essays on Liberty, Civil and Religious, and Other Important Subjects*, 4 vols. (London: printed for T. Woodward et al., 1748), no. 90 (August 18, 1722), 3:201. See also no. 20 (March 11, 1721), and no. 60 (January 6, 1722).

174. See Robert Molesworth, *An Account of Denmark, with Francogallia and Some Considerations for the Promoting of Agriculture and Employing of the Poor*, ed. Justin Champion (Indianapolis: Liberty Fund, 2011), 18. As this title indicates, Molesworth also translated François Hotman's *Franco-Gallia*, one of the French Huguenot "Monarchomach" texts. Both Trenchard and Molesworth attended Trinity College, Dublin (along with Sir Thomas Molyneux); as Caroline Robbins observed, these "Real Whigs greatly extended the application of general statements of right so frequent in English constitutional pronouncements [ . . . ] to all of mankind": *Eighteenth-Century Commonwealthman*, 9–10.

175. *Cato's Letters*, no. 26 (April 22, 1721), 1:195.

176. *Cato's Letters*, no. 33 (June 17, 1721), 1:257.

177. *Cato's Letters*, no. 55 (December 2, 1721), 2:169; emphasis added.

178. This interpretation of the Trenchard/Gordon divide might be challenged by the passage (cited by Zuckert) in letter 62 (January 20, 1722), that "[t]he entering into political society, is so far from a departure from his natural right, that to preserve it was the sole reason why men

did so" (2:245). In most editions, including this one (and the Liberty Fund edition), this letter is attributed to Gordon. But this attribution is doubtful, since the author of letter 62 begins by noting that he has shown "in a late paper, wherein consists the difference between free and arbitrary governments." This was the topic of letter 61, written by Trenchard. It would moreover have been surprising if Gordon had changed his mind about the status of rights in society within the space of two months. He would remain committed to the transfer regime of rights later in life: see Gordon, *An Essay of Government* (London: Roberts, 1747), 8–11.

179. See most notably Garry Wills, *Inventing America: Jefferson's Declaration of Independence* (New York: First Mariner Books, 2002). On Hutcheson, see also Haakonssen, *Natural Law and Moral Philosophy*.

180. Hutcheson, *An Inquiry into the Original of Our Ideas of Beauty and Virtue* (1725), ed. Wolfgang Leidhold (Indianapolis: Liberty Fund, 2004), treatise II, sec. VII, § X, p. 193. Subsequent page references to this work are provided in line. Hutcheson's arguments about rights are fairly similar to those of his teacher Gershom Carmichael, as laid out in his *Supplements and Observations upon Samuel Pufendorf's On the Duty of Man and Citizen according to the Law of Nature, composed for the use of students in the Universities* (Edinburgh, 1724), in *Natural Rights on the Threshold of the Scottish Enlightenment: The Writings of Gershom Carmichael*, ed. James Moore and Michael Silverthorne (Indianapolis: Liberty Fund, 2002). See, for instance, his claim that "God has granted to man those natural rights whose transfer in part to a ruler constitutes civil government" (155); see also 70 (on the abridgment of rights), and 77–78 (on their preservation).

181. On the supposed "unthinkability" of the revolutionary rights regime in the early eighteenth century, see Peter de Bolla, *The Architecture of Concepts: The Historical Formation of Human Rights* (New York: Fordham University Press, 2013).

### Chapter III

1. Data from ARTFL-FRANTEXT database, the "Tout Voltaire" database, and the Electronic Enlightenment Project. Montesquieu texts include the *Lettres persanes* (1721), the *Considérations sur les causes de la grandeur des Romains* (1734), and *De l'esprit des lois* (1748). On this point in Montesquieu, see also Michael Zuckert, "Natural Rights and Modern Constitutionalism," *Northwestern Journal of International Human Rights* 2, no. 1 (2004), http://scholarlycommons .law.northwestern.edu/njihr/vol2/iss1/4. For an exception in Voltaire, see below.

2. Thémiseul de Saint-Hyacinthe, *Entretiens dans lesquels on traite des entreprises de l'Espagne, des prétentions de M. le Chevalier de S. George, et de la renonciation de sa majesté catholique* (The Hague: chez A. de Rogissart, 1719), 186–87. This passage reappears verbatim in Gaspard de Réal de Curban's posthumous work, *La Science du gouvernement*, 8 vols. (Aix-la-Chapelle, 1761–65), 1:342. Despite emphasizing the necessary transfer of rights, Thémiseul does suggest that this transfer is not a total loss: "When Man subjects himself to Government, he does not completely abandon the Rights of Nature; he only derogates them, out of the necessity to entrust them in hands capable of conserving them for him." See Elisabeth Carayol, *Thémiseul de Saint-Hyacinthe, 1684–1746* (Oxford: Voltaire Foundation, 1984).

3. Andrew Michael Ramsay, *Essay de politique où l'on traite de la nécessité, de l'origine des droits, des bornes & des différentes formes de la souveraineté selon les principes de l'auteur de Télémaque* (La Haye: H. Scheurleer, 1719). A second edition of this work was published as *Essai sur le gouvernement civil* (London, 1722). On this text, see Andrew Mansfield, "Fénelon's Cuckoo: Andrew Michael Ramsay and the Archbishop Fénelon," in *Fénelon in the Enlightenment: Traditions,*

*Adaptations, and Variations*, ed. Christoph Schmitt-Maaß, Stefanie Stockhorst, and Doohwan Ahn (Amsterdam: Rodopi, 2014), 77–97.

4. Samuel von Pufendorf, *Le Droit de la nature et des gens*, trans. Jean Barbeyrac (Amsterdam: G. Kuyper, 1706); this text went through five subsequent editions in the eighteenth century; an English translation, including Barbeyrac's notes, appeared in 1710. See also Pufendorf, *Les Devoirs de l'homme et du citoien, tels qu'ils lui sont prescrits par la loi naturelle* (Amsterdam: H. Schelte, 1707); six further editions followed in the eighteenth century; an English translation with Barbeyrac's notes was published in 1716.

5. See Pufendorf, *Les Devoirs de l'homme et du citoien*, 2.12; 321; English translation, *The Whole Duty of Man According to the Law of Nature*, trans. Andrew Tooke (1691), ed. Ian Hunter and David Saunders (Indianapolis: Liberty Fund, 2003), 224.

6. The marginal note in the English edition simply reads "Form." The marginal notes to the French edition were likely added by Barbeyrac, as they do not feature in the original Latin: compare *De Officio hominis et civis juxta legem naturalem libri duo* (New York: Oxford University Press, 1927; reprod. of the 1692 edition), 142.

7. William Wollaston, *Ebauche de la religion naturelle, traduite de l'anglais avec un supplément et autres additions considérables* (The Hague: Jean Swart, 1726), 257; English passage from the original, *The Religion of Nature Delineated* (London, 1724), 7.6, p. 150.

8. Alberto Radicati, *Recueil de pièces curieuses sur les matières les plus intéressantes* (Rotterdam: Veuve Thomas Johnson, 1736), 15. He did defend the right of resistance against tyrants who subjected individuals to their power without their consent: see the tenth Discourse, 185–87 (where Radicati defends an argument that bears more resemblance to the transfer thesis). See Silvia Berti, "Alberto Radicati di Passerano," trans. Joan B. Sax, in *Encyclopedia of the Enlightenment*, ed. Alan Charles Kors (Oxford: Oxford University Press, 2002); accessible online through Oxford Reference.

9. Gerhard Noodt, *Du pouvoir des souverains et de la liberté de conscience, en deux discours*, trans. Jean Barbeyrac (Amsterdam: Pierre Humbert, 1724), 243. First edition, 1707; another edition appeared in 1775, alongside a re-edition of Abbadie's *Défense de la nation britannique*.

10. *La Henriade de Mr. de Voltaire* (London: Woodman & Lyon, 1728), n.p.

11. Jean-Baptiste Boyer d'Argens, *Lettres juives*, 6 vols. (La Haye: P. Gautier, 1736–37), letter 100, 4:125. On Boyer d'Argens, see notably Julia Gasper, *The Marquis d'Argens: A Philosophical Life* (Plymouth, UK: Lexington Books, 2014).

12. César de Missy to Voltaire, 18 November 1742 (D2689). On Missy, see his entry by John Patrick Lee in the *Dictionnaire des journalistes (1600–1789)*, http://dictionnaire-journalistes.gazettes18e.fr/journaliste/580-cesar-de-missy.

13. Voltaire, *Le Siècle de Louis XIV*, 2 vols. (London: R. Dodsley, 1752), 2:124. On the tendency to read this document as a progressive step forward for plantation slaves, see Malick Ghachem, *The Old Regime and the Haitian Revolution* (Cambridge: Cambridge University Press, 2012). I return to the topic of slavery and rights in chapter 5. The expression "droits de l'humanité" also appears in a passage about Mme de Montespan (2:49). In his *Essai sur les mœurs et l'esprit des nations* (1756; Geneva, 1769), Voltaire describes how, in the fourteenth century, "all the Italian cities recovered their natural rights [rentrent dans leurs droits naturels] and raised the flag of liberty" (2:77). See also Louis-Sébastien Mercier, *Histoire d'Izerben, poëte arabe* (Amsterdam: Cellot, 1756), 69.

14. Rousseau, *Discours sur l'inégalité*, in *Œuvres complètes*, 5 vols., ed. Bernard Gagnebin and Marcel Raymond (Paris: Pléiade, 1964), 3:118, p. 189. Subsequently abridged as *JJR*.

15. "Economie," *Encyclopédie, ou dictionnaire raisonné des sciences, des arts et des métiers, etc.*,

ed. Denis Diderot and Jean le Rond d'Alembert (Chicago: ARTFL Encyclopédie Project, 2013), ed. Robert Morrissey, http://encyclopedie.uchicago.edu/, 5:339; see also the discussion of "droits de l'état de nature" (5:342). This article would later be published as the *Discours sur l'économie politique* (Geneva: E. Du Villard fils, 1758).

16. "Droit naturel," *Encyclopédie*, 5:116.

17. See Helvétius, *De l'Esprit* (Paris: Durand, 1758), 2.17, 175, note *e*; 2.30, p. 464, note *a*; see also 1.3, p. 21, note *c*.

18. Montesquieu, *De l'Esprit des loix*, in *Œuvres de Monsieur de Montesquieu* (Amsterdam: chez Arkstée et Merkus, 1764), 434.

19. On the broader interest in natural law (*droit naturel*) in the French Enlightenment, see chapter 4.

20. See notably Dale K. Van Kley, *The Damiens Affair and the Unraveling of the Ancien Régime, 1750–1770* (Princeton, NJ: Princeton University Press, 1984); Keith Baker, *Inventing the French Revolution: Essays on French Political Culture in the Eighteenth Century* (Cambridge: Cambridge University Press, 1990); and Colin Jones, *The Great Nation: France from Louis XV to Napoleon* (London: Penguin, 2002).

21. Richard Tuck's *Natural Rights Theories: Their Origins and Development* (Cambridge: Cambridge University Press, 1979), in a characteristic statement, claims to help readers "understand more fully the characteristics of the natural rights theories available to the men of the Enlightenment" (book jacket). See also below, on Locke.

22. This distaste must be situated within the broader anti-pedantic current of Enlightenment France: see notably Blandine Barret-Kriegel, *La Défaite de l'érudition* (Paris: PUF, 1988).

23. Simon-Nicholas-Henri Linguet, *Théorie des lois civiles ou principes fondamentaux de la société* (1767; ARTFL Electronic Edition, 2009), 15.

24. Gabriel Bonnot de Mably, *Des droits et des devoirs du citoyen* (Paris, 1789), 73 (and 21).

25. Diderot, "Droit naturel"; compare Antoine-Gaspard Boucher d'Argis, "Droit naturel," 5:115 and 5:131–34, respectively. Diderot wrote his article in response to the latter: see Jacques Proust, *Diderot et l'Encyclopédie* (Paris: Armand Colin, 1962), 384–93.

26. *Discours sur l'inégalité*, in *JJR*, 3:124. On Rousseau's knowledge of the natural right canon, see in particular Robert Derathé, *Jean-Jacques Rousseau et la science politique de son temps* (1950; Paris: Vrin, 1995); and Helena Rosenblatt, *Rousseau and Geneva: From the First 'Discourse' to 'The Social Contract,' 1749–1762* (Cambridge: Cambridge University Press, 1997).

27. For the indictment of the (anonymous) philosopher, see *Discours sur l'inégalité*, in *JJR*, 3:156.

28. Diderot, "Droit naturel," *Encyclopédie*, 5:115.

29. Jean-Baptiste-Claude Delisle de Sales, *De la philosophie de la nature* (Amsterdam, 1770), xxvi [ARTFL].

30. *Poème sur la Loi naturelle* (1756), in *Œuvres complètes de Voltaire*, ed. David Beeson et al. (Oxford: Voltaire Foundation, 2007), 32B: 51: "Ecartons ces romans qu'on appelle systèmes; / Et pour nous élever descendons dans nous-mêmes."

31. See, e.g., Sophie Wahnich, *L'Impossible citoyen* (Paris: Albin Michel, 1997); and Marc Belissa, *Fraternité universelle et intérêt national (1713–1795): les cosmopolitiques du droit des gens* (Paris: Kimé, 1998), 80, 110.

32. Peter Laslett wrote that Mazel's translation "was reprinted a dozen times in the next [eighteenth] century": see the introduction to his edition of Locke's *Two Treatises of Government* (1960; Cambridge: Cambridge University Press, 1988), 12. This number is repeated in S. J. Savonius, "Locke in French: The *Du Gouvernement Civil* of 1691 and Its Readers," *Historical*

*Journal* 47, no. 1 (2004): 47-79 (69), with a reference to Laslett. See also Ross Hutchinson, *Locke in France, 1688-1734*, Studies on Voltaire and the Eighteenth Century, vol. 290 (Oxford: Voltaire Foundation, 1991).

33. The number twelve may come from the fact that the Bibliothèque nationale de France holds double copies of the 1691, 1755, and 1794 editions; these copies are catalogued separately but appear to be (at most) the product of separate print runs (the 1755 and 1794 doubles are by the same printer). I found one reference to a 1718 Amsterdam edition on WorldCat, but suspect a data entry error, since I have never seen any mention of this edition elsewhere.

34. See Baker, *Inventing the French Revolution*, 89; and Margaret Jacob, "In the Aftermath of Revolution: Rousset de Missy, Freemasonry, and Locke's *Two Treatises of Government*," in *L'Età dei lumi: studi storici sul settecento europeo in onore di Franco Venturi*, 2 vols. (Naples: Jovene, 1985), 1:489-521; she also suggests, *contra* Baker, that the 1754 edition was the work of Rousset de Missy (510-14). See also Jacob, *The Radical Enlightenment: Pantheists, Freemasons and Republicans* (London: George Allen and Unwin, 1981), 236-37.

35. These first two texts were both translated by Pierre Coste as the *Essai philosophique concernant l'entendement humain* (Amsterdam, 1700), and *De l'éducation des enfans* (Amsterdam, 1695).

36. These books are Simon Linguet's *Théorie des lois civiles ou principes fondamentaux de la société* (1767); Delisle de Sales's *Philosophie de la nature* (1769); and d'Holbach's *Système social ou principes naturels de la morale et de la politique avec un examen de l'influence du gouvernement sur les moeurs* (1773). The Locke of the *Second Treatise of Government* is cited, respectively, 11, 8, and 7 times in these works. The other four works in the database that reference the "political" Locke are Rousseau's *Discours sur l'inégalité* (2 mentions), his *Lettres écrites sur la montagne* (2 mentions), Helvétius's *De l'homme* (1 mention), and Diderot's *Essai sur la vie de Sénèque* (1 mention).

37. At the time of this writing, for instance, it does not contain Mably's *Droits et devoirs du citoyen*.

38. This claim is based on an analysis of the nearly 300 mentions of Locke in the *Voltaire électronique* database, and the 32 references in Voltaire's correspondence (searchable on the *Electronic Enlightenment* database). A few illuminating details offer further evidence that Voltaire did not think of Locke as a political writer: even his *Poème sur la Loi naturelle* refers only to Locke the metaphysician, and in the *Questions sur l'Encyclopédie*, s.v. "Superstition," Voltaire writes, "I challenge you to show me a single philosopher from Zoroaster to Locke who ever roused the people to rebel [qui ait jamais excité une sédition], who joined in an attack on a king's life, who ever troubled society"—a curious assertion for someone who had read Locke's chapter on the right of resistance.

39. On the basis of the *Bibliothèque de Voltaire*, Hutchinson claims that Voltaire owned a copy of the 1691 David Mazel translation of *Du gouvernement civil*: *Locke in France*, 206. But that work is not in fact listed in the catalog (see 563-64). Voltaire did possess a copy of the *Œuvres diverses de M. Locke*, 2 vols., ed. J[ean]-F[rédéric] Bernard (Amsterdam, 1732), but the *Second Treatise* is not included there. It is of course always possible that Voltaire owned a copy that was then lost or read the work elsewhere. For a similar assessment, see Theodore Besterman, *Voltaire* (New York: Harcourt, Brace and World, 1969), 298.

40. Montesquieu did not possess a copy of Mazel's translation, though the Académie de Bordeaux owned both the 1724 and the 1749 editions: see Hutchinson, *Locke in France*, 84 (who also suggests that Montesquieu is more likely to have picked up secondhand knowledge of Locke through Barbeyrac). In the *Spicilège*, Montesquieu's commonplace book, Locke is mentioned twice, but never with respect to his political theory. Some commentators have read indirect

references to the *Second Treatise* in the *Persian Letters*. But the arguments ascribed here to "les anglois" (letter 104) are generic and not unique to Locke: see *Lettres persanes*, vol 1. of *Œuvres complètes de Montesquieu*, ed. Pierre Rétat and Catherine Volpilhac-Auger (Oxford: Voltaire Foundation, 2004), 414n1; and Ursula Haskins Gonthier, *Montesquieu and England: Enlightened Exchanges, 1689-1755* (London: Routledge, 2010), 24-25, 35. The absence of any clear evidence that Montesquieu was familiar with Locke's political philosophy has not stopped scholars from insisting on the latter's influence: see, e.g., Thomas Pangle, *Montesquieu's Philosophy of Liberalism: A Commentary on "The Spirit of the Laws"* (Chicago: University of Chicago Press, 1989); Paul Rahe, *Montesquieu and the Logic of Liberty* (New Haven, CT: Yale University Press, 2009); and Belissa, *Fraternité universelle.* My thanks to Céline Spector for her help with this question.

41. See Mably, *Des droits et devoirs*, 21. For the quote, see J. Kent Wright, *A Classical Republican in Eighteenth-Century France: The Political Thought of Mably* (Stanford, CA: Stanford University Press, 1997), 78; see also Baker, *Inventing the French Revolution*, 89-90.

42. See, for instance, Derathé, *Jean-Jacques Rousseau*, 90. See also Tim Hochstrasser, "Conscience and Reason: The Natural Law Theory of Jean Barbeyrac," *Historical Journal* 36, no. 2 (1993): 289-308; and David Saunders, "The Natural Jurisprudence of Jean Barbeyrac: Translation as an Art of Political Adjustment," *Eighteenth-Century Studies* 36, no. 4 (2003): 473-90.

43. See Jean-Jacques Burlamaqui, *Principes du droit naturel* (Geneva, 1747), and the posthumous *Principes du droit politique* (Amsterdam, 1751). On Burlamaqui, Barbeyrac, and Locke, see Ray Forrest Harvey, *Jean-Jacques Burlamaqui: A Liberal Tradition in American Constitutionalism* (Chapel Hill: University of North Carolina Press, 1937); Derathé, *Jean-Jacques Rousseau*; and Peter Korkman, introduction to Burlamaqui, *The Principles of Natural and Politic Law*, trans. Thomas Nugent, ed. Peter Korkman (Indianapolis: Liberty Fund, 2006).

44. See Savonius, "Locke in French."

45. See Dan Edelstein, Robert Morrissey, and Glenn Roe, "To Quote or Not to Quote: Citation Strategies in the *Encyclopédie*," *Journal of the History of Ideas* 74, no. 2 (2013): 213-36. At least thirty-eight passages from the *Second Treatise* are quoted (in the French translation) in nine different articles. The most important of these include "Etat de nature," "Gouvernement," "Pouvoir," "Prérogative," "Tyrannie," and "Usurpation."

46. All nine of the *Encyclopédie* articles in which the *Second Treatise* is quoted were written (or compiled) by Jaucourt, with the possible exception of "Pouvoir" (whose authorship remains unknown). The argument about a "subversive style" of non-citation is developed in Edelstein, Morrissey, and Roe, "To Quote or Not to Quote."

47. This description of the effects of authorship draws on Michel Foucault, "What Is an Author?" in *The Foucault Reader*, ed. Paul Rabinow (New York: Pantheon Books, 1984), 101-20.

48. See esp. John Lough, *Essays on the 'Encyclopédie' of Diderot and d'Alembert* (Oxford: Oxford University Press, 1968), 439 (for both quotes). Lough also comments how "[i]t is probable that by 1750-1 Diderot was familiar with at least the Barbeyrac translations of Grotius and Pufendorf, if not also with Locke's *Two Treatises.*"

49. "Autorité politique," *Encyclopédie*, 1:899.

50. "Autorité politique," *Encyclopédie*, 1:900.

51. See Lough, *Essays*, 439-40.

52. "We must speak out against senseless laws until they're reformed and, in the meanwhile, abide by them": Diderot, *Political Writings*, ed. and trans. John Hope Mason and Robert Wokler (Cambridge: Cambridge University Press, 1992), 74. For the French, see *Supplément au voyage de Bougainville*, in *Œuvres*, ed. André Billy (Paris: Pléiade, 1951), 1001.

53. Baker, *Inventing the French Revolution*, 323n13.

54. See Derathé, *Jean-Jacques Rousseau*, 117–19; and also Joshua Cohen, *Rousseau: A Free Community of Equals* (Oxford: Oxford University Press, 2010), 52–53.

55. See in particular Quentin Skinner, *Foundations of Modern Political Thought*, vol. 2 (Cambridge: Cambridge University Press, 1978). See also Baker, *Inventing the French Revolution*, 90, notably on the influence of Sidney's *Discourses on Government*, which Voltaire, Mably, Rousseau, Helvétius, and d'Holbach all read and referenced.

56. R. R. Palmer, *Catholics and Unbelievers in Eighteenth-Century France* (Princeton, NJ: Princeton University Press, 1939). On Palmer's thesis (and the Jesuit connection more broadly), see Dan Edelstein, *The Enlightenment: A Genealogy* (Chicago: University of Chicago Press, 2010), 65–66.

57. Francis Hutcheson, *Recherches sur l'origine des idées que nous avons de la beauté & de la vertu*, 2 vols. (Amsterdam [Paris: Durand], 1749).

58. Hutcheson, *An Inquiry into the Original of Our Ideas of Beauty and Virtue*, second treatise, 7.10–14.

59. Hutcheson, *Recherches*, second treatise, 7.6, 2:353–59.

60. Hutcheson, *Recherches*, second treatise, 7.8, 2:366.

61. s.v. "Eidous, Marc-Antoine," in *Biographie universelle ancienne et moderne*, ed. Louis-Gabriel Michaud (Paris: Thoisnier Desplaces, 1843), 12:321.

62. Hutcheson, *Recherches*, second treatise, 7.8, 2:373; emphasis added.

63. Sections from this translation would be excerpted in the article "Droit," in *Dictionnaire universel des sciences morale, économique, politique et diplomatique*, ed. Jean Robinet (London, 1780), 16:403–5.

64. "To vindicate the Deity from the impious charge of protecting Tyrants, to maintain the cause of Liberty, and shew its blessings, to assert the rights of men [défendre les droits des hommes] [ . . . ] is the design of these discourses": Thomas Gordon, introduction to *Political Discourses upon Tacitus* (1728), in *Thomas Gordon's Political Discourses on Tacitus and Sallust: Tyranny, Empire, War, and Corruption (1728–1744)*, ed. David M. Hart (Indianapolis: Liberty Fund, 2013), 128. For the French, see *Discours historiques, critiques et politiques sur Tacite*, 3 vols., trans. Pierre Daudé (Amsterdam: F. Changuion, 1751), 1:xvii–xviii.

65. See Voltaire's *Lettres philosophiques* (Amsterdam, 1734), letter 22, p. 113. See also d'Holbach, *Système social ou principes naturels de la morale et de la politique* (1773; ARTFL electronic edition, 2009), 224n.

66. Gordon, *Political Discourses*, 129, 58, 57; Gordon, *Discours sur Tacite*, xx, 1:118, 1:106.

67. Keith Michael Baker, "Transformations of Classical Republicanism in Eighteenth-Century France," *Journal of Modern History* 73, no. 1 (2001): 32–53; see also Rachel Hammersley, *French Revolutionaries and English Republicans: The Cordeliers Club, 1790–1794* (Woodbridge, UK: Boydell Press, 2005), 161.

68. See Algernon Sidney, *Discours sur le gouvernement*, trans. P.-A. Samson (The Hague: L. et H. Van Dole, 1755)—same translation (and publisher) as the first edition. A subsequent edition appeared in 1793. On Sidney's rights regime, see chapter 2.

69. Burlamaqui, *Principes du droit naturel*.

70. See Derathé, *Jean-Jacques Rousseau*, 85–88. For a more positive assessment of Burlamaqui's thought, see Bruno Bernardi, *Le Principe d'obligation: sur une aporie de la modernité politique* (Paris: Vrin/EHESS, 2007), chap. 5.

71. See Rosenblatt, *Rousseau and Geneva*.

72. Jean-Jacques Burlamaqui, *The Principles of Natural Law*, trans. Thomas Nugent (London: J. Nourse, 1748). This translation would undergo six reeditions before 1800.

73. See Harvey, *Jean-Jacques Burlamaqui*.

74. See Burlamaqui, *The Principles of Natural Law*, in *The Principles of Natural and Politic Law*, trans. Thomas Nugent, ed. Petter Korkman (Indianapolis: Liberty Fund, 2006), 2.4.23, pp. 162–63 (French ed., pp. 202–3). See also 1.7.8.

75. Burlamaqui, *Principles of Politic Law*, 3.4.5, p. 416; emphasis added. See also 1.7.12, p. 310; 1.7.53, p. 321; 2.6.33, p. 376; 3.4.14, p. 418; 4.3.24, p. 473. He made an exception for property rights: see 3.5.4, p. 432.

76. One still finds this claim in another major natural law treatise of this period, Emmerich de Vattel's *Le droit des gens, ou Principes de la loi naturelle, appliqués à la conduite et aux affaires des Nations et des Souverains*, 2 vols. (London, 1758). See, for instance, his discussion of sovereignty, which "originally and essentially belonged to the body of the society, to which each member submitted, and ceded his natural right of conducting himself in every thing as he pleased according to the dictates of his own understanding, and of doing himself justice": Vattel, *The Law of Nations, or Principles of the Law of Nature . . .* (1758), ed. Béla Kapossy and Richard Whatmore, trans. Thomas Nugent (Indianapolis: Liberty Fund, 2008), 1.4.38, p. 97.

77. Helvétius [false attribution], *Le vrai sens du 'Système de la Nature,'* in *Œuvres complètes de M. Helvétius*, 4 vols. (London, 1777), 1.12, 4:184; emphasis added. On the misattribution of this work (which largely rehashed d'Holbach's own *Système de la Nature*), see François Moureau, *La Plume et le plomb: espaces de l'imprimé et du manuscrit au siècle des lumières* (Paris: PUPS, 2006), 92–93.

78. See in general Georges Weulersse, *Le Mouvement physiocratique en France de 1756 à 1770*, 2 vols. (Paris: Alcan, 1910); Elizabeth Fox-Genovese, *The Origins of Physiocracy: Economic Revolution and Social Order in Eighteenth-Century France* (Ithaca, NY: Cornell University Press, 1976); Catherine Larrère, *L'Invention de l'économie au XVIIIe siècle: du droit naturel à la physiocratie* (Paris: PUF, 1992); Peter Groenewegen, *Eighteenth-Century Economics: Turgot, Beccaria and Smith and Their Contemporaries* (London: Routledge, 2002), chaps. 12–14; Michael Sonenscher, "Physiocracy as Theodicy," *History of Political Thought* 23, no. 2 (2002): 326–39; Sonenscher, *Sans-Culottes: An Eighteenth-Century Emblem in the French Revolution* (Princeton, NJ: Princeton University Press, 2008), esp. 248–60; Paul Cheney, *Revolutionary Commerce: Globalization and the French Monarchy* (Cambridge, MA: Harvard University Press, 2010), chap. 5; and Liana Vardi, *The Physiocrats and the World of the Enlightenment* (Cambridge: Cambridge University Press, 2012).

79. Dan Edelstein, *The Terror of Natural Right* (Chicago: University of Chicago Press, 2009), part 1. In this book, however, I did not consider the role of natural rights in Physiocratic writings.

80. See notably Larrère, *Invention de l'économie au XVIIIe siècle*, who draws heavily on Villey and Tuck in her analysis; Groenewegen, *Eighteenth-Century Economics*, chap. 12; and Vardi, *Physiocrats and the World of the Enlightenment*, 130–36.

81. For biographical details about Quesnay, see Jacqueline Hecht, "La vie de François Quesnay," in *François Quesnay et la physiocratie*, 2 vols. (Paris: Institut National d'Etudes Démographiques, 1958), 1:211–94.

82. Peter Groenewegen detects a few hints of Quesnay's future interest in economics: see "From Prominent Physician to Major Economist: Some Reflections on Quesnay's Switch to Economics in the 1750s," in *Physicians and Political Economy: Six Studies of the Work of Doctor Economists*, ed. P. Groenewegen (London: Routledge, 2001), 105–6.

83. Quesnay, *Essai physique sur l'œconomie animale*, 3 vols. (Paris: Cavelier, 1747), § 3, chap. XVIII, 3:349–73 (349 for quote). Subsequent page references are provided in-line. On this text, see Larrère, *Invention de l'économie au XVIIIe siècle*; Groenewegen, "From Prominent Physician

to Major Economist," 103–6; and Vardi, *The Physiocrats and the World of the Enlightenment*, 68–69.

84. Quesnay, *Essai physique*, 3:364.

85. *The Digest of Justinian*, trans. Charles Henry Monro (Cambridge: Cambridge University Press, 1904), 1.8.2.1.

86. From the table of contents, in Quesnay, *Essai physique*, 3:609.

87. See in particular the works by Villey, Strauss, and Tuck, discussed in chapter 1.

88. On Quesnay's appreciation of Aristotle, whom he read at a young age (Hecht, "Vie de François Quesnay," 214), see notably Paul P. Christensen, "Fire, Motion, and Productivity: The Proto-Energetics of Nature and Economy in François Quesnay," in *Natural Images in Economic Thought: 'Markets Read in Tooth & Claw,'* ed. Philip Mirowski (Cambridge: Cambridge University Press, 1994), 249–88; and Olivier Perru, "Les Physiocrates: 'La communauté est-elle de droit naturel?'" *Revue philosophique de Louvain* 95, no. 4 (1997): 617–38.

89. See Fred D. Miller, *Nature, Justice, and Rights in Aristotle's "Politics"* (Oxford: Oxford University Press, 1995).

90. See Weulersse, *Mouvement physiocratique en France*, 2:111–19; and Sonenscher, "Physiocracy as Theodicy."

91. See, e.g., Fox-Genovese, *Origins of Physiocracy*, 49, 56. Quesnay discusses Locke's *Essay Concerning Human Understanding* in his *Essai physique*, 3:250, but I came across no evidence that he read *Du gouvernement civil* (as the French translation of the *Second Treatise* was called). He only cites Locke once (and the passage is borrowed from another source) in all his economic writings: see Quesnay, "Fermiers," in *Œuvres économiques complètes et autres textes*, ed. Christine Théré, Loïc Charles, and Jean-Claude Perrot (Paris: Institut national d'études démographiques [INED], 2005), 156. On this article, see Groenewegen, *Eighteenth-Century Economics*, chap. 13.

92. I discuss the disappearance of the social contract in *Terror of Natural Right*, chap. 2; see also Larrère, *Invention de l'économie au XVIIIe siècle*, 197.

93. For an overview of the older scholarship on this question, see Sonenscher, "Physiocracy as Theodicy," 327.

94. Fox-Genovese, *Origins of Physiocracy*, 86. She also points to Burlamaqui as a possible influence, but that is unlikely as his *Principes de droit naturel* came out the same year as Quesnay's *Essai physique* (in 1747), and Quesnay in fact owned the 1748 edition: see *Œuvres économiques complètes*, 1448. Her conclusion that "Quesnay's early forays into natural law theory platitudinously reflect the common discussion of his day" is curiously unfounded (87).

95. *Le Droit naturel* (1765), 6n6.

96. See, for instance, the imagined "objection" to his argument (367), and compare *De Cive*, chap. 2. On the reception of Hobbes in eighteenth-century France, see Yves Glaziou, *Hobbes en France au XVIIIe siècle* (Paris: PUF, 1993). Of Hobbes's major political works, only *De Cive* was translated into French before the twentieth century: see *Élémens philosophiques du citoyen*, trans. Samuel Sorbière (Amsterdam: J. Blaeu, 1649).

97. See Michael Sonenscher, *Before the Deluge: Public Debt, Inequality, and the Intellectual Origins of the French Revolution* (Princeton, NJ: Princeton University Press, 2009), 216–17; on Mirabeau and Stoicism, see also Vardi, *Physiocrats and the World of the Enlightenment*, 99. See also Weulersse, *Mouvement physiocratique en France*, 2:117–18; and Heiner Roetz, "On Nature and Culture in Zhou China," in *Concepts of Nature: A Chinese-European Cross-Cultural Perspective*, ed. Hans Ulrich Vogel and Gunter Dux (Leiden: Brill, 2010), 198–219.

98. See Hecht, "Vie de François Quesnay," 214; and Quesnay, *Œuvres économiques complètes*, 1449.

99. Cicero, *Les Offices de Cicéron, traduits en françois sur la nouvelle édition latine de Grae-vius*. . . , trans. and ed. Philippe Goibaud-Dubois (Paris: J.-B. Coignard, 1691), 3.3, 326; and 3.11, 367–68; see also 3.6, 361.

100. Aristotle, *Politics*, 1.2.

101. Hecht, "Vie de François Quesnay," 215.

102. See in particular Akiteru Kubota, "Quesnay, disciple de Malebranche," in *François Quesnay et la physiocratie*, 1:169–96; and Catherine Larrère, "Malebranche revisité: l'économie naturelle des Physiocrates," *Dix-huitième siècle* 26 (1994): 117–38.

103. Malebranche, *Recherche de la vérité*, in *Œuvres de Malebranche*, ed. Jules Simon (Paris: Entier, 1871), 3:134–35. See Patrick Riley, *The General Will Before Rousseau* (Princeton, NJ: Princeton University Press, 1986), 120–21; and Riley, "Malebranche and Natural Law," in *Early Modern Natural Law Theories: Context and Strategies in the Early Enlightenment*, ed. T. J. Hochstrasser and Peter Schröder (Dordrecht: Kluwer Academic Publishers, 2003), 67.

104. Malebranche, *Conversations chrétiennes* (Brussels: Henry Fricx, 1677), 35.

105. See Steven Nadler, *Occasionalism: Causation among the Cartesians* (Oxford: Oxford University Press, 2010), chap. 3. Thanks to Keith Baker for his helpful comments on occasionalism.

106. Malebranche, *Recherche de la vérité*, 3:172.

107. I return to Malebranche, along with other predecessors to Quesnay (including Jean Domat and Pierre le Pesant de Boisguilbert) in the following chapter.

108. See Pierre-Maxime Schuhl, "Malebranche et Quesnay," *Revue philosophique de la France et de l'étranger* 125, nos. 3/4 (1938): 313–15.

109. Hecht, "Vie de François Quesnay," 260.

110. See Steven L. Kaplan, *Bread, Politics and Political Economy in the Reign of Louis XV*, rev. ed. (1976; New York: Anthem, 2015). On the controversies, see especially Arnaud Orain, "Figures of Mockery: The Cultural Disqualification of Physiocracy (1760–1790)," *European Journal of the History of Economic Thought* 22, no. 3 (2015): 383–419.

111. Families "s'accoutument à se voir, la confiance s'établit entr'eux, ils s'entr'aident, ils s'allient par des marriages, & forment en quelque sorte des Nations particulieres, où tous sont ligués pour leur defense commune," Quesnay, *Droit naturel*, 27. Again, the similarities with Aristotle's *Politics* are significant.

112. See chapter 6.

113. Locke, *Second Treatise*, § 6.

114. On social naturalism and socioeconomic rights, see the discussion of Jean Domat in chapter 5; on socioeconomic rights in the French Revolution, see Dupont de Nemours's *cahier* and contribution to the National Assembly's debate on the Declaration of Rights, discussed in chapter 7.

115. As he argues here, "a government that is obviously to the greatest advantage of people" is one that "guarantees to complete and full enjoyment of all their natural rights . . .": Pierre Samuel Dupont de Nemours, *De l'origine et des progrès d'une science nouvelle* (Paris: Desaint, 1768), 364.

116. Nicolas Baudeau, ed., *Ephémérides du citoyen, ou Bibliothèque raisonnée des sciences morales et politiques* (Paris: N. A. Delalain, 1768), 55. On Baudeau, see Thomas McStay Adams, *Bureaucrats and Beggars: French Social Policy in the Age of the Enlightenment* (Oxford: Oxford University Press, 1990).

117. Victor Riqueti, marquis de Mirabeau, *La science, ou Les droits et les devoirs de l'homme* (Lausanne: Grasset, 1774): Man has a natural right, Mirabeau argues, "which is the enjoyment of those things acquired by his labor," and this right is "the root of all his other rights" (6–7).

118. Helvétius's letter is lost, but see Le Mercier's response of December 15, 1767, in Helvétius's

correspondence (letter n. 624 *ter*). For Voltaire, see letter of January 29, 1768 (D14704). For a franker assessment, see his letter of October 16, 1767, to Damilaville (D14490). Voltaire would subsequently pen a satire of Physiocratic thought, *L'Homme aux quarante écus* (1768), though he would also express more sympathetic views, notably in his correspondence with Dupont de Nemours (see, e.g., his letter of June 7, 1769; D15679). On Voltaire's complex relations with the Physiocrats, see Benoît Malbranque, introduction to *Ecrits économiques de Voltaire* (Paris: Institut Coppet, 2013); see also Albert Farchadi, "La bonne fortune de M. André: une lecture de *L'Homme aux quarante écus*," in *Etre riche au siècle de Voltaire*, ed. Jacques Berchtold and Michel Porret (Geneva: Droz, 1996), 219–36.

119. See notably Samuel Moyn, "A Powerless Companion: Human Rights in the Age of Neo-liberalism," *Law and Contemporary Problems* 77, no. 4 (2014): 148–69. On liberalism and the Physiocrats, in addition to the works cited above, see also Henry C. Clark, *Compass of Society: Commerce and Absolutism in Old-Regime France* (Lanham, MD: Lexington Books, 2007); and Arnault Skornicki, *L'économiste, la cour et la patrie: l'économie politique dans la France des Lumières* (Paris: CNRS, 2011). On liberalism in eighteenth-century France more generally, see Annelien de Dijn, *French Political Thought from Montesquieu to Tocqueville: Liberty in a Levelled Society?* (Cambridge: Cambridge University Press, 2008); and Raf Geenens and Helena Rosenblatt, eds., *French Liberalism from Montesquieu to the Present Day* (Cambridge: Cambridge University Press, 2012), though neither work devotes much attention to the Physiocrats.

120. Honoré-Gabriel Riqueti, comte de Mirabeau, *Essai sur le despotism*; 2nd ed. (London, 1776), 36, 152. After his nearly three-year imprisonment in the donjon de Vincennes, thanks to a *lettre de cachet* signed by his father, Mirabeau would repeatedly invoke "les droits de l'espèce humaine" (1:xi) and the "droits naturels de l'homme" (1:54) in his (anonymous) two-volume *Des Lettres de cachet et des prisons d'état*, 2 vols. (Hambourg, 1782). On this work, see François Quastana, *La Pensée politique de Mirabeau, 1771–1789: républicanisme classique et régénération de la monarchie* (Aix-en-Provence: Presses universitaires d'Aix-Marseille, 2007), esp. 191–212; see also Jeffrey Freedman, " 'Wounded Imagination': Fears of Imprisonment in Enlightenment France" (manuscript).

121. From the Preamble, 2nd para. This passage was introduced by the Frenchman René Cassin: see Johannes Morsink, *The Universal Declaration of Human Rights: Origins, Drafting, and Intent* (Philadelphia: University of Pennsylvania, 1999), and conclusion.

122. I return to this argument in chapter 7.

123. See Keith M. Baker, *Condorcet: From Natural Philosophy to Social Mathematics* (Chicago: University of Chicago Press, 1975); Emma Rothschild, *Economic Sentiments: Condorcet, Adam Smith, and the Enlightenment* (Cambridge, MA: Harvard University Press, 2001); and David Williams, *Condorcet and Modernity* (Cambridge: Cambridge University Press, 2004).

124. See Kaplan, *Bread, Politics and Political Economy*.

125. See esp. Adams, *Bureaucrats and Beggars*, chap. 7. More generally, see Camille Bloch, *L'Assistance et l'état en France à la veille de la Révolution* (Paris: Alphonse Picard, 1908); Gaston V. Rimlinger, *Welfare Policy and Industrialization in Europe, America, and Russia* (New York: John Wiley, 1971), chap. 2; and Lisa DiCaprio, *The Origins of the Welfare State: Women, Work, and the French Revolution* (Urbana: University of Illinois Press, 2007), chap. 1. For an even longer perspective on welfare projects, see Howard M. Solomon, *Public Welfare, Science and Propaganda in 17th-Century France: The Innovations of Theophraste Renaudot* (Princeton, NJ: Princeton University Press, 1972).

126. See notably Daniel Hickey, *Local Hospitals in Ancien Régime France: Rationalization, Resistance, Renewal, 1530–1789* (Montreal: McGill-Queen's University Press, 1997). This is also

the topic of Michel Foucault, *Madness and Civilization: A History of Insanity in the Age of Reason* (New York: Random House, 1965).

127. "Fondation," *Encyclopédie*, 7:73–75. For an interesting discussion of Turgot's article in this context, see Rimlinger, *Welfare Policy and Industrialization in Europe, America, and Russia*, 26–27.

128. *Archives parlementaires de 1787 à 1860*, ed. M. J. Mavidal et al (Paris: P. Dupont, 1862–), 4:162. See chapter 7. On the authorship of this *cahier*, see Stéphane Rials, *La Déclaration des droits de l'homme et du citoyen* (Paris: Hachette, 1988), 37. For his biography of Turgot, see below.

129. In general, see Baker, *Condorcet*.

130. On Condorcet and natural rights, see Williams, *Condorcet and Modernity*, chap. 2; and Vicenzo Ferrone, *Storia dei diritti dell'uomo: L'Illuminismo e la costruzione del linguaggio politico dei moderni* (Rome: Laterza, 2014). Neither relate Condorcet's defense of natural rights to his Physiocratic leanings.

131. Condorcet, *Lettres sur le commerce des grains* (Paris: chez Couturier père, 1774), 21.

132. Condorcet, *Réflexions sur le commerce des bleds* (London, 1776), 134, 80–81, 131–32. For the attack on Necker, see 208. Necker had published an essay in 1775, *Sur la législation et le commerce des grains*, that was critical of Turgot's reforms.

133. Condorcet, *Réflexions sur l'esclavage des nègres* (Neufchâtel: Société typographique, 1781), 14.

134. Condorcet, *Réflexions sur l'esclavage*, 13. On this point, see Madeleine Dobie, *Trading Places: Colonization and Slavery in Eighteenth-Century French Culture* (Ithaca, NY: Cornell University Press, 2010), esp. chap. 6. I return to slavery and natural rights/law in chapter 5.

135. According to Condorcet, Cassini liked to reminisce about his time in Austria with the then-archduke Joseph, who wanted to "rétablir les habitans de ses vastes états dans ces droits naturels de l'homme dont l'intolérance & la tyrannie féodale les avoient privés trop long-temps": "Eloge de M. Cassini de Thury," *Histoire de l'Académie royale des sciences . . .* (Paris: Imprimerie Royale, 1784), 59.

136. See, respectively, Condorcet, *Influence de la révolution de l'Amérique sur les opinions et la législation de l'Europe* (1788), 16; and *Essai sur la Constitution et les fonctions des Assemblées provinciales* (1788), 4. See also his *Lettres d'un citoyen des États-Unis à un Français, sur les affaires présentes* (1788): "Quel but se sont proposés les hommes en se réunifiant en sociétés régulières, en se soumettant à des loix, c'est sans doute de s'assurer par ces mêmes loix la jouissance de leurs droits naturels" (5–6).

137. Condorcet, "Sur l'admission des femmes au droit de cité," *Journal de la Société de 1789* (July 3, 1790): 2.

138. *Contra* Lynn Hunt, *Inventing Human Rights: A History* (New York: Norton, 2007); I discuss Hunt's thesis in chapter 5. On Condorcet's rational justification for women's rights, see Guillaume Ansart, "Condorcet, Social Mathematics, and Women's Rights," *Eighteenth-Century Studies* 42, no. 3 (2009): 347–62.

139. Dupont de Nemours, *Mémoires sur la vie et les ouvrages de M. Turgot, ministre d'Etat*, 2 vols. (Philadelphia, 1782), 1:149. In reality, Turgot opposed funding the American revolutionaries.

140. See *Constitutions des treize états-unis de l'Amérique* (Paris: Ph.-D. Pierres, 1783).

141. See in general Vardi, *Physiocrats and the World of the Enlightenment*; and Orain, "Figures of Mockery." Many commentators claim that Galiani changed Diderot's mind about Physiocracy with the publication of his *Dialogues sur le commerce des blés* (London, 1770). As I argue in *The Terror of Natural Right* (chap. 2), however, this conclusion overlooks the very Physiocratic ideas about government found in Diderot's *Supplément au Voyage de Bougainville*, written in 1772. See

also Proust, *Diderot et l'Encyclopédie*; and Anthony Strugnell, *Diderot's Politics: A Study of the Evolution of Diderot's Political Thought after the 'Encyclopédie'* (The Hague: Martinus Nijhoff, 1973).

142. As Weulersse points out, Quesnay always maintained friendly relations with the *philosophes*, while the marquis de Mirabeau detested them (though he did correspond with Rousseau): see *Mouvement physiocratique en France*, 1:108–11.

143. See Diderot, *Première lettre d'un citoyen zélé qui n'est ni chirurgien, ni médecin* (1748), 8; this letter is cited in Hecht, "Vie de François Quesnay," 238.

144. According to Proust, "dès 1756 ses [Diderot's] liens avec les pionniers de la physiocratie sont assurés": *Diderot et l'Encyclopédie*, 458–59. Quesnay was also to have authored the articles "Intérêt de l'argent," "Hommes," and "Impôts" (460).

145. Vardi has cast doubt on the claim that Mme de Pompadour joined these gatherings (the apartment was notoriously cramped): see Vardi, *Physiocrats and the World of the Enlightenment*, 41–42. But the Physiocrats and the *philosophes* may also have met in the salon of Mme de Pompadour, who received *gens de lettres* and *gens de science* on Sundays: see Alan Charles Kors, *D'Holbach's Coterie: An Enlightenment in Paris* (Princeton, NJ: Princeton University Press, 1976), 174. Like Quesnay, Marmontel was himself a Pompadour protégé and resided in Versailles from 1753–58. See also Groenewegen, *Eighteenth-Century Economics*, 250–51. Helvétius was previously connected to Quesnay through his father (d. 1755), who had been the primary doctor to Queen Marie Leszczyńska, Louis XV's wife. On Helvétius's intellectual debts to Quesnay, see Ian Cumming, *Helvétius: His Life and Place in the History of Educational Thought* (Abingdon, UK: Routledge, 1955).

146. On this salon, see in particular Kors, *D'Holbach's Coterie*. More generally, see Antoine Lilti, *Le Monde des salons: sociabilité et mondanité à Paris au XVIIIe siècle* (Paris: Fayard, 2005).

147. This debate first peaked in the years 1763–64, when the minister Henri Bertin introduced measures liberalizing the grain trade: see Kaplan, *Bread, Politics and Political Economy*; and John Shovlin, *The Political Economy of Virtue: Luxury, Patriotism, and the Origins of the French Revolution* (Ithaca, NY: Cornell University Press, 2007), chap. 3. Voltaire famously immortalized this sudden fascination for agriculture among the chattering classes: "Vers l'an 1750, la nation, rassasiée de vers, de tragédies, de comédies, d'opéras, de romans, d'histoires romanesques, de réflexions morales plus romanesques encore, et de disputes théologiques sur la grâce et sur les convulsions, se mit enfin à raisonner sur les blés." "Bled ou blé," *Questions sur l'Encyclopédie*, in *Œuvres complètes de Voltaire*, ed. Nicholas Cronk and Christiane Mervaud (Oxford: Voltaire Foundation, 2008), 39:402–19 (412–13 for quote).

148. See Koen Stapelbroek, *Love, Self-Deceit, and Money: Commerce and Morality in the Early Neapolitan Enlightenment* (Toronto: University of Toronto Press, 2008), 209–12.

149. Morellet, *Réfutation de l'ouvrage qui a pour titre Dialogues sur le commerce des bleds* (London, 1770). Morellet was commissioned by the French government to write this work, but was genuinely committed to free-trade ideas.

150. See Hecht, "Vie de François Quesnay," 272. On Saint-Lambert, Physiocracy, and abolitionism, see chapter 5.

151. See Kors, *D'Holbach's Coterie*, 17–18 and *passim*; on Le Roy's relations with Quesnay, see Christine Théré and Loïc Charles, "The Writing Workshop of François Quesnay and the Making of Physiocracy," *History of Political Economy* 40, no. 1 (2008): 1–42.

152. "Vingtième," *Encyclopédie*, 17:855–90 (published in 1765). Attributed to the conveniently deceased Nicolas Boulanger (1722–1759), an early member of d'Holbach's circle, Friedrich Melchior von Grimm (himself part of the coterie) acknowledged Damilaville as the author, with important additions ("the best parts") by Diderot: see Proust, *Diderot et l'Encyclopédie*,

487–91; John Lough, "*L'Encyclopédie* and the *Contrat Social*," in *Reappraisals of Rousseau: Studies in Honour of R. A. Leigh*, ed. Simon Harvey (Manchester: Manchester University Press, 1980), 66–68; and Gerolama Imbruglia, "From Utopia to Republicanism: The Case of Diderot," in *The Invention of the Modern Republic*, ed. Biancamaria Fontana (Cambridge: Cambridge University Press, 1994), 63–85. On Damilaville, see Frank Kafker, *The Encyclopedists as a Group: A Collective Biography of the Authors of the Encyclopédie*, Studies on Voltaire and the Eighteenth Century, vol. 345 (Oxford: Voltaire Foundation, 1996), 110. Kors lists him as an occasional guest: *D'Holbach's Coterie*, 41. On the *vingtième* itself, see Michael Kwass, *Privilege and the Politics of Taxation in Eighteenth-Century France: Liberté, Egalité, Fiscalité* (Cambridge: Cambridge University Press, 2006).

153. See Ian Davidson, *Voltaire: A Life* (London: Profile Books, 2010), chap. 26.

154. "Vingtième," *Encyclopédie*, 17:872.

155. "Vingtième," *Encyclopédie*, 17:866, p. 875. Proust emphasizes the Physiocratic tone of this article: *Diderot et l'Encyclopédie*, 491.

156. Scholars have not devoted much study to d'Holbach's Physiocratic borrowings, though his sympathy toward the group was noted at the time: see Vardi, *Physiocrats and the World of the Enlightenment*, 142n126. Older sources recognized the influence of Physiocracy on his ideas: see John Lough, "Helvétius and d'Holbach," *Modern Language Review* 33, no. 3 (1938): 360–84 (379); Everett C. Ladd Jr., "Helvetius and d'Holbach: 'La Moralisation de la Politique,'" *Journal of the History of Ideas* 23, no. 2 (1962): 221–38 (235); and Robert Anchor, *The Enlightenment Tradition* (Berkeley: University of California, 1967), 74–78. More generally, see Mark Curran, *Atheism, Religion and Enlightenment in Pre-Revolutionary Europe* (Woodbridge, UK: Boydell & Brewer, 2012).

157. [D'Holbach], *Système de la nature, ou des loix du monde physique & du monde moral*, 2 vols. (London [Amsterdam], 1770). See Robert Darnton, *The Forbidden Best-Sellers of Pre-Revolutionary France* (New York: Norton, 1995), 63, drawing on the archives of the Société typographique de Neuchâtel (STN). The French Book Trade in Enlightenment Europe project (FBTEE) corroborates this finding: for the decade 1770–80, this work comes in eleventh place. See their "STN Online Database Archive" at http://fbtee.uws.edu.au/stn/interface/.

158. Quotes from baron d'Holbach, *Système de la nature* (London, 1775), 2:262, 2:307, 1:253, 2:302, 2:405, 2:407. See also 1:336, 2:206, 2:358, 2:362.

159. [Baron d'Holbach,] *La politique naturelle, ou Discours sur les vrais principes du gouvernement*, 2 vols. (London, 1773); and *Système social, ou Principes naturels de la morale et de la politique, avec un examen de l'influence du gouvernement sur les moeurs*, 3 vols. (London, 1773); *La morale universelle, ou Les devoirs de l'homme fondés sur sa nature*, 2 vols. (Amsterdam: M.-M. Rey, 1776).

160. Jonathan Israel, *Democratic Enlightenment: Philosophy, Revolution, and Human Rights, 1750–1790* (Oxford: Oxford University Press, 2011). Despite passing mentions of Quesnay, the older Mirabeau, Le Mercier de la Rivière, and Dupont de Nemours, Israel does not discuss or cite any Physiocratic texts in this work (nor in any others of his that I consulted). This neglect is particularly odd given the attention he showers on the younger Mirabeau.

161. Spinoza, *Theological-Political Treatise*, trans. Samuel Shirley (Indianapolis: Hackett, 2011), chap. 16, p. 179.

162. See d'Holbach, *Système de la nature*, 2:152–53. For d'Holbach, the founding social contract can just be "tacit" and does not necessarily involve any explicit vote or agreement.

163. See notably Dupont de Nemours on "les Loix de l'ordre que Dieu a établi pour servir de régles à la société," in "Discours de l'éditeur," in *Physiocratie, ou constitution naturelle du gouvernement le plus avantageux au genre humain*, ed. Dupont de Nemours (Paris: Merlin, 1768), lxxxv.

164. As Kors notes in his study of d'Holbach's group, very few of the attendees were atheists: see *D'Holbach's Coterie*, 49.

165. Jean-François Marmontel, *Bélisaire* (Paris: Merlin, 1767), chap. 15 (on religion), p. 73, for quote. This novel also reflects Physiocratic ideas about agriculture: see Nathaniel Wolloch, *History and Nature in the Enlightenment: Praise of the Mastery of Nature in Eighteenth-Century Historical Literature* (Farnham, UK: Ashgate, 2011), 118–19.

166. Jean-François Marmontel, *Les Incas, ou La destruction de l'empire du Pérou*, 2 vols. (Paris: chez Lacombe, 1777), 1:14, 1:163. This argument is echoed throughout the book: see, for instance, the letter from a Spanish defector to Francisco Pizarro: "Vous trouverez en moi un médiateur, un ami, si vous respectez avec eux les droits de la nature; un ennemi, si, par la force, le brigandage & la rapine, vous violez ces droits sacrés" (1:251).

167. See d'Holbach, *Système de la nature*, 1.9, 1:163. See also d'Holbach, *Système social*, 2.1, 2:96, 2:100.

168. Pierre-Paul Le Mercier de la Rivière, *L'ordre naturel et essentiel des sociétés*, 2 vols. (London: Jean Nourse, 1767), 440; see also 37, 77–78, 441–42, 454, and *passim*.

169. Dupont de Nemours, *De l'origine et des progrès d'une science nouvelle*, 346.

170. On these relations, see Kors, *D'Holbach's Coterie*, 21–22 and *passim*. A great deal has been written about Raynal's work: some classic studies include Hans Wolpe, *Raynal et sa machine de guerre; l'"Histoire des deux Indes" et ses perfectionnements* (Stanford, CA: Stanford University Press, 1957); and Michèle Duchet, *Diderot et l'"Histoire des deux Indes": ou, L'écriture fragmentaire* (Paris: A.-G. Nizet, 1978). More recently, see Sankar Muthu, *Enlightenment against Empire* (Princeton, NJ: Princeton University Press, 2003), chap. 3; J. G. A. Pocock, *Barbarians, Savages and Empires*, vol. 4 of *Barbarism and Religion* (Cambridge: Cambridge University Press, 2005), chaps. 13–17; and Anoush Fraser Terjanian, *Commerce and Its Discontents in Eighteenth-Century French Political Thought* (Cambridge: Cambridge University Press, 2012).

171. On Raynal's resistance to Physiocracy, see Vardi, *Physiocrats and the World of the Enlightenment*, 142n126.

172. Guillaume-Thomas Raynal, *Histoire philosophique et politique des établissemens et du commerce des européens dans les deux Indes*, 10 vols. (Geneva, 1780).

173. Raynal, *Histoire philosophique et politique*, 5.15, 3:90; 6.13, 3:361; 6.1, 3:260; 8.14, 4:249.

174. Raynal, *Révolution de l'Amérique* (London: Lockyer Davis, 1781), 37. On the depiction of the American Revolution found here, see notably Keith M. Baker, "Revolution 1.0," *Journal of Modern European History* 11, no. 2 (2013): 187–219.

175. "Qui peut donc avoir mis entre nous et leur trône / Cet immense intervalle, et ravir aux mortels / Leur dignité première et leurs droits naturels?" Voltaire, *Les loix de Minos* (Paris: Valade, 1773); II, I, p. 31. This was an unauthorized edition of a play Voltaire had probably written in 1771.

176. Voltaire, *L'évangile du jour contenant: l'examen de la nouvelle histoire de Henri IV de M. de Bury, par M. le marquis de B\*\*\*, lu dans une séance d'académie, avec des notes; l'A, B, C, en seize entretiens, ou dialogues curieux traduits de l'anglois de M. Huet* (1775), "Neuvième entretien: Des esprit serfs," 139.

177. Edelstein, *Terror of Natural Right*, part 1.

178. Jacob-Nicolas Moreau, *Les devoirs du prince réduits à un seul principe, ou discours sur la justice* (Versailles: Impr. du Roi, 1775). On Moreau, see Keith Baker, "Controlling French History: The Ideological Arsenal of Jacob-Nicolas Moreau," in *Inventing the French Revolution*, 59–85.

179. Émile Bos, *Les avocats aux conseils du roi: étude sur l'ancien régime judiciaire de la France* (Paris: Marchal, Billard, 1881), 456 (on Moreau more generally, see 447–68). Bos gives 1773 as the first publication date, but I could not find an earlier edition than 1775 (which addresses Louis XVI

as king, an impossibility before 1774). See also Bernard Hours, "Moreau et Proyart, pédagogues en attente du prince et éducateurs de la nation," *Histoire de l'éducation* 132 (2011): 153–76.

180. On this theme, and with respect to Moreau in particular, see Jeffrey Merrick, "The Body Politics of French Absolutism," *From the Royal to the Republican Body: Incorporating the Political in Seventeenth- and Eighteenth-Century France*, ed. Sara E. Melzer and Kathryn Norberg (Berkeley: University of California Press, 1998), 11–31.

181. Moreau had mocked the *philosophes* in his *Nouveau mémoire pour servir à l'histoire des Cacouacs* (1757). See Bos, *Avocats aux conseils du roi*, 450. On the composition of a *parti philosophique*, see Maria Comsa, Melanie Conroy, Dan Edelstein, Chloe Edmondson, and Claude Willan, "The French Enlightenment Network," *Journal of Modern History* 88, no. 3 (2016): 495–534.

182. See notably Durand Echeverria, *The Maupeou Revolution: A Study in the History of Libertarianism: France, 1770–1774* (Baton Rouge: Louisiana State University Press, 1985).

183. See Dale Van Kley, "The Estates General as Ecumenical Council: The Constitutionalism of Corporate Consensus and the *Parlement*'s Ruling of September 25, 1788," *Journal of Modern History* 61, no. 1 (1989): 1–52; David A. Bell, *Lawyers and Citizens: The Making of a Political Elite in Old Regime France* (Oxford: Oxford University Press, 1994), 149ff.

184. See Van Kley, "Estates General as Ecumenical Council."

185. See Bell, *Lawyers and Citizens*, 118; and David A. Bell, *Cult of the Nation in France: Inventing Nationalism, 1680–1800* (Cambridge, MA: Harvard University Press, 2001), 58.

186. Vattel, *Le droit des gens*, 1.3.

187. See, for instance, Pierre Jurieu: "Les Officiers de la Cour & de la Couronne ont eu plus ou moins de pouvoir, mais c'est par rapport au Roy: les Droits de la Nation sont toujours demeurez en leur entier." "Neuvième mémoire," *Les soupirs de la France esclave qui aspire après la liberté* (Amsterdam, 1690), 131.

188. *Mémoire instructif sur la requeste présentée au Roy contre les Princes legitimez* (Paris: Ganeau, 1716), 40 [G'BOOKS]. On this affair more broadly, see Jones, *The Great Nation*.

189. Jean de La Chapelle, *Réflexions politiques et historiques sur l'affaire des Princes* (n.p., n.d.), 49 [G'BOOKS].

190. There was also a direct English influence on the French conception of national rights: the expression "droits de la nation" often appears in the context of discussions of English politics.

191. See the "déclaration des droits de la nation" of the Paris Parlement, May 3, 1788; in Rials, *Déclaration des droits*, 522.

192. See Dale Van Kley, "From the Lessons of French History to Truths for All Times and All People: Origins of an Anti-Historical Declaration," in *The French Idea of Freedom: The Old Regime and the Declaration of Rights of 1789*, ed. Dale Van Kley (Stanford, CA: Stanford University Press, 1994), 72–113; Bell, *Cult of the Nation*, 71; Paul Friedland, *Political Actors: Representative Bodies and Theatricality in the Age of the French Revolution* (Ithaca, NY: Cornell University Press, 2002), 94ff.

193. While d'Antraigues occasionally implies that the people retain individual rights, he broadly subscribes to the transfer regime: "Pour ceux qu'il [Dieu] appelloit à se réunir en société, sans doute il exigea & il sanctionna le sacrifice de cette indépendance sans limite [natural liberty], mais il la remplaça par une autre plus difficile peut-être à conserver, mais tout aussi sacrée. Il soumit l'homme à la loi, & ne le soumit jamais qu'à elle." *Mémoire sur les Etats-généraux, leurs droits, et la manière de les convoquer* (1788), 8.

194. See in particular Friedland, *Political Actors*, 97–99.

195. See chapter 6.

196. See Bell, *Cult of the Nation*, 73.

197. *Dictionnaire de l'Académie française* (1694), s.v. "nation."

198. See Henri de Boulainvilliers, *Etat de la France*, 3 vols. (London: Palmer, 1727); more generally, see Harold Ellis, *Boulainvilliers and the French Monarchy: Aristocratic Politics in Early Eighteenth-Century France* (Ithaca, NY: Cornell University Press, 1988).

199. Quesnay, *Le droit naturel* (1756), 27 (see also 26–28 more generally).

200. On social naturalism, see chapters 4–5.

201. Emmanuel Joseph Sieyès, *Qu'est-ce que le tiers-état?*, ed. E. Champion (Paris: Société de l'Histoire de la Révolution Française, 1888), 27 [ARTFL]. See notably William H. Sewell Jr., *A Rhetoric of Bourgeois Revolution: The Abbé Sieyes and What Is the Third Estate?* (Durham, NC: Duke University Press, 1994); Friedland, *Political Actors*, 114–22.

202. See, e.g., Sewell, *Rhetoric of Bourgeois Revolution*, 46; Van Kley, " From the Lessons of French History," 95.

203. See Keith M. Baker, "Sovereignty," in *A Critical Dictionary of the French Revolution*, ed. François Furet and Mona Ozouf, trans. Arthur Goldhammer (Cambridge, MA: Harvard University Press, 1989), 851.

204. Rousseau, *Social Contract*, 1.5, p. 48.

205. See also Sieyès's first draft for a declaration of rights: "l'ordre social est comme une suite, comme un complément de l'ordre naturel," though here he does make room for a "contrat réciproque." In Rials, *Déclaration des droits*, 594. On his relations with Physiocracy, see Catherine Larrère, "Sieyès, lecteur des physiocrates: droit naturel ou économie?" in *Figures de Sieyès*, ed. Pierre-Yves Quiviger, Vincent Denis, and Jean Salem (Paris: Sorbonne, 2008), 195–211.

206. The French original is difficult to translate: "La loi, en protégeant les droits communs de tout citoyen, protège chaque citoyen dans tout ce qu'il peut être, jusqu'au moment où ce qu'il veut être commencerait à nuire au *commun* intérêt." Sieyès, *Qu'est-ce que le tiers-état?*, 89. This idea would resurface in Sieyès's drafts for the Declaration of the Rights of Man and of the Citizen, where he does refer to "natural rights" but defines "l'objet d'une association politique" as "le plus grand bien de tous" (art. 2): in Rials, *Déclaration des droits*, 602. In other respects, however, the drafts present a somewhat different account of rights than that found in *Qu'est-ce que le tiers-état?*, probably reflecting the greater attention given to individual rights after spring 1789: see chapter 7.

207. Hannah Arendt, *On Revolution* (New York: Penguin, 2006), 154–55. For a helpful discussion of her claims, albeit in a different context, see Joshua Braver, "Hannah Arendt in Venezuela: The Supreme Court Battles Hugo Chávez over the Creation of the 1999 Constitution," *I•CON* (2016): 1–29.

208. Jason Frank, *Constituent Moments: Enacting the People in Postrevolutionary America* (Durham, NC: Duke University Press, 2009), 46–50.

209. See his draft declaration: "Tous les pouvoirs publics, sans distinction, sont une émanation de la volonté générale; tous viennent du peuple, c'est-à-dire de la nation. Ces deux termes doivent être synonymes." In Rials, *Déclaration des droits*, 601.

210. See chapter 6.

211. Locke, *Second Treatise*, § 135.

## Part II

1. See, for instance, in Guillaume-Thomas Raynal, *Histoire philosophique et politique des établissemens et du commerce des européens dans les deux Indes*, 10 vols. (Geneva, 1780), 8.22, 4:271.

Earlier, d'Holbach had defended "les droits naturels de l'homme," in *Système social ou principes naturels de la morale et la politique* (London, 1773), 96; the same expression can be found in Mirabeau, *La science, ou Les droits et les devoirs de l'homme* (1774), 115, whereas his son evoked "les droits de l'homme," in *Essai sur le despotisme* (1775), 152.

2. See Emile Boutmy, "La Déclaration des droits de l'homme et du citoyen et M. Jellinek," *Annales des sciences politiques* 17 (1902): 419–43. For Georg Jellinek, see *The Declaration of the Rights of Man and of the Citizen*, trans. Max Farrand (New York: Henry Holt, 1901). For a good overview of the Jellinek/Boutmy debate, see Keith Baker, "The Idea of a Declaration of Rights," in *The French Idea of Freedom: The Old Regime and the Declaration of Rights of 1789*, ed. Dale Van Kley (Stanford, CA: Stanford University Press, 1997), 154–96; see also Duncan Kelly, "Revisiting the Rights of Man: Georg Jellinek on Rights and the State," *Law and History Review* 22, no. 3 (2004): 493–529.

3. See, e.g., the narrative proposed by Jonathan Israel, in *A Revolution of the Mind: Radical Enlightenment and the Intellectual Origins of Modern Democracy* (Princeton, NJ: Princeton University Press, 2009).

4. "Loi naturelle" occurs in 10 works (by 8 authors) published between 1770 and 1779 in the FRANTEXT database, for a total of of 88 occurrences and a frequency of 0.17 per 10,000 words; in the same decade, "droits naturels" appears in 6 works (by 3 authors), for a total of 8 occurrences and a word frequency of 0.01 per 10,000 words.

"Droit naturel" in the singular is more ambiguous, as it could be used to designate both an individual right (e.g., "mon droit naturel") or the overall corpus of natural law (e.g., "le droit naturel"). The latter use seems to have been far more common. For the same decade, this expression appeared in 12 works (by 10 authors) with a frequency of 0.05 per 10,000 words.

5. Knud Haakonssen, "From Natural Law to the Rights of Man: A European Perspective on American Debates," in *A Culture of Rights: The Bill of Rights in Philosophy, Politics, and Law—1791 and 1991*, ed. Michael J. Lacey and Knud Haakonssen (Cambridge: Woodrow Wilson International Center for Scholars and Cambridge University Press, 1991), 20. Samuel Moyn develops this insight in "Giuseppe Mazzini in (and beyond) the History of Human Rights," in *Revisiting the Origins of Human Rights*, ed. Pamela Slotte and Miia Halme-Tuomisaari (Cambridge: Cambridge University Press, 2015), 119–39; see also Moyn, "Rights vs. Duties: Reclaiming Civic Balance," *Boston Review* (May 16, 2016): http://bostonreview.net/books-ideas/samuel-moyn-rights-duties.

6. Fred Block and Margaret R. Somers, *The Power of Market Fundamentalism: Karl Polanyi's Critique* (Cambridge, MA: Harvard University Press, 2014), 102.

7. See notably Francis Oakley, *Natural Law, Laws of Nature, Natural Rights: Continuity and Discontinuity in the History of Ideas* (New York: Continuum, 2005); see also Lorraine Daston and Fernando Vidal, eds., *The Moral Authority of Nature* (Chicago: University of Chicago Press, 2010). I discuss this process further in section 2 of this chapter.

8. Cicero, *De legibus*, 1.6 and 1.56; trans. Clinton Walker Keyes (Cambridge, MA: Harvard University Press/Loeb, 1928), 316, 360–61. See also Dirk Baltzly, "Stoic Pantheism," *Sophia* 42, no. 3 (2003): 3–33.

9. Hugo Grotius, *The Rights of War and Peace* (1625), ed. Richard Tuck, trans. John Morrice et al. (Indianapolis: Liberty Fund, 2005), Prolegomena, §VIII, p. 86.

10. This reading differs from that of Richard Tuck: see his *Natural Rights Theories: Their Origins and Development* (Cambridge: Cambridge University Press, 1979), 73.

11. See Peter Gay, *The Enlightenment: An Interpretation*, 2 vols. (New York: Norton, 1966), 1:296–304.

NOTES TO PAGES 107-108

## Chapter IV

1. Cicero, *De legibus*, trans. Clinton Walker Keyes (Cambridge, MA: Harvard University Press/Loeb, 1928), 1.35, pp. 334–35.

2. Jon Miller, "Stoics, Grotius, and Spinoza on Moral Deliberation," in *Hellenistic and Early Modern Philosophy*, ed. J. Miller and Brad Inwood (Cambridge: Cambridge University Press, 2003), 120. See also Bo Lindberg: authors writing in this vein express "a moral attitude to life characterized by the effort to control one's desires and feelings and to prepare for the adversities and vicissitudes of life." "Stoicism in Political Humanism and Natural Law," in *(Un)masking the Realities of Power: Justus Lipsius and the Dynamics of Political Writing in Early Modern Europe*, ed. Erik De Bom (Leiden: Brill, 2011), 73–93 (73).

3. See Richard H. Popkin, *The History of Scepticism: From Savonarola to Bayle*, rev. ed. (Oxford: Oxford University Press, 2003); see also Anton M. Matytsin, *The Specter of Skepticism in the Age of Enlightenment* (Baltimore: Johns Hopkins University Press, 2016).

4. See José Ruysschaert, *Juste Lipse et les Annales de Tacite: une méthode de critique textuelle au XVIe siècle* (Turnhout: Brepols Press, 1949); Jacqueline Lagrée, ed., *Juste Lipse et la restauration du stoïcisme* (Paris: Vrin, 1994); Justus Lipsius, *Politica: Six Books of Politics or Political Instruction*, ed. and trans. Jan Waszink (Assen: Royal Van Gorcum, 2004); and De Bom, *(Un)masking the Realities of Power*, particularly the articles by Bo Lindberg, "Stoicism in Political Humanism and Natural Law," 73–93, and Jacob Soll, "A Lipsian Legacy? Neo-Absolutism, Natural Law and the Decline of Reason of State in France, 1660–1760," 301–23. More generally, see Gerhard Oestreich, *Neostoicism and the Early Modern State*, ed. Brigitta Oestreich and H. G. Koenigsberger, trans. David McLintock (Cambridge: Cambridge University Press, 1982); Pierre-François Moreau, ed., *Le Stoïcisme au XVIe et au XVIIe siècle* (Paris: Albin Michel, 1999); Denise Carabin, *Les Idées stoïciennes dans la littérature morale des XVIᵉ et XVIIᵉ siècles (1575–1642)* (Paris: H. Champion, 2004); Alexandre Tarrête, ed., *Stoïcisme et Christianisme à la Renaissance* (Paris: Éditions Rue d'Ulm, 2006); and Christopher Brooke, *Philosophic Pride: Stoicism and Political Thought from Lipsius to Rousseau* (Princeton, NJ: Princeton University Press, 2012).

5. Montaigne, "To the Reader," in *The Complete Essays of Montaigne*, trans. Donald M. Frame (Stanford, CA: Stanford University Press, 1957), 2. See Pierre Villey, *Les Sources & l'évolution des 'Essais' de Montaigne*, 2 vols. (Paris : Hachette, 1908); Quentin Skinner, *The Foundations of Modern Political Thought*, 2 vols. (Cambridge: Cambridge University Press, 1978), 2:275–81; Marcel Conche, *Montaigne et la philosophie* (Paris: Mégare, 1987); J. B. Schneewind, "Montaigne on Moral Philosophy and the Good Life," in *The Cambridge Companion to Montaigne*, ed. Ullrich Langer (Cambridge: Cambridge University Press, 2005), 207–25; and John D. Lyons, *Before Imagination: Embodied Thought from Montaigne to Rousseau* (Stanford, CA: Stanford University Press, 2005), chap. 1.

6. "The laws of conscience, which we say are born of nature, are born of custom": Montaigne, "Of Custom, and Not Easily Changing an Accepted Law," in *Complete Essays*, 1.23; 83. Montaigne's argument that disagreements among natural law theorists invalidate their project would resurface in Rousseau's second *Discourse*: see chapter 3. On Montaigne's skepticism, see Popkin, *History of Scepticism*, chap. 3.

7. As is argued in Conche, *Montaigne et la philosophie*, 111; and Schneewind, "Montaigne on Moral Philosophy," 217–18.

8. Montaigne, "Apology for Raymond Sebond," in *Complete Essays*, 437.

9. Hugo Grotius, *The Rights of War and Peace* (1625), 3 vols., ed. Richard Tuck, trans. John Morrice et al. (Indianapolis: Liberty Fund, 2005), Preliminary Discourse, § 5. On Grotius and

Skepticism, see notably Richard Tuck, *The Rights of War and Peace* (Oxford: Oxford University Press, 1999). More generally, see Hans Blom and Laurens C. Winkel, eds., *Grotius and the Stoa* (Assen: Royal Van Gorcum, 2004); and Benjamin Straumann, *Roman Law in the State of Nature: The Classical Foundations of Hugo Grotius' Natural Law* (Cambridge: Cambridge University Press, 2015).

10. Grotius, *Rights of War and Peace*, Preliminary Discourse, § 6.

11. Pufendorf justifies his definition of the natural law as a command for sociableness with a long citation from Seneca: see *Of the Law of Nature and Nations* (1672), trans. Basil Kennett, ed. Jean Barbeyrac (London: Walthoe et al., 1729), 2.3.15, p. 138. On Pufendorf's Stoicism, see T. J. Hochstrasser, *Natural Law Theories in the Early Enlightenment* (Cambridge: Cambridge University Press, 2000), 60ff.

12. Rom. 2:14-15; English translation from New International Version.

13. See notably Michael Bertram Crowe, *The Changing Profile of the Natural Law* (The Hague: Nijhoff, 1977), chap. 3.

14. For Aquinas, see *Summa theologica* Q. 90, Art. 3, obj. 1; and Q. 94, Art. 6; in *Treatise on Law*, trans. Richard J. Reagan (Indianapolis: Hackett, 2000). For Francisco Suárez, see *On the Laws and God the Lawgiver*, in *Selections from Three Works of Suárez*, 2 vols., trans. and ed. Gwladys L. Williams et al. (Oxford: Clarendon Press, 1944), 2.5.10.

15. See notably Jean de Silhon, *Deux vérités* (1629; ARTFL Electronic Edition, 2009), 46; Pierre Nicole, *Essais de morale* (1675; Paris: G. Desprez, 1701) [ARTFL], 3:50.

16. See esp. Tarrête, *Stoïcisme et Christianisme*.

17. See Jean-François Senault, *De l'usage des passions* (1641; ARTFL Electronic edition), 23. On Senault, see notably Jean-Pierre Cavaillé, "Jean-François Senault, de l'usage politique des passions," *Rue Descartes* 12/13, (1995): 57-73.

18. Senault, *Usage des passions*, 16.

19. On Abbadie, see Alan Charles Kors, *Atheism in France, 1650-1729*, vol. 1, *The Orthodox Sources of Disbelief* (Princeton, NJ: Princeton University Press, 1990), 91-96; Ruth Whelan, "From Christian Apologetics to Enlightened Deism: The Case of Jacques Abbadie (1656-1727)," *Modern Language Review* 87, no. 1 (1992): 32-40; and Isaac Nakhimovsky, "The Enlightened Epicureanism of Jacques Abbadie: *L'Art de se connoître soi-même* and the Morality of Self-Interest," *History of European Ideas* 29, no. 1 (2003): 1-14.

20. Letter to Bussy-Rabutin, August 13, 1688, in Mme de Sévigné, *Correspondance, 1680-1696*, 3 vols., ed. Roger Duchêne (Paris: Pléiade, 1978), 3:347.

21. *Défense de milord Bolingbroke*, in *Œuvres complètes de Voltaire*, ed. Louis Moland (Paris: Garnier, 1877-1885), 23:532. Elsewhere Voltaire recognized that Abbadie was "célèbre pour son traité *de la Religion chrétienne*": "Catalogue des écrivains," in *Le Siècle de Louis XIV*, in *Œuvres complètes de Voltaire*, ed. Diego Venturino (Oxford: Voltaire Foundation, 2017), 12:47.

22. See Kors, *Atheism in France*. Abbadie was still a point of reference for the authors of the *Encyclopédie*, who cited him on thirteen occasions (in four articles).

23. Jacques Abbadie, *Traité de la vérité de la religion chretienne*, 2 vols. (Rotterdam: R. Leers, 1684), 1:248, 1:187.

24. Abbadie, *Traité de la vérité*, 2.5, 1:178.

25. See esp. Whelan, "From Christian Apologetics to Enlightened Deism."

26. Abbadie, *Traité de la vérité*, 2.6, 1:180.

27. Cicero, *De legibus*, 1.14, p. 340. See Laurel Fulkerson, *No Regrets: Remorse in Classical Antiquity* (Oxford: Oxford University Press, 2013).

28. On the reception of Stoicism in the French Enlightenment, see generally Peter Gay, *The*

*Enlightenment: An Interpretation* (New York: Norton, 1966), vol. 1; Thomas Kavanaugh, *Enlightened Pleasures: Eighteenth-Century France and the New Epicureanism* (New Haven, CT: Yale University Press, 2010); Derek Beales, *Enlightenment and Reform in Eighteenth-Century Europe* (London: I. B. Tauris, 2005), 62–63; Brooke, *Philosophic Pride*; and Nathaniel Wolloch, "Cato the Younger in the Enlightenment," *Modern Philology* 106, no. 1 (2008): 60–82.

29. "La nature a fourni d'une main salutaire / Tout ce qui dans la vie à l'homme est nécessaire": Voltaire, *Poème sur la Loi naturelle*; English translation in *The Works of Voltaire*, 21 vols., trans. William F. Fleming (New York: St Hubert Guild, 1901), 10:24. Available online through the Liberty Fund: http://oll.libertyfund.org/titles/2240.

30. See also Voltaire's article on "Conscience," in *Questions sur l'Encyclopédie*, in *Œuvres complètes de Voltaire*, vol. 40, ed. Nicholas Cronk and Christiane Mervaud (Oxford: Voltaire Foundation, 2009), 190–98.

31. Boyer d'Argens made a similar argument in his *Lettres juives*: "je ne puis m'imaginer que Dieu, juste dans ses arrêts, et miséricordieux dans ses graces, punisse des hommes, qui, obéïssant au législateur interne, je veux dire à la loi de la nature, et à celle de la conscience." *Lettres juives* (The Hague: Pierre Paupie, 1736), letter 33, 2:21.

32. See d'Alembert, "Discours préliminaire des éditeurs," *Encyclopédie*, 1:iii, xi, xiv. For English translation, see "Preliminary Discourse," trans. Richard N. Schwab and Walter E. Rex, in *The Encyclopedia of Diderot & d'Alembert Collaborative Translation Project* (Ann Arbor: Michigan Publishing, University of Michigan Library, 2009), http://hdl.handle.net/2027/spo.did2222.0001.083.

33. Brooke, *Philosophic Pride*, chap. 8; see also Thomas Pfau, "The Letter of Judgment: Practical Reason in Aristotle, the Stoics, and Rousseau," *Eighteenth Century* 51, no. 3 (2010): 289–316.

34. Jean-Jacques Rousseau, *Emile, or On Education*, trans. Allan Bloom (New York: Basic Books, 1979), 472.

35. *Emile*, 473.

36. *Emile*, 286–87.

37. See Diderot, "Droit naturel," *Encyclopédie*, 5:115.

38. Another interesting case is Montesquieu, though his Stoic interests may have had less to do with natural law theory: see Catherine Larrère, "Montesquieu et le stoïcisme," *Lumières* 1 (2003): 59–83.

39. This is particularly true in a number of literary works: see, for instance, Philippe Gérard, *Comte de Valmont* (Paris: Moutard, 1787) [ARTFL], letter 21, 469.

40. See *The Meditations of the Emperor Marcus Aurelius Antoninus*, trans. Francis Hutcheson and James Moor (Glasgow: Robert Foulis, 1742); for Smith, see Charles L. Griswold, *Adam Smith and the Virtues of Enlightenment* (Cambridge: Cambridge University Press, 1998), chap. 8.

41. See, e.g., James Griffin, who argues that during the eighteenth century "there was the continued secularization of the doctrines of natural law and natural rights, following the expanding role of human reason": *On Human Rights* (Oxford: Oxford University Press, 2008), 11. See also Micheline Ishay, who describes the "secular and relatively more egalitarian approach to universal Europe" that "spread throughout the world under the revolutionary banner of the Enlightenment": *The History of Human Rights: From Ancient Times to the Globalization Era* (Berkeley: University of California Press, 2004), 64.

42. Cf. Brooke, *Philosophic Pride*, chap. 6. But Brooke's only example of an atheist in this chapter is Diderot.

43. See *Emile*, 308.

44. "Mais, me direz-vous, où est le dépôt de cette volonté générale? Où pourrai-je la consulter? . . . Dans les principes du droit écrit de toutes les nations policées; dans les actions sociales

des peuples sauvages & barbares; dans les conventions tacites des ennemis du genre humain entr'eux; & même dans l'indignation & le ressentiment, ces deux passions que la nature semble avoir placées jusque dans les animaux pour suppléer au défaut des lois sociales & de la vengeance publique." Diderot, "Droit naturel," *Encyclopédie*, 5:115.

45. See, for instance, "ni des dieux inconstans, ni leurs prêtres dont les intérêts varient à chaque instant, ne peuvent être les modèles ou les arbitres d'une morale, qui doit être aussi constante et aussi sûre que les loix invariables de la nature auxquelles nous ne la voyons jamais déroger." Baron d'Holbach, *Système de la nature* (London, 1775), part 2, § 9, p. 286. More generally, see Lorraine Daston and Fernando Vidal, eds., *Moral Authority of Nature* (Chicago: University of Chicago Press, 2004).

46. *Œuvres complètes de Voltaire*, 32B:57.

47. Jean-Baptiste-Claude Delisle de Sales, *De la philosophie de la nature* (Amsterdam, 1770) [ARTFL], xxx.

48. See Rousseau, *Discours sur l'inégalité*, in *Œuvres complètes*, 5 vols., ed. Bernard Gagnebin and Marcel Raymond (Paris: Pléiade, 1964), 3:156. Subsequently abridged as *JJR*.

49. *Emile*, 235. On the passions more generally, see the second *Discourse* and Rousseau's justification of his claim that "[q]uoiqu'en disent les moralistes, l'entendement humain doit beaucoup aux passions": *Discours sur l'inégalité*, in *JJR*, 3:143.

50. See the preface to the second *Discourse*, in *JJR*, 3:126–27; see also *Emile*, in *JJR*, 4:523.

51. See Condorcet, *Lettres d'un bourgeois de New-Haven à un citoyen de Virginie*, in *Œuvres de Condorcet*, ed. Arthur Condorcet O'Connor and François Arago (Paris: Firmin Didot, 1847), vol. 9, let. 2, p. 14. See more generally, David Williams, *Condorcet and Modernity* (Cambridge: Cambridge University Press, 2004), chap. 2.

52. See, e.g., David Denby, *Sentimental Narrative and the Social Order in France, 1760–1820* (Cambridge: Cambridge University Press, 1994); Anne Vila, *Enlightenment and Pathology: Sensibility in the Literature and Medicine of Eighteenth-Century France* (Baltimore: Johns Hopkins University Press, 1998); Lynn Festa, *Sentimental Figures of Empire in Eighteenth-Century Britain and France* (Baltimore: Johns Hopkins University Press, 2006); Henry Martyn Lloyd, ed., *The Discourse of Sensibility: The Knowing Body in the Enlightenment* (Cham, Switzerland: Springer, 2013).

53. Lynn Hunt, *Inventing Human Rights: A History* (New York: Norton, 2007). I return to Hunt's thesis in the following chapter.

54. Abbadie, *Traité de la vérité*, 2.8; 1:203.

55. Nicole, *Essais de morale*, 3:50. Like Jean Domat, Nicole was also closely associated with the Jansenist school of Port-Royal. On Jansenist ideas of justice (if not natural law), see Jean Mesnard, "Pascal et la justice à Port-Royal," *Commentaire* 121, no. 1 (2008): 163–74. On Jansenism and natural law, see chapter 5.

56. Rousseau uses the expression on numerous occasions: see, e.g., "Ô vertu! Science sublime des âmes simples, faut-il donc tant de peines et d'appareil pour te connoître? Tes principes ne sont-ils pas gravés dans tous les coeurs, et ne suffit-il pas pour apprendre tes loix de rentrer en soi-même et d'écouter la voix de sa conscience dans le silence des passions?" First *Discourse*, part 2, in *JJR*, 3:30. See also Rousseau, "Toutes les régles du droit naturel sont mieux gravées dans les cœurs des hommes que dans tout le fatras de Justinien," *Considérations sur le gouvernement de Pologne*, in *JJR*, 3:1001. For the *parlementaires*, see Claude Mey and Gabriel-Nicolas Maultrot: "Le droit primitif gravé dans le cœur de tous les hommes leur a fait connoître la nature du gouvernement, & le motif fondamental de son institution." *Maximes du droit public françois*, 2 vols. (1772; Amsterdam: M.-M. Rey, 1775), 1:7. On this text, see chapter 3.

57. Abbadie, *Traité de la vérité*, 1.4; 1:29.

58. Letter from Charles Bonnet to Montesquieu, November 14, 1753, in Montesquieu, *Œuvres complètes* (Paris: Nagel, 1955), 3:1478. This comparison was fairly commonplace: see Jessica Riskin, *Science in the Age of Sensibility: The Sentimental Empiricists of the French Enlightenment* (Chicago: University of Chicago Press, 2002), 144. See also Catherine Larrère, "In Search of the Newton of the Moral World: The Intelligibility of Society and the Naturalist Model of Law from the End of the Seventeenth Century to the Middle of the Eighteenth Century," trans. Nieves Claxton, in *Natural Law and Laws of Nature in Early Modern Europe: Jurisprudence, Theology, Moral and Natural Philosophy*, ed. Lorraine Daston and Michael Stolleis, rev. ed. (London: Routledge, 2016), chap. 15.

59. "Jus naturale est quod natura omnia animalia docuit": *Institutes*, 1.2.

60. See R. G. Collingwood, *The Idea of Nature* (Oxford: Oxford University Press, 1960), 8; discussed in Francis Oakley, *Natural Law, Laws of Nature, Natural Rights: Continuity and Discontinuity in the History of Ideas* (New York: Continuum, 2005), 38–39.

61. See Aquinas, *Summa theologica*, I–II, Q. 91, Arts. 1–2; for translation, see *Treatise on Law*, 7–9.

62. Cicero, *De legibus*, 1.42.

63. Robert Boyle, *The Christian Virtuoso*, in *The Philosophical Works of The Honourable Robert Boyle*, 2 vols. (London: Innys, 1725), 2:245. Discussed in Oakley, *Natural Law*, 36.

64. On Descartes, and for some pre-Cartesian examples, see Jane Ruby, "The Origins of Scientific 'Law,'" in *Laws of Nature: Essays on the Philosophical, Scientific, and Historical Dimension*, ed. Friedel Weinert (Berlin: Walter de Gruyter, 1995), 289–315.

65. Descartes, *Principes de la philosophie* (1644; ARTFL Electronic Edition, 2009); 2.37; 77. For the English, see *Principles of Philosophy*, trans. and ed. Valentine Rodger Miller and Reese P. Miller (Dordrecht: Kluwer Academic Publishers, 1982), 59 (translation modified, as it omits the italicized passage).

66. *Principes de la philosophie*, 2.38; *Principles*, 60.

67. See "these few suppositions seem to me sufficient for all effects of this world to result from them in accordance with the laws of nature explained previously, as if they were the causes of these effects": *Principes de la philosophie*, 2.47; *Principles*, 107. On the divine origin of these laws, see Descartes, *Le Monde ou traité de la lumière* (1633; ARTFL Electronic Edition, 2009), chap. 7, p. 12.

68. See "les regles suivant lesquelles se font ces changemens [dans la nature], je les nomme les Loix de la Nature": Descartes, *Monde*, chap. 7, p. 12.

69. J. R. Milton, "Laws of Nature," in *The Cambridge History of Seventeenth-Century Philosophy*, ed. Daniel Garber (686). Ruby, "Origins of Scientific 'Law'"; John Henry, "Metaphysics and the Origins of Modern Science: Descartes and the Importance of Laws of Nature," *Early Science and Medicine* 9, no. 2 (2004): 73–114; Lorraine Daston and Michael Stolleis, eds., *Natural Laws and Laws of Nature in Early-Modern Europe* (Farnham, UK: Ashgate, 2009); and Walter Ott, *Causation and Laws of Nature in Early Modern Philosophy* (Oxford: Oxford University Press, 2009), chap. 7.

70. Milton, "Laws of Nature," 680.

71. See Newton, *The Mathematical Principles of Natural Philosophy*, 2 vols., trans. Andrew Motte (London: Benjamin Motte, 1729), bk. 1, "Axioms and Laws of Motion," 1:14ff.

72. See Alan C. Kors, *Naturalism and Unbelief in France, 1650–1729* (Cambridge: Cambridge University Press, 2016), 14.

73. Kors, *Naturalism and Unbelief in France*, 20.

74. See Jonathan Sheehan and Dror Wahrman, *Invisible Hands: Self-Organization and the*

*Eighteenth Century* (Chicago: University of Chicago, 2015), though they surprisingly do not consider the place of natural law in this story.

## Chapter V

1. See Diderot, "Droit naturel," *Encyclopédie*, 5:115. Translation by Stephen J. Gendzier, in *Encyclopedia of Diderot & d'Alembert Collaborative Translation Project* (Ann Arbor: Michigan Publishing, University of Michigan Library, 2009), http://hdl.handle.net/2027/spo.did2222.0001 .313. The French phrase ("rendre à chacun ce qui lui appartient") was commonplace and can already be found in Bodin, Charron, Montaigne, Scipion Dupleix, Honoré d'Urfé, Mersenne, Poulain de la Barre, Bossuet, and many others. Rousseau uses it in *Emile*, in *Œuvres complètes*, 5 vols., ed. Bernard Gagnebin and Marcel Raymond (Paris: Pléiade, 1964), 4:593–94, 4:818. Subsequently abridged as *JJR*.

2. See Arthur M. Wilson, *Diderot: The Testing Years, 1713–1759* (New York: Oxford University Press, 1957), 27.

3. Boucher d'Argis, "Droit romain," *Encyclopédie*, 5:141. More generally, see Peter Stein, *Roman Law in European History* (Cambridge: Cambridge University Press, 1999).

4. Montesquieu, *The Spirit of the Laws*, trans. and ed. Anne M. Cohler, Basia C. Miller, and Harold S. Stone (Cambridge: Cambridge University Press, 1989), 28.38, p. 591. In keeping with his relativist approach, Montesquieu did not consider Roman law as a perfect legal code for all peoples, but he viewed its rediscovery in the eleventh century as a key step in the progressive rationalization of the law. See Céline Spector, " 'Il faut éclairer l'histoire par les lois et les lois par l'histoire': statut de la romanité et rationalité des coutumes dans *L'Esprit des lois* de Montesquieu," in *Généalogie des savoirs juridiques: le carrefour des Lumières*, ed. M. Xifaras (Brussels: Bruylant, 2007), 15–41.

5. Harold J. Berman, *Law and Revolution: The Formation of the Western Legal Tradition* (Cambridge, MA: Harvard University Press, 1983), 123.

6. See Aldo Schiavone, *The Invention of Law in the West*, trans. Jeremy Carden and Antony Shugaar (Cambridge, MA: Harvard University Press, 2012). See also Marcia L. Colish, *The Stoic Tradition from Antiquity to the Early Middle Ages* (Leiden: Brill, 1985), vol. 1, chap. 6. Colish disputes the claim that Roman law was indebted to Stoicism.

7. See Paolo Grossi, *A History of European Law*, trans. Laurence Hooper (Chichester, UK: Wiley-Blackwell, 2010).

8. On the German context, see James Q. Whitman, *The Legacy of Roman Law in the German Romantic Era: Historical Vision and Legal Change* (Princeton, NJ: Princeton University Press, 1990).

9. One major exception is Damiano Canale, Paolo Grossi, and Hasso Hofmann, eds., *A History of the Philosophy of Law in the Civil Law World, 1600–1900*, vol. 9 of *A Treatise of Legal Philosophy and General Jurisprudence*, ed. Enrico Pattaro (Dordrecht: Springer, 2009). See also Benjamin Straumann, *Roman Law in the State of Nature: The Classical Foundations of Hugo Grotius' Natural Law* (Cambridge: Cambridge University Press, 2015).

10. Budé published his *Annotations on the Pandects* in 1508. See Donald Kelley, *Foundations of Modern Historical Scholarship* (New York: Columbia University Press, 1970), 53–86 (67–76, on Budé's contributions to Roman law). See also Jean-Louis Halpérin, "French Legal Science in the 17th and 18th Centuries: To the Limits of the Theory of Law," in *History of the Philosophy of Law*, 43–67; Grossi, *History of European Law*.

11. Scipion Dupleix, *L'éthique ou philosophie morale* (1610; ARTFL Electronic Edition, 2009),

bk. 4, chap. 10, p. 151. This work was written in the context of Dupleix's preceptorship of Henri IV's illegitimate son, Antoine de Bourbon-Bueil.

12. Antoine Loisel, *Institutes coutumières* (Paris: Henry Le Gras, 1637).

13. See also William F. Church, "The Decline of the French Jurists as Political Theorists, 1660–1789," *French Historical Studies* 5, no. 1 (1967): 1–40.

14. For instance, Voltaire, in his "Catalogue des écrivains" of the seventeenth century, describes Domat as a "célèbre jurisconsulte. Son livre des *Lois civiles* a eu beaucoup d'approbation": *Siècle de Louis XIV*, in *Œuvres complètes de Voltaire*, ed. Diego Venturino (Oxford: Voltaire Foundation, 2017), 12:96. Domat would be referenced in thirteen *Encyclopédie* articles. Montesquieu borrowed the title of his *Spirit of Laws* from Domat (see section 2 of this chapter). The French revolutionaries still regarded Domat as an authority on legal matters: the jurist Pierre-Toussaint Durand de Maillane singled out the "principes immuables et éternels" that Domat had "si bien distingués," in *Archives parlementaires*, April 17, 1793, 62:402–7 (406 for quote). In the early nineteenth century, the reactionary vicomte Louis Gabriel Ambroise de Bonald lauded "le célèbre Domat, qui est à nos philosophes récens les plus vantés ce que la raison est à l'esprit": *Législation primitive*, 3 vols. (Paris: chez Le Clere, 1802), 1:156. On Domat, see Church, "Decline of the French Jurists," 13–22; Jacob Viner, *Religious Thought and Economic Society*, ed. Jacques Mélitz and Donald Winch (Durham, NC: Duke University Press, 1978), 130–50; Halpérin, "French Legal Science," 48ff.

15. See Church, "Decline of the French Jurists," 13–16.

16. See *A Treatise of the First Principles of Laws in General*, trans. Thomas Wood (London, 1705), a partial translation, not attributed to Domat. A complete translation was undertaken by William Strahan, *The Civil Law in Its Natural Order*, 2 vols. (1722; 2nd ed., 1737).

17. See David J. Bederman, *The Classical Foundations of the American Constitution: Prevailing Wisdom* (Cambridge: Cambridge University Press, 2008), 11.

18. See, most notably, Aquinas, *Summa theologica*, Q. 94, Art. 4, rpl. 1; in *Treatise on Law*, trans. Richard J. Reagan (Indianapolis: Hackett, 2000), 40. See also *Leviathan*, 1.14.

19. Domat, *Civil Law in Its Natural Order*, 1:ii–iii; for the French, see Domat, *Les loix civiles dans leur ordre naturel*, 3 vols. (Paris: Aubouin et al., 1697), "Traité des loix," 1.3, 1:v. Domat's definition may have drawn on Pascal, who had argued, "All men are in search of happiness. [ ... ] They all aim for this goal"; but "[God] alone is our true good." See Blaise Pascal, *Penseés and Other Writings*, trans. Honor Levi (Oxford: Oxford University Press, 1999), § 181 (Sellier edition), pp. 51–52.

20. Aquinas had also declared that "the ultimate end of human life is happiness or blessedness," but had not elevated this telos to a natural law: see *Summa theologica*, I–II, Q. 90, Art. 2; in *Treatise on Law*, 3.

21. *Civil Law in Its Natural Order*, 1:iii; *Loix civiles*, 1:v.

22. See Pascal on diversion (*divertissement*): "I have often said that man's unhappiness springs from one thing alone, his incapacity to stay quietly in one room." *Penseés*, § 168, p. 44.

23. Pascal, *Penseés*, § 94, pp. 23–24. On "cette belle raison humaine," see the discussion in chapter 2 of Montaigne's "Apologie de Raymond Sebond."

24. Pufendorf, *Of the Law of Nature and Nations* (1672), trans. Basil Kennett, ed. Jean Barbeyrac (London: Walthoe et al., 1729), 2.3.11, p. 131.

25. *Civil Law in Its Natural Order*, 1:xxviii–xxix; *Loix civiles*, "Traité des loix," 11.1, 1:lvi–lvii.

26. See Gilbert Faccarello, *The Foundations of Laissez-Faire: The Economics of Pierre de Boisguilbert*, trans. Carolyn Shread (London: Routledge, 1999), 23, 48. Domat's friend and fellow Jansenist Pierre Nicole also espoused a traditional Christian approach to natural law: "la

connoissance de nous-mêmes [ . . . ] nous fait découvrir dans le fond de nos cœurs l'impression de la loi naturelle qui nous défend de faire aux autres ce que nous ne voudrions pas qu'ils nous fissent." "De la connoissance de soi-même," *Essais de morale*, 3 vols. (1675; Paris: Desprez, 1701), 3:50.

27. *Civil Law in Its Natural Order*, 1:ii; *Loix civiles*, "Traité des loix," 1.2, 1:iii.

28. *Civil Law in Its Natural Order*, 1:xxi; *Loix civiles*, "Traité des loix," 9.5, 1:xli.

29. *Civil Law in Its Natural Order*, 1:248; *Loix civiles*, 1.18.1.3, 1:493. Domat cites Rom. 2:14–15 in the introductory "Traité des loix," 9.5, 1:xli, note *a*; *Civil Law in Its Natural Order*, 1:xxi. He still insisted on the need for revelation: "quoyque ces principes ne nous soient connus que par la lumière de la Religion, elle nous les fait voir dans nôtre nature même avec tant de clarté, qu'on voit que l'homme ne les ignore que parce qu'il s'ignore lui-même" (1:iii). Pascal had rewritten these same biblical verses in a way that restricted knowledge of the divine law to the chosen people alone: "[Jesus Christ] had to produce a great people, elect, holy, and chosen [ . . . ] give laws to this people, engrave these laws on their hearts [graver ces lois dans leur cœur]; offer himself to God for them and sacrifice himself for them . . ." *Pensées*, ed. and trans. Roger Ariew (Indianapolis: Hackett, 2004), § 504, p. 160.

30. *Civil Law in Its Natural Order*, 1:x, 1:vi; *Loix civiles*, "Traité des loix," 4.1, 1:xviii; 2.3, 1:xi.

31. Domat even develops an interesting proto-Levi-Straussian argument about the universality of the incest taboo based on his matrimonial theory of society: see *Loix civiles*, "Traité des loix," 4.1, 1:xviii. On these points in Pufendorf, see Istvan Hont, "The Language of Sociability and Commerce: Samuel Pufendorf and the Theoretical Foundations of the 'Four-Stages Theory,'" in *The Languages of Political Theory in Early-Modern Europe*, ed. Anthony Pagden (Cambridge: Cambridge University Press, 1987), 253–76; and T. J. Hochstrasser, *Natural Law Theories in the Early Enlightenment* (Cambridge: Cambridge University Press, 2000), chap. 2.

32. Pufendorf, *Of the Law of Nature and Nations*, 6.1.1; 559. On this point in particular (and on the discussion of Domat's debt to Pufendorf more generally), my thanks to David Grewal.

33. For Pufendorf, two covenants were needed: *Of the Law of Nature and Nations*, 7.2.7–8.

34. *Civil Law in Its Natural Order*, 1:xii, 1:xxii; *Loix civiles*, "Traité des loix," 4.6, 1:xxiii; 9.7, 1:xliii.

35. The epistle is not found in the English translation: *Loix civiles*, n.p.

36. Paul, Rom. 13:1; cited in Domat, *Loix civiles*, "Traité des loix," 9.7, 1:xliii, note *b*; *Civil Law in Its Natural Order*, 1:xxii, note *m*. Contrast Pufendorf: "no Sovereignty can be actually establish'd, unless some human Deed or Covenant precede." *Of the Law of Nature and Nations*, 3.2.8, p. 231.

37. Pufendorf had explicitly rejected the idea that society could come about through a "natural way" and "that these [first human] Engagements found a Family, which by constant Increase from new Births, with that Love of Society implanted in Men by Nature, and improved by Neighbourhood and Alliance, at length furnish'd out a civil State": *Of the Law of Nature and Nations*, 7.1.5, 627. He attributes this view to Georgius Hornius.

38. *Civil Law in Its Natural Order*, 1:xxi; *Loix civiles*, "Traité des loix," 9.6, 1:xli–xlii. See Faccarello, *Foundations of Laissez-Faire*, 32–33.

39. For Malebranche, "tous les êtres qu'il [Dieu] a faits tiennent les uns aux autres": *Recherche de la vérité*, 3:137. While Pufendorf rejects Grotius's *etiamsi daremus* hypothesis, insisting that "the Obligation of natural Law proceeds from God himself," his account of natural sociability remains more anthropological: *Of the Law of Nature and Nations*, 2.3.14, 136 (on natural sociability), and 2.3.20, 143–46 (on the divine origins of natural law).

40. See in particular Hobbes, as discussed in chapter 2.

41. See David Grewal, "The Political Theology of *Laissez-Faire*: From *Philia* to Self-Love in Commercial Society," *Political Theology* 17, no. 5 (2016): 417–33 (419).

42. *Civil Law in Its Natural Order*, 1:liii; *Loix civiles*, "Traité des loix," 14.1, 1:civ.

43. *Civil Law in Its Natural Order*, 1:xix–xx; *Loix civiles*, "Traité des loix," 9.1–3 (1:xxxvii–xl for quotes). This passage draws on Pierre Nicole's essay "De la charité et de l'amour-propre": "l'amour-propre imite les principales actions de la charité." *Essais de morale*, 3:162. See also Faccarello, *Foundations of Laissez-Faire*, 24–28.

44. Pascal, *Pensées*, § 244, p. 75; see also § 243. See Albert Hirschman, *The Passions and the Interests: Political Arguments for Capitalism before Its Triumph* (Princeton, NJ: Princeton University Press, 1977), 16–17 note *b*; and Grewal, "Political Theology of *Laissez-Faire*," 421–24. See also Isaac Nakhimovsky, "The Enlightened Epicureanism of Jacques Abbadie: *L'Art de se connoître soi-même* and the Morality of Self-Interest," *History of European Ideas* 29, no. 1 (2003): 1–14.

45. See Nicole, "De la grandeur," in *Essais de morale*, 3 vols. (1671; Paris: Desprez, 1701), 1.6, 2:186. See also his essay "De la charité et de l'amour-propre." More generally, see Viner, *Religious Thought*, 131–38; Dale Van Kley, "Pierre Nicole, Jansenism, and the Morality of Self-Interest," in *Anticipations of the Enlightenment in England, France, and Germany*, ed. Alan C. Kors and Paul J. Korshin (Philadelphia: University of Pennsylvania Press, 1987), 69–85; and Pierre Force, *Self-Interest before Adam Smith: A Genealogy of Economic Science* (Cambridge: Cambridge University Press, 2003), 76–78.

46. Nicole did not share Domat's naturalistic account of government: "L'ordre politique est donc une *invention admirable* que les hommes ont trouvée," he writes in "De la grandeur," in *Essais de morale*, 2:187.

47. For Nicole, self-love only imitates charity if it is regulated by a political order: "si on la laisse à elle-même, elle n'a ni bornes, ni mesures. Au-lieu de servir à la société humaine, elle la détruit. [ . . . ] Il a donc fallu trouver un art pour régler la cupidité, et cet art consiste dans l'ordre politique qui la retient par la crainte de la peine, et qui l'applique aux choses qui sont utiles à la société." "De la grandeur," in *Essais de morale*, 2:187.

48. There is a "preliminary book" before this one, but the rest of the first book (and volume) deals with "engagements volontaires & mutuels par les conventions." Book 2 is similarly dedicated to "engagements," but without conventions. Together, these two books form part one of Domat's work. The third volume (and book) constitutes the second part and is devoted to inheritances.

49. *Civil Law in Its Natural Order*, 1:33; *Loix civiles*, 1.1, 1:61.

50. *Leviathan*, 1.15, p. 220.

51. Domat describes a convention as having the value of "une loy d'executer ce qu'ils se promettent": *Loix civiles*, 1:61.

52. See, e.g., *Loix civiles*, 1.3.15, 1:86.

53. See also Viner, *Religious Thought*, 138–39.

54. See Jonathan Sheehan and Dror Wahrman, *Invisible Hands: Self-Organization and the Eighteenth Century* (Chicago: University of Chicago Press, 2015).

55. "Il n'est point question de faire de miracle pour former au Roy cent millions de rente plus qu'il n'a, en rétablissant à ses Sujets le double de leurs biens, tels qu'ils les avoient autrefois, *il est seulement nécessaire de laisser agir la Nature*, en cessant de lui faire une perpétuelle violence par des intérêts indirects . . .": Pierre le Pesant de Boisguilbert, *Le Détail de la France sous le règne présent* (1707, 2nd ed.), 119 (emphasis added). For details about his education, see Félix Cadet, *Pierre de Boisguilbert, précurseur des économistes, 1646–1714: sa vie—ses travaux—son influence* (Paris: Librairie Guillaumin, 1871); and Jacqueline Hecht, "Pierre de Boisguilbert ou la naissance de l'économie politique," *Population* 22, no. 1 (1967): 111–16. On Boisguilbert's debts to Domat, see

Faccarello, *Foundations of Laissez-Faire*; and Grewal, "Political Theology of *Laissez-Faire*." For a different account of Boisguilbert's sources, see Paul P. Christensen, "Epicurean and Stoic Sources for Boisguilbert's Physiological and Hippocratic Vision of Nature and Economics," *History of Political Economy* 35, annual Supplement (2003): 101–28.

56. Hecht, "Pierre de Boisguilbert," 113.

57. On Boisguilbert's legacy, see esp. Peter Groenewegen, "Boisguilbert and Eighteenth-Century Economics," in *Eighteenth-Century Economics: Turgot, Smith, Beccaria, and Their Contemporaries* (London: Routledge, 2002), 111–24; and Arnaud Orain, "The Second Jansenism and the Rise of French Eighteenth-Century Political Economy," *History of Political Economy* 46, no. 3 (2014): 463–90 (esp. 470–77).

58. It forms the topic of two forthcoming books: Jacob Soll, *Free Market: The History of a Dream* (New York: Basic Books, forthcoming); and David Grewal, *The Invention of the Economy* (Cambridge, MA: Harvard University Press, forthcoming).

59. *Civil Law in Its Natural Order*, 1:xi; *Loix civiles*, "Traité des loix," 4.4, 1:xxi.

60. For the Physiocrats, see chapter 3; for the French Revolution, see chapter 7.

61. Charles Augustin Sainte-Beuve, *Port-Royal*, 3 vols. (1842; Paris, Hachette, 1860), 2:173.

62. On this "worldly style," see Dan Edelstein, Robert Morrissey, and Glenn Roe, "To Quote or Not to Quote: Citation Strategies in the *Encyclopédie*," *Journal of the History of Ideas* 74, no. 2 (2013): 213–36.

63. Keith Baker, "Ideological Origins," in *Inventing the French Revolution: Essays on French Political Culture in the Eighteenth Century* (Cambridge: Cambridge University Press, 1990), 25–27 (25 for quote).

64. The obvious exception here might appear to be Rousseau, but *The Social Contract* ultimately makes little use of natural law theory. In general, when they were advanced at all, arguments about *who* should have the authority to make the law tended to be presented in a historical and constitutional vein (as can be seen with Boulainvilliers and, to a lesser extent, Montesquieu).

65. See Pierre-Paul Le Mercier de la Rivière, *L'ordre naturel et essentiel des sociétés politiques*, 2 vols. (London: Jean Nourse, 1767); and discussion in Dan Edelstein, *The Terror of Natural Right* (Chicago: University of Chicago Press, 2009), chap. 2.

66. See Quesnay and Mirabeau's *Traité de la monarchie*, ed. Gino Longhitano (c. 1757; Paris: L'Harmattan, 1999). On this work, see Elizabeth Fox-Genovese, *The Origins of Physiocracy: Economic Revolution and Social Order in Eighteenth-Century France* (Ithaca, NY: Cornell University Press, 1976), 167–201; Michael Sonenscher, "Physiocracy as Theodicy," *History of Political Thought* 23, no. 2 (2002): 326–39; and Liana Vardi, *The Physiocrats and the World of the Enlightenment* (Cambridge: Cambridge University Press, 2012), chap. 5.

67. Diderot, *Supplément au Voyage de Bougainville*, in *Political Writings*, ed. and trans. John Hope Mason and Robert Wokler (Cambridge: Cambridge University Press, 1992), 74.

68. In this regard, the *philosophes* perpetuated a tradition that goes back at least to Montaigne and Descartes. The latter had similarly claimed that it was possible to criticize unjust laws, all the while obeying them: see Descartes, *Discours de la méthode* (Paris: Gallimard, 1991), 95–96. Montaigne advocated a similar "Stoic" stance: see Quentin Skinner, *The Foundations of Modern Political Thought*, 2 vols. (Cambridge: Cambridge University Press, 1978), 2:275–84. When the *philosophes* did criticize royal authority, it was usually for ignoring or violating the law (e.g., the many charges of royal despotism).

69. Diderot, *Supplément*, in *Political Writings*, 67, 71.

70. Victor de Riqueti, marquis de Mirabeau, *L'ami des hommes, ou, Traité de la population* (Avignon, 1756) [ARTFL], 3.5; 237.

71. Voltaire, *Traité sur la tolérance*, in *Œuvres complètes de Voltaire*, 56C:158.

72. I analyze this movement in *The Terror of Natural Right*, part I.

73. Diderot, *Supplément*, in *Political Writings*, 41.

74. See Michèle Duchet, *Anthropologie et histoire au siècle des lumières* (Paris: Albin Michel, 1971); and Christopher Miller, *The French Atlantic Triangle: Literature and Culture of the Slave Trade* (Durham, NC: Duke University Press, 2007). More broadly, see David Brion Davis, *The Problem of Slavery in Western Culture*, rev. ed. (New York: Oxford University Press, 1988).

75. Lynn Hunt, *Inventing Human Rights: A History* (New York: Norton, 2007).

76. See Pierre Choderlos de Laclos, *Les liaisons dangereuses* (Paris: Gallimard, 2003), letter 173 (pp. 471–74). The chevalier de Danceny publishes two of Merteuil's letters and gives the rest to a third party: see letter 169 (pp. 461–64).

77. For a similar contemporary assessment of empathy's limits, see Paul Bloom, *Against Empathy: The Case for Rational Compassion* (New York: Ecco, 2016).

78. Rousseau, *Emile, or On Education*, trans. Allan Bloom (New York: Basic Books, 1979), 224–25. Hunt does not discuss Rousseau's theory of pity. On Rousseau's attitudes toward slavery, see esp. Miller, *French Atlantic Triangle*, chap. 3.

79. See David A. Bell, "Questioning the Global Turn: The Case of the French Revolution," *French Historical Studies* 37, no. 1 (2014): 1–24; see also Anoush Fraser Terjanian, *Commerce and Its Discontents in Eighteenth-Century French Political Thought* (Cambridge: Cambridge University Press, 2012).

80. See Sue Peabody, *'There Are No Slaves in France': The Political Culture of Race and Slavery in the Ancien Régime* (Oxford: Oxford University Press, 1996).

81. See Laurent Dubois, "An Enslaved Enlightenment: Rethinking the Intellectual History of the French Atlantic," *Social History* 13, no. 1 (2006): 1–14; see also Madeleine Dobie, *Trading Places: Colonization and Slavery in Eighteenth-Century French Culture* (Ithaca, NY: Cornell University Press, 2010).

82. Jonathan Glover, *Humanity: A Moral History of the Twentieth Century* (London: Jonathan Cape, 1999), 28.

83. Adam Smith, *The Theory of Moral Sentiments*, ed. Knud Haakonssen (Cambridge: Cambridge University Press, 2002), 1.1.1.10, p. 15.

84. Smith, *Theory of Moral Sentiments*, 1.1.3.4, p. 22.

85. Smith, *Theory of Moral Sentiments*, 3.3.4, pp. 157–58. See discussion in Hunt, *Inventing Human Rights*, 210.

86. Diderot makes a similar point in his *Lettre sur les aveugles*: "Nous-mêmes, ne cessons-nous pas de compatir, lorsque la distance ou la petitesse des objets produit le même effet sur nous, que la privation de la vue sur les aveugles?" In *Œuvres complètes de Diderot*, 20 vols., ed. J. Assézat and Maurice Tourneux (Paris: Garnier frères, 1875–77), 1:289.

87. See Emma Rothschild, "Adam Smith in the British Empire," in *Empire and Modern Political Thought*, ed. Sankar Muthu (Cambridge: Cambridge University Press, 2013), 184–98 (196); quoted in Jennifer Pitts, "Irony in Adam Smith's Critical Global History," *Political Theory* 45, no. 2 (2015): 1–23.

88. Voltaire, *Candide*, trans. Theo Cuffe (London: Penguin, 2005), chap. 19, p. 52. See more generally Duchet, *Anthropologie et histoire*; Claudine Hunting, "The *Philosophes* and Black Slavery: 1748–1765," *Journal of the History of Ideas* 39, no. 3 (1978): 405–18; and Jean Ehrard, *Lumières et esclavage: l'esclavage colonial et l'opinion publique en France au XVIII<sup>e</sup> siècle* (Paris: André Versaille, 2008).

89. Montesquieu, *Spirit of the Laws*, 15. 2, p. 248. Following the practice of earlier translations,

I refer to this work in the text as *The Spirit of Laws* (without the direct article), which is more faithful to the French title. References in the notes, however, are to the Cambridge translation, which includes the direct article. For an excellent overview of the literature on Montesquieu and slavery, see Céline Spector, "'Il est impossible que nous supposions que ces gens-là soient des hommes': la théorie de l'esclavage au livre XV de *L'Esprit des lois*," *Lumières*, no. 3 (2004): 15–51. See also Russell P. Jameson, *Montesquieu et l'esclavage* (Paris: Hachette, 1911); Davis, *Problem of Slavery*; Miller, *French Atlantic Triangle*; Ehrard, *Lumières et esclavage*; Andrew Curran, *The Anatomy of Blackness: Science and Slavery in an Age of Enlightenment* (Baltimore: Johns Hopkins University Press, 2011); and Dobie, *Trading Places*. On his use of natural law theory in particular, see also Mark H. Waddicor, *Montesquieu and the Philosophy of Natural Law* (The Hague: Martinus Hijoff, 1970), though Waddicor claims, incorrectly, that Montesquieu opposed slavery in the name of "natural law and natural rights" (149). As we will see, Montesquieu does not, in fact, invoke natural rights in his discussion of slavery.

90. See Céline Spector, "Montesquieu et la crise du droit naturel moderne. L'exégèse straussienne," *Revue de métaphysique et de morale* 77, no. 1 (2013): 65–78.

91. See Ehrard, *Lumières et esclavage*, 159.

92. *Spirit of the Laws*, 15.7, p. 252. Book 15, chapter 6, provided a justification for slavery in despotic governments, but this was clearly slavery of a different sort.

93. *Spirit of the Laws*, 15.8, p. 253.

94. *Spirit of the Laws*, 15.5, p. 250. On this chapter, see Catherine Volpilhac-Auger, "Pitié pour les nègres," *L'Information littéraire* 55, no. 1 (2003): 11–16.

95. See Davis, *Problem of Slavery*.

96. See Jameson, *Montesquieu et l'esclavage*, 77–78; Ehrard, *Lumières et esclavage*, 141–46; and Spector, "Il est impossible." Pufendorf has a lengthy discussion of Roman and Aristotelian arguments about slavery and natural law in *Of the Law of Nature and Nations*, 3.2.8. Montesquieu had already copied down (in French) this passage from the *Institutes* in a 1728 *Pensée*: see Ehrard, *Lumières et esclavage*, 145.

97. My thanks to Darrin McMahon for calling this passage to my attention.

98. Jean Bodin to some degree anticipates Montesquieu's argument, as he grants that "if the common law of peoples is unjust, the prince can depart from it in edicts made for his kingdom and forbid his subjects to use it." He then uses the abolition of slavery (and serfdom) by Louis X as an example: "That is the way the law of slavery was handled in this kingdom, even though it was common to all peoples." See Bodin, *Six Livres de la République* (1576), i.1; translation from *On Sovereignty*, trans. and ed. Julian Franklin (Cambridge: Cambridge University Press, 1992), 45. But Bodin's logic is premised on the possibility that the law of nations can and often does violate natural law, whereas a century later, this premise would be rejected.

99. Hugo Grotius, *Le droit de la guerre et de la paix*, 3 vols., trans. and ed. Jean Barbeyrac (1724; Basel: Thourneisen, 1746), 1.1.14 (for Grotius quote), n. 3 (for Barbeyrac's comment), 1:56. English translation in Grotius, *The Rights of War and Peace* (1625), 3 vols., ed. Richard Tuck, trans. John Morrice et al. (Indianapolis: Liberty Fund, 2005), 1:163.

100. Montesquieu, *Lettres persanes* (Paris: Folio, 2003), letter XCV, p. 218.

101. *Spirit of the Laws*, 15.2.

102. Emmerich de Vattel, *The Law of Nations, or Principles of the Law of Nature . . .* (1758), ed. Béla Kapossy and Richard Whatmore, trans. Thomas Nugent (Indianapolis: Liberty Fund, 2008), Preliminaries, § 6. While Vattel accepted certain practices (such as the right of reprisals) that appalled some of his contemporaries, notably Voltaire, he never explicitly recognized that these practices might stand in violation of natural law. He also rejects as unlawful the "ancient" practice

of enslaving prisoners of war (i.e., the Roman law justification of slavery): see *Law of Nations*, 3.8.152–54, pp. 556–57. More generally, see Emmanuelle Jouannet, *Emer de Vattel et l'émergence doctrinale du droit international classique* (Paris: Editions A. Pédone, 1998); Ian Hunter, "Vattel's Law of Nations: Diplomatic Casuistry for the Protestant Nation," *Grotiana* 31 (2010): 108–40; and Dan Edelstein, "Enlightenment Rights Talk," *Journal of Modern History* 84, no. 3 (2014): 1–36.

103. Boucher d'Argis, "Droit des gens," *Encyclopédie*, 5:127. I discuss this conflation further (and the exceptions, such as Vattel) in *Terror of Natural Right*.

104. Pufendorf, *Of the Laws of Nature and Nations*, 2.3.23, pp. 149–50.

105. Hobbes, *On the Citizen*, ed. and trans. Richard Tuck and Michael Silverthorne (Cambridge: Cambridge University Press, 1998), 14.4, p. 156.

106. "It was not until 1765, however, when the editors arrived at 'Traite des negrès,' that de Jaucourt was able to rise above the qualifications engendered by Montesquieu's tolerance for institutional differences": Davis, *Problem of Slavery*, 415–16. See also Curran, *Anatomy of Blackness*, 182. The article "Liberté naturelle" also concludes with a condemnation of "l'esclavage des negres": see *Encyclopédie*, 9:472.

107. Jaucourt, "Esclavage," *Encyclopédie*, 5:936–97; trans. Naomi J. Andrews, *Encyclopedia of Diderot & d'Alembert Collaborative Translation Project*, http://hdl.handle.net/2027/spo.did2222 .0000.667.

108. See Ehrard, *Lumières et esclavage*, 169.

109. Cf. *Spirit of the Laws*, 15.17 ("What a people, whose civil law ceased to cling to natural law!" p. 260).

110. See, for instance, "Tous les hommes naissent libres; dans le commencement ils n'avoient qu'un nom, qu'une condition; [ … ] la nature les avoit fait tous égaux; mais on ne conserva pas long-tems cette égalité [replacing *liberté*] naturelle"; and "Cependant le Christianisme commençant à s'accréditer . . ."; cf. Jean Mallet, *Mémoire pour Jean Boucaux* (Paris, 1738), 1–3. On this text, see Peabody, *'There Are No Slaves in France,'* chap. 2 (who does not mention its recycling by Jaucourt).

111. Mallet, *Mémoire pour Jean Boucaux*, 3. Montesquieu also credited Christianity with having done away with slavery in Europe but did not provide any names or dates: see *Spirit of the Laws*, 15.7, p. 252.

112. Jaucourt, "Esclavage," *Encyclopédie*, 5:936. Montesquieu had already used the abolition of serfdom in the name of Christianity to point out the hypocrisy of slavery in the *Persian Letters* (see letter LXXV).

113. Jaucourt, "Esclavage," *Encyclopédie*, 5:936. This edict was in fact far more limited than eighteenth-century admirers tended to consider it: see Marc Bloch, *Rois et serfs et autres écrits sur le servage* (Paris: Champion, 1920).

114. See Charles-Jean-François Hénault, *Nouvel abrégé chronologique de l'histoire de France* (Paris: Prault, Desaint & Saillant, 1749), 649. The quotation from Louis X is truncated in exactly the same places in both texts. Jaucourt cites Hénault openly in a number of other articles (e.g., "Nantes," "Vénalité des charges").

115. See Ehrard, *Lumières et esclavage*, 173.

116. On such borrowed passages, see Edelstein, Morrissey, and Roe, "To Quote or Not to Quote."

117. David Brion Davis pointed to similarities between Jaucourt's 1765 article, "Traite des negrès," and George Wallace's *A System of the Principles of the Law of Scotland*, published in 1760, in "New Sidelights on Early Antislavery Radicalism," in *From Homicide to Slavery: Studies in American Culture* (New York: Oxford University Press, 1986), chap. 10.

118. See, e.g., Curran, referencing Davis: "the violent 'Traite des nègres' flows almost directly from Wallace's text. [ . . . ] [I]t is no exaggeration to state that it was actually Wallace and not Jaucourt who was responsible for one of the first real denunciations of the colonial project in French thought." *Anatomy of Blackness*, 182.

119. It also bears noting how indebted Wallace himself was to Montesquieu, whom he cites at great length (in French): see George Wallace, *A System of the Principles of the Law of Scotland* (London: Printed for A. Millar, D. Wilson and T. Durham, 1760), 93, 97–98. As always with Jaucourt, it is possible that his additions were pulled from another, yet unidentified source.

120. Jaucourt, "Traite des nègres," *Encyclopédie*, 16:532; trans. Stephanie Noble, *Encyclopedia of Diderot & d'Alembert Collaborative Translation Project*, http://hdl.handle.net/2027/spo.did2222 .0000.114; translation modified.

121. With one exception in his chapter on slavery: "Every man has a natural right to his liberty" (91). As Davis notes, Wallace also drew on Francis Hutcheson.

122. Cf. *Spirit of the Laws*, 26.16, p. 512.

123. Davis, *Problem of Slavery*, 416.

124. Wallace, *System of the Principles*, 96.

125. Wallace (and Jaucourt after him) had also made an economic argument for abolition, fairly similar to Montesquieu's.

126. In *Les Saisons, poème par Saint-Lambert. L'Abenaki, Sara Th . . . , Ziméo, contes* (n.p., 1769) [GALLICA], 226–59. Discussed in Miller, *French Atlantic Triangle*, 103–4; see also Dobie, *Trading Places*, 258–61; and Pratima Prasad, *Colonialism, Race, and the French Romantic Imagination* (New York: Routledge, 2009). There is some debate about whether the story as a whole conveys an abolitionist message, but the conclusion is unambiguous (as we will see).

127. See Jacqueline Hecht, "La vie de François Quesnay," in *François Quesnay et la physiocratie*, 2 vols. (Paris: Institut National d'Etudes Démographiques, 1958), 1:272; and Vardi, *Physiocrats and the World of the Enlightenment*.

128. See Dupont de Nemours, *Éphémérides du citoyen, ou Chronique de l'esprit national*, vol. 6, no. 2 (1771): 178–246. Dobie similarly remarks upon the "economic subtext" of *Ziméo* but does not connect its arguments with the Physiocrats (despite also discussing Dupont de Nemours's reaction): *Trading Places*, 261.

129. Dupont de Nemours, *Éphémérides du citoyen*, 181.

130. Condorcet, *Réflexions sur l'esclavage des nègres* (Neufchâtel: Société typographique, 1781). See chapter 3.

131. It is of course important to note, as does Dobie, that abolitionism was not tantamount to anti-colonialism.

132. See in particular Lucien Jaume, ed., *Les Déclarations des droits de l'homme* (Paris: Flammarion, 1989), 54; see also Marcel Gauchet, *La Révolution des droits de l'homme* (Paris: Gallimard, 1989).

133. See notably Donald R. Kelley, *Historians and the Law in Postrevolutionary France* (Princeton, NJ: Princeton University Press, 1984).

134. As noted in chapter 3, histories of French liberalism have tended to overlook Physiocracy: see, e.g., Annelien de Dijn, *French Political Thought from Montesquieu to Tocqueville: Liberty in a Levelled Society?* (Cambridge: Cambridge University Press, 2008); and Raf Geenens and Helena Rosenblatt, eds., *French Liberalism from Montesquieu to the Present Day* (Cambridge: Cambridge University Press, 2012). For an interesting parallel with twentieth-century neoliberals, see Quinn Slobodian, *Globalists: The End of Empire and the Birth of Neoliberalism* (Cambridge, MA: Harvard University Press, 2018).

135. See Johannes Morsink, *The Universal Declaration of Human Rights: Origins, Drafting, and Intent* (Philadelphia: University of Pennsylvania Press, 1999), 281–328; Stefan-Ludwig Hoffman, "Human Rights and History," *Past & Present* 232, no. 1 (2016): 279–310; and, more generally, the conclusion.

## Part III

1. *Constitutions des treize États Unis de l'Amérique* (Paris, 1783). The state constitutions that included declarations were (in order of passage) Virginia, Pennsylvania, Delaware, Maryland, North Carolina, and Massachusetts. I discuss some of these state declarations in chapter 6. Connecticut and Rhode Island did not compose new constitutions after independence, but their colonial charters were included in this translation.

2. Filippo Mazzei, *Recherches historiques et politiques sur les États-Unis de l'Amérique septentrionale*, 4 vols. (Paris, 1788); 1:154–63. More broadly, see Durand Echeverria, *Mirage in the West: A History of the French Image of American Society* (Princeton, NJ: Princeton University Press, 1957).

3. See Jefferson's letter of January 12, 1789, to James Madison, in *The Papers of Thomas Jefferson Digital Edition*, ed. Barbara B. Oberg and J. Jefferson Looney (Charlottesville: University of Virginia Press/Rotunda, 2008), 14:436–38. More generally, see Lloyd S. Kramer, *Lafayette in Two Worlds: Public Cultures and Personal Identities in an Age of Revolutions* (Chapel Hill: University of North Carolina Press, 2000).

4. Georg Jellinek, *The Declaration of the Rights of Man and of Citizens*, trans. Max Farrand (New York: Henry Holt, 1901), 20. On Jellinek, see the introduction to Part II.

5. A topic that Jellinek's adversary, Emile Boutmy, pursued at length: see "La Déclaration des droits de l'homme et du citoyen et M. Jellinek," *Annales des sciences politiques* 17 (1902): 419–43. More recently, see Stéphane Rials, *La Déclaration des droits de l'homme* (Paris: Hachette, 1988).

6. See chapter 7.

7. See chapter 2.

## Chapter VI

1. Compare "a long train of abuses and usurpations, pursuing invariably the same Object evinces a design to reduce them under absolute Despotism" (Jefferson) with "a long train of abuses, prevarications and artifices, all tending the same way, make the design visible to the people": Locke, *Second Treatise*, § 225.

2. For a classic statement of this "liberal" interpretation, see Louis Hartz, *The Liberal Tradition in America* (New York: Harcourt, Brace & World, 1955). This interpretation has become closely identified with scholars in the orbit of Leo Strauss, whose own *Natural Right and History* (Chicago: University of Chicago Press, 1953) defended this thesis as well: see Allan Bloom, *The Closing of the American Mind* (New York: Simon and Schuster, 1987); Michael Zuckert, "Natural Rights in the American Revolution: The American Amalgam," in *Human Rights and Revolutions*, 2nd ed., ed. Jeffrey N. Wasserstrom, Greg Grandin, Lynn Hunt, and Marilyn B. Young (Lanham, MD: Rowman & Littlefield, 2007); Zuckert, *The Natural Rights Republic* (Notre Dame, IN: University of Notre Dame Press, 1996); and Scott Douglas Gerber, *To Secure These Rights: The Declaration of Independence and Constitutional Interpretation* (New York: New York University Press, 1996). But historians without any Straussian affiliations have also proposed different versions of this thesis: see notably James T. Kloppenberg, "The Virtues of Liberalism: Christianity, Republicanism, and Ethics in Early American Political Discourse," *Journal of American History* 74, no. 1 (1987): 9–33.

3. James H. Hutson, "The Emergence of the Modern Concept of a Right in America: The Contribution of Michel Villey," *American Journal of Jurisprudence* 39, no. 1 (1994): 183–224 (216).

4. Knud Haakonssen, "From Natural Law to the Rights of Man," in *Natural Law and Moral Philosophy: From Grotius to the Scottish Enlightenment* (Cambridge: Cambridge University Press, 1996), 328; see also Jack Rakove, *Original Meanings: Politics and Ideas in the Making of the Constitution* (New York: Vintage, 1996), 290.

5. Daniel T. Rodgers, *Contested Truths: Keywords in American Politics since Independence* (Cambridge, MA: Harvard University Press, 1998), 45–79 (47 for quote).

6. See, e.g., Bernard Bailyn, who acknowledged the extent to which colonists cited Locke, but argued that their knowledge was "at times superficial" and could just as easily be used to defend Loyalist positions: *The Ideological Origins of the American Revolution* (Cambridge, MA: Harvard University Press, 1967), 28–29; for similar assessments, see Gordon Wood, *The Creation of the American Republic, 1776–1787* (Chapel Hill: University of North Carolina Press, 1969), 14; and John Pocock, *The Machiavellian Moment* (Princeton, NJ: Princeton University Press, 1975), 527. More generally, see Isaac Kramnick, "Republican Revisionism Revisited," *American Historical Review* 87, no. 3 (1982): 629–64; and Joyce Appleby, *Liberalism and Republicanism in the Historical Imagination* (Cambridge, MA: Harvard University Press, 1992), esp. 124–60; and for a critical account of this "republican" historiography on Locke, see Steven M. Dworetz, *The Unvarnished Doctrine: Locke, Liberalism, and the American Revolution* (Durham, NC: Duke University Press, 1989).

7. Roscoe Pound, *The Formative Era of American Law* (Boston: Little, Brown, 1938), 104.

8. John Phillip Reid, *Constitutional History of the American Revolution* (Madison: University of Wisconsin Press, 1995), 15.

9. Eric Slauter, "Rights," in *The Oxford Handbook of the American Revolution*, ed. Jane Kamensky and Edward G. Gray (Oxford: Oxford University Press, 2012), 447–64.

10. See chapter 2. On the American reception of this legal/constitutional tradition, see also Bernadette Meyler, "Towards a Common Law Originalism," *Stanford Law Review* 59 (2006): 551–600.

11. See chapter 3.

12. James Otis, *The Rights of the British Colonies Asserted and Proved* (Boston: Edes and Gill, 1764), 12.

13. The exception is Benjamin Lord, who argued that "Men's natural rights [were] given up to Community, whereby, those may be exercised for the Good of every one; as they cannot be, while in the Hands of Individuals themselves." *Religion and Government Subsisting Together in Society, Necessary to Their Compleat Happiness and Safety* (New London, CT: Timothy Green, 1752), 3. The situation changed somewhat after 1765, with various authors insisting that men must "give up" some of their natural rights and "deposit them" in government: see Hutson, "Emergence of the Modern Concept of a Right," 221–23.

14. See Richard Overton, *An Arrow against all Tyrants* (1646), and the discussion in chapter 2.

15. William Penn, *The Peoples Ancient and Just Liberties Asserted in the Tryal of William Penn, and William Mead . . .* (1670), 48–49.

16. See esp. Penn, *The Excellent Priviledge of Liberty and Property Being the Birth-right of the Free-born Subjects of England* (Philadelphia: Bradford, 1687).

17. *A Letter to B.G. from One of the Members of Assembly of the Province of New-Jersey* (Philadelphia: Benjamin Franklin, 1739), 2. As we will see, statements such as these were commonplace in colonial America.

18. Haakonssen, *Natural Law and Moral Philosophy*, 322 (emphasis added).

19. See Reid, *Constitutional History*, 14.

20. See, respectively, Thomas Paine, *Common Sense* (London: Penguin, 1976), 98; and the Declaration of Independence.

21. For this chapter, I relied primarily on the Early American Imprints database, Series I: Evans, produced by Readex.

22. John Wise, *A Vindication of the Government of New-England Churches* (Boston: J. Allen, for N. Boone, 1717) [EVANS]. On Wise's role in the Ipswich rebellion, see notably John McWilliams, *New England's Crises and Cultural Memory: Literature, Politics, History, Religion, 1620–1860* (Cambridge: Cambridge University Press, 2004), 156.

23. Wise, *Vindication of the Government*, 39, 61.

24. John Wise, *The Churches Quarrel Espoused* (New York: William Bradford, 1713); reprinted in 1715 in Boston by Nicholas Boone. See in particular the passage on how "many of their [English] Incautelous Princes have endeavoured to Null all their Charter Rights and Immunities, and aggrandize themselves in the Servile state of their Subjects [ . . . ] yet they have all a long paid Dear for their Attempts" (120–21).

25. For Wise's gloss of Romans 2:14, see *Vindication of the Government*, 34; on Puritan invocations of this verse, see John D. Eusden, "Natural Law and Covenant Theology in New England, 1620–1670," *Natural Law Forum*, paper 47 (1960), 21 (accessible at http://scholarship.law.nd.edu /nd_naturallaw_forum/47). On impact of the Glorious Revolution in the colonies, see Rakove, *Original Meanings*, 20.

26. See *A Discourse on Government and Religion* (Boston: Daniel Fowle, 1750); the attribution to Peter Annet is found in this work's WorldCat entry. The full quote reads, "[W]e now enjoy that natural and reasonable liberty, which is the natural and reasonable right of mankind, and reason therefore may speak without fear: But when *tyrants* reign, reason is suppressed; because it is feared" (7). The entire work is filled with similar claims.

27. William Homes, *Proposals of Some Things to Be Done in Our Administring [sic] Ecclesiastical Government* (Boston: B. Gray, 1732), 11 [EVANS].

28. John Barnard, *The Throne Established by Righteousness: A Sermon Preach'd Before His Excellency Jonathan Belcher* (Boston,1734), 24 [EVANS].

29. Nathaniel Appleton, *The Origin of War Examin'd and Applied, in a Sermon . . .* (Boston: T. Fleet, 1733), 14 [EVANS].

30. John Williams, *Several Arguments, Proving, that Inoculating the Small Pox is not Contained in the Law of Physick, either Natural or Divine, and therefore Unlawful* (Boston: J. Franklin, 1721), 2–3 [EVANS].

31. Barnard, *The Throne Established by Righteousness*, 41.

32. James Logan, *The Latter Part of the Charge Delivered from the Bench to the Grand Inquest . . .* (Philadelphia: Benjamin Franklin, 1733), 1.

33. Edwin Wolf, *James Logan, 1674–1751, Bookman Extraordinary* (Philadelphia: Library Company, 1971).

34. Tom Shachtman, *Gentlemen Scientists and Revolutionaries: The Founding Fathers in the Age of Enlightenment* (New York: St. Martin's Press, 2014).

35. [Benjamin Franklin], *A Letter to a Friend in the Country, Containing the Substance of a Sermon Preach'd at Philadelphia* (Philadelphia: B. Franklin, 1735), iv [EVANS]. See also the letter he published four years later: "no Government can be legally established in any of the Plantations but on the Basis of an *English Constitution*; otherwise our natural Rights could not be preserved." *A Letter to B.G.*, 2 [EVANS]. And see the broadsheet accusing the governor of having amassed excessive executive power: "Such great Incroachments on the natural Rights and Liberties of the

People, could never have been made if their Representatives had not given their Consent." *To the Freeholders of the Province of Pennsylvania* (n.p., n.d. [1743]) [EVANS].

36. See, e.g., the Maryland Lower House of Assembly's address to Governor Samuel Ogle: "We sincerely wish there had been no occasion of applying to your Excellency about Aggrievances, but many such having been laid before us of a most oppressive Nature, we could not but think it incumbent on us to endeavour to restore and preserve our natural Rights and Privileges"; April 26, 1740, *Votes and Proceedings of the Lower House of Assembly of the Province of Maryland* (Annapolis: Jonas Green, 1740), 208 [EVANS].

37. See Eusden, "Natural Law and Covenant Theology"; and Dworetz, on the "theistic liberalism" of Puritans, *Unvarnished Doctrine*, chap. 5.

38. See "The 1723 Catalogue," in *The Printed Catalogues of the Harvard College Library, 1723–1790*, ed. W. H. Bond and Hugh Amory (Boston: Colonial Society of Massachusetts, 1996), A79, A57, A106 (respectively). The Library possessed the three-volume *Works of John Locke Esq.* (London: A. Churchill and A. Manship, 1722), the second volume of which contained the *Two Treatises*. More generally, see Arthur E. Sutherland, *The Law at Harvard: A History of Ideas and Men, 1817–1967* (Cambridge, MA: Belknap Press of Harvard University Press, 1967).

39. Benjamin Franklin, *Proposals Relating to the Education of Youth in Pensilvania* (Philadelphia: Franklin and Hall, 1749), 23 [EVANS].

40. See notably Frank Lambert, *Inventing the "Great Awakening"* (Princeton, NJ: Princeton University Press, 2001); and Thomas S. Kidd, *The Great Awakening* (New Haven, CT: Yale University Press, 2007). George Whitefield arrived in Boston in 1740. On rights and the Great Awakening, see also Hutson, "Emergence of the Modern Concept of a Right," 214.

41. Elisha Williams, *The Essential Rights and Liberties of Protestants* (Boston: S. Kneeland and T. Green, 1744), 46. See also his brother Solomon Williams, *Christ, the King and Witness of Truth, and the Nature, Excellency, and Extent of his Kingdom, as Founded in Truth, and only Promoted by it* (Boston: Rogers and Fowle, 1744), 80.

42. See Williams, *Essential Rights and Liberties*, 5–6; quoting Locke, *Second Treatise*, chap. 9, §§ 128–30. Also see chapter 2.

43. See chapter 2.

44. For another take on the Americanization of Locke, see Dworetz, *Unvarnished Doctrine*, esp. chap. 5.

45. Ebenezer Pemberton, *A Sermon Delivered at the Presbyterian Church in New-York* (New York: James Parker, 1746), 21 [EVANS]. See Lambert, *Inventing the "Great Awakening,"* 126.

46. Charles Chauncy, *Civil Magistrates Must Be Just, Ruling in the Fear of God* (Boston, 1747), 35 [EVANS]. See Kidd, *The Great Awakening*, 120–21; see also John Corrigan, *The Hidden Balance: Religion and the Social Theories of Charles Chauncy and Jonathan Mayhew* (Cambridge: Cambridge University Press, 2006).

47. Jonathan Mayhew, "The Right and Duty of Private Judgment," in *Seven Sermons* (Boston: Rogers and Fowle, 1749), 57–58 [EVANS].

48. Jonathan Mayhew, *A Discourse Concerning Unlimited Submission and Non-Resistance to the Higher Powers* (Boston, 1750), 12; see also Electronic Texts in American Studies, Paper 4: http://digitalcommons.unl.edu/etas/44.

49. See *The Works of John Adams*, 10 vols., ed. Charles Francis Adams (Boston: Little, Brown, 1856), 10:301.

50. A full account of this tax debate can be found in Paul S. Boyer, "Borrowed Rhetoric: The Massachusetts Excise Controversy of 1754," *William and Mary Quarterly* 21, no. 3 (1964): 328–51. See also, and more generally, Alvin Rabushka, *Taxation in Colonial America* (Princeton,

NJ: Princeton University Press, 2008), 559n20; and William Cuddihy, *The Fourth Amendment: Origins and Original Meaning* (New York: Oxford University Press, 2009).

51. Quoted in an opposition pamphlet, *The Relapse* (Boston, 1754) [EVANS]; see also Boyer, "Borrowed Rhetoric," 333.

52. *The Voice of the People* (Boston, 1754), 3 [EVANS].

53. Samuel Cooper, *The Crisis* (Boston, 1754), 5 [EVANS].

54. Daniel Fowle, *An Appendix to the Late 'Total Eclipse of Liberty'* (Boston, 1756), 20–21 [EVANS].

55. See Boyer, "Borrowed Rhetoric," 347.

56. Fowle, *Appendix*, 22. Fowle also quotes, without attribution, from John Shebbeare and Daniel Defoe, among others.

57. See the quotes in Fowle, *Appendix*, 4–5.

58. Rusticus, *The Good of the Community Impartially Considered, in a Letter to a Merchant in Boston* (Boston, 1754), 32 (for the Locke citation). For the identification of the author, see John R. Vile, "Excise Tax of 1754 (Massachusetts)," in *Encyclopedia of the Fourth Amendment*, ed. John R. Vile and David L. Hudson Jr. (Thousand Oaks, CA: CQ Press, 2013), 1:247. Fletcher would be voted out of office, due to his support of the tax: see William Pencak, *War, Politics & Revolution in Provincial Massachusetts* (Boston: Northeastern University Press, 1981), 145n94.

59. Rusticus, *Good of the Community Impartially Considered*, 39.

60. Boyer is mistaken, then, in his assertion that for Fletcher "there is no appeal from within an organized society to natural rights unless one is willing to return to a state of nature": "Borrowed Rhetoric," 348.

61. See Jonathan Mayhew, *Two Discourses delivered November 23d. 1758* (Boston: R. Draper, Edes & Gill, and Green & Russell, 1758), 9 [EVANS]; and *A Discourse Occasioned by the Death of King George II* (Boston: Edes & Gill, 1761), 33 [EVANS].

62. *All Canada in the Hands of the English* (Boston: B. Mecom, 1760), 3–4 [EVANS].

63. *Journal of the Honourable House of Representatives, of His Majesty's Province of the Massachusetts-Bay* (Boston: Samuel Kneeland, 1757), December 16, 1757, p. 209; emphasis added [EVANS]. On this controversy, see Alan Rogers, *Empire and Liberty: American Resistance to British Authority, 1755–1763* (Berkeley: University of California Press, 1974), chap. 7; Francis Jennings, *Empire of Fortune: Crowns, Colonies, and Tribes in the Seven Years War in America* (New York: Norton, 1990), 304–5; and Peter James Marshall, *The Making and Unmaking of Empires: Britain, India, and America c. 1750–1783* (Oxford: Oxford University Press, 2005), 102–3.

64. See Maurice Henry Smith, *The Writs of Assistance Case* (Berkeley: University of California Press, 1970).

65. Letter to William Tudor, June 1, 1818, in *Works of John Adams*, 10:314–17. Adams had written "An Abstract of the Argument" at the time, though it does not contain this section on natural rights: see *Works of John Adams*, 2:521–25. For an astute discussion of Otis, Adams, and natural law, see Mark Somos, "Boston in the State of Nature, 1761–1765: The Birth of an American Constitutional Trope," *Jus Gentium: Journal of International Legal History* 3, no. 1 (2018): 63–113.

66. In James Otis's *The Rights of British Colonists Asserted* (Boston, 1764), he famously defended the natural rights of slaves: "The Colonists are by the law of nature free born, as indeed all men are, white or black" (43). This line clearly echoes Montesquieu's denunciation of slavery in *The Spirit of Laws* (see chapter 5); unsurprisingly, Otis references Montesquieu in the following sentence.

67. See letters to Dr. J. Morse, November 29, 1815, in *Works of John Adams*, 10:183–84; to William Tudor, March 29, 1817, 10:247; to H. Niles, January 14, 1818, 10:275–76.

68. See, for instance, Daniel Rodgers: "The term [natural rights] was injected into the center of political argument by the crisis over Parliament and taxes": *Contested Truths*, 47; see also T. H. Breen, who argued that Otis "advanced what was at the time an extraordinarily radical theory of natural right": "Subjecthood and Citizenship: The Context of James Otis's Radical Critique of John Locke," *New England Quarterly* 71, no. 3 (September 1998): 378–403 (379).

69. James Otis, *A Vindication of the Conduct of the House of Representatives of the Province of the Massachusetts-Bay* (Boston, 1762), 15. Subsequent pagination for this reference is given in-line.

70. Adams gives a good summary of this incident in his letter to William Tudor of April 5, 1818, in *Works of John Adams*, 10:300–12.

71. Otis quoted § 22 in chap. 4 ("Of Slavery") of Locke's *Second Treatise*; then excerpted lengthily from chap. 11, "Of the Extent of the Legislative Power," and chap. 14, "Of Prerogative."

72. Otis, *Rights of the British Colonies*, 12. See also, "The law of nature, was not of man's making, nor is it in his power to mend it, or alter its course. He can only perform and keep, or disobey and break it. The last is never done with impunity, even in this life . . ." (31).

73. Otis writes that "[t]he people will bear a great deal, before they will even murmur against their rulers; but when once they are thoroughly roused, and in earnest, against those who would be glad to enslave them, their power is irrepressible," concluding this passage with a note referring to "Mr. Locke on the Dissolution of Government [*Second Treatise*, chap. 19]." See also the long quote on pp. 33–35, about how "there remains still *in the people a supreme power to remove or alter the legislative*, when they find the *legislative* act contrary to the trust reposed in them," and how the people "will always have a right to preserve, what they have not a power to part with; and to rid themselves of those, who invade this fundamental, sacred, and unalterable law of *self-preservation*, for which they entered into society." Cf. *Second Treatise*, chap. 13, § 149. Otis concludes with another quote from chap. 19 (misidentified as chap. 9), which includes this passage: "Whensoever therefore, the legislative shall transgress this fundamental rule of society [ . . . ] they forfeit the power the *people* had put into their hands for quite contrary ends, and it devolves to the people, who have a right to resume their original liberty, and by the establishment of a new legislative (such as they shall think fit) provide for their own safety and security, which is the end for which they are in society" (§ 222).

74. "Those who expect to find any thing very satisfactory on this subject in particular, or with regard to the law of nature in general, in the writings of such authors as *Grotius* and *Pufendorf* will find themselves much mistaken" (38). See chapter 3.

75. On the reach of Otis's pamphlet, see Elaine K. Ginsberg, who describes it as "the most widely read statement in the period between the passage of the Sugar Act and that of the Stamp Act": "The Patriot Pamphleteers," in *American Literature, 1764–1789: The Revolutionary Years*, ed. Everett H. Emerson (Madison: University of Wisconsin Press, 1997), 19–38 (34). In 1767 John Dickinson sent a copy of his *Letters from a Farmer in Pennsylvania* to Otis, writing, "whenever the Cause of American Freedom is to be vindicated, I look towards the Province of Massachusetts Bay." Letter of December 6, 1767, in *Warren-Adams Letters* (Boston: Massachusetts Historical Society, 1917), 1:3.

76. Francis Bowen, "Life of James Otis," in *The Library of American Biography*, ed. Jared Sparks (Boston: Charles Little & James Brown, 1846), 2:14.

77. See *A Vindication of the British Colonies* (Boston: Edes and Gill, 1765), which praises "Mr. Blackstone's accurate and elegant analysis of the laws of England" (9). As Gerald Stourzh has noted, this was not a description of Blackstone's *Commentaries*, which had not yet crossed the Atlantic, but the citation of his 1756 work: see "William Blackstone: Teacher of Revolution," in

*From Vienna to Chicago and Back: Essays on Intellectual History and Political Thought in Europe and America* (Chicago: University of Chicago Press, 2007), 60–79 (78). On the specific passages quoted by Otis, see Horst Dippel, "Blackstone's *Commentaries* and the Origins of Modern Constitutionalism," in *Re-Interpreting Blackstone's Commentaries: A Seminal Text in National and International Contexts*, ed. Wilfrid Prest (Oxford: Hart, 2009), 199–214 (200).

78. For Adams and Dickinson, see Stourzh, "William Blackstone," 78; Hamilton's reference is in *The Federalist Papers*, no. 84. On Jefferson, see Jessie Allen, "Blackstone in the Twenty-First Century and the Twenty-First Century through Blackstone," in *Re-Interpreting Blackstone's Commentaries*, 227.

79. Edmund Burke, "Speech on Conciliation with America," in *The Works of the Right Honourable Edmund Burke*, 3 vols. (London: Dodsley, 1792), 2:43. My thanks to David Armitage for first bringing this speech to my attention. More generally on this point, see Dippel, "Blackstone's *Commentaries* and the Origins of Modern Constitutionalism."

80. See, e.g., Linda Colley, *Britons: Forging the Nation, 1707–1837* (New Haven, CT: Yale University Press, 2005), 108.

81. The expression, as far as I can tell, appears only in the preliminary "Discourse on the Study of the Law" (1758): "in the northern parts of our own island, where also the municipal laws are frequently connected with the civil, it is difficult to meet with a person of liberal education, who is destitute of a competent knowledge in that science which is to be the guardian of his natural rights and the rule of his civil conduct." William Blackstone, *An Analysis of the Laws of England* (Oxford: Clarendon Press, 1756), xvii–xviii.

82. Blackstone, *Analysis of the Laws of England*, 1.1.6–8, p. 7. On this work, see Wilfrid R. Prest, *William Blackstone: Law and Letters in the Eighteenth Century* (Oxford: Oxford University Press, 2008), 142–44.

83. See esp. *Analysis of the Laws of England*, 1.1.2–5.

84. See notably Charles Phineas Sherman, *Roman Law in the Modern World* (Boston: Boston Book Co., 1917), 1:381. In the *Commentaries*, Blackstone would also cite Jean Domat's "treatise of laws"; on this work, see chapter 5.

85. My thanks, again, to David Armitage for a discussion on the differences between the *Analysis* and the *Commentaries*.

86. For Locke, see *Commentaries on the Laws of England* (Oxford: Clarendon Press, 1765), 1:52, 122, 157, 172, 206, 236, 244. For Grotius, see 1:61, 247, 286, 436. And for Pufendorf (whom Blackstone refers to as "Puffendorf"), 1:59, 251, 436, 438.

87. Blackstone does not cite Montesquieu on natural law matters but draws heavily on the discussion of the English constitution in *The Spirit of Laws* (11.6; see below).

88. *Commentaries*, 1.1, p. 119; emphasis added.

89. *Commentaries*, 1.1, p. 120; emphasis in original. In fact, like many of the American authors above, Blackstone acknowledged that the passage from a state of nature into civil society exacted a toll: "every man, when he enters into society, gives up a part of his natural liberty, as the price of so valuable a purchase" (121). In a later chapter, he even recognized the power of law to restrain at least some natural rights: see *Commentaries* (1766), 2.27, 2:411. But by distinguishing between natural *liberty* and natural rights (as Pufendorf and Locke before him), Blackstone avoided the transfer and abridgment regimes of rights, and emphasized, with Locke, the liberating power of the law: *Commentaries*, 1.1, p. 122; referencing *Second Treatise*, § 57—"where there is no law, there is no freedom."

90. See *An Interesting Appendix to Sir William Blackstone's 'Commentaries on the laws of England'* ([Philadelphia] America: Robert Bell, 1773). More generally, see Iain Hampsher-Monk,

"British Radicalism and the Anti-Jacobins," in *Cambridge History of Eighteenth-Century Political Thought*, ed. Mark Goldie and Robert Wokler (Cambridge: Cambridge University Press, 2006), 660–87.

91. *Commentaries*, 1.1, p. 125. On this point, see Meyler, "Towards a Common Law Originalism."

92. *Commentaries*, 1.1, pp. 140–41; referencing Montesquieu, *Spirit of Laws*, 11.5 (a typo or error, as M.'s discussion of England is in chap. 6).

93. *Commentaries*, 1.1, pp. 137–38.

94. Book 2, on property; book 3, on civil procedure; book 4, on criminal law. This structure mirrors the breakdown of Blackstone's *Analysis*.

95. *Commentaries*, 1.1, p. 140.

96. *Commentaries*, 2.1, pp. 3, 7. *Contra* Locke, however, Blackstone insists on occupancy alone as the primary step in establishing ownership (see p. 8).

97. *Commentaries*, 2.2, p. 18.

98. "All mankind had by the original grant of the Creator a right to pursue and take any fowl or insect of the air, any fish or inhabitants of the waters, and any beast or reptile of the field: and this natural right still continues in every individual, unless where it is restrained by the civil laws of the country." *Commentaries*, 2.26, p. 403.

99. *Commentaries*, 1.1, p. 139. On this topic more generally, see Steven J. Heyman, "Natural Rights and the Second Amendment," *Chicago-Kent Law Review* 76, no. 1 (2000): 237–90 (252–59).

100. The Convention Parliament insisted instead that James II had "abdicated," when he left the throne "vacant": see Steven Pincus, *1688: The First Modern Revolution* (New Haven, CT: Yale University Press, 2009), 284–85.

101. In his discussion of legitimate resistance, Locke quotes the jurist William Barclay: "Self-defence is a part of the law of nature." *Second Treatise*, § 233.

102. *Commentaries*, 1.7, p. 244.

103. See *Second Treatise*, § 166.

104. See notably Edmund S. Morgan and Helen M. Morgan, *The Stamp Act Crisis: Prologue to Revolution*, rev. ed. (Chapel Hill: University of North Carolina Press, 1995).

105. See R. R. Palmer, *The Age of the Democratic Revolution: A Political History of Europe and America, 1760–1800*, rev ed. (Princeton, NJ: Princeton University Press, 2014), 120.

106. Daniel Dulany, *Considerations on the Propriety of Imposing Taxes in the British Colonies* (Annapolis: Jonas Green, 1765; repr., New York: John Holt, 1765; Boston: William M'Alpine, 1766). On this work, see Morgan and Morgan, *Stamp Act Crisis*, chap. 6 (though the Morgans downplay the role of natural rights: see 87–88). Dulany was educated at Cambridge University.

107. Richard Bland, *An Inquiry into the Rights of the British Colonies* (Williamsburg, [VA]: Alexander Purdie, 1766), 26.

108. John Joachim Zubly, *An Humble Enquiry into the Nature of the Dependency of the American Colonies upon the Parliament of Great-Britain* ([Charleston, SC?], 1769), 19. For a very similar argument, see William Hicks, *The Nature and Extent of Parliamentary Power Considered* (Philadelphia: [William and Thomas Bradford?], 1768), 23.

109. See Michael Warner, *The Letters of the Republic: Publication and the Public Sphere in Eighteenth-Century America* (Cambridge, MA: Harvard University Press, 1990); and William B. Warner, *Protocols of Liberty: Communication Innovation and the American Revolution* (Chicago: University of Chicago Press, 2013).

110. On the declaration "genre," see David Armitage, *The Declaration of Independence: A Global History* (Cambridge, MA: Harvard University Press, 2007), 13–15.

111. See Edmund Morgan, *Prologue to Revolution: Sources and Documents on the Stamp Act Crisis, 1764–1766* (Chapel Hill: University of North Carolina Press, 2004), 47–51.

112. *Votes and Proceedings of the House of Representatives of the Province of Pennsylvania* (Philadelphia: B. Franklin, 1765); session of September 21, 1765, p. 68.

113. William Knox, *The Controversy between Great-Britain and Her Colonies Reviewed* (Boston: Mein and Fleeming, 1769), 6–7. Knox was "one of the many sub-ministers in the British bureaucracy who had sought to reform the empire but had been stymied by Whig politicians reluctant to enhance the Crown's power": *The American Revolution: Writings from the Pamphlet Debate 1764–1772*, ed. Gordon S. Wood (New York: Library of America, 2015), pamphlet 16.

114. See the Massachusetts Resolves of October 29, 1765, arts. 1, 2, 12; in Morgan, *Prologue to Revolution*, 56–57. This resolution is also discussed in Knox, *The Controversy between Great-Britain and Her Colonies Reviewed*, 9.

115. "Declaration of Rights and Grievances," preamble; in Morgan, *Prologue to Revolution*, 62.

116. See notably the *Journal of the Honourable House of Representatives, of His Majesty's province of the Massachusetts-Bay* (Boston: Green and Russell, 1768–69), appendix 7. It also features in the minutes of the Pennsylvania, North Carolina, and New Hampshire assemblies.

117. *The Speeches of His Excellency Governor Hutchinson, to the General Assembly of the Massachusetts-Bay* (Boston: Edes and Gill, 1773), 10.

118. *Social Contract*, 3.15.

119. The Assembly's response was given by a committee consisting of William Brattle, Harrison Gray, James Pitts, James Humphrey, and Benjamin Greenleaf. See *Speeches of His Excellency Governor Hutchinson*, 30; emphasis added.

120. *Speeches of His Excellency Governor Hutchinson*, 61.

121. See also the case of Edward Bancroft, who sought to rebut Knox in his *Remarks on the Review of the Controversy between Great Britain and Her Colonies* (New London, Conn., 1769); Bancroft would subsequently become a British spy.

122. See H. T. Dickinson, "Britain's Imperial Sovereignty," in *Britain and the American Revolution*, ed. H. T. Dickinson (London: Routledge, 2014), 64–96 (73 for quote); see also Wood, *Creation of the American Republic*, chap. 5. More recently, see Eric Nelson, *The Royalist Revolution: Monarchy and the American Founding* (Cambridge, MA: Harvard University Press, 2014).

123. Dickinson, "Britain's Imperial Sovereignty," 77.

124. Text reproduced at the Avalon Project of the Yale Law School: http://avalon.law.yale.edu/18th_century/mass_circ_let_1768.asp.

125. Otis, *Rights of the British Colonies*, 37; emphasis in original. For Otis's thoughts on the social contract, see 5–7.

126. Knox, *The Controversy between Great-Britain and Her Colonies Reviewed*, 32.

127. Text available through the Avalon Project at Yale University: http://avalon.law.yale.edu/18th_century/resolves.asp.

128. On Jefferson's debt to the Virginia Declaration, see Pauline Maier, *American Scripture* (New York: Vintage, 1998), 105, 165, and *passim*.

129. "A Declaration of Rights," art. 3. See also the Constitution of Delaware, art. 25: "The common law of England, as-well as so much of the statute law as has been heretofore adopted in practice in this State, shall remain in force, unless they shall be altered by a future law of the legislature." More broadly, on this point see Forrest McDonald: "Twelve of the states provided, by statute or constitution, for the continuation of the common law as it had been received before 1776." *Novus Ordo Seclorum: The Intellectual Origins of the Constitution* (Lawrence: University Press of Kansas, 1985), 40. See also Bailyn, *Ideological Origins*, 196–97.

130. See Akhil Reed Amar, *The Bill of Rights: Creation and Reconstruction* (New Haven, CT: Yale University Press, 1998), chap. 5; see also Rakove, *Original Meanings*, 294–95.

131. See also Virginia, § 8; Pennsylvania, § 9; Massachusetts, art. 15; Vermont, art. 10.

132. *Commentaries on the Laws of England*, 3.23, 3:350.

133. *Commentaries on the Laws of England*, 1.1.

134. See Carl Ubbelohde, *The Vice-Admiralty Courts and the American Revolution*, rev. ed. (Chapel Hill: University of North Carolina Press, 2012).

135. VA § 10, PA § 10, DE § 17, MD § 23, NC § 11, VT § 9, MA § 14.

136. VA § 9, DE § 16, MD § 22, NC § 10, VT § 2.25, MA § 26.

137. VA § 8, PA § 9, DE § 14, MD § 19, NC § 7, VT § 10, MA § 12.

138. See DE § 11, MD § 15, NC § 24.

139. Wood, *Creation of the American Republic*, 271.

140. See Herbert J. Storing, ed., *The Complete Anti-Federalist*, 7 vols. (Chicago: University of Chicago, 1981), 1:70; and Philip Hamburger, "Natural Law, Natural Rights, and American Constitutions," *Yale Law Journal* 102 (1993): 907–60.

141. There were, in fact, a number of motions to do so, including by George Mason, who had drafted the Virginia Declaration: see Wendell Bird, *Press and Speech under Assault: The Early Supreme Court Justices, the Sedition Act of 1798, and the Campaign against Dissent* (Oxford: Oxford University Press, 2016), 28n229.

142. Jeff Broadwater, *George Mason, Forgotten Founder* (Chapel Hill: University of North Carolina Press, 2009), 235. The text of this draft is available in *The Founders' Constitution*, vol. 5, doc. 9: http://press-pubs.uchicago.edu/founders/documents/bill_of_rightss9.html.

143. See, e.g., Amar, *Bill of Rights*.

144. See, e.g., Hon. Diarmuid F. O'Scannlain, "The Natural Law in the American Tradition," *Fordham Law Review* 79 (2011): 1513–28.


## Chapter VII

1. Keith M. Baker, *Inventing the French Revolution: Essays on French Political Culture in the Eighteenth Century* (Cambridge: Cambridge University Press, 1990), 127.

2. On Burke's attitude toward the American Revolution, see notably Richard Bourke, *Empire and Revolution: The Political Life of Edmund Burke* (Princeton, NJ: Princeton University Press, 2015), chap. 6.

3. Edmund Burke, *Reflections on the Revolution in France*, in *Revolutionary Writings*, ed. Iain Hampsher-Monk (Cambridge: Cambridge University Press, 2014), 59, 17, 34.

4. Marcel Gauchet, *La Révolution des droits de l'homme* (Paris: Gallimard, 1989), 41; for a comparison of French and American rights, see 36–59.

5. Gauchet, *Révolution des droits de l'homme*, 19–28.

6. Gauchet, *Révolution des droits de l'homme*, 201.

7. See chapter 6.

8. On the aspirations vs. reality of absolutism, see notably James Collins, *The State in Early Modern France* (Cambridge: Cambridge University Press, 2015). On legal reform movements in Europe, see Harold J. Berman, *Law and Revolution: The Formation of the Western Legal Tradition* (Cambridge, MA: Harvard University Press, 1983); and more generally chapter 5.

9. See Gauchet, *Révolution des droits de l'homme*, 21; see also Lucien Jaume, ed., *Les Déclarations des droits de l'homme* (Paris: Flammarion, 1989).

10. See the discussion of Domat in chapter 5.

11. Again, see chapter 5.

12. Thomas Paine, *Common Sense* (London: Penguin, 1976), 65.

13. To some extent, it informed the "natural republican" utopias of Fénelon or Sylvain Maréchal, though even in these cases, governmental institutions remained crucial: see Dan Edelstein, *The Terror of Natural Right* (Chicago: University of Chicago Press, 2009), part I.

14. See Eric Slauter, *The State as a Work of Art: The Cultural Origins of the Constitution* (Chicago: University of Chicago Press, 2009).

15. I am drawing here on Roland Barthes's definition of political myth as an object that transforms a historical contingency into a natural necessity: see "Myth Today," in *Mythologies* (Paris: Seuil, 1957).

16. Gauchet, *Révolution des droits de l'homme*, chap. 1; this was also François Furet's argument in *Interpreting the French Revolution*, trans. Elborg Forster (Cambridge: Cambridge University Press, 1981). As Samuel Moyn has shown, this interpretation of the Revolution owed a great deal to Claude Lefort: see "On the Intellectual Origins of François Furet's Masterpiece," *Tocqueville Review/La Revue Tocqueville* 29, no. 2 (2008): 1–20.

17. See chapter 3 and, more generally, David A. Bell, *The Cult of the Nation in France: Inventing Nationalism, 1680–1800* (Cambridge, MA: Harvard University Press, 2001).

18. Cf. Harold A. Ellis, *Boulainvilliers and the French Monarchy: Aristocratic Politics in Early Eighteenth-Century France* (Ithaca, NY: Cornell University Press, 1988).

19. Discussed in chapter 3.

20. See Jonathan Israel, *Revolutionary Ideas: An Intellectual History of the French Revolution from The Rights of Man to Robespierre* (Princeton, NJ: Princeton University Press, 2014), 57–58. Israel does not address the demands for a declaration of rights in the *Cahiers*.

21. These *cahiers* were identified by a proximity word search for "déclaration droits" on the ARTFL version of the *Archives parlementaires*: http://artfl-project.uchicago.edu/node/144. This method does not yield exhaustive results.

22. One additional *cahier* was compiled jointly by the nobility and the Third Estate, and one more by all three estates.

23. See [Laclos,] *Instruction donnée par S.A.S. Monseigneur le duc d'Orléans* (Paris, 1789), 4–5. On this work, see Stéphane Rials, *La Déclaration des droits de l'homme et du citoyen* (Paris: Hachette, 1988), 95n59.

24. Sieyès, *Délibérations à prendre pour les assemblées de bailliages*, in [Laclos,] *Instruction donnée*, 36.

25. See Rials, *Déclaration des droits*, 31.

26. All three of his drafts can be found in Rials, *Déclaration des droits*, 528, 567, 590. On Jefferson and Lafayette's collaboration, see notably Dumas Malone, *Jefferson and the Rights of Man*, vol. 2 of *Jefferson in His Time* (1951; Charlottesville: University of Virginia Press, 2006), 223–25.

27. *Archives parlementaires de 1787 à 1860*, ed. M. J. Mavidal et al. (Paris: P. Dupont, 1862–), 4:214; henceforth abbreviated as *AP*. This *cahier* also lamented "l'oubli des droits de l'homme" (4:191), a phrase that would recur in the Preamble of the Declaration ("l'oubli ou le mépris des droits de l'Homme sont les seules causes des malheurs publics et de la corruption des Gouvernements").

28. See Keith M. Baker, *Condorcet: From Natural Philosophy to Social Mathematics* (Chicago: University of Chicago Press, 1975), 265; *AP*, 3:661.

29. "Discours de M. le chevalier Alexandre de Lameth, prononcé à l'assemblée générale du bailliage de Péronne, et imprimé sur la demande des trois ordres," in *AP*, 5:366.

30. See Robert F. Haggard, "The Politics of Friendship: Du Pont, Jefferson, Madison, and the

Physiocratic Dream for the New World," *Proceedings of the American Philosophical Society* 153, no. 4 (2009): 419–40.

31. See Olivier Blanc, "Cercles politiques et 'salons' du début de la Révolution (1789–1793)," *Annales historiques de la Révolution française* 344 (2006): 63–92.

32. Nicholas Hans, "UNESCO of the Eighteenth Century: *La Loge des Neuf Sœurs* and Its Venerable Master, Benjamin Franklin," *Proceedings of the American Philosophical Society* 97, no. 5 (1953): 513–24. Duport may also have been a member (522).

33. See session of August 18, 1789; *AP*, 8:453.

34. See Gilbert Shapiro and John Markoff, *Revolutionary Demands: A Content Analysis of the "Cahiers de Doléances" of 1789* (Stanford, CA: Stanford University Press, 1998), table 14.8, p. 277.

35. See, for example, the *Cahiers de la ville et pays-état d'Arles* (*AP*, 2:57); *Cahier des remontrances de l'ordre de la noblesse du bailliage d'Aval* (*AP*, 2:139); *Cahier des plaintes, doléances et remontrances du clergé du bailliage de Beauvais* (*AP*, 2:287); *Instruction que l'assemblée de l'ordre du clergé du bailliage de Clermont en Beauvoisis remet à son député aux Etats généraux* (*AP*, 2:746); *Cahier du tiers-état de la sénéchaussée de Marsan* (*AP*, 4:34); and *Cahier des vœux, doléances et supplications du tiers-état de la sénéchaussée de Montpellier* (*AP*, 4:49).

36. In a fairly typical example, the Third Estate of Gardanne, near Aix, expressed its desire that "[l]es droits naturels et imprescriptibles de l'homme et du citoyen quel qu'il soit, seront inviolablement reconnus et assurés aux Etats généraux" (*AP*, 6:280). The same formulation can be found in the *Cahier des doléances de la communauté de Carri et le Rouet* (today, Carry-le-Rouet), a neighboring town (*AP*, 6:293).

37. Rials, *Déclaration des droits*, 277n7.

38. *Discours au roi, prononcé à Versailles, par M. l'archevêque de Narbonne, à la clôture de l'assemblée du clergé, le dimanche 27 juillet 1788*; in *AP*, 1:387.

39. *AP*, 2:287.

40. See *AP*, 2:488 and 2:746, respectively.

41. *AP*, 2:486.

42. See the conclusion.

43. *AP*, 2:219. This phrasing reappears in several *cahiers*: see 5:29, 5:220, 5:531, 5:641, 6:15.

44. *AP*, 2:659.

45. Third Estate, Châtellerault, *AP*, 2:691; all three orders, Bayonne, 3:100.

46. Rials, *Déclaration des droits*, 275n5.

47. Sieyès, *Délibérations à prendre*, in [Laclos,] *Instruction donnée*, 32–36.

48. Alexis-François Pison du Galand, in *AP*, 8:135, June 19, 1789.

49. July 27, 1789; *AP*, 8:283.

50. See, for instance, the speech by Talleyrand on July 7, 1789, where he notes how "[d]ans la suite, lorsque la constitution aura été bien affermie, et qu'il existera une déclaration des droits qui pourra servir de boussole aux bailliages, les mandats seront nécessairement beaucoup plus restreints quant à l'objet" (*AP*, 8:201).

51. See, e.g., the report by Champion de Cicé on July 27, 1789, in the name of the constitutional committee: "nous avons cru devoir commencer par l'examen de ces volontés [de nos commettants], consignées dans les cahiers que nous avons pu consulter" (*AP*, 8:281).

52. For more details, see Antoine de Baecque, "'Le choc des opinions': Le débat des droits de l'homme, juillet-août 1789," in *L'An 1 des droits de l'homme*, ed. Antoine de Baecque, Wolfgang Schmale, and Michel Vovelle (Paris: Presses du CNRS, 1989), 7–37 (11).

53. See Rials, *Déclaration des droits*, 120. On Mounier's pre-revolutionary past, see notably Simon Schama, *Citizens* (New York: Vintage, 1989), 272–80.

54. *AP*, 8:217.

55. *AP*, 8:216.

56. See Rials, *Déclaration des droits*, 134–37, 201, 215.

57. July 11, 1789; *AP*, 8:221.

58. July 14, 1789; *AP*, 8:231.

59. See speeches by Malouet, on August 1, 1789 (8:322); Guiot, on August 19 (8:457); and the vicomte de Mirabeau, on August 20 (8:462).

60. For instance, it is in the same terms that the *conventionnels* described the role of the Declaration in 1793: see my *Terror of Natural Right*, chap. 4.

61. July 11, 1789; *AP*, 8:221.

62. "Le comité a cru qu'il serait convenable, pour rappeler le but de notre constitution, de la faire précéder par une déclaration des droits des Hommes; mais de la placer, en forme de préambule, au-dessus des articles constitutionnels, et non de la faire paraître séparément" (*AP*, 8:216).

63. See the comte de Lally-Tollendal, on July 11, 1789 (*AP*, 8:222).

64. See, e.g., Marie-Joseph Chenier, in December 1792 (*AP*, 54:145).

65. For a similar argument, see Lally-Tollendal: "songer encore combien la différence est énorme, d'un peuple naissant qui s'annonce à l'univers, d'un peuple colonial qui rompt les liens d'un gouvernement éloigné, à un peuple antique, immense, l'un des premiers du monde, qui depuis quatorze cents ans s'est donné une forme de gouvernement" (*AP*, 8:222).

66. *Contra* Hannah Arendt, *On Revolution* (New York: Viking, 1963), chap. 5 ("The rupture between king and parliament indeed threw the whole French nation into a 'state of nature'"; 180). On the golden age topos, see my *Terror of Natural Right*, chap. 3. As I show there, Arendt's claim is better suited to the political situation following August 1792, when the monarchy was toppled.

67. *AP*, 8:217.

68. *AP*, 8:221.

69. July 27, 1789; *AP*, 8:281.

70. August 1, 1789; *AP*, 8:318.

71. August 3, 1789; *AP*, 8:334.

72. On the role of sentimentalism during the August 4 debates, see notably William Reddy, *The Navigation of Feeling: A Framework for the History of Emotions* (Cambridge: Cambridge University Press, 2001), 182–84; and more generally Michael Fitzsimmons, *The Night the Old Regime Ended: August 4, 1789, and the French Revolution* (University Park: Penn State University Press, 2003).

73. See Georg Jellinek, *The Declaration of the Rights of Man and of the Citizen*, trans. Max Farrand (New York: Henry Holt, 1901).

74. This right was missing from the first draft that Lafayette shared with Jefferson, though was in the second, unpublished draft of June 1789; see Rials, *Déclaration des droits*, 567. More generally, see Micah Alpaugh, "The Right of Resistance to Oppression: Protest and Authority in the French Revolutionary World," *French Historical Studies* 39, no. 3 (2016): 567–98.

75. See Rials, *Déclaration des droits*, 591. This was an idea that had been in Lafayette's first draft, albeit worded somewhat differently: "Toute souveraineté réside essentiellement dans la nation" (Rials, *Déclaration des droits*, 528).

76. More generally, see J. Kent Wright, "National Sovereignty and the General Will: The Political Program of the Declaration of Rights," in *The French Idea of Freedom: The Old Regime and the Declaration of Rights of 1789*, ed. Dale Van Kley (Stanford, CA: Stanford University Press, 1994), 199–233.

77. For a more detailed discussion of this session, see Rials, *Déclaration des droits*, 134–48.

78. *AP*, 8:282.

79. Art. 19 in Sieyès's draft (Rials, *Déclaration des droits*, 604); it would become part of art. 7.

80. *AP*, 8:340. See Keith M. Baker, "The Idea of a Declaration of Rights," in *The French Idea of Freedom*, ed. Van Kley, 177–82.

81. See, e.g., Rials, *Déclaration des droits*, 162–75.

82. For the French translation, see *Les Devoirs de l'homme et du citoyen: tels qu'ils lui sont prescrits par la loi naturelle*, trans. Jean Barbeyrac (Amsterdam, 1707).

83. See, e.g., Wesley Hohfeld, *Fundamental Legal Concepts* (New Haven, CT: Yale University Press, 1919).

84. *AP*, 8:340.

85. The preamble would indeed refer to both: "que cette Déclaration, constamment présente à tous les Membres du corps social, leur rappelle sans cesse leurs droits et leurs devoirs."

86. Timothy Tackett, *Becoming a Revolutionary: The Deputies of the French National Assembly and the Emergence of a Revolutionary Culture (1789–1790)* (Princeton, NJ: Princeton University Press, 1996), 20.

87. See *AP*, 8:458.

88. The best discussion and analysis of the Sixth Bureau's draft is in Rials, *Déclaration des droits*, 212–17.

89. *L'An 1 des droits de l'homme*, 188.

90. *AP*, 8:489.

91. *AP*, 8:465.

92. "C'est là [dans la Constitution] que sera prononcé le mot sacré et saint de religion catholique," in *L'An 1 des droits de l'homme*, 171. The *Archives parlementaires* do not capture the discussion of article 10 exactly, but this edition contains a much better reconstruction.

93. The wording for the first half of this article came from the comte Boniface de Castellane; the bishop Jean-Baptiste Gobel contributed the second half. Translation from the Avalon Project at Yale University: http://avalon.law.yale.edu/18th_century/rightsof.asp.

94. On property rights in the Declaration, and the French Revolution more generally, see Rafe Blaufarb, *The Great Demarcation: The French Revolution and the Invention of Modern Property* (Oxford: Oxford University Press, 2016), chap. 2.

95. *L'An 1 des droits de l'homme*, 195. The author of this proposal is not listed here, but two years later, Dupont de Nemours identified himself: see *AP*, 29:267 (Aug. 8, 1791). He had made a similar suggestion in the *cahier* he drafted for the Third Estate of Nemours:

> Tout homme dans l'état d'enfance, impuissance, caducité, infirmité, a droit à des secours gratuits de la part des autres hommes; car il n'y a pas un d'entre eux qui n'ait à payer, à cet égard, une dette qui dure autant que sa vie, puisqu'il n'y en a point qui ne doive la vie à une multitude de secours gratuits qu'il a reçus au moins dans son enfance. (*AP*, 4:162)

On the Physiocratic origins of this idea, see chapter 3.

96. See in particular "Les secours publics sont une dette sacrée. La société doit la subsistance aux citoyens malheureux, soit en leur procurant du travail, soit en assurant les moyens d'exister à ceux qui sont hors d'état de travailler" (article 21). The demand for public assistance did not come out of nowhere: it had figured repeatedly in the *Cahiers de doléance*: See, e.g., *AP*, 2:405, 4:20, 4:162, 4:477, 5:394. Some deputies, such as Sieyès, had included them in their draft declarations: see, e.g., Sieyès, *Préliminaire de la constitution* (Versailles: Ph.-D. Pierres, 1789): society "augmente [les moyens particuliers] par le concours inestimable des travaux & des secours publics" (5). See also Stephen P. Marks, "From the 'Single Confused Page' to the 'Decalogue for Five Billion

Persons': The Roots of the Universal Declaration of Human Rights in the French Revolution," *Human Rights Quarterly* 20, no. 3 (1998): 459–514.

97. *AP*, 8:453 (August 18, 1789). Mirabeau acknowledged that "these are not M. the abbé Sieyes' statements." The passage in question appears to come from Mirabeau himself: see the dedication to *De la monarchie prussienne sous Frédéric le Grand* (London, 1788), 2 vols., 1:4–5 (unpaginated). This passage in the dedication is emphasized, so it is possible that Mirabeau was quoting his father (the dedicatee) or Quesnay, though I was unable to locate any other source.

98. See articles 1, 2, 4, 6, 11, 12, 14–17. Some of these rights, however, are expressed collectively: see articles 6, 14, 15.

99. See articles 4–11.

100. See Pierre Lascoumes, Pierrette Poncela, and Pierre Lenoël, *Au nom de l'ordre: une histoire politique du Code pénal* (Paris: Hachette, 1989).

101. Indeed, the American articles banning *ex post facto* laws were similarly phrased: for instance, the Delaware Declaration states, "That retrospective laws, punishing offences committed before the existence of such laws, are oppressive and unjust, and ought not to be made" (§ 11). For comparable language see Maryland, art. 15; and North Carolina, § 24.

102. See the two *projets de déclaration anonymes*, as well as the drafts by Thouret and Gallot, collected in Rials, *Déclaration des droits*, §§ 31, 40, 42, 44.

103. In addition to Mounier's July 9 speech (see above), see Antoine-François Delandine's proposal that the declaration begin with "l'examen des droits de la nation, antérieurs à tout autre, et dont tout autre émane . . ." (August 1, 1789; *AP*, 8:325).

104. See, e.g., the marquis de Sillery: "Une sage Constitution établie, dans laquelle les droits de la nation et ceux du monarque seront irrévocablement fixés, ne sera-t-elle pas le rempart assuré du bonheur des peuples?" (September 7, 1789; *AP*, 8:600).

105. On article 3, see Wright, "National Sovereignty and the General Will."

106. See the discussion in chapter 3.

107. This was the Physiocratic understanding of the nation: see chapter 3.

108. See, e.g., Lynn Hunt, *Inventing Human Rights: A History* (New York: Norton, 2007), 18, 178.

109. *Recueil des actes du Comité de salut public*, ed. François-Alphonse Aulard (Paris: Imprimerie nationale, 1894), 7:493 (October 18, 1793).

110. "Ah ! qu'il est beau, ce siècle où je respire ! . . . / Ce siècle, où de la liberté, / Sur les droits de l'humanité, / Mes yeux ont vu fonder l'empire !" Gabriel Bouquier and Pierre-Louis Moline, *La réunion du dix août, ou L'inauguration de la république française* (Paris: chez R. Vatar, an II [1793?]), 3–4.

111. 18 floréal an II; *Réimpression de l'ancien Moniteur*, 31 vols. (Paris: H. Plon, 1858–63), 20:416.

112. Edelstein, *Terror of Natural Right*, chap. 3.

113. May 8, 1793; in *Œuvres de Maximilien Robespierre*, 10 vols., ed. Société des études robespierristes (Ivry: Phénix éditions, 2000), 9:487–88.

114. November 17, 1789; *AP*, 10:84. For similar uses, see Gaultier de Biauzat's speech on November 19, 1789 (*AP*, 10:123), and the "Adresse des jeunes citoyens de la ville de Bordeaux," March 4, 1790 (*AP*, 12:20).

115. *AP*, 10:35. See also Nicholas Bergasse's letter refusing the *serment civique*: "le serment qu'on ose me commander attente aux droits des législatures, attente aux droits de la nation" (February 6, 1790; *AP*, 11:459).

116. Interestingly, it was the more conservative deputies who continued to invoke national

rights *against* the Assembly: see the abbé Maury, April 19, 1790 (*AP*, 13:108); and the comte de Sérent, May 16, 1790 (*AP*, 15:527).

117. April 12, 1790; *AP*, 12:700. He is referring here to the decree nationalizing Church property, passed on November 2, 1789.

118. August 7, 1790; *AP*, 17:655.

119. September 30, 1790; *AP*, 19:325.

120. October 20, 1790; *AP*, 20:25-27. The creation of this court had been mandated by the National Assembly on July 23, 1789 (*AP*, 8:267). Until the Constitution established the structure and location of this court, the Assembly decided, on October 14, 1789, that crimes of *lèse-nation* would be heard by the Châtelet court (*AP*, 9:445). See Charles Walton, *Policing Public Opinion in the French Revolution: The Culture of Calumny and the Problem of Free Speech* (Oxford: Oxford University Press, 2009), esp. 173-79; and Anne Simonin, *Le Déshonneur dans la République* (Paris: Grasset, 2008), 233-37; see also G. A. Kelly, "From Lèse-Majesté to Lèse-Nation: Treason in Eighteenth-Century France," *Journal of the History of Ideas* 42, no. 2 (1981): 269-86; and Barry Shapiro, *Revolutionary Justice in Paris, 1789-90* (Cambridge: Cambridge University Press, 1993).

121. "C'est un principe incontestable que les droits politiques des citoyens, et par conséquent les droits de la nation, ne peuvent point être soumis ni au pouvoir exécutif, ni au pouvoir administratif. [ ... ] Le Corps législatif au contraire doit juger des qualités politiques et individuelles, parce que ce sont là les véritables intérêts du peuple" (March 5, 1791; *AP*, 23:674). See also March 9, 1791; *AP*, 23:746; and August 10, 1791; *AP*, 29:326-27.

122. September 1, 1791; *AP*, 30:139.

123. August 23, 1791; *AP*, 29:656. At the moment the Constituent Assembly was disbanding, Robespierre charged the revolutionary clubs and societies with defending the rights of the nation (September 29, 1791; *AP*, 31:619). Once he was again in government, however, he again assumed the personal burden of defending these rights: "C'est moi dont le nom fut lié avec les noms de tous ceux qui defendirent avec courage les droits du peuple" (September 25, 1792; *AP*, 52:132-33).

124. *AP*, 53:396, 645; *AP*, 54:150, 179, 266; *AP*, 57:431.

125. December 3, 1792; *AP*, 54:76.

126. See, e.g., Robespierre: "Quelles sont les lois qui la remplacent [la constitution monarchique]? celles de la nature; celle qui est la base de la société même, le salut du peuple, le droit de punir le tyran et celui de le détrôner, c'est la même chose" (*AP*, 54:75). I discuss the place of natural law arguments during the king's trial in *Terror of Natural Right*, chap. 3.

127. During the trial, deputies invoked the rights of the people on at least 23 occasions, compared to 3 references to rights of the nation. Data are taken from volume 54 of the *Archives parlementaires*, which contains most of the speeches delivered on this occasion. By 1793, *droits de la nation* had largely faded from use, reflecting the predominance of *droits du peuple*, which features roughly 16 times more often in the *Archives parlementaires* for that year (214 vs 13 hits, on uncorrected OCR). It would even make it into the Declaration of Rights of 1793: "Quand le gouvernement viole les droits du peuple, l'insurrection est, pour le peuple et pour chaque portion du peuple, le plus sacré des droits et le plus indispensable des devoirs" (art. 35). The people also replaced the nation as source of sovereignty: "La souveraineté réside dans le peuple" (art. 25).

128. *Droits du peuple* features less than 20 times per year in the *Archives parlementaires* between 1789 and 1791; there are 76 instances in 1792, and 129 in 1793. The expression "ennemi* du peuple" appears in 8 laws passed between January 1, 1793, and 9 Thermidor year II (in the Baudouin collection), including the infamous law of 22 prairial. In the sixteenth century, Huguenot revolutionaries already used this term: see chapter 2.

129. See October 9 and 24, 1789, in *AP*, 9:394-96, 517.

130. *Réimpression de l'ancien Moniteur*, 20:695.

131. See my *Terror of Natural Right*, chap. 4.

132. See François Furet, "The Revolution Is Over," in *Interpreting the French Revolution*, trans. Elborg Forster (Cambridge: Cambridge University Press, 1981), 1–79.

133. Gauchet, *Révolution des droits de l'homme*; and Jaume, *Déclarations des droits de l'homme*.

134. Dale Van Kley similarly originates this term in parliamentary discourse, though he only identifies actual uses in the late 1780s: see *The Religious Origins of the French Revolution: From Calvin to the Civil Constitution, 1560–1791* (New Haven, CT: Yale University Press, 1996), 325–26.

135. *Mémoires de l'abbé Terrai . . .* ([Paris?:] A la Chancellerie, 1776), 315. On this text, see Steven L. Kaplan, *Bread, Politics and Political Economy in the Reign of Louis XV*, rev. ed. (New York: Anthem, 2015), 650. In Robert Darnton's ranking (based on sales of the Société typographique de Neuchâtel), Coquereau's book comes in ninth: see *The Forbidden Best-Sellers of Pre-Revolutionary France* (New York: Norton, 1995), 63.

136. *AP*, 4:282.

137. See David A. Bell, *Lawyers and Citizens: The Making of a Political Elite in Old Regime France* (Oxford: Oxford University Press, 1994), 187. As Bell also notes, "Eight of the 36 electors chosen to draft the formal grievances of the city of Paris were barristers."

138. See Rials, *Déclaration des droits*, 256; and Hunt, *Inventing Human Rights*, 133–44.

### Chapter VIII

1. See, respectively, Martti Koskenniemi, *The Gentle Civilizer of Nations: The Rise and Fall of International Law 1870–1960* (Cambridge: Cambridge University Press, 2001); David P. Forsythe, *The Humanitarians: The International Committee of the Red Cross* (Cambridge: Cambridge University Press, 2005); and Susan Pedersen, *The Guardians: The League of Nations and the Crisis of Empire* (New York: Oxford University Press, 2015).

2. I discuss both of these examples below.

3. On the idea of the declaration as speech act, see Keith M. Baker, "The Idea of a Declaration of Rights," in *The French Idea of Freedom: The Old Regime and the Declaration of Rights of 1789*, ed. Dale Van Kley (Stanford, CA: Stanford University Press, 1994), 157. See also Quentin Skinner, "Meaning and Understanding in the History of Ideas," *History and Theory* 8, no. 1 (1969): 3–53.

4. See notably Marco Duranti, *The Conservative Human Rights Revolution: European Identity, Transnational Politics, and the Origins of the European Convention* (Oxford: Oxford University Press, 2016).

5. I borrow this expression from Valentine Zuber, *Le Culte des droits de l'homme* (Paris: Gallimard, 2014).

6. This is an argument that Samuel Moyn has been developing in his many studies on the history of human rights, starting with *The Last Utopia*. I engage with, and cite, his other relevant articles and books below. For a related criticism of Moyn, see Stefan-Ludwig Hoffman, "Human Rights and History," *Past & Present* 232, no. 1 (2016): 279–310.

7. On Maritain, see notably Guðmundur S. Alfreðsson and Asbjørn Eide, eds., *The Universal Declaration of Human Rights: A Common Standard of Achievement* (The Hague: Martinus Nijhoff Publishers, 1999), 46–49; Mary Ann Glendon, *A World Made New: Eleanor Roosevelt and the Universal Declaration of Human Rights* (New York: Random House, 2001), 51, 87, 147. For recent work on the Catholic Church, see Thomas D. Williams, *Who Is My Neighbor? Personalism and the Foundations of Human Rights* (Washington, DC: Catholic University of America Press, 2005); John Witte Jr. and Frank S. Alexander, eds., *Christianity and Human Rights: An*

*Introduction* (Cambridge: Cambridge University Press, 2010); Samuel Moyn, *Christian Human Rights* (Philadelphia: University of Pennsylvania Press, 2015); and Giuliana Chamedes, "Pius XII, Rights Talk, and the Dawn of the Religious Cold War," in *Religion and Human Rights*, ed. Devin Pendas (Oxford: Oxford University Press, forthcoming). See also the responses to Moyn's book in "The Immanent Frame" forum dedicated to it: https://tif.ssrc.org/category/exchanges/book-blog /book-forums/christian-human-rights/, and the *Journal of the History of Ideas* special issue on Christian human rights. Most of my comments here are taken from my contributions to these two collections.

8. Quote from Pius XII, Christmas Day message, 1942; quoted in Moyn, *Christian Human Rights*, 2.

9. Moyn, *Christian Human Rights*, 2–3.

10. For Vitoria, see *De Indis et iure belli relectiones*, ed. Ernest Nys, trans. John P. Bate (Washington, DC: Carnegie Institution, 1917); and Anthony Pagden, "Dispossessing the Barbarian: The Language of Spanish Thomism and the Debate over the Property Rights of the American Indians," in *The Languages of Political Theory in Early-Modern Europe*, ed. Anthony Pagden (Cambridge: Cambridge University Press, 1987). On Soto, see Annabel Brett: "Soto, while preserving this objective sense of right [found in Aquinas] also uses the subjective sense which gives rights of action to individuals, and he takes over from Aquinas's discussion of natural *law* his most fundamental natural *right*, the right of preserving one's own being." As she goes on to note, for Soto, this right "always figures as the right that overrides every other right [ . . . ] it can never be 'trumped.' " *Liberty, Right and Nature: Individual Rights in Later Scholastic Thought* (Cambridge: Cambridge University Press, 1997), 21. For Suárez, see *On the Laws and God the Lawgiver*, in *Selections from Three Works of Suárez*, 2 vols., trans. and ed. Gwladys L. Williams et al. (Oxford: Clarendon Press, 1944), 1:30 (1.3.9); and Brian Tierney, *The Idea of Natural Rights: Studies on Natural Rights, Natural Law, and Church Law, 1150–1625* (Atlanta: Scholars Press, 1997), chap. 12.

11. See Jacques Maritain, *The Rights of Man and Natural Law*, in *Christianity and Democracy, the Rights of Man and Natural Law*, rev. ed. (San Francisco: Ignatius Press, 2011), 103; and for Moyn, *Christian Human Rights*, 83 (see also: "the Thomist movement had [ . . . ] long and unanimously rejected modern rights").

12. Commission pontificale "Justitia et pax," *L'Eglise et les droits de l'homme* (Vatican, 2011), 15.

13. *Adeo nota*, in *Collection générale des brefs et instructions de Notre Très-Saint Père le Pape Pie VI, relatifs à la Révolution françoise*, 2 vols., ed. N. S. Guillon (Paris: Le Clere, 1798), 2:38. On this encyclical, see notably Mary Elsbernd, "Rights Statements: A Hermeneutical Key to Continuing Development in Magisterial Teaching," *Ephemerides Theologicae Lovanienses* 62, no. 4 (1986): 308–32; Gérard Pelletier, *Rome et la Révolution française: la théologie et la politique du Saint-Siège devant la Révolution française, 1789–1799* (Rome: École française de Rome, 2004); and Williams, *Who Is My Neighbor?*, 33.

14. For a tendential, yet detailed, history of Avignon during the French Revolution, see Charles L. Souvay, "The French Papal States during the Revolution," *Catholic Historical Review* 8, no. 4 (1923): 485–96 (488). More recently, see Edward Kolla, "The French Revolution, the Union of Avignon, and the Challenges of National Self-Determination," *Law and History Review* 31, no. 4 (2013): 717–47; and also Kolla, *Sovereignty, International Law, and the French Revolution* (Cambridge: Cambridge University Press, 2017).

15. See Souvay, "French Papal States during the Revolution," 487.

16. *Adeo nota*, 2:70.

17. See Dale Van Kley, *The Religious Origins of the French Revolution: From Calvin to the Civil Constitution, 1560–1791* (New Haven, CT: Yale University Press, 1996); and Nigel Aston,

*Religion and Revolution in France, 1780-1804* (Washington, DC: Catholic University of America Press, 2004).

18. Translation (modified) from the Avalon Project: http://avalon.law.yale.edu/18th_century /rightsof.asp. Pius acknowledges that the Declaration granted citizens the right "not to be disturbed for religious matters" (turbari scilicet circa religionem non debeat), and also to "think, discuss, write, and publish" whatever they wished (quidquid velit, opinari, loqui, scribere, ac typis etiam evulgare): *Quod aliquantum,* in *Collection générale des brefs et instructions,* ed. Guillon, 1:124.

19. *Quod aliquantum,* 124-28.

20. See *Quod aliquantum:* "ad pristinum civilem statum redintegrentur" (130).

21. See *Allocutio habita in Consistorio secreto,* March 9, 1790, in *Collection générale des brefs et instructions,* ed. Guillon, 1:2.

22. See Umberto Benigni, "Spedalieri, Nicola," in *Catholic Encyclopedia,* ed. Charles G. Herbermann et al. (New York: Robert Appleton, 1912), 14:213; Bernard Plongeron, *Théologie et politique au siècle des Lumières (1770-1820)* (Geneva: Droz, 1973); Hanns Gross, *Rome in the Age of Enlightenment: The Post-Tridentine Syndrome and the Ancien Regime* (Cambridge: Cambridge University Press, 1990), 262-63; Pelletier, *Rome et la Révolution française;* and Dale Van Kley, "From the Catholic Enlightenment to the Risorgimento: The Exchange between Nicola Spedalieri and Pietro Tamburini, 1791-1797," *Past and Present* 224 (2014): 109-62.

23. As Pelletier writes, Spedalieri enjoyed "protection in high places": *Rome et la Révolution française,* 253; Van Kley speaks of "unofficial papal sponsorship" in "From the Catholic Enlightenment to the Risorgimento," 122.

24. Spedalieri, *De' diritti dell'uomo* (Assisi [Rome], 1791), 81, 93; Pelletier, *Rome et la Révolution française,* 253. On Mariana, see chapter 2. A critical "exam" of Spedalieri found in the archives of the Congregation for the Doctrine of the Faith underscores this point. Written by Francesco Forti, and dedicated to Tommaso Maria Mamachi (the censor who had refused to grant the original imprimatur), this assessment mainly focuses on Spedalieri's "scandalous" argument that the people can overthrow their ruler ("S. Tomaso non ha gianmai insegnata la dottrina della deposizione de' sovrani"). On the topic of rights, however, Forti is laudatory: "La definizione è ottima . . ." See *Esame de' Diritti dell' uomo di Nicola Spedalieri,* in *Censorum librorum ab anno 1803, A.D. 1806,* ACDF C.L. 1803-1806 3 (16 and 49, respectively).

25. Benigni, "Spedalieri, Nicola," 213.

26. Spedalieri, *De' diritti dell'uomo,* 346.

27. See Plongeron, *Théologie et politique au siècle des Lumières,* 122; and Van Kley, "From the Catholic Enlightenment to the Risorgimento," 123.

28. Elsbernd, "Rights Statements," 309-10.

29. Pius IX, *Respicientes,* in *Acta Sanctae Sedis* 6 (1870): 136-45 (142).

30. Leo XIII, *Rerum novarum,* paras. 15, 51.

31. See Ernest L. Fortin, *Human Rights, Virtue, and the Common Good: Untimely Meditations on Religion and Politics,* ed. J. Brian Benestad (Lanham, MD: Rowman & Littlefield, 1996), 191; and Witte and Alexander, *Christianity and Human Rights.* Moyn alludes to this encyclical but does not discuss how its contents foreshadow Pius XI's own pronouncements: see his *Christian Human Rights,* 76.

32. For the original Italian, I consulted the third edition, which contains many additions to the original 1890 edition: Pasquale Fiore, *Il Diritto internazionale codificato a la sua sanzione giuridica* (Turin: Unione Tipografico editrice, 1900). An English translation, based on the fifth edition, appeared in 1918: *International Law Codified and Its Legal Sanction: Or, The Legal*

*Organization of the Society of States*, trans. Edwin Borchard (New York: Baker, Voorhis and Co, 1918). On this text, see Koskenniemi, *Gentle Civilizer of Nations*, 54–57. See also Duranti, *Conservative Human Rights Revolution*, 68–69.

33. See Fiore, *International Law Codified*, §§ 67–69 (109), § 10 (30).

34. "All the acts of the great French Revolution, and of those revolutions which succeeded and imitated it, were a consequence of the *Declaration of the Rights of Man*": Giuseppe Mazzini, *The Duties of Man* (London: Chapman & Hall, 1862), 4; the Italian original was published in 1860. See also Samuel Moyn, "Giuseppe Mazzini in (and beyond) the History of Human Rights," in *Revisiting the Origins of Human Rights*, ed. Pamela Slotte and Miia Halme-Tuomisaari (Cambridge: Cambridge University Press, 2015).

35. David Armitage, *The Declaration of Independence: A Global History* (Cambridge, MA: Harvard University Press, 2007).

36. Linda Colley, "Empires of Writing: Britain, America and Constitutions, 1776–1848," *Law and History Review* 32, no. 2 (2014): 237–66.

37. See chapter 2, and more generally Quentin Skinner, *The Foundations of Modern Political Thought*, vol. 2 (Cambridge: Cambridge University Press, 1978); and Francis Oakley, *The Conciliarist Tradition: Constitutionalism in the Catholic Church 1300–1870* (Oxford: Oxford University Press, 2003).

38. Vicenzo Ferrone, *Storia dei diritti dell'uomo: L'Illuminismo e la costruzione del linguaggio politico dei moderni* (Rome: Laterza, 2014), esp. 292–356.

39. Vincenzo Ferrone, *The Politics of Enlightenment: Constitutionalism, Republicanism, and the Rights of Man in Gaetano Filangieri*, trans. Sophus Reinert (London: Anthem Press, 2014). Filangieri's *Scienza della legislazione* (1783–86) was translated as *La science de la législation*, 6 vols., trans. J.-A. Gallois (Paris: Cuchet, 1786–91) and would be cited repeatedly in the National Assembly.

40. Lynn Hunt, *Inventing Human Rights: A History* (New York: Norton, 2007), 177. On this point, see also Samuel Moyn, "On the Genealogy of Morals," in *Human Rights and the Uses of History* (London: Verso, 2014), 13–14. In a more recent text, Hunt also pointed to republican constitutionalism as a source of rights talk in the nineteenth century: "Revolutionary Rights," in *Revisiting the Origins of Human Rights*, ed. Slotte and Halme-Tuomisaari, 116.

41. As claimed in Samuel Moyn, *The Last Utopia: Human Rights in History* (Cambridge, MA: Belknap Press of Harvard University Press, 2010), 26.

42. See, e.g., Jon Elster and Rune Slagstad, eds., *Constitutionalism and Democracy* (Cambridge: Cambridge University Press, 1988); see also Jan-Erik Lane, *Constitutions and Political Theory* (Manchester: Manchester University Press, 1996), esp. 137–42.

43. As William Schabas notes, this is a fairly standard clause in human rights conventions: see *The European Convention on Human Rights: A Commentary* (Oxford: Oxford University Press, 2015), 84.

44. Moyn makes this point (in these terms) most clearly in "Giuseppe Mazzini in (and beyond) the History of Human Rights," 119–39.

45. Charles Walton, *Policing Public Opinion in the French Revolution: The Culture of Calumny and the Problem of Free Speech* (Oxford: Oxford University Press, 2009).

46. Human Rights Watch, for instance, routinely issues statements condemning nations for violating the right to a fair trial. See, more generally, Helen Stacy, *Human Rights for the 21st Century: Sovereignty, Civil Society, Culture* (Stanford, CA: Stanford University Press, 2009).

47. See notably Laurent Dubois, *Avengers of the New World: The Story of the Haitian Revolution* (Cambridge, MA: Harvard University Press, 2004), 242–46.

48. See in general see John Lynch, *The Spanish American Revolutions, 1808–1826* (New York: Norton, 1986).

49. See Anthony McFarlane, *Colombia Before Independence: Economy, Society, and Politics under Bourbon Rule* (Cambridge: Cambridge University Press, 1978), 285–87.

50. This declaration is available on Wikisource: https://es.wikisource.org/wiki/Firma_del _Acta_de_la_Declaraci%C3%B3n_de_Independencia_de_Venezuela.

51. *Venezuelan Declaration of Independence and Constitution* (Longman and Co., 1812), 248. Available online: https://scholarship.rice.edu/jsp/xml/1911/9253/1/aa00032.tei.html#div2030.

52. See Jaime E. Rodríguez O., *The Independence of Spanish America* (Cambridge: Cambridge University Press, 1998), 51.

53. See Lynch, *Spanish American Revolutions*, 197.

54. In *El Libertador: Writings of Simón Bolívar*, trans. Frederick H. Fornoff, ed. David Bushnell (Oxford: Oxford University Press, 2003), 6.

55. On this constitution, see Lynch, *Spanish American Revolutions*, 246ff.

56. Constitución de las Provincias Unidas de Sudamérica, available online: https://es.wiki source.org/wiki/Constituci%C3%B3n_de_la_Naci%C3%B3n_Argentina_(1819). Almost all of the "particular rights" found in the 1819 Constitution would be repeated in the 1826 Constitution, in the eighth section on "Disposiciones generales."

57. See *Constitutive Acts of the Mexican Federation* (Mexico, 1824), art. 30; p. 65. The *Acta Constitutiva* (promulgated in January 1824) served as a draft from the Federal Constitution of the United Mexican States (ratified by Congress in October 1824). On these documents, see George Athan Billias, *American Constitutionalism Heard Round the World, 1776–1989: A Global Perspective* (New York: NYU Press, 2009), 130.

58. In *Primeras constituciones latinoamericanas* (Barcelona: Linkgua, 2017), 453.

59. Translation in *The Mexican Constitution of 1917 Compared with the Constitution of 1857*, trans. and ed. H. N. Branch (Philadelphia: American Academy of Political and Social Science, 1917).

60. See Richard Herr, "The Constitution of 1812 and the Spanish Road to Parliamentary Monarchy," in *Revolution and the Meanings of Freedom in the Nineteenth Century*, ed. Isser Woloch (Stanford, CA: Stanford University Press, 1996), 65–102.

61. For some differences between the French and Spanish constitutions, see Nigel Townson, "Anticlericalism and Secularization: A European Exception?" in *Is Spain Different? A Comparative Look at the 19th and 20th Centuries*, ed. Nigel Townson (Eastbourne, UK: Sussex Academic Press, 2015), chap. 3.

62. This article is a near-direct translation of art. 11 of the DRMC: "The free communication of ideas and opinions is one of the most precious of the rights of man." The Portuguese Constitution can be accessed online: https://www.parlamento.pt/Parlamento/Documents/CRP-1822.pdf. See Gabriel B. Paquette, *Imperial Portugal in the Age of Atlantic Revolutions: The Luso-Brazilian World, c. 1770–1850* (Cambridge: Cambridge University Press, 1998), esp. 133–34.

63. Costituzione della Repubblica romana (Liber Liber Electronic edition, 1999): http://www .liberliber.it/mediateca/libri/r/repubblica_romana_1849/costituzione_della_repubblica_etc/pdf /costit_p.pdf.

64. 1848 French Constitution online: https://fr.wikisource.org/wiki/Constitution_du_4 _novembre_1848. See Zuber, *Culte des droits de l'homme*.

65. Samuel Moyn, "The Universal Declaration of Human Rights of 1948 in the History of Cosmopolitanism," *Critical Inquiry* 40, no. 4 (2014): 365–84 (372).

66. Typically, social rights are described as a late development of political rights: see, for

instance, Stein Kuhnle and Anne Sander: "Prior decades had seen the spread of democracy and political rights. Directly or indirectly, these now smoothed the way for social rights": "The Emergence of the Western Welfare State," in *The Oxford Handbook of the Welfare State*, ed. Francis G. Castles, Stephan Leibfried, Jane Lewis, Herbert Obinger, and Christopher Pierson (Oxford: Oxford University Press, 2010), 63. On social naturalism, see chapters 4–5.

67. See, e.g., Stephen P. Marks, "From the 'Single Confused Page' to the 'Decalogue for Five Billion Persons': The Roots of the Universal Declaration of Human Rights in the French Revolution," *Human Rights Quarterly* 20, no. 3 (1998): 459–514; and Rory O'Connell, "Recovering the History of Human Rights: Public Finances and Human Rights," in *Human Rights and Public Finance: Budgets and the Promotion of Economic and Social Rights*, ed. Aoife Nolan, Rory O'Connell, and Colin Harvey (Oxford: Hart Publishing, 2013), 107–22 (115).

68. "Il sera créé et organisé une Instruction publique commune à tous les citoyens, gratuite à l'égard des parties d'enseignement indispensables pour tous les hommes . . ." French Constitution of 1791, title 1. Camille Bloch, in his classic study *L'assistance et l'état en France à la veille de la Révolution* (Paris: Alphonse Picard, 1908), is one of the few to point to this Constitution as a source of social rights (ii).

69. See chapter 3, notably on Turgot.

70. See, e.g., Bernard Poyet, *Mémoire sur la nécessité de transférer et reconstruire l'Hôtel-Dieu de Paris* (Paris, 1785); and Jean-Sylvain Bailly's reports in response to Poyet's proposals: discussed in Edwin Burrows Smith, "Jean-Sylvain Bailly: Astronomer, Mystic, Revolutionary 1736–1793," *Transactions of the American Philosophical Society* 44, no. 4 (1954): 427–538 (501–6).

71. As Stephen Marks observed, in the eighteenth century, "the essence of these [social and economic] rights involves distributive justice": "From the 'Single Confused Page,'" 503. In his "Fondation" article, Turgot does however write, "Le pauvre a des droits incontestables sur l'abondance du riche" (73): see chapter 3.

72. See Christopher Guyver, *The Second French Republic 1848–1852: A Political Reinterpretation* (London: Palgrave Macmillan, 2016), 151–53.

73. See Kees van Kersbergen and Barbara Vis, *Comparative Welfare State Politics: Development, Opportunities, and Reform* (Cambridge: Cambridge University Press, 1998), 38–39; Kuhnle and Sander, "Emergence of the Western Welfare State," chap. 5; and Manfred Nowak, *Human Rights or Global Capitalism: The Limits of Privatization* (Philadelphia: University of Pennsylvania Press, 2017), 14–15.

74. *Rerum novarum* (1891), § 33; English translation: http://w2.vatican.va/content/leo-xiii/en /encyclicals/documents/hf_l-xiii_enc_15051891_rerum-novarum.html.

75. "Justice is the constant and perpetual will to give to each his due [ius suum cuique tribuens]": *Institutes*, 1.1.

76. See Gaston V. Rimlinger, *Welfare Policy and Industrialization in Europe, America, and Russia* (New York: John Wiley, 1971), chap. 3.

77. In general, see Dzovinar Kévonian, "Les juristes, la protection des minorités, et l'internationalisation des Droits de l'homme: le cas de la France (1919–1939)," *Relations internationales* 149, no. 1 (2012): 57–72.

78. Fiore, *International Law Codified*, § 241; and Fiore, *Diritto internazionale codificato*, § 491 (1890 ed.).

79. See, e.g., Gabriella Silvestrini, "Justice, War and Inequality: The Unjust Aggressor and the Enemy of the Human Race in Vattel's Theory of the Law of Nations," *Grotiana* 31 (2010): 44–68. Fiore cites Vattel on two occasions: see *International Law Codified*, §§ 114, 1421.

80. See, e.g., Grotius: "Kings . . . have a Right to exact Punishments, not only for Injuries

committed against themselves, or their Subjects, but likewise, for those which do not peculiarly concern them, but which are, in any Persons whatsoever, grievous Violations of the Law of Nature or Nations." *The Rights of War and Peace*, trans. from Barbeyrac's 1724 edition, ed. Richard Tuck (Indianapolis: Liberty Fund, 2005), 2.20.40 (p. 1021).

81. From a speech at the National Assembly on September 18, 1789; *AP*, 9:33.

82. Fiore, *Diritto internazionale codificato*, § 29; quote not found in first edition. The Borchard English translation takes this quote as its epigraph; it also appears at §§ 38, 425, 556.

83. On André Mandelstam, see Jan Herman Burgers, "The Road to San Francisco: The Revival of the Human Rights Idea in the Twentieth Century," *Human Rights Quarterly* 14, no. 4 (1992): 447–77; Paul Gordon Lauren, *The Evolution of International Human Rights: Visions Seen*, rev. ed. (Philadelphia: University of Pennsylvania Press, 2013), 114; Dzovinar Kévonian, "André Mandelstam and the Internationalization of Human Rights (1869–1949)," in *Revisiting the Origins of Human Rights*, ed. Slotte and Halme-Tuomisaari, 239–66; and Helmut Philipp Aust, "From Diplomat to Academic Activist: André Mandelstam and the History of Human Rights," *European Journal of International Law* 25, no. 2 (2014): 1105–21.

84. On the Institut de droit international, see Koskenniemi, *Gentle Civilizer of Nations*, chap. 1. The best source for biographical information on Mandelstam is Kévonian, "André Mandelstam."

85. André Mandelstam, *Le Sort de l'empire Ottoman* (Lausanne: Payot, 1917), 445–47.

86. Mandelstam, *Sort de l'empire Ottoman*, 574; see also 584.

87. See Burgers, "The Road to San Francisco," 452–53; and Kévonian, "André Mandelstam," 259–60.

88. André Mandelstam, "La Déclaration des Droits Internationaux de l'Homme," *Esprit International: The International Mind* 4, no. 14 (1930): 232–43.

89. See George Finch, "The International Rights of Man," *American Journal of International Law* 35, no 41 (1941): 662–65 (663–64); cited in Moyn, *Last Utopia*, 294n7.

90. See John Peters Humphrey, who mentions the draft by the Institut de droit international as one of those he consulted: *Human Rights and the United Nations: A Great Adventure* (Dobbs Ferry, NY: Transnational Publishers, 1984), 32.

91. See Dzovinar Kévonian, "Question des réfugiés, droits de l'homme: éléments d'une convergence pendant l'entre-deux-guerres," *Matériaux pour l'histoire de notre temps* 72 (2003): 40–49 (42–43); Stéphane Pinon, "Boris Mirkine-Guetzévitch et la diffusion du droit constitutionnel," *Droits* 46, no. 2 (2007): 183–212; and Moyn, *Christian Human Rights*, 28–33.

92. On these Russian and French leagues, see below.

93. Boris Mirkine-Guetzévitch, "Dans les prisons soviétiques," *Cahiers des droits de l'homme* 25, no. 13 (1925): 299–300.

94. "Conscience" would feature prominently in the UDHR, appearing both in the Preamble ("disregard and contempt for human rights have resulted in barbarous acts which have outraged the conscience of mankind"), and in article 1 ("All human beings are born free and equal in dignity and rights. They are endowed with reason and conscience and should act towards one another in a spirit of brotherhood.")

95. Boris Mirkine-Guetzévitch, "Les droits de l'homme en russie soviétique," *CDH* 26, no. 20 (1926): 459–63.

96. Boris Mirkine-Guetzévitch, *Les Constitutions de l'Europe nouvelle*, rev. ed. (1928; Paris: Delagrave, 1930). This same paragraph also appears in "Les nouvelles tendances du droit constitutionnel," *Revue du droit public* 45, no. 1 (1928): 5–53 (42). This article would later be incorporated as the first chapter in a book-length study of the same name: *Les Nouvelles tendances du droit constitutionnel* (Paris: M. Giard, 1931).

97. In addition to *Constitutions de l'Europe nouvelle,* see also the volume Mirkine-Guetzévitch coedited with Alphonse Aulard, *Les Déclarations des Droits de l'Homme: Textes constitutionnels concernant les droits de l'homme et les garanties des libertés individuelles dans tous les pays* (Paris: Payot, 1929). Michel Rosenfeld and András Sajó credit Mirkine-Guetzévitch as the field's founder: see introduction to *The Oxford Handbook of Comparative Constitutional Law* (Oxford: Oxford University Press, 2012), 5; see also, in the same volume, Laurence Morel: "These comments by Mirkine-Guetzévitch written in 1931 have not lost their timeliness" (on referenda), in "Referendum," 501–28 (527).

98. Mirkine-Guetzévitch, *Constitutions de l'Europe nouvelle,* 5, 34; repeated in "Les nouvelles tendances du droit constitutionnel," 39.

99. "Presque toutes les constitutions nouvelles donnent une liste détaillée des droits des citoyens": Mirkine-Guetzévitch, "Les nouvelles tendances du droit constitutionnel," 40.

100. Following the French Revolution (described as the "source fondamentale du droit constitutionnel moderne"), human and civil rights were incorporated into constitutions, "avec l'obligation correspondante pour l'État de respecter ces droits et de les garantir": Mirkine-Guetzévitch, *Nouvelles tendances du droit constitutionnel,* 82–83.

101. "Les historiens de la Déclaration des Droits ont raison d'insister sur le caractère mobile de la liste française des libertés individuelles," Mirkine-Guetzévitch writes, referring to a work by Alphonse Aulard that I was unable to track down (*L'Evolution de la Déclaration des Droits de l'Homme,* 1927; non-existent in the WorldCat and BnF catalogs): see *Nouvelles tendances du droit constitutionnel,* 38, 84–88. Moyn offers a somewhat different reading of Mirkine-Guetzévitch's constitutionalism in *Christian Human Rights,* 30.

102. Mirkine-Guetzévitch and Aulard, *Déclarations des Droits de l'Homme,* 7.

103. See Emmanuel Naquet, "La Ligue des droits de l'Homme: une association en politique (1898–1840)" (PhD diss., Institut d'études politiques de Paris, 2005); and Naquet, "Un républicain en droits de l'Homme: le cas du philosophe-sociologue Célestin Bouglé," *Les Études Sociales* 165, no. 1 (2017): 6–30. See also William Irvine, *Between Justice and Politics: The Ligue des Droits de l'Homme, 1898–1945* (Stanford, CA: Stanford University Press, 2007). As Irvine notes, this name was originally adopted by a group of French politicians in 1888 to defend republican values in the face of General Boulanger's threatened coup (5).

104. Naquet, "La Ligue des droits de l'Homme," 77. This attachment to French Revolutionary principles was further underscored by Aulard's participation in the LDH.

105. Irvine, *Between Justice and Politics,* 1.

106. Naquet, "La Ligue des droits de l'Homme," 433; and Naquet,, "L'action de la Fédération internationale des Ligues des droits de l'Homme (FIDH) entre les deux guerres," *Matériaux pour l'histoire de notre temps* 95, no. 3 (2009): 53–64 (55).

107. See Zuber, *Culte des droits de l'homme,* 252ff.

108. Moyn, *Last Utopia,* 38; see also Moyn, "Universal Declaration of Human Rights," 371. Naquet also challenges Moyn on this point: see his review of *Last Utopia* in *Annales: Histoire, Sciences sociales* 69, no. 3 (2015): 801–3.

109. Moyn, *Christian Human Rights,* 27, 31. See also Moyn, *Last Utopia,* 64–66.

110. *Bulletin officiel de la Ligue des droits de l'Homme* (March 1, 1901); emphasis added; quoted in Naquet, "L'action de la Fédération internationale," 53.

111. Irvine, *Between Justice and Politics,* 1.

112. See Emmanuel Naquet, "Paix, humanitaire et droits de l'homme: Notes sur des acteurs de la société civile au tournant des XIXe et XXe siècles," *Cahiers d'histoire: Revue d'histoire critique* 127 (2015): 33–50.

113. In Naquet, "L'action de la Fédération internationale," 56 (Annex); emphasis added. A version in the archives of the FIDH reads somewhat differently, omitting the specific reference to 1789 and 1793: see Archives de la Ligue des Droits de l'Homme (ALDH), Bibliothèque de Documentation Internationale Contemporaine (BDIC), F delta res 798/54, "Statuts de la fédération." On the FIDH, see also Naquet, "La Ligue des droits de l'Homme," 431ff. An earlier attempt to found an international federation had foundered in 1915.

114. Quoted in Emile Kahn, "L'Action de la Ligue pour la paix," *CDH* 25, no. 24 (1925): 555–72 (566). Again, an archived version reads somewhat differently: "Ce qui nous unit, c'est le respect des Droits de la personne humaine." See ALDH, BDIC, F delta res 798/54, "Appel aux Peuples pour les Droits de l'Homme et la Paix," art. 6.

115. See Moyn, "The Secret History of Human Dignity," in *Christian Human Rights*, chap. 1.

116. Moyn, *Christian Human Rights*, 69.

117. See, e.g., the passage cited above, Fiore, *Diritto internazionale codificato*, § 491 (1890 ed.). He also invokes the "personalità dell'uomo."

118. See, respectively, Amédée Dunois: "Vera et ses amis réunissaient autour d'eux des paysans ou des ouvriers, leur apprenaient à lire, les initiaient à la notion des droits sacrés de toute personne humaine": "A propos de Vera Zassoulitch," *Bulletin communiste* 2, no. 31 (1921): 509–11; Antoine Pillet, *Principes de droit international privé* (Paris: Pedone, 1903); and *Etats généraux du féminisme* (Paris, 1929), 167.

119. See also Victor Basch's comment: "il n'y a pas les droits 'de l'homme,' mais seulement les droits 'de l'être humain.' Il y a des citoyens, mais aussi des citoyennes, il faut donc indiquer par un moyen quelconque que l'on entend légiférer pour la femme aussi bien que pour l'homme." In *CDH*, January 20, 1933, 36.

120. See Naquet, "La Ligue des droits de l'Homme," 193; and Irvine, *Between Justice and Politics*, 68 and *passim*.

121. Meeting of the executive council of the FIDH on January 20,1930: ALDH, BDIC, F delta res 798/54, "Comité internationale, Séance du 20 janvier." This meeting is mentioned in Kévonian, "André Mandelstam," 262.

122. ALDH, BDIC, F delta res 798/54, "Compte-rendu de la séance du Conseil du 26 janvier 1931."

123. The minutes of this Congress can be found in *CDH*, January 20, 1933. Subsequent in-line quotes in this paragraph are taken from this source.

124. See Naquet, "La Ligue des droits de l'Homme," 731. For Mandelstam's intervention, see *CDH*, January 20, 1933, 33–35. On Mandelstam's own proposal for a new international declaration, and on Mirkine-Guetzévitch's *CDH* articles, see above.

125. See ALDH, BDIC, F delta res 798/54, "Convocation, 22 fevrier 1936." See also Naquet, "La Ligue des droits de l'Homme"; Naquet, "L'action de la Fédération internationale," 62; and Kévonian, "André Mandelstam," 262. The text of this declaration can be found in *CDH*, May 20, 1936, 327.

126. *CDH*, May 20, 1936, 323–26. See also Georges-Etienne's speech at the LDH's Dijon Congress that year: Ligue des droits de l'Homme, *Le Congrès national de 1936: compte rendu sténographique (Dijon, juillet 1936)* (Paris: LDH, 1936), 218–20. Mirkine-Guetzévitch had originally been chosen by the LDH to represent France at the Luxembourg conference, but he declined (*Congrès national de 1936*, 206).

127. See Naquet, "La Ligue des droits de l'Homme," 432.

128. *CDH*, May 20, 1936, 324; see also LDH, *Congrès national de 1936*, 225–26. Another draft proposal, proposed by the Alpes-Maritime delegation, made this complementary approach even

more explicit, by incorporating all its changes to the original seventeen articles of the 1789 Declaration (260–63). See also Naquet, "La Ligue des droits de l'Homme," 733.

129. LDH, *Congrès national de 1936*, 264.

130. The modified proposal was published in the *CDH*, June 10, 1936, 387–88.

131. See LDH, *Congrès national de 1936*, 218 ff. [GALLICA]. For the final text of the Complement, see 418–22.

132. See, e.g., Glenda Sluga, "René Cassin: *Les droits de l'homme* and the Universality of Human Rights, 1945–1966," in *Human Rights in the Twentieth Century*, ed. Stefan-Ludwig Hoffmann (Cambridge: Cambridge University Press, 2011), 107–24 (110). It is true that LDH members played a leading role in the FIDH (for example, Victor Basch, president of the LDH, presided over the Luxembourg Congress): see Naquet, "La Ligue des droits de l'Homme," 434–36. But demands for a new declaration had undeniably come from all across Europe, as the 1930–31 executive council debates demonstrate (see above). In 1935, at the Hyères Congress, the LDH had signaled its own desire to prepare a new Declaration of Human Rights: see LDH, *Congrès national de 1936*, 276.

133. Some of the *ligueurs* argued in favor of this method: see in particular the counterproposal by Gustave Rodrigues: *Congrès national de 1936*, 237–44.

134. In its conclusion, the *Complément* issued a call "to the world, on the model of the French Revolution, to bring about the reign of reason and fraternity."

135. See Emmanuel Naquet, "La Ligue des droits de l'Homme et l'école de la République dans la première moitié du XXe siècle," *Histoire@Politique* 3, no. 9 (2009): 1–18 (16). On Cassin and his role in drafting the UDHR, see Johannes Morsink, *The Universal Declaration of Human Rights: Origins, Drafting, and Intent* (Philadelphia: University of Pennsylvania Press, 1999); Morsink, *Inherent Human Rights: Philosophical Roots of the Universal Declaration* (Philadelphia: University of Pennsylvania Press, 2009); Glendon, *World Made New*, 60–70; Sluga, "René Cassin"; and Jay Winter and Antoine Prost, *René Cassin and Human Rights: From the Great War to the Universal Declaration* (Cambridge: Cambridge University Press, 2013). For an important reappraisal, see A. J. Hobbins, "René Cassin and the Daughter of Time: The First Draft of the Universal Declaration of Human Rights," *Fontanus* 2 (1989): 7–26.

136. See René Cassin, "Souvenirs sur B. Mirkine-Guetzévitch," in *Hommage à Boris Mirkine-Guetzévitch* (New York: Ecole Libre des Hautes Etudes, n.d.), 29–34.

137. Cassin proposed calling it a "universal" declaration, as opposed to merely "international": "Looking Back on the Universal Declaration of 1948," *Review of Contemporary Law*, no. 1 (1968): 13–26 (22).

138. Hobbins, "René Cassin and the Daughter of Time," 10. This article contains Humphrey's draft, which is also available online: http://www.un.org/en/ga/search/view_doc.asp?symbol=E/CN.4/AC.1/3. The "Documented Outline" is available as well: http://www.un.org/en/ga/search/view_doc.asp?symbol=E/CN.4/AC.1/3/ADD.1. See also Humphrey, *Human Rights and the United Nations*, 31–32.

139. Morsink, *Universal Declaration of Human Rights*, 8. Cassin's draft is available in a number of sources: see, e.g., Marc Agi, *René Cassin, Prix Nobel de la Paix (1887–1976)* (Paris: Perrin, 1998), annexe 9 (pp. 358–65). An English translation is available through the UN: http://www.un.org/en/ga/search/view_doc.asp?symbol=E/CN.4/21 (annex D). I have taken the chapter translations from this source.

140. Both Morsink and Moyn downplay Cassin's contributions: for Morsink, see above; for Moyn, *Last Utopia*, 65. For a contrary view, which stresses Cassin's editorial importance, see Glendon, *World Made New*, 61.

141. Blaise Pascal, *Pensées and Other Writings*, trans. Honor Levi (Oxford: Oxford University Press, 1995), § 575, 132.

142. See Morsink, *Universal Declaration of Human Rights*, 332.

143. For the list of constitutions, see "Documented Outline," 1–4. Cassin refers to "the celebrated English, American, and French declarations of human rights of the 18th century and [ . . . ] almost all of the national constitutions of the nineteenth and twentieth centuries": "Looking Back," 18. Cassin's recollections contain some historical errors and embellish his own role in the drafting process, but his list of the committee's sources fits with other accounts.

144. See Morsink, *Universal Declaration of Human Rights*, chap. 8; Marks, "From the 'Single Confused Page,'" 469, 511; Hunt, *Inventing Human Rights*, 203–6; and O'Connell, "Recovering the History of Human Rights," 119.

145. Koskenniemi, *Gentle Civilizer of Nations*, 100.

146. See esp. Moyn, "The Secret History of Human Dignity," in *Christian Human Rights*, chap. 1.

147. Again, see Moyn on "the striking prominence of Christian social thought among the framers": *Last Utopia*, 64; and also *Christian Human Rights*.

148. See in particular Michael Rosen, *Dignity: Its History and Meaning* (Cambridge, MA: Harvard University Press, 2012); and Jeremy Waldron, *Dignity, Rank, and Rights* (Oxford: Oxford University Press, 2012).

149. Charles Beitz, *The Idea of Human Rights* (Oxford: Oxford University Press, 2009), 19–21.

150. See Cassin: "it is important to show that the unreligious character of the Declaration is in direct relation to its universalness": "Looking Back," 23.

151. Maritain also contributed a very emotional piece to the *Hommage à Boris Mirkine-Guetzévitch*.

152. See, e.g., Cassin's wry comment: "Had I not heard a canon of Irish origin speak eulogiously of the French Revolution because it brought something new to the conception of human rights?" "Looking Back," 14.

153. With John XXII's 1963 encyclical, *Pacem in Terris*. See esp. Duranti, *Conservative Human Rights Revolution*.

# Selected Bibliography of Secondary Sources on the History of Human Rights

NB: The works listed below combine both classical and more recent studies on the history of human rights. They are meant to provide an introduction to the field, and in no way constitute an exhaustive list. A full bibliography is available online: http://press.uchicago.edu/sites/edelstein/.

## Rights Theory

Beitz, Charles. *The Idea of Human Rights*. Oxford: Oxford University Press, 2009.

Donnelly, Jack. *Universal Human Rights in Theory and Practice*. Ithaca, NY: Cornell University Press, 2002.

Dworkin, Ronald. *Taking Rights Seriously*. Cambridge, MA: Harvard University Press, 1977.

Hart, H. L. A. "Are There Any Natural Rights?" *Philosophical Review* 64 (1955): 175–91.

Hohfeld, Wesley. *Fundamental Legal Concepts*. New Haven, CT: Yale University Press, 1919.

Lyons, David. "The Correlativity of Rights and Duties." *Noûs* 4 (1970): 45–55.

## Medieval and Early Modern Period

Brett, Annabel. *Liberty, Right and Nature: Individual Rights in Later Scholastic Thought*. Cambridge: Cambridge University Press, 1997.

Höpfl, Harro. *Jesuit Political Thought: The Society of Jesus and the State, c. 1540–1630*. Cambridge: Cambridge University Press, 2004.

Lee, Daniel. *Popular Sovereignty in Early Modern Constitutional Thought*. Oxford: Oxford University Press, 2016.

Oakley, Francis. *Natural Law, Laws of Nature, Natural Rights: Continuity and Discontinuity in the History of Ideas*. New York: Continuum, 2005.

Skinner, Quentin. *The Foundations of Modern Political Thought*. 2 vols. Cambridge: Cambridge University Press, 1978.

Straumann, Benjamin. *Roman Law in the State of Nature: The Classical Foundations of Hugo Grotius' Natural Law*. Cambridge: Cambridge University Press, 2015.

Tierney, Brian. *The Idea of Natural Rights: Studies on Natural Rights, Natural Law, and Church Law, 1150–1625*. Atlanta: Scholars Press, 1997.

Tuck, Richard. *Natural Rights Theories: Their Origins and Development.* Cambridge: Cambridge University Press, 1979.

Villey, Michel. "La genèse du droit subjectif chez Guillaume d'Occam." *Archives de philosophie du droit* 9 (1964): 97–127.

### Seventeenth-Century Natural Law Theorists

Den Uyl, Douglas J. *Power, State and Freedom: An Interpretation of Spinoza's Political Philosophy.* Assen: Van Gorcum, 1983.

Foxley, Rachel. *The Levellers: Radical Political Thought in the English Revolution.* Manchester: Manchester University Press, 2013.

Hoekstra, Kinch. "Hobbes on Law, Nature, and Reason." *Journal of the History of Philosophy* 41, no. 1 (2003): 111–20.

Malcolm, Noel. *Aspects of Hobbes.* Oxford: Oxford University Press, 2002.

McClure, Kirstie M. *Judging Rights: Lockean Politics and the Limits of Consent.* Ithaca, NY: Cornell University Press, 1996.

Simmons, A. John. *The Lockean Theory of Rights.* Princeton, NJ: Princeton University Press, 1992.

Skinner, Quentin. *Hobbes and Republican Liberty.* Cambridge: Cambridge University Press, 2008.

Tuck, Richard. *The Rights of War and Peace.* Oxford: Oxford University Press, 1999.

Tuckness, Alex. *Locke and the Legislative Point of View.* Princeton, NJ: Princeton University Press, 2002.

Waldron, Jeremy. *The Right to Private Property.* Oxford: Oxford University Press, 1988.

### Enlightenment

Bernardi, Bruno. *Le principe d'obligation: sur une aporie de la modernité politique.* Paris: Vrin/ EHESS, 2007.

Cohen, Joshua. *Rousseau: A Free Community of Equals.* Oxford: Oxford University Press, 2010.

Faccarello, Gilbert. *The Foundations of Laissez-Faire: The Economics of Pierre de Boisguilbert.* Translated by Carolyn Shread. London: Routledge, 1999.

Ferrone, Vicenzo. *Storia dei diritti dell'uomo: L'Illuminismo e la costruzione del linguaggio politico dei moderni.* Rome: Laterza, 2014.

Haakonssen, Knud. *Natural Law and Moral Philosophy: From Grotius to the Scottish Enlightenment.* Cambridge: Cambridge University Press, 1996.

Hochstrasser, Tim. *Natural Law Theories in the Early Enlightenment.* Cambridge: Cambridge University Press, 2000.

Hunt, Lynn. *Inventing Human Rights: A History.* New York: Norton, 2007.

Larrère, Catherine. *L'invention de l'économie au XVIIIe siècle: du droit naturel à la physiocratie.* Paris: PUF, 1992.

Spector, Céline. "'Il est impossible que nous supposions que ces gens-là soient des hommes': la théorie de l'esclavage au livre XV de *L'Esprit des lois*." *Lumières*, no. 3 (2004): 15–51.

### American Colonies and Revolution

Amar, Akhil Reed. *The Bill of Rights: Creation and Reconstruction.* New Haven, CT: Yale University Press, 1998.

Dworetz, Steven M. *The Unvarnished Doctrine: Locke, Liberalism, and the American Revolution.* Durham, NC: Duke University Press, 1989.

Lacey, Michael J., and Knud Haakonssen, eds. *A Culture of Rights: The Bill of Rights in Philosophy, Politics and Law—1791 and 1991.* Cambridge: Woodrow Wilson International Center for Scholars and Cambridge University Press, 1991.

Prest, Wilfrid, ed. *Re-Interpreting Blackstone's Commentaries: A Seminal Text in National and International Contexts.* Oxford: Hart, 2009.

Rakove, Jack. *Original Meanings: Politics and Ideas in the Making of the Constitution.* New York: Vintage, 1996.

Reid, John Phillip. *Constitutional History of the American Revolution.* Madison: University of Wisconsin Press, 1995.

Rodgers, Daniel T. *Contested Truths: Keywords in American Politics since Independence.* Cambridge, MA: Harvard University Press, 1998.

Shain, Barry Alan, ed. *The Nature of Rights at the American Founding and Beyond.* Charlottesville: University of Virginia Press, 2007.

Zuckert, Michael. *Natural Rights and the New Republicanism.* Princeton, NJ: Princeton University Press, 1994.

## French Revolution

Baecque, Antoine de, Wolfgang Schmale, and Michel Vovelle, eds. *L'An 1 des droits de l'homme.* Paris: Presses du CNRS, 1989.

Baker, Keith M. *Inventing the French Revolution: Essays on French Political Culture in the Eighteenth Century.* Cambridge: Cambridge University Press, 1990.

Bell, David A. *The Cult of the Nation in France: Inventing Nationalism, 1680–1800.* Cambridge, MA: Harvard University Press, 2001.

Blaufarb, Rafe. *The Great Demarcation: The French Revolution and the Invention of Modern Property.* Oxford: Oxford University Press, 2016.

Gauchet, Marcel. *La Révolution des droits de l'homme.* Paris: Gallimard, 1989.

Jaume, Lucien. *Les Déclarations des droits de l'homme.* Paris: Flammarion, 1989.

Kolla, Edward James. *Sovereignty, International Law, and the French Revolution.* Cambridge: Cambridge University Press, 2017.

Rials, Stéphane. *La Déclaration des droits de l'homme et du citoyen.* Paris: Hachette, 1988.

Van Kley, Dale, ed. *The French Idea of Freedom: The Old Regime and the Declaration of Rights of 1789.* Stanford, CA: Stanford University Press, 1994.

Walton, Charles. *Policing Public Opinion in the French Revolution: The Culture of Calumny and the Problem of Free Speech.* Oxford: Oxford University Press, 2009.

## From 1800 to 1948

Duranti, Marco. *The Conservative Human Rights Revolution: European Identity, Transnational Politics, and the Origins of the European Convention.* Oxford: Oxford University Press, 2016.

Glendon, Mary Ann. *A World Made New: Eleanor Roosevelt and the Universal Declaration of Human Rights.* New York: Random House, 2001.

Hoffmann, Stefan-Ludwig, ed. *Human Rights in the Twentieth Century.* New York: Cambridge University Press, 2011.

Koskenniemi, Martti. *The Gentle Civilizer of Nations: The Rise and Fall of International Law 1870–1960*. Cambridge: Cambridge University Press, 2001.

Marks, Stephen P. "From the 'Single Confused Page' to the 'Decalogue for Five Billion Persons': The Roots of the Universal Declaration of Human Rights in the French Revolution." *Human Rights Quarterly* 20, no. 3 (1998): 459–514.

Morsink, Johannes. *The Universal Declaration of Human Rights: Origins, Drafting, and Intent*. Philadelphia: University of Pennsylvania Press, 1999.

Moyn, Samuel. *Christian Human Rights*. Philadelphia: University of Pennsylvania Press, 2015.

———. *The Last Utopia: Human Rights in History*. Cambridge, MA: Belknap Press of Harvard University Press, 2010.

Naquet, Emmanuel. "La Ligue des droits de l'Homme: une association en politique (1898–1840)." PhD diss., Institut d'études politiques de Paris, 2005.

Zuber, Valentine. *Le Culte des droits de l'homme*. Paris: Gallimard, 2014.

# Index